T0333322

WAR DIARY
OF THE
UKRAINIAN
RESISTANCE

WAR DIARY
OF THE
UKRAINIAN RESISTANCE

THE KYIV INDEPENDENT

This edition is published by arrangement with Nouveau Monde éditions and is an updated edition of *Carnet de bord de la résistance ukrainienne*, Nouveau Monde éditions, 2022

This English-language edition first published 2023

FLINT is an imprint of The History Press
97 St George's Place, Cheltenham,
Gloucestershire, GL50 3QB
www.flintbooks.co.uk

© *The Kyiv Independent*, 2023
Preface and Introduction by Maria Poblete and Frédéric Ploquin, translated from the French by Alan McKay
Timeline © Flint Books

The right of *The Kyiv Independent* to be identified as the Author of this work has been asserted in accordance with the Copyright, Designs and Patents Act 1988.

All rights reserved. No part of this book may be reprinted or reproduced or utilised in any form or by any electronic, mechanical or other means, now known or hereafter invented, including photocopying and recording, or in any information storage or retrieval system, without the permission in writing from the Publishers.

British Library Cataloguing in Publication Data.
A catalogue record for this book is available from the British Library.

ISBN 978 1 80399 324 9

Typesetting and origination by The History Press
Printed and bound in Great Britain by TJ Books Limited, Padstow, Cornwall.

Trees for Life

CONTENTS

PREFACE

Four months before the Russian invasion of Ukraine, a small group of journalists and editorial staff made a decision: to stick together and spread the truth. They became *The Kyiv Independent*, and this book is the result of the small team's dedication to their cause. Under a hail of Russian bullets, bombs and missiles, its thirty members have held fast (and continue to hold) to their mission: to inform. This task is all the more vital given that the invader, Vladimir Putin's Russia, is a past master in the art of disinformation. Such disinformation has the power to paralyse or blind public opinion, to sway elections or to convince people of the righteousness of war; it can be overt or more subversive, but either way it is, unfortunately, rather successful.

Informing is resisting. Reporting the facts, day in, day out, hour after hour, gives air to those who have had to hole up to get away from the shooting; it also seriously spurs on those with the strength and the courage to rise up against the annihilation and the capitulation of their country, with whatever means they have at their disposal. In this case, it is the pen. It is the pen that history has shown has the power to topple dictatorships; and here it is once again the pen that tells of the extraordinary feats of these ordinary Ukrainians, informing the world, in English, and which has inspired millions. It is the pen that documents and shores up the reality, whose truth the aggressor would not hesitate to stamp out.

They are: Illia Ponomarenko, from Donbas, a reporter in charge of defence, who knows everything there is to know about what's going on in the ranks of the army; Daria Shulzhenko, a former lifestyle chronicler turned war correspondent; Anastasiia Lapatina, barely 20 years old and already a war correspondent; Anna Myroniuk, head of investigations, who managed to get her family out of Bucha just in time and reports on the tragedy daily; Alexander Query, a former business reporter turned war correspondent; Oleg Sukhov, the political reporter, who fled his native Russia in 2014; Igor Kossov, a Russian-Ukrainian born in Kyiv and raised in New York, who writes frontline dispatches and analytical war stories; Asami Terajima, of Japanese origin who grew up in Ukraine; Lili Bivings, who takes over at night in the United States where she's studying; Olena Goncharova, a correspondent in Canada where there's a large Ukrainian community; Thaisa Semenova, who joined *The Kyiv Independent* on the eve of the war before mixing with the flood of refugees; and not forgetting the editor-in-chief, Olga Rudenko, her deputy, Toma Istomina, and senior editor, Oleksiy Sorokin. They are in their 20s and 30s, all of them bound to Ukraine like arteries to the heart.

Those who could donned war correspondent clothes on the morning of 24 February 2022, not to cover some conflict breaking out far from home, in a country whose language and history were unfamiliar, but to report on the end of their own street. While one chose to slip into uniform and join up to defend his country with weapons in his hands, the others got organised. They were determined to carry on doing the job of journalist with conviction: after all, if Ukraine lost the war, the Ukrainians would lose Ukraine. There was fear, too: that a loved one, living in a stricken zone, would suffer. From these first moments of war, they were convinced that defeat was never to be contemplated. And that their lives would never be the same again.

These journalists are able to testify better than anybody else, being as close as possible to the facts. They work from home and have solutions to all the problems, which is not always the case with special correspondents from the international press. As chronicles of the pre-war period and the war on a day-to-day basis, their reports will be food for tomorrow's historians.

THE KYIV INDEPENDENT TEAM

 Lili Bivings, contributing editor. From 2017 to 2020 she served as a Peace Corps volunteer in Ukraine, after which she interned with the Atlantic Council's Eurasia Center. Lili worked as a business reporter and later editor at the old *Kyiv Post* and *The Kyiv Independent*. Based in New York, she is set to receive a Master's degree from Columbia University in 2023.

 Natalia Datskevych, business reporter. Formerly the *Kyiv Post* business reporter, she studied economic theory at Kyiv National Economic University and holds a PhD in economic science.

 Francis Farrell, reporter. Francis has worked as managing editor at the online media project Lossi 36, and as a freelance journalist and documentary photographer. He has previously worked in OSCE (Organization for Security and Co-operation in Europe) and Council of Europe field missions in Albania and Ukraine.

 Olena Goncharova, development manager, Canadian correspondent. Olena first joined the *Kyiv Post* as a staff writer in 2012 and later became Canadian correspondent in 2018. She has a Master's degree in publishing and editing from Taras Shevchenko National University of Kyiv and was a 2016 Alfred Friendly Press Partners fellow.

 Anastasiya Gordiychuk, news reporter. Anastasiya has previously worked as an associate business and labour editor at *The Varsity* and holds a Bachelor's degree in journalism from the University of Toronto. Her work has also been published in *Maclean's*, *Global Summitry Project* and *The Toronto Observer*.

Toma Istomina, deputy chief editor. Toma joined the *Kyiv Post* in 2017, as a staff writer and later taking on editorial roles. As a co-founder of *The Kyiv Independent*, she was featured on the Forbes 30 Under 30 Europe list in 2022. She holds a Master's degree in international journalism from Taras Shevchenko National University of Kyiv.

Dinara Khalilova, news reporter. Dinara has previously worked as a fixer and local producer for Sky News. She holds a BA in journalism from Taras Shevchenko National University of Kyiv and a Master's degree in media and communication from Bournemouth University.

Alexander Khrebet, reporter. Alexander has previously covered Ukrainian foreign policy, the Middle East and North Africa. He was published in the *ZN.UA*, *Washington Times* and *Atlantic Council*.

Artur Korniienko, culture reporter. Artur previously reported on the cultural scene at the *Kyiv Post*, and later *The Kyiv Independent*, until the outbreak of the full-scale war, when he decided to join the Territorial Defense to protect the country from Russia. He is still on the front line.

Igor Kossov, reporter. Igor has covered conflicts in the Middle East, investigated corruption in Ukraine and environmental damage in South East Asia. He holds a Master's degree in journalism from the City University of New York and has written for *USA Today*, *The Atlantic*, *Daily Beast* and *Foreign Policy*.

Anastasiia Lapatina, reporter. Anastasiia previously held the same position at the *Kyiv Post* and focused on politics and human rights, publishing articles on Crimea, Donbas and conflict zones in the Middle East. She has been included in the Forbes 30 under 30 Europe list and Teen Vogue 21 Under 21.

Olena Makarenko, video reporter. Since November 2015, Olena has been covering the events in Ukraine for foreign audiences. She has authored two short documentaries: *The Court* (2018), about establishing the Anti-Corruption Court in Ukraine, and *Life-Long City* (2020), about an activist in Kryvyi Rih.

Brooke Manning, community manager. Brooke previously worked as a field organiser in California and as an English teacher in Ukraine. She holds a Bachelor's degree in international studies and communication from the University of Washington and a Master's degree in investigative journalism from Arizona State University.

Iryna Matviyishyn, video reporter. Iryna was previously an analyst, video producer and project coordinator at *UkraineWorld*. She studied journalism in Lviv and holds a Master's degree in human rights and democratisation from the Global Campus of Human Rights in Europe.

Anna Myroniuk, head of investigations. Anna has investigated corruption, smuggling and misconduct in the armed forces. When the full-scale invasion started, she did some of *The Kyiv Independent*'s most important war reporting. She has a Master's degree in investigative journalism from City, University of London. As a co-founder of *The Kyiv Independent*, she was featured on the Forbes 30 Under 30 Europe list in 2022.

Jakub Parusinski, chief financial officer. Jakub holds an MBA from INSEAD business school and spent three years at McKinsey's London office, before co-founding Jnomics Media consultancy.

Teah Pelechaty, contributing editor. Teah is a former intern at the *Kyiv Post* and is completing a Master's degree in global affairs with a specialisation in global security and digital governance at the University of Toronto and Sciences Po.

Illia Ponomarenko, defence reporter. Illia covers national security. He was embedded with Ukrainian combat formations near the front line, and visited Palestine and the Democratic Republic of Congo to follow UN peacekeepers. He won the Alfred Friendly Press Partners fellowship and was selected to work as *USA Today*'s guest reporter at the US Department of Defense. Illia is the most followed Ukrainian journalist abroad.

Zakhar Protsiuk, chief development officer. Zakhar is also a co-founder and managing editor at The Fix Media, a media outlet about the European publishing sector. Before joining *The Kyiv Independent*, he worked as a senior project lead at Jnomics Media consultancy.

Alexander Query, reporter. Alexander previously covered business at the *Kyiv Post* and has worked as an anchorman at UATV in Ukraine. Born in France, he opened a *Reporter sans Frontières* (RSF, Reporters Without Borders) outpost in Lviv when the full-scale war had just begun.

Olga Rudenko, editor-in-chief. Before co-founding *The Kyiv Independent*, Olga spent ten years at the *Kyiv Post*. She has written for numerous international publications. In 2021, she held a fellowship at the University of Chicago Booth School of Business. In May 2022, she appeared on the cover of *Time* magazine, named one of that year's Next Generation Leaders.

Thaisa Semenova, reporter. Thaisa joined the team a few days before the full-scale war started. She has been covering current affairs and human interest stories. She has a Master's degree in journalism from the Ukrainian Catholic University and worked as a staff writer for the *Kyiv Post* until November 2021.

Daryna Shevchenko, CEO. Daryna has over ten years' experience as a media manager, trainer and media consultant. She worked at the *Kyiv Post*, Media Development Foundation, TV channel ZIK and investigative media Slidstvo.info before joining Jnomics Media consultancy as partner.

Daria Shulzhenko, reporter. Daria was a lifestyle reporter at the *Kyiv Post* until November 2021. She graduated from Kyiv International University with a Bachelor's degree in linguistics, specialising in translation from English and German languages. She has previously worked as a freelance writer and researcher. At *The Kyiv Independent*, she covers stories on the human toll and personal tragedies of the war.

Oleksiy Sorokin, senior editor. Oleksiy has a degree from the University of Toronto and has published numerous articles on the government and judiciary, as well as investigative reports about the former Ukrainian president and the current prosecutor general. As a co-founder of *The Kyiv Independent*, he was featured on the Forbes 30 Under 30 Europe list in 2022.

Oleg Sukhov, political reporter. A former reporter for *The Moscow Times* and holder of a Master's degree in history from Moscow State University, Oleg moved to Ukraine in 2014 because of the crackdown on independent media in Russia.

Asami Terajima, reporter. Of Japanese origin, Asami has lived in Kyiv for much of her life. Since the start of the full-scale invasion of Ukraine, she has been covering the war. She writes a daily update on the battlefield developments, *Ukraine War Latest*.

Anna Yakutenko, head of video. Anna started out as a journalist for the *Kyiv Post* in 2015, launching the video department there in 2018. She has spent six months working with newsrooms in the US as an Alfred Friendly Press Partners fellow. She holds a Bachelor's degree in journalism from the Taras Shevchenko National University of Kyiv.

Helen Yushchenko, newsroom assistant. Helen has previously worked as a news writer and content manager at the ADASTRA analytical center. She holds a Bachelor's degree in international relations.

INTRODUCTION

With its mission statement of upholding the ideals of free press and informing the international community of the real events in Ukraine as they unfold, *The Kyiv Independent* leapt into the limelight from its inception. But nearly every member of *The Kyiv Independent* team came from the first English-language media in Ukraine, the *Kyiv Post*. Set up in 1995, in 2018 it had come into the ownership of Adnan Kivan, a Syrian-born magnate who was made rich by investing in real estate in the southern Ukrainian port of Odesa.

'Silence is golden', the small-time tycoon had dared to whisper to his editorial team. But could the *Post* keep its prestige and reputation while under the thumb of a boss who wanted his team to shut up on command? The businessman's ethics clashed with the values of his journalists, whose principles of a free and independent press were instilled a long time ago by an editor-in-chief from Missouri, Brian Bonner.

The situation suddenly grew more tense in November 2020, when the newspaper published an article criticising the public prosecutor Iryna Venediktova, who was appointed by President Zelensky. After threats of proceedings for defamation against the *Post* and a criminal lawsuit against its owner, an article put online on 12 January 2022 by *The Kyiv Independent* tells us:

> Soon after, Kivan said he would be expanding the paper by launching a Ukrainian language edition run by a handpicked TV presenter from his non-independent TV channel in Odesa. Fearing a loss of editorial independence, the *Kyiv Post* staff demanded that the person in charge of the Ukrainian edition go through a rigorous job interview. Several weeks later, Kivan announced that he was closing the paper, firing everyone and reopening it under new management. Venediktova stated in November that she never pressured anybody or even met Kivan, who has also denied allegations of pressure.

The break came in November 2021 and it was brutal. Fired overnight by the oligarch, most of the editorial staff agreed to continue on their own. From a makeshift raft, they created a dreadnought, christened, naturally, *The Kyiv Independent*. This was on 11 November 2021, the founding date of a very clear declaration of values to 'serve as the backbone' of the new venture:

- The new publication will serve its readers and community, and nobody else.
- *The Kyiv Independent* won't be dependent on a rich owner or an oligarch. The publication will depend on fundraising from readers and donors and later on, commercial activities.
- The newsroom will decide and execute the publication's editorial policy in the community's best interests. Attempts to influence it from outside will not be tolerated.
- *The Kyiv Independent* will always be at least partly owned by its journalists.
- *The Kyiv Independent* will strive to reach financial sustainability to preserve its independence in the future.

Olga Rudenko, 32, who'd been with the *Post* for ten years or so, took over the new press outlet, hand in hand with Toma Istomina, the *Post*'s former lifestyle editor, and Oleksiy Sorokin, the *Post*'s former political reporter; Daryna Shevchenko and Jakub Parusinski took over the management, as well as the titles of CEO and CFO. The first editorial meetings took place at a café in central Kyiv, before the team could afford an office.

It didn't take long for the newspaper's dedication to editorial independence and its principled approach to journalism to catch the attention of the wider community, and the team was given the Journalist of the Year award on 15 December 2021. This is a prestigious annual award given by prominent Ukrainian news outlet *Ukrainska Pravda*, whose editor-in-chief Sevgil Musayeva announced at the prize-giving:

It was a shock and a big disappointment to learn our colleagues were fired without explanation from a newspaper that they had been publishing for so many years.

We were astonished by how fast the team made a decision to launch a new project. The story of *The Kyiv Independent* is one of journalists who have shown their adherence to principles, remained faithful to their profession and chosen to serve the society rather than the owner and his fears.

'We are overwhelmed by the amount of support we have been receiving from the community,' replied Rudenko. 'It is especially humbling to receive this award from *Ukrainska Pravda*, a news outlet that has a special significance for any journalist in Ukraine, which has paid a higher price for its journalism than any other newsroom in Ukraine.'

During *Ukrainska Pravda*'s twenty-two years of existence, two of its journalists have been killed. The co-founder of the publication, Georgiy Gongadze, was kidnapped and murdered in 2000, allegedly on the orders of former president Leonid Kuchma, and became a symbol of journalistic courage. Another member of *Ukrainska Pravda*'s editorial staff, Belarusian-born Pavel Sheremet, was killed by a car bomb in central Kyiv in 2016. In both cases, the culprits remain unknown and unpunished.

According to the Institute for Mass Information (IMI), there have been 229 violations of the freedom of expression recorded in 2020, 171 of which involved physical aggression against journalists.

All that was before the war, when the only deadline was electoral.

Since the Russian invasion, pro-Putin voices have been isolated and the habits of all journalists have been shattered. From then on it was from bombs and other firearms that they had to shelter, and creative arrangements had to be made to allow them to continue informing about a war that was turning more murderous every day. They turned their reporting from Covid numbers to civilian and military casualties, then to Russian losses – of men, tanks, artillery, rocket launchers, missiles, planes, helicopters, ships, petrol tanks, drones – the new yardstick of the Ukrainian resistance's effectiveness.

Understandably, many editorial staff members scattered, some of them deciding it was more prudent to put a border between themselves and the invaders. One of them, a Russian national, left because he hadn't stopped criticising Russia in public since he'd left it in 2014, another because their family history made him a choice target for kidnappers, and a third prioritised taking her children to safety.

But the trauma of these movements and arrangements would pale in comparison to reports civilians gave to journalists on the ground. They would tell of how Russian soldiers ordered them to salute like Nazis and swear allegiance to Vladimir Putin, before carrying out a fake execution in the middle of an empty village. They would tell how their loved ones were tortured and killed.

It is to these wounded people, whose pain and humiliation has done nothing to dull the strength of their national sentiment, that we dedicate this logbook of a total war at the gates of Europe. We wish long life to *The Kyiv Independent* team, to whom we owe this very personal, poignant account, imbued with indispensable journalistic detachment. As the war approaches its first anniversary, it can only be hoped that *The Kyiv Independent*'s dedication to free press and informing the international community about the horrors of this war will ultimately help bring Ukraine's people the support they need to beat back oppressors and ensure that truth is the final word.

MAPS

Donbas, comprising Luhansk and Donetsk oblasts, and its surroundings.

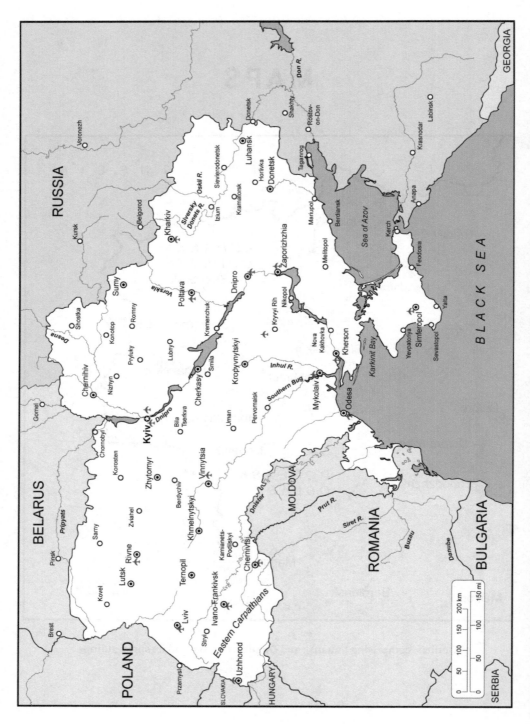

Ukraine, its cities and surrounding territories.

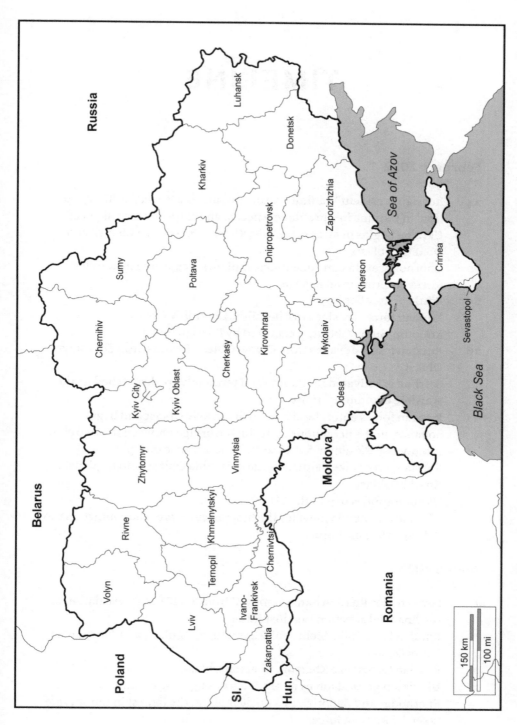

Ukraine's oblasts (administrative areas).

TIMELINE

February 2022

24   Russian President Vladimir Putin announces a 'special military operation' in Ukraine in a pre-dawn speech, and the all-out invasion of Ukraine begins in attacks on Kyiv, Kharkiv, Kherson, Luhansk and Donetsk oblasts
Chornobyl exclusion zone (nuclear plant) is captured by Russian forces entering from Belarus

25   Battle of Kyiv begins
Russian forces lay siege to Chernihiv, Chernihiv Oblast
Konotop, Sumy Oblast, is captured by Russian forces

26   Russian forces advance from Gomel Oblast, Belarus, into Zhytomyr Oblast
Starlink is activated in Ukraine and terminals are dispatched to aid wartime communications

27   Russian forces enter the city of Bucha in Kyiv Oblast and begin advance on the neighbouring Irpin; the bridge between the two cities is blown by Ukrainian forces to stall the advance on Irpin
Russian forces take Berdiansk, Zaporizhzhia Oblast, and Kupiansk, Kharkiv Oblast

28   Ukraine applies to join the EU
Ukraine and Russia meet for the first peace talks of the conflict on the Belarus–Ukraine border

March 2022

1   Seven major Russian banks removed from SWIFT in an escalation of the financial sanctions against Russia
Russian forces take Melitopol, Zaporizhzhia Oblast, and Trostianets, Sumy Oblast

2   Russian forces take Kherson, Kherson Oblast

3   Ukrainian ground forces retake Bucha as fighting continues
Enerhodar and Zaporizhzhia nuclear plant, the largest in Europe, are taken by Russian forces

Ukraine and Russia meet for peace talks on the Belarus–Ukraine border

5 Russian forces capture Bucha, Hostomel and Vorzel, Kyiv Oblast

7 Ukraine and Russia meet for peace talks on the Belarus–Ukraine border

8 Ukrainian military claim to have killed the first Wagner Group member since the start of the Russian invasion; this organisation is alleged to have been ordered to assassinate President Zelensky in the lead-up to the all-out invasion of Ukraine in February and will be involved in many of the major Russian offensives throughout the war

9 Large-scale evacuation of Kyiv Oblast takes place

10 Ukraine and Russia meet for peace talks in Turkey

12 Russian forces fully occupy Bucha

14 Ukraine and Russia meet again for peace talks in Turkey

16 Ukrainian forces begin counter-attack in Bucha and other Russian-held locations

24 First prisoner-of-war exchange takes place between Ukrainian and Russian forces

28 Ukrainian forces regain complete control of Irpin after over a month of heavy fighting

31 Russian forces end their occupation of Bucha and withdraw from the city

The end of the Battle of Kyiv with Russian withdrawal

April 2022

1 Evidence emerges of the mass murder of Ukrainian civilians and prisoners of war in Bucha

Russian forces take Izium, Kharkiv Oblast

Russian troops completely withdraw from the Chornobyl exclusion zone

2 Ukrainian officials declare Zhytomyr Oblast clear of Russian forces

4 Russian forces withdraw from Chernihiv Oblast, ending the siege of Chernihiv

6 Russian forces withdraw from Sumy Oblast

8 Russian forces withdraw from occupied territories in northern Ukraine

The battle for Mykolaiv ends in Russian defeat

Russian missiles strike Kramatorsk railway station

14 Russian warship *Moskva* is sunk in the Black Sea

18 Battle of Donbas begins

Kreminna, Luhansk Oblast, is taken by Russian forces

May 2022

6	Russian forces move to take Sievierodonetsk, Luhansk Oblast
12	Russian forces take Rubizhne, Luhansk Oblast
13	First war crimes trial against Russian army sergeant Vadim Shysimarin is held in Kyiv
20	The close of the siege of Mariupol, which began on the first day of Russia's all-out invasion of Ukraine, ending with Ukrainian surrender
27	Russian forces take Lyman, Donetsk Oblast, ending the First Battle of Lyman
31	Major Russian bank Sberbank is removed from SWIFT

June 2022

2	Zelensky reports that Russian forces hold 'almost 20 per cent' of Ukrainian territory
23	Ukraine is granted candidate status for membership of the EU
25	Sievierodonetsk fully occupied by Russian forces

July 2022

3	Russian forces capture Lysychansk, bringing all of Luhansk Oblast under their control
12	Ukraine becomes associate member of NATO's Multilateral Interoperability Program
13	Ukrainian Foreign Minister Dmytro Kuleba states that peace talks are frozen
22	Ukraine and Russia agree the Black Sea Grain Initiative, facilitated by the UN and Turkey, to allow grain exports previously blockaded by Russia in Ukrainian Black Sea ports
23	Russia launches missiles at Odesa sea trade port
26	Vuhlehirska power station, Svitlodarsk, Donetsk Oblast, is captured by Russian forces

August 2022

1	Main assault on Bakhmut, Donetsk Oblast, begins First ship carrying grain leaves Odesa under the Black Sea Grain Initiative
15	Wagner Group base in Popasna, Luhansk Oblast, is hit by a HIMARS rocket
29	Ukraine launches a counter-offensive in the south, in Kherson Oblast

September 2022

4	The beginning of the Kharkiv counter-offensive by Ukrainian forces
10	Second Battle of Lyman commences
	Izium, Kharkiv Oblast, and Kreminna, Luhansk Oblast, are retaken by Ukrainian forces
11	Zaporizhzhia nuclear plant shuts down last reactor
19	Bilohorivka returns to Ukrainian control and ends the total Russian occupation of Luhansk Oblast
23	436 bodies are recovered from a mass grave in Izium, Kharki Oblast, some of which showed evidence of torture
29	Kupiansk, Kharkiv Oblast, is fully retaken by Ukrainian forces
30	Russian president Vladimir Putin announces the annexation of parts of Donetsk, Luhansk, Kherson and Zaporizhzhia oblasts after sham referendums
	Ukraine submits formal application for membership of NATO

October 2022

1	Ukrainian forces liberate Lyman, Donetsk Oblast, after Russian forces withdraw
2	Battle of the Svatove–Kreminna line begins
3	Kharkiv Oblast is fully retaken by Ukrainian forces, ending Russian occupation of the area
6	Two mass graves are discovered in Lyman, Donetsk Oblast
10	Widespread Russian missile attacks across Ukraine, including on the nation's capital, Kyiv
12	UN Resolution is made not to recognise the sham referendums held by Russia declaring the annexation of Donetsk, Luhansk, Kherson and Zaporizhzhia oblasts

November 2022

10	Russian forces withdraw from Snihurivka, Mykolaiv Oblast
11	Ukraine announce liberation of Kherson, Kherson Oblast
15	Air defence missile originating in Ukraine crosses into Polish territory and kills two civilians

December 2022

9   Velyky Potyomkinsky Island, near Kherson, in the Dnipro River, is
    occupied by Russian forces
26 The Governor of Donetsk, Pavlo Kyrylenko, claims that over 60 per
    cent of Bakhmut's infrastructure has been damaged or destroyed

January 2023

2   Ukrainian flags are raised on the occupied Velyky Potyomkinsky
    Island, near Kherson
14 Russian missile attacks on Dnipro, Dnipropetrovsk, hit an apartment
    block, killing 40 and injuring 75 people, with 46 people reported
    missing
20 Ukrainian forces repel Russian attacks on sixteens settlements in
    Donetsk, Luhansk and Zaporizhzhia oblasts
25 Ukraine acknowledges the loss of Soledar, Donetsk Oblast, to Russian
    forces, in the first significant Russian advance since July 2022 and pro-
    viding a significant tactical advantage for the assault on Bakhmut

15 February 2022

Even if Russia attacks, Ukraine's fall is not predestined

Illia Ponomarenko

It's important not to lose the battle before it even begins.

Right now, the Russia-instigated security crisis in Ukraine is threatening to become an all-out war of occupation. Against all the voices of reason, Russia's military force, over 130,000 strong, might be days or hours away from attacking Ukraine.

It is unbelievable this is happening in Europe in the year 2022. Those who cried 'Why can't we give Russia what it deserves' can thank Vladimir Putin in Moscow for this.

What may happen soon would go down in history as one of the most tragic pages of this century.

The occupation of most of Ukraine, the downfall of a young democracy, millions of refugees fleeing west, killings, a pro-Russian puppet ruler in Kyiv, the death of all hopes and dreams for the Ukrainian nation.

To many in the world, Ukraine seems to be doomed. But I refuse to accept that the situation is that simple. It's not because I blindly deny the danger.

In this complex reality, our path towards complete downfall is not going to be as straight and inevitable as the media sometimes presents it to be.

In other words, Ukraine's fall is not predestined – at least, as long as the nation does not accept it without a fight.

We in Ukraine might be standing at the gate of hell, but Russia is facing a nightmare as well. Millions of things can go wrong, turning another one of the Kremlin's 'splendid little wars' into a nationwide catastrophe for Russia.

This is not 2014, when Russia took Ukraine by surprise. Ukraine is not easy prey any more.

The maps published in the media showing giant arrows of Russia's multi-pronged strikes towards Ukrainian cities look scary. But they shouldn't be taken literally.

The problem is that, for instance, as part of their rush between Belarus across the Chornobyl Zone to Zhytomyr (as predicted by many media outlets), Russian troops would have to pass hundreds of kilometers of dense forests and swamps. Not a very good lane for a supposed blitzkrieg.

Also, near Zhytomyr, Russians would have to deal with the famous 95th Airborne Brigade, one of Ukraine's best combat formations.

South of Kyiv, in Bila Tserkva, there would be the 72nd Mechanized Infantry Brigade – one of Ukraine's most battle-hardened and aggressive formations, with which I have spent some time in the trenches of Donbas.

In Dnipro, Russian forces can expect a hot welcome from the legendary 93rd Mechanized and the 25th Airborne brigades. In Mykolaiv, the 79th Airborne is on guard.

Scary invasion maps published in Western media somehow fail to mention all this.

And we've only touched on several formations out of Ukraine's nearly 250,000-strong military, plus nearly 50,000 National Guard troops, many of whom have real hard-won combat experience from 2014–2015. Add to that tens of thousands of combat-hardened veterans in civilian life, who also know what to do if the worst comes.

Back in 2014, when Russia took Crimea and started a war in Donbas, the nation was beheaded and disorganized, and the military barely existed as an organized institution.

Even so, Ukrainian society produced dozens of self-organized volunteer battalions of former taxi drivers and programmers that fought fiercely, often dressed in sneakers and hunting fatigues.

Ukraine has proved once already that it can self-mobilize and fight. Just try and imagine what happens if Russia unleashes an all-out war. According to estimates, Ukraine might end up with nearly 500,000 armed men and women.

Don't forget that Ukrainian combatants would be fighting on their land – unlike their Russian adversaries, many of whom would be taken from Russia's Far East. I don't recommend underestimating the rage of the doomed fighting for their families and their homes.

Thinking Russian tanks will make it to Kyiv in a couple of hours like a Ford Focus on a good highway is wrong.

It is true that Ukraine's military is still full of flaws and problems. But morale is very high, the organization is strong, and the command team led by Lieutenant General Valerii Zaluzhnyi is the best it's ever been since the war began.

Similarly, the relationship between the military and the Defense Ministry led by Oleksiy Reznikov is strong like never before.

It is true that Russia would certainly enjoy full supremacy in the air and start its offensive with devastating missile attacks – Ukraine's woeful air defense will have a hard time countering these.

But even here, there's a possible antidote.

The most basic option is to use small groups tactics. To put it simply, the Ukrainian military and paramilitary could disperse into small squads, barely noticeable to enemy reconnaissance.

They would exhaust the Russians with surprise harassment, striking seemingly from nowhere. They would disrupt Russian supply chains, bogging them down in a long and extremely brutal war no one wants to be in.

It's also time to mention the Western-provided advanced anti-tank and anti-aircraft weaponry. Behind every ruin, tree and blade of grass, there may be a Ukrainian squad with launchers, waiting, ready to turn Russian armored convoys into smoldering piles of scrap.

A smart plan of blitzkrieg, as it usually happens in history, would prove to be smart only on the military headquarters maps. And time would be on our side.

Western media sometimes wonder why Ukrainians are not freaking out or going panic shopping. The thing is that, in the face of the grave threat, the general population remains calm and stable.

While Russia's massive psychological operation is disturbing the international diplomatic and business communities in Ukraine, it's not meeting its goal to demoralize and divide the Ukrainian population.

It's just not 2014 anymore.

Notice how no one's even mentioning the old concept of '*Novorossiya*' ('New Russia') extending from Odesa to Kharkiv. After eight years of war in Donbas, pro-Russian sentiments in Ukraine are lower than ever before.

It goes without saying that an all-out war will force Russia to face an angry population of 40 million distributed through a country the size of France. According to a 15 February poll, 58% of Ukrainians say they are ready to offer resistance to Russian occupation; 37% of them said they'd want to take up arms. Ukrainians' decisiveness grows: in a December poll, these numbers were 50% and 33%, respectively.

According to estimates by Ukraine's military and many defense specialists, the Russian military force of over 80 battalion tactical groups, or nearly 130,000 personnel, concentrated near Ukraine, in Belarus, and occupied areas of Ukraine is not even close to being enough to fully occupy the country.

And without occupation, any plans to install a pro-Russian puppet government in Kyiv are just not realistic. Without Russia's constant, indefinite military presence, such a collaborationist leadership would have zero chance to survive even one day in Ukraine.

Should Putin make the decision to invade, the Russian nation faces a horrific prospective as well. Tens of thousands of soldiers' coffins coming back to all parts of Russia, crushing economic sanctions directly affecting the lives of regular people, complete political isolation and status as rogue nation waging an openly aggressive war of conquest.

This is not going to be the war in Donbas, where Russian paratroopers were killed in Debaltseve and buried secretly, with their families paid for their silence. And this is not going to be Syria, with the involvement of Wagner mercenaries no one cares about.

In addition, the Russian war on Ukraine would be the ground zero for a global economic crisis affecting many industries ranging from air transportation to gas and oil. It would cause food shortages around the globe, cutting people off from Ukraine's bountiful harvests.

Considering just these very basic factors, a full-fledged Russian invasion is like an equation with so many unknown variables, its solution cannot be predicted.

The situation, for all of its complexity, leaves Ukraine with many stepping stones to use against Russia in any scenario.

In other words, even if Russia throws its armies at Ukraine, nothing is over. No defeat or catastrophe would be final.

Even if Putin kisses the last bits of common sense goodbye and gives the order for the military to attack Ukraine tomorrow – can we be sure that the Russian military, and especially the Kremlin's inner circle of multibillionaires, would gladly jump to execute it?

General Valeriy Gerasimov, Russia's chief of general staff, knows such an action would be a disaster. For Russia's top billionaires behind the throne, with all of their kitsch mansions in London, their villas in the French Riviera, their luxury apartments in Miami, their kids in Oxford and their billions in Swiss banks, it's the last thing they want.

Are we sure they would not stage a silent palace coup to save what they have stolen from the Russian people if the Kremlin lunatic decides to make his worst mistake?

Nothing is predestined for Ukraine, even if the worst is to come.

THE WAR DIARY

THE WAR DIARY

24 February 2022

Putin declares war on Ukraine

The Kyiv Independent News Desk

Russian President Vladimir Putin announced that Russia will conduct 'a special military operation' to 'demilitarize' Ukraine, effectively declaring a major war on the country.

In a televized announcement that aired just before 5 a.m. Kyiv time, Putin said that NATO was threatening the existence of Russia and that, to protect it, he is sending Russian military into Ukraine.

Immediately after people in many Ukrainian cities, including Kharkiv and Odesa, began reporting hearing loud explosions.

Russian forces began shelling Ukraine, namely Donetsk, Zaporizhzhia, Luhansk, Odesa, Kherson, Mykolaiv, Poltava, Chernihiv, Zhytomyr, and Kyiv oblasts. At the airfields of Melitopol and Ozerne village of Zhytomyr Oblast one plane was blown up. Information about the shelling is coming constantly.

'There have just been missile strikes on the centers of the military administration, airfields, military depots, near Kyiv, Kharkiv, and Dnipro. There is shelling of our borders,' Anton Geraschenko, an advisor for the Interior Minister of Ukraine wrote on Facebook.

Ukraine introduced martial law, President Volodymyr Zelensky said in an impromptu video address he released on Facebook. Zelensky also said he held a phone call with US President Joe Biden. 'The United States already began consolidating international support,' Ukraine's President added.

As of 6 a.m., the State Emergency Service (SES) received information about the detonation of the locator at the airport in Odesa, on the territory of the military unit in Ananiv town.

A fire took place in Revne village of Kyiv Oblast – territory of a military unit – and two billboards in the central part of the city were blown up in Kyiv.

As of 6.10 a.m., there was a report of an explosion in Kharkiv near the station, while surveillance cameras recorded the crossing of Russian troops on the border of Sumy and Kyiv oblasts (exclusion zone). The command and control point of the Nizhyn airfield was blown up.

State Border Guard of Ukraine said Ukraine's border with Belarus and Russia was attacked: 'Russian troops supported by Belarus.'

Russian and Belarusian forces attack border units, border patrols and checkpoints with artillery, heavy equipment and small arms. This is happening within Luhansk, Sumy, Kharkiv, Chernihiv and Zhytomyr oblasts, and also in Russia-occupied Crimea.

Ukraine's forces shot down five enemy planes and one helicopter in Luhansk and Donetsk oblasts, said the General Staff of the Armed Forces of Ukraine. 'The combined forces give a worthy rebuff to the armed forces of the Russian Federation. Military units in their positions. The enemy suffers losses,' the Facebook statement said.

At the same time, Kyiv City Administration said there was an air threat in Kyiv and urged Kyivans to immediately find shelter when they hear sirens. Users on social media have posted videos of air raid sirens already sounding in Kyiv.

Kyiv City Council also said schools and kindergartens are now closed, while all medical infrastructure begins operating on high alert.

Parts of Kyiv are now collapsing under traffic, as many flee Kyiv after Russia's airstrikes.

In Luhansk Oblast, two villages – Horodyshche and Milove – were taken over by Russian forces.

The Kremlin's declaration of war comes days after Russia recognized its enclaves in eastern Ukraine's Luhansk Oblast and Donetsk Oblast as independent states on 21 February. Russia has been occupying territories in eastern Ukraine and the peninsula of Crimea since 2014.

Following the 'recognition', the Kremlin-installed leaders of the occupied areas of eastern Ukraine requested that Russia provides military protection from the supposed attack of the Ukrainian army, of which there has been no evidence.

Responding to their address, Putin announced the beginning of the 'special military operation'.

Biden said he will be meeting with leaders of the G7 on 24 February, adding that the US and its allies will be imposing 'severe sanctions' on Russia. He also said Russia's attack on Ukraine was 'unprovoked and unjustified'.

25 February 2022

Dozens of Ukrainians killed within hours of Russian invasion
Anna Myroniuk

Dozens of people were killed by Russian fire, and at least 19 went missing as of 1 p.m. on 24 February, just seven hours after Russia started the all-out invasion of Ukraine from several directions.

One civilian was killed by Russian shelling in Mariupol, Donetsk Oblast.

Six people were killed during the attack on the city of Podilsk in Odesa Oblast, Ukraine's Interior Ministry reported at 9 a.m.

A Ukrainian border guard was killed by missile shelling coming from the occupied Crimea.

The State Border Guard Service reported that Russia had fired arms on them from occupied Crimea onto Preobrazhenka village, Kherson Oblast.

Three civilians were killed by shelling in the city of Vuhledar in Donetsk Oblast, the Interior Ministry reported at 11 a.m.

Russian bombardment killed **a child** in the city of Chuhuiv, Kharkiv Oblast, the Interior Ministry reported at 12 p.m.

Eighteen people were killed during Russia's shelling of Lypetske village in Odesa Oblast, local authorities reported.

Six people were killed in Russia's morning shelling of Kyiv's suburb of Brovary, the city's mayor said to Suspilne media outlet.

One civilian was killed by Russian shelling in Uman, Cherkasy Oblast, local authorities reported.

Oleksiy Arestovych, advisor to the head of the President's Office, said that **over 40 Ukrainian soldiers** were killed since the morning, according to *Ukrainska Pravda*. This number hasn't been confirmed yet.

26 February 2022

Kyiv residents calm after heavy night fighting

Igor Kossov

As morning rose over the battered capital city, the streets were emptied out but people were still going about their business.

Sporadic sirens and bangs went off throughout the capital from the morning, into the early afternoon.

After the night's fighting, which has injured 35 people, including two children, Kyivans were curt and untalkative yet determined and unafraid. When asked how they felt throughout the night as Russian rockets and troops attacked the city, they mostly responded with a simple '*normalno*', which means 'I'm fine'.

Such was the case with Varvara, who declined to give her last name. She was standing in line for the one open pharmacy within a several-block area. Varvara and her husband spent their night in a shelter, obeying instructions from the city.

'As soon as [mayor Vitali] Klitschko told us to go, we followed the instructions and went,' she said. The couple does not intend to leave Kyiv.

Getting basic goods has become more of a challenge, as many stores have closed and many Kyivans have left the city, turning the roads west into sprawling convoys dozens of kilometers long. Sporadically people could be seen packing their vehicles or moving around with large backpacks, presumably to find somewhere safer or to leave on 26 February.

At a local Silpo supermarket, people were getting what was on the shelves and forming longer lines than usual at the cash registers. The store, like many others, was completely out of bread but contained many other goods. Queues for food and pharmacies were quiet and orderly.

One man, buying a bunch of Red Bull cans and cigarette packs was speaking on the phone to someone, saying, 'Yeah, I just grabbed my passport, going to head for the Territorial Defense.' After a pause, he replied, 'I don't know, I'll be fighting everywhere.'

'Everything's okay, everything's calm, you need to stop worrying,' he soon added.

Fighting has spread close to this neighborhood, close to Kyiv's Peremohy (Victory) Square. Elena Kozlova, a local pensioner, said she heard multiple rounds of automatic fire, likely from assault rifles, as well as single shots very close to her building, from the direction of the intersection of Poltavska and Sichovykh Striltsiv streets.

'It seemed like they were shooting right outside our windows,' she said. 'Then again, it was night and the city is a lot quieter than usual.'

When asked how she felt, she gave the same confidence, 'I'm fine,' before switching the subject to the reported build-up of Russian tanks near the village of Kazarovichi, where her family has a *dacha*, a sort of summer home with a garden, popular with Ukrainians, on the edge of the Kyiv Reservoir, known locally as the Kyiv Sea. Ukrainian forces blew the approaches to Kyiv and the tanks can't make headway for now, she said.

Some locals believe that the shooting in the neighborhood came from what Ukrainians call 'diversionary forces' or 'saboteurs' – essentially special operations units who are sent ahead to destabilize an area.

The shooting provoked fury among some. A taxi driver who declined to give his name for safety's sake went on a profanity-laden tirade against the attackers.

'These diversionary forces should be shot and left to lie in the street to send a message,' he said. 'What the f*ck are they doing here? Don't they f*cking know that we are an independent nation and don't want what they're offering?'

27 February 2022

Everyone is important in the war against Putin

Nataliia Steblyna

As I write this, Kyiv defenders are fighting on the streets and on the outskirts of the city. A Russian missile hit a residential apartment. There are air raid alerts in Vinnytsya, Kherson, Cherkasy, Kharkiv, Lviv, Rivne, Lutsk, air strikes in Uman. Chernihiv is preparing for street fights. The Ministry of Internal Affairs sent instructions for every Ukrainian citizen to make 'Molotov' cocktails.

In Odesa people woke up because of air defense: our border guards were bringing down some drone-scouts along the Black Sea coast. There is almost no place in Ukraine where people can feel safe. And everyone should be ready to confront the enemy.

Therefore, I'm asking myself, what can I do with all this hell on my beloved and peaceful land? How can I protect my colleagues, my students and all my compatriots from Russian rockets, jets and helicopters, Grads and Uragans?

What everyone can do to help Ukraine, to save our civilization, democratic values and to stop Putin. I don't know how to fire, but I know how to write. I have friends abroad. And I can ask everyone to help. Because everyone is important. Everyone can contribute.

Here in Ukraine, we will be repeating this over and over again: Russia's war isn't only about our country. This is about all of us. Because of Russian hybrid warfare everyone who values freedom, democracy and justice is a potential target. Thus, we should stand together. Please, don't be indifferent. Contribute. Even small steps may be significant. We will win the war against Putin all together ...

At 5 a.m. two days ago we were terrified. Blasts were reported in many Ukrainian cities and towns. And we still couldn't believe that Russians would do this to us. However, our military started to fight back. They were prepared, they were strong and unbreakable. And so are we now. This is our land. We will fight for it in any way possible. However, it's hard to do it alone. Please, lend Ukraine a shoulder. Let's stop darkness, despair, fear, injustice, death. Let's stop Putin together.

28 February 2022

Here's how to support the Ukrainian military

Daria Shulzhenko

Ukraine has been defending itself from Russia's all-out invasion since 24 February.

While Ukraine has so far been successful at pushing back Russian forces, Russia's advance into Ukraine continues on multiple fronts as heavy fighting takes place in different cities and regions.

There are several options to help the Ukrainian military.

The National Bank of Ukraine launched a special account to raise money to support the Ukrainian military on 24 February. A day after it was launched, NBU raised almost Hr 300 million (Ukrainian hryvnia) and the support continues to come.

The bank also notes that it's better to donate via the international payment order system SWIFT, from which Russia is expected to be cut off soon.

Also, Ukrainians who got Hr 1,000 from the government for getting their coronavirus shots can transfer the money to support the military as well.

Another option is donating to the Come Back Alive (Povernys Zhyvym), one of the most accountable and trustworthy charities working for the military in Ukraine since 2014. The charity has been providing the military with auxiliary equipment, specialized software, drones, personal body protection, training, and other supplies ever since the foundation's inception.

Earlier, on 22 February, Ukrainians donated a record Hr 20.5 million (over $707,000) to Come Back Alive. It happened right after Russian President Vladimir Putin sent troops into the Kremlin-occupied territories of Donetsk and Luhansk oblasts in eastern Ukraine, after officially recognizing them as independent states.

It was more than the charity received over the year 2021.

Many Ukrainians have since then lambasted Putin's actions on social media, sharing the link to the charity's website, urging others to support the Ukrainian military.

The Ukrainian IT platform DOU was the first one to start the so-called 'flashmob', says Oleg Karpenko, the charity's partner manager. DOU's head donated Hr 5 million to the charity on 22 February.

Other Ukrainian IT companies, businesses, and citizens followed soon, Karpenko says.

'The level of financial support that the foundation has received over the past few weeks is another indication that Ukraine and Ukrainians are ready to fight Russia in all possible forms,' the charity's head Taras Chmut wrote on Facebook.

The charity has already transferred 200 thermal imagers and thermal weapon sights to Ukrainians protecting Kyiv from the invasion.

Another Kyiv-based charity Army SOS raises money to support the Ukrainian military with necessary ammunition, shields, communication devices, and more. They say they focus on providing direct assistance to those soldiers who are on the very front line.

Those who live in Ukraine, foreigners included, can also join the new Territorial Defense Force that is currently successfully helping defend their local communities as part-time soldiers.

1 March 2022

Hundreds of thousands of refugees flee Ukraine as war rages on

Thaisa Semenova

Tears streamed down Margaryta Chornobryvets's face as she entered a refugee hostel in Krakow, Poland.

The 16-year-old, from Kyiv, was now safe from the bombs and rockets unleashed by Russian President Vladimir Putin on Ukraine on 24 February but was desperate at being separated from her family.

'My mother brought me to Krakow, got a little sleep, and went back to Ukraine to help orphans. My brother and father stayed there. I am with my sister, who managed to flee earlier as she was in Lviv. I cannot believe all this is real,' she told me on 27 February.

Marauders tried to attack Margaryta and her mother several times during their 28-hour-long trip to the Polish border, trying to block their path on the highway so they could steal the car.

They avoided the bandits, but eventually had to leave the car in the bordertown Grushiv and make the rest of the trip on foot. The line to the border stretched for kilometers and did not move for hours.

The United Nations Refugee Agency (UNHCR) said on 28 February that about 520,000 people had fled the country into bordering nations like Poland, Hungary, Moldova, Romania and Slovakia since the start of Russia's invasion.

Thousands more are still trying to get through the clogged borders, waiting in the cold for hours on end in cars or on foot with only minimal belongings.

Among those fleeing into Poland was Anastasiia Kotenko, 25, who carried her almost 2-year-old son in her arms for five hours while walking 11 kilometers on foot to the border.

Her husband drove them from the Ukrainian capital to the border on the first day of the war. The road took almost a day as there was constant shelling in the cities they passed by, and they had to constantly adjust their route.

Anastasiia tried to remain calm in front of her son so he wouldn't get upset, but she couldn't help herself.

'When Roma would hear explosions, I was saying "bam-bam", as if it was something that fell on the ground. Although when the whole car vibrates from the flash, a child can guess that this is not normal,' Anastasiia said.

When they finally arrived near the border, Anastasiia couldn't even hug her husband goodbye. She said that people were allowed to cross the border in groups of 20–30 people, and foreigners were treated horribly – they were pushed, and nobody tried to communicate with them.

'Somehow, we broke through. I was not even allowed to hug my husband in farewell because the crowd simply pushed me out. Immediately behind us, the gate closed. My husband was pushed away and shouted at.'

She told me that many volunteers brought food, medicine, and warm blankets for Ukrainian refugees on the Polish side of the border. Some of them offered a free ride to other cities in Poland and helped find a place to stay.

'This is nothing compared to war, but it is so much compared to our quiet lives,' she said.

Those who don't own cars have sought their way to Poland on trains.

Lyubava Boiko from Ternopil decided to leave the country on 25 February, bringing her dog with her. When she got to the station, she heard the announcement that the train would not go to Poland. The next one didn't go either, so she got on the one to Lviv, hoping she could catch another train there.

She said there were a few air sirens, but many people refused to hide in the shelter so they wouldn't lose their place in the line for the train.

When Lyubava came back from the shelter, even more people were on the platform: 'I thought people just would not fit on the platform and would fall on the track.'

According to her, people started to scream at each other and even physically fight for places on the train. Police officers were helping children get up inside, but some of them then realized their mothers were left on the platform.

'It is so scary when a child is standing in the middle of this chaos and doesn't understand what's going on,' she added.

Eventually, Lyubava was able to board the train.

'From the window, I looked at the people who didn't manage to get on the train. At that very moment, I broke down and cried.'

2 March 2022

Kyivans hide in subways as Russian forces bombard the capital
Igor Kossov

As Russian missiles rain down on their homes, many people of Kyiv have moved permanently into the safe shelter of the metro.

After being thrown back from the capital numerous times over the past week, Russian forces have decided to revert to their doctrinal terror tactics of pounding the city with bombs, rockets and artillery to try to break the defenders and their will.

On 1 March, at least two missiles aimed for Kyiv's TV tower struck the neighborhood of Dorohozhychy, damaging several buildings, killing five people and temporarily shutting down TV. One missile struck next to the historic Babyn Yar memorial to the victims of Nazi atrocities from the Second World War, the last time Europe saw a conflict on a scale so large.

Tetiana Boyko, 20, saw them coming. 'I was on the street. We were returning home to pick up some necessities. We were literally approaching the street crossing when we saw the missile. I thought it was a plane at first because it was winged,' Boyko said, as her husky, Curry, watched plaintively.

Thinking there was just the one missile, Boyko thought about returning to the safety of the Dorohozhychy metro station, where hundreds have been taking shelter in the past week. Then the second missile came and she sprinted back for the cover of her nearby apartment building.

'People began to panic and run for cover. Someone was just walking calmly, with no regard for his life, because death was very close,' she said.

The aftermath of the attack was plain to see – blackened buildings, twisted beams, and thousands of chunks of shattered glass and stone.

Fortunately, Kyiv's extremely deep metro tunnels are a perfect place to hide. Descending into the cavernous cool of the Dorohozhychy station, one is greeted with the sight of wall-to-wall blankets, tents, piles of personal goods and people sitting or lying on the floor, with their children and their pets, waiting and hoping that the Russians will be defeated and that they can have their lives back.

Around 11 a.m. the day after the missile attack, the place was emptier than usual. Many people go out during the day, to attend to their business, go home, wash up or change clothes, said Volodymyr Borodyansky, 70, a resident who does the same. Yesterday's missile exploded behind him as he was coming back from his house and entering the metro, making him sprint down the stairs.

But at night, when the danger is greatest, the place is packed with hundreds and hundreds of people. Children in neighboring spots on the floor chatter and play with one another. Cats and dogs perch on blankets by their owners, also adapting to this strange new normal in their lives.

Kateryna Belytska, 25, has been here for seven days: 'Here it's safer than on the street so it's relatively okay, but I'm worried for those who are on the street,' as well as people trapped in besieged cities towards the east.

Some of those people are her family members. They've been trapped in the town of Volnovakha in Donetsk Oblast, which saw extremely heavy fighting since Russia invaded and was reportedly almost completely destroyed and on the verge of humanitarian catastrophe.

'The Russians aren't allowing them a green corridor' to escape, she said. 'They're trapped there, they have no light and no food. When people tried to leave, they were shot at.'

In contrast, it's relatively decent in the metro, interviewees said. Volunteers deliver food, water and hot tea. Belytska and her sister praised the tasty pilaf that some local Uzbeks whip up for the people taking shelter. But, lacking appetite, they have to force themselves to eat when they start feeling light-headed from hunger.

Boyko said the same of Curry, who often refuses to eat and sometimes has to be forced. The dog is as on edge as the people and its sight of the outside world is limited to 15-minute morning walks when things are quiet.

The young woman is sheltering with her mother and sisters while her father serves with the city's Territorial Defense units. They never know where he is but, so far, they've stayed in contact and he's doing okay, Boyko said.

Olga Kuznetsova, 34, has the added challenge of taking care of her 4-year-old daughter. Kuznetsova and her family ran to the metro when they heard the first explosions and sirens over Kyiv, eventually deciding that it would be best to stay here full time, for now. Sometimes they take turns going home to grab stuff, change clothes or wash up.

'Down here it's very calm, a lot of Territorial Defense, police, we feel safe here. There are children here, they play amongst themselves, that's why it's relatively good,' she said.

When asked how her little girl is taking it, Kuznetsova said that she's okay, as she's too young to understand what's going on. 'But yesterday, when the tower was attacked, I got scared and started crying, that's when she felt my state and got scared too.'

Still, the presence of so many others in the same boat helps the locals stay strong.

'Here we talk to people whom we hadn't previously known, trying to watch the news, supporting what our army's doing, and worrying,' Borodyansky said.

When asked if he has anything to add, Borodyansky scrunches up his face in thought: 'I think that people should support Ukraine and Kyiv, which is the mother of the cities of Rus. The capital must be free.'

Over the past week, the majority of the world offered a tremendous out-pouring of support for Ukraine and moved to sanction Russia into the Middle Ages. But Borodyansky thinks that the support is a little late. 'I have to say, if [the support and sanctions] came at least six months ago, none of this would have happened,' he said. 'Our "Russian brothers" would never have come here. It's good, at least, that the world is doing it now.'

Interview with Artur Korniienko, culture reporter

'I volunteered for the army to defend my family, my friends, my town, my country, but I'm not a hero.'

What did you imagine your work would be like with The Kyiv Independent *before you joined the army on 22 February*?
I worked at first as a cultural journalist for the *Kyiv Post* in which I also wrote articles on social matters. I carried on with this work within *The Kyiv Independent*, which we co-founded with the team. I saw my task as being simple: help my fellow Ukrainians promote their culture and make it popular throughout the world. I like to think we were doing a good job: every year the world understood our country and our way of life better.

Why and when did you decide to give up journalism and join the Ukrainian Army?
During the months prior to the Russian invasion of Ukraine, I felt that there was a risk we'd lose all we'd worked for, in spite of all our efforts. I felt powerless. As a journalist, I could not see what I could do to stop the biggest country in the world from coming and killing our people and destroying our towns. We could only rely on our armed forces, tiny in comparison to the Russians. On 22 February, I therefore enrolled in the Territorial Defense so I'd be as useful as possible to the resistance, just in case the invasion took place. And two days later that is what happened: as my girlfriend and I entered the air raid shelter at 7 a.m., I was called up. Without any previous training, that same evening, I found myself patrolling Kyiv with an assault rifle.

As a journalist would you have felt you were not being useful to your country?
At that critical moment for my country, under very serious threat, I indeed felt I'd be more useful as a member of the armed forces. I felt powerless as a journalist. Two months later I still feel the same thing, but as soon as I sense that my journalist's job will be more useful, I'll be back. Fortunately I am still on *The Kyiv Independent*'s editorial staff; it's a young team that relies on being transparent, on managing democratically and on the potential of innovating its journalism. Once a journalist, always a journalist. Even though I know that anything can happen in wartime.

In the name of what did you join the ranks of the Territorial Defense, a branch of the Ukrainian armed forces? In the name of democracy?

I joined up to defend my family, my friends, my community, my quarter, my town, my country, my people and our culture. All that is under direct threat. I don't think about liberty and democracy every moment of the day just because I'm being threatened by bullets and bombs. But they are an integral part of our way of life, which is what is being attacked. By defending ourselves we defend these values.

Did you think through your decision?

Russia's war against Ukraine has now lasted for more than eight years and I have often thought about what I would do if the Russian army attacked my town and my family. In most of the situations I saw myself fleeing with my girlfriend, but I decided that if people did resist and I was armed, I'd fight. So I suppose that I was getting ready for this eventuality but I didn't really see it happening one day. I don't know how you get yourself ready mentally for a situation in which you can get killed or be forced to kill somebody. You can only try to be rational by trying to find a reason to give up your life or to take somebody else's. It's easier when you're defending your country and you have the feeling that justice is on your side, with the support of most of the civilized world. I'm a pacifist who is opposed to killing and to destruction, but not opposing this evil would only cause more death and suffering. In the first weeks, the cold and the stress did get the better of my strength.

Did you talk about your choice with your loved ones?

I talked about it only with my girlfriend, who also stayed in Kyiv and volunteered to help the military. But I never told my mother about it. She believes that I'm filling in papers somewhere in army headquarters. She is very worried and sends me a text message after each bombing. My friends and colleagues back me up.

How do you make yourself into a member of the armed forces?

We had lessons in civil defense at school and university where I learnt how an AK-47 worked and I was able to shoot a bit at the time. I didn't like it. My friends also showed me how to use air guns several times. But I had to follow a sped-up course when I was given the AK-47. My brothers in arms helped me and I learnt as I went along.

Putting down your notepad and pen and taking up such a weapon instead is hardly neutral. What is it that bonds together those who have made such a choice?

The civilians did what they could: by leaving the town they prevented the Russians from terrorizing them. Those who remained carried out a huge amount of work, especially in terms of intelligence gathering, but also by evacuating the civilians who wanted to go. As for the soldiers, we have certainly done enough — after all, the battle has been won. I don't want to be described as a hero. I simply answered my country's call as it considered me fit for combat. We did what we could to defend our country and our people, bonded by two attitudes: anger towards Russian atrocities, which freed a form of hatred; and pride in our people for the unity we have been able show.

Did your people's attitude astonish you?

We knew that our people would fight until we won or until our last breath. Our armed forces were ready and our effectiveness wasn't a surprise, given the Russian army's mediocre performance. However, what did surprise me was seeing Volodymyr Zelensky choosing to remain in the country and becoming the symbol of the resistance. Whatever happens, the Ukrainians are still fighting and that has without any doubt greatly helped our president, who was ready to make huge concessions to Putin, to acquire the status of resistance leader. The man has changed, he has become the symbol of the determination of his people and this is admirable.

Journalist only have words. Are they enough?

Sometimes, indeed, words aren't enough. For years we, the journalists, have tried speaking to the whole world about our country and of the Russian threat. We have obtained some results, especially our country's unity and solidarity from most civilized countries. But we haven't managed to beat censorship or propaganda in Russia. When the Russians, with their brains carefully washed, arrived in our country, the only way we had to defend ourselves was to take up our weapons. We had to do this whether we were singers, political experts, salesmen, farmers, computer scientists, waiters or journalists.

(Interview by Maria Poblete and Frédéric Ploquin)

3 March 2022

Kyiv under shelling: 'First thing I heard was my child's scream'
Anna Myroniuk

One week since Russia began its full-scale war against Ukraine, the civilian death toll is in the hundreds, while thousands have been left injured.

According to the United Nations, over 600 civilians have died as a result of Russia's aggression.

Russian troops have shelled residential areas, hitting civilian targets such as schools, kindergartens and nurseries. Thousands have been forced out of their homes.

Houses of ordinary Ukrainians have been shattered by airstrikes, Grad rocket launchers and cruise missiles fired from Russian and Belarusian territory.

This is the story of two families who were nearly killed by shelling.

Lucky to survive
It was eight o'clock on 26 February. The family of Maksym Karaush gathered for breakfast in the kitchen of their Kyiv apartment.

A few minutes into the meal, a Russian missile hit their bedroom.

'The light went out instantly, it turned black, smoke filled the room,' Karaush, a father of two, recalled. 'The first thing I heard was a child's scream. My youngest son, he was lucky. He was sitting behind the wall. The wall is strong, it held the strike.'

Maksym and his son Georgiy, 11, were spared. But his wife, Iryna, and their oldest son, Marko, 19, were severely injured. They were standing in the doorway when the strike occurred.

'The shot wave knocked them off their feet. Bricks, gravel, debris fell from above,' Karaush said.

He found Georgiy and asked a neighbor to get the child out of the building. Then he dug up his son and wife from the rubble and put splints on their legs. Together with rescuers, they took Iryna and Marko down the stairs.

The shelling left Iryna with a broken leg. She went through a surgery. A few more are ahead. Marko has a spinal injury and a broken leg. His condition is of the most concern. The first surgery was successful – the doctors managed to save his leg.

Now Karaush is running in between two hospitals to help his loved ones.

'We were lucky to survive,' he said. 'So many people in Kyiv either were killed or lost their relatives in the bombardments.'

What saved them is breakfast, Karaush said. 'There is almost nothing left from our apartment but the kitchen,' he said.

Head full of glass

The next morning, 27 February, was no different from the one before – Russia shelled people's homes in Kyiv.

Same time, different place.

It was around 8 a.m. when Lyudmyla Honcharenko, 59, a concierge at a Kyiv residential building was sitting on a sofa next to a TV set at her workplace.

'Suddenly, out of the blue, I hear a bang, then a flash,' she recalled. That was a Russian missile hitting the ground next to the entrance to the building. Seven cars parked outside caught fire.

'Glass rained down right on me from the window. Good thing I had blinds there. They saved me,' she said. 'I had blood all over my face, my head was full of glass. You can't imagine.'

The explosion was so heavy, she said, that it tore out an iron door.

The residents immediately rushed to the bomb shelter.

'People were screaming and crying. Pregnant women, people with children, with little babies,' she said. 'There was a lot of panic.'

She did not follow them and immediately ran home to her son.

'I was in sweatpants and in slippers,' Honcharenko said. 'As I was walking home, I was trembling out of fear so badly,' she added.

She was stunned by the explosion but otherwise escaped in one piece.

'I do not know how much longer we can stand this,' Honcharenko said.

4 March 2022

In the nation's darkest hours, Ukrainians look out for each other
Daria Shulzhenko

Sixteen-year-old Ukrainian Anna Liutyk will never forget that early morning when she woke up to her mother screaming the most terrifying words she had ever heard.

'The war has started,' Liutyk's mother cried out. 'Putin started a war.'

Multiple Ukrainian cities were shelled that same day on 24 February, as Russia declared a major war on Ukraine, attacking the country with missiles, helicopters, tanks, and ships.

Russian troops have already killed hundreds of civilian Ukrainians, destroying multiple objects of critical societal infrastructure.

But in the face of great adversity, Ukrainians showed unprecedented unity.

Civilians all across the country do whatever it takes to help each other: they deliver medicine and food for those hiding in bomb shelters. Regular citizens and restaurant chefs prepare meals for the military, refugees, and civilians. People adopt abandoned animals and offer shelters and rides to fellow Ukrainians.

Liutyk is no exception: the girl, together with her mother and best friend, has been offering warm food and drinks for free to fleeing Ukrainians who are spending exhausting hours in lines on the border with Poland in Lviv Oblast, where she lives.

'Such difficult times either break the nation or, just like in our case, unite it entirely,' Liutyk says.

Teenagers supporting refugees

On the first day of war, Liutyk didn't go to school, and neither did other children all over Ukraine.

She and her mother spent the entire day monitoring the news and getting in touch with their loved ones.

As they left the house later that day, the family saw hundreds of people heading to the border checkpoint nearby. Liutyk noticed a lot of foreigners among them.

According to the United Nations, 1 million people have already fled Ukraine in an attempt to escape the brutal war. Ukrainians flee to neighboring countries such as Poland, Moldova, Hungary, Romania, and others. Over 50,000 foreigners have also left Ukraine since 24 February.

Most of them spent hours if not days in enormously long lines to cross the border.

'I was just standing on the street, crying, as I realized that this was an actual war and people were leaving,' Liutyk says.

The number of people increased as night fell. As Liutyk looked out of the window at around 10 p.m., she noticed the line stretching right to her house, located about 15 kilometers from the state border.

'We were slightly scared to see so many strangers at first,' Liutyk says. 'So we were sitting quietly in our house, with the lights off.'

Liutyk soon learned her mother's friend started helping the refugees, offering them overnight shelter and some food. They decided to help as well.

As the line kept growing on the next day, Liutyk noticed an exhausted old woman with two grandchildren, looking for a restroom. She invited them in. The woman sat near the front door, holding her grandson and shuddering every time she heard some loud noise.

'That was shocking,' Liutyk says.

She called her friend Yaryna to help. The girls started walking along the line and offering hot tea and coffee to people trying to get through the clogged borders. The next day, they put a table outside Liutyk's house and began offering people hot dishes like traditional Ukrainian *borshch*, *salo* (salted pork fat) with bread and pickles, as well as sweets and hot drinks.

Liutyk says she has never hugged so many people and has never heard so many kind words from strangers.

'It inspires and gives hope that we will win,' she says.

Although there are almost no lines now, Liutyk continues supporting those in need: she helps to take care of adults and kids staying at the refugee shelter set up in a local school. Her mother and her friends are also on board.

In those kind words, comforting hugs, and gratuitous mutual support, Liutyk sees the unity of the Ukrainian people. And that, she says, is something that defines Ukraine.

'We, Ukrainians, are so strong,' Liutyk says. 'We try to help each other however we can because it is who we are,' she adds. 'It is in our veins.'

Free psychological aid

24 February was one of the scariest days for Kyiv-based psychologist Julia Naista.

Her 3-year-old baby boy wasn't sleeping well at night 'as if feeling something was coming', Naista says. When she saw the light from explosions out of her window, Naista immediately checked the news.

Her worst nightmare proved to be true. Putin had launched a war on Ukraine.

'I was very scared,' she says.

Naista and her husband decided to leave the capital as soon as possible. 'I realized that we either leave Kyiv now or never,' Naista says.

Early morning on 25 February, the family headed to Mukachevo, Naista's home town in western Ukraine. She did not have a go-bag prepared for the emergency, only some documents packed the day before. The rest, she says, they were packing in complete chaos, just throwing some clothes into the suitcase. She forgot to put in many necessities like socks or underwear for her baby.

When locals found out she was in need of clothes for her son they brought her even more of it than she needed.

'People were so kind, I had to ask them to stop bringing clothes as we already had too much,' she says, adding that she was impressed and grateful for the support.

She, too, decided to step in and help others.

Psychologist Naista reached out to all of her former and current patients, asking them if they needed support in such a difficult time.

She's currently offering free psychological aid for anyone who needs it.

She joined the group of volunteers in Mukachevo to provide refugees and their children with psychological assistance. She also holds online consultations helping people overcome anxiety and stress caused by the war.

Besides psychological help, she also occasionally helps fleeing people find petrol and accommodation to relocate to in western Ukraine.

She says this social support is essential in handling tough situations. 'Before [the war] we could get this support from family members. But now we get it from all the people of Ukraine,' she says. 'We are united, we are together and it gives hope that everything will be fine.'

Entrepreneur-turned-volunteer

On 23 February, Kyiv citizen Valeria Kuzmenko was a successful entrepreneur, co-owning a beauty salon and a law firm. But just like millions of other Ukrainians, Kuzmenko's life changed drastically overnight when Russia began a major war on Ukraine.

'My whole life collapsed,' Kuzmenko says.

Kuzmenko, 24, says she wasn't afraid for her life, only for the lives of her loved ones. So she brought her mother and their beloved dog to a place safer than their home on the outskirts of Kyiv. She decided not to stay with them, but to come back to her home town and support those who were left alone there.

Kuzmenko reached out to her friend in the military, asking how she could help them. She ended up purchasing all hygiene products from a local store and donated them to the army.

It took her several days to turn from a successful entrepreneur into a fearless volunteer.

Not only does she volunteer for the military, raising money to purchase various goods like slippers, yellow fabric for armbands for Territorial Defense units, cigarettes, and more, but she also delivers food and medicine to those civilians who are unable to leave their apartments or bomb shelters.

'I get a lot of requests from citizens who are [hiding] in basements and are hungry or need some special medicines,' Kuzmenko says.

She uses her Instagram account as a platform to look for those who need help, as well as find those who can help.

Thousands of regular Ukrainians along with influencers began using their accounts on social media as platforms to help each other since the outbreak of war. They spread the word online to find lost relatives, rare medicine for the elderly or kids, or a simple ride or a place to sleep.

Kuzmenko says she gets requests not only from Kyiv and Kyiv Oblast but from other regions as well. She tries to help those in Kyiv immediately and looks for volunteers in other regions.

But it's not only people she assists: Kuzmenko says she also rescues pets abandoned by their owners due to war. Her military base is now home not only to soldiers and volunteers but to rescued cats and dogs as well.

Surrounded by many strangers every day, Kuzmenko says she hasn't seen a quarrel or an argument among them ever since the war started. 'Everyone just rushes to help each other,' Kuzmenko says.

Every day she learns about the death of an acquintance. And every day she cries after returning home. Yet these tragedies motivate Kuzmenko to keep helping others and fight 'for the future of her family, nation, and country'.

'For my beloved and great Ukraine.'

5 March 2022

Ukrainian loses parent to Russian propaganda: 'I can consider myself an orphan'

Thaisa Semenova

'I woke up from a call from a friend. He told me Russia was bombing Kyiv,' says Artem Basistiy, a 29-year-old from Crimea, who had lived in Kyiv for the last four years. 'Then I heard a siren going off, quickly grabbed the dog, and ran to the shelter. After the air raid was over, I called my mom to tell her I was alive. She answered, "What are you talking about? Of course, you are. Putin is trying to save you."'

Basistiy has been regularly speaking with his mother, who continues to live in the Russia-occupied peninsula. Since 24 February, when Russia launched its full-scale war against Ukraine, Basistiy says he isn't succeeding at convincing his mother of how much danger he is in.

According to the United Nations, nine days of Russia's war have already killed 752 civilians. Footage of Russian shelling of residential areas, including schools, kindergartens and hospitals has been making rounds all over the internet. However, people living in Russia and Russian-occupied areas such as Crimea and Donbas have been blindsided.

Russian President Vladimir Putin claimed to have 'no ill intentions towards neighboring countries' and denied firing missiles on the civil infrastructure during what he calls a 'special military operation' to 'disarm and de-Nazify' Ukraine.

The statement fits well into Moscow's age-old tactic, inherited from the Soviet Union, to construct a false reality in an attempt to hide facts and alleged war crimes.

The USSR called the Soviet invasion of Finland a 'liberation campaign', the Soviet–Afghan war an 'operation of providing international assistance' to Afghanistan, while Russia's previous major war, the invasion of Georgia, was branded as a campaign 'to force to peace'.

This time, to mute dissent and limit the Russian people's access to information, the Kremlin took new heights.

On 4 March, Russia stepped up censorship by passing a law punishing the spreading of 'false information' about Russia's armed forces with up to 15 years in prison. The law criminalized calling the Russian war against Ukraine a 'war' on social media or any news article or broadcast.

As a result, the semi-independent media outlets, the Echo of Moscow radio station and the TV Rain television channel shut down, Facebook and Twitter were officially banned, while those media outlets that decided to keep operating, such as *Novaya Gazeta*, agreed to take down coverage of Russia's war on the Kremlin's request.

TV channels, which are still the main source of information for 62% of the country's population according to Levada's center poll, have been making baseless claims that Ukrainians indiscriminately bombed their own hospitals and killed their civilians.

For many Ukrainians it means very tough conversations with relatives in Russia or in Russia-occupied territories of Ukraine, who don't believe their first-hand accounts of Russian attacks.

'I begged my mom not to watch Russian propaganda and to open other sources – Ukrainian, American, or British, doesn't matter. But she told me they were zombifying us,' Artem said.

He knew his mother was a Russia supporter long before the all-out war began. Unlike him, she was happy when the Russian flag was raised over the building of the Crimean parliament in 2014. She praised Putin for being a strong leader and mocked Ukraine's Volodymyr Zelensky, calling him a 'clown'.

But Basistiy hoped that, in the end, she would believe him, her own son, over the TV propaganda.

On the fourth day of the war, he decided to join the Territorial Defense Forces of Ukraine. So far, he has not entered its ranks, waiting for his turn.

'I called her again in a few days, hoping she followed my advice, read some independent news outlets, and watched videos I sent her,' Artem said. 'Unfortunately, nothing changed at all. Even after the destroyed apartment buildings in Kyiv, Kharkiv, Cherkasy, Sumy … She said we were hitting our own citizens with high-precision artillery.'

At the end of the conversation, he said to his mother 'the same thing Ukrainian defenders told the Russian warship'. On the first day of war, Ukrainian guards of the Zmiiny (Snake) Island in the Black Sea famously told a Russian warship that demanded that they surrender to 'go f*ck yourself'.

Later Basistiy posted a story on Instagram saying: '02/03/2022, the day I lost my mom.'

He was devastated, wanted to tear everything, throw things, cry, bang his head against the wall. He was having a nervous breakdown, he said. He hoped that at least his father would support and believe him, but he couldn't know for sure as there was no way to reach him.

'My father works on a drilling rig in the Black Sea between Crimea and Odesa. His team was supposed to be replaced the day before the invasion, but they are still at sea, and I still haven't talked to him,' he said.

Basistiy's father is from Grozny, Chechnya, the city war-torn by Russia twice, in 1994–1996 and 1999–2000, what is known as the First and Second Chechen War. His family fled to Crimea accompanied by soldiers, having only minimal belongings.

'My father knows what war is firsthand. I really hope that we will get in touch soon and he will understand everything and be able to convey this to my mom. Otherwise, I can consider myself an orphan with 100% certainty.'

6 March 2022

Kyiv resident gives birth during war: 'I forgot about the bombings only in labor'

Thaisa Semenova

A cold basement with a corridor and small rooms on both sides, previously used as a wardrobe for the hospital staff. Chairs, worn benches, and cradles for newborns. This is where Mariia Shostak, 25, met her son for the first time.

He was born in Kyiv on 25 February, or just 'the second day' of Russia's all-out war.

The news about Russia's further invasion into Ukraine found Shostak in the hospital ward at 6 a.m. a day earlier, in the pathology pregnancy department of the Kyiv city maternity hospital in Solomianskyi district, where she was put to monitor her high-risk pregnancy.

The doctor tried to remain calm, joking: 'Don't be afraid. Women gave birth even in besieged Leningrad.' But the nurses looked confused and whispered that they had no instructions on how to act.

Shostak was having light contractions when the siren went off. The nurses helped her get on a wheelchair and come down to the hospital bomb shelter.

It was very crowded inside. In addition to all the patients and staff, residents of neighboring homes had come there to hide from Russian missiles. After a few hours, she returned to the ward but was told to be ready to hide any moment again.

She didn't sleep that night as her contractions became more and more intense, and she was losing her nerve from constantly scrolling through newsfeeds on her phone.

In the morning, Shostak had to go to the shelter again. Soon afterwards the doctor examined her and said she would be delivering the baby right there. She called her husband, asked him to buy some medicine and groceries on the way to the hospital, but he couldn't get there in time as he was stuck in traffic.

'I was so pissed off he didn't go to the pharmacy in advance, and he wasn't there when I went into labor,' Shostak recalled. 'I will not delve into all medical details, but during the delivery, it was probably the only time in this horrible week I forgot about the war raging on.'

Shostak tried for a natural delivery for five hours but eventually agreed to surgery under anesthesia: 'Through the sleep, I heard my son's weight – 4.09 kilograms.'

There was another air raid alert when her husband showed up at the hospital's bunker. He came together with the nurse who held their son, and Shostak finally got a chance to meet him properly.

Soon after that, Russian forces struck a residential building near the hospital.

In the next three days, Shostak and her family spent the vast majority of their time in the shelter. She was in so much pain after the surgery she could barely speak, let alone walk up the stairs. And the elevator always had a line.

'My husband and I sat in the shelter's hallway, rocking the baby in turns. It was the hardest time for me because before and after delivery, my legs were terribly swollen. I just wanted to get into bed,' she said.

Shostak told me that there were enough medical supplies in the hospital shelter and devices for fetal CTG, but mixtures for feeding babies were in short supply. Due to the stress, many mothers did not get colostrum or milk immediately, and the hospital, according to Shostak, provided one milk mixture bottle for two or three babies.

Several times in the bunker, Shostak felt she could not sit anymore, so her husband took her upstairs, where she managed to get some sleep. All days in the maternity ward merged into one, she said, as it was hard to distinguish day from night, and it felt like the war had lasted at least for a few months already. She tried to calm down by not reading the news about the shelling and bombing. But it was hardly possible to ignore the sound of missiles hitting nearby, she said.

'Sometimes it helped to focus on my thoughts and desires.' Shostak remembers she wanted coffee so bad she could smell it from another room. She asked her husband to get some from the nurses. 'They poured us custard coffee, soluble coffee, and even gave us a pack of cookies. Our money was flatly refused. It was probably the most delicious instant coffee of my life,' she recalled.

On 1 March, Shostak and her son were discharged from the hospital.

'Of course, I imagined all of this very differently. I wanted to be surrounded by family, friends, flowers, to take some photos,' Shostak said. 'But in reality, my husband drove the car as close as possible to the hospital's exit, and we jumped into it, accompanied by a Territorial Defense Forces soldier, and left.'

7 March 2022

Civilians flee in terror as Ukraine's military deter Russia in Irpin

Illia Ponomarenko

Hundreds of terrified people cautiously walk through the debris of concrete and twisted metal, trying to cross the Irpen River on foot.

'Come on, no need to rush, careful,' a Ukrainian soldier says while helping civilians onto concrete blocks leading to a stairway.

Mothers hold up their crying babies, young men drag their bicycles, and elderly people carry bags of essentials. Ukrainians and foreigners, all fleeing a brutal war that came in its full destructive power in just a snap.

The rolling thunder sound of heavy fighting reaches from the north.

This messy water crossing used to be a bridge connecting Kyiv and Irpin, a satellite city of 60,000 people just northwest of Ukraine's capital.

Only 10 days earlier, Irpin was a blossoming, comfortable suburb booming with housing developments. Now, along with nearby cities of Hostomel and Bucha, it is one of the worst hotspots of Russia's full-fledged invasion of Ukraine that was unleashed on 24 February.

The bridge is in shambles after being blown up by Ukrainian forces in an attempt to slow the approach of Russian forces.

One of the final frontiers of deterring the enemy advance to the heart of the capital city, it is at the same time the only way for many to flee on foot ...

So people flee.

They flee by their cars packed to the full, bringing out all they can, and crossing the destroyed bridge by foot.

Civilian volunteers marking their cars with signs reading 'Children' and 'Evacuation' shuttle between the city and the bridge in the hope to rescue as many as possible. On their way back to Irpin were vehicles full of smiling Ukrainian soldiers holding on to their rifles and NLAW tank killers provided by the United Kingdom.

As of 4 March, the streets of Irpin were almost totally empty but still almost intact. Some civilians even preferred to stay in the city, standing in long queues for food and medicine at stores.

The sounds of heavy fighting, however, were getting closer from the north. Yet another artillery duel between Ukrainian and Russian forces is in full throttle.

As groups of Territorial Defense fighters marked by yellow armlets gather together at a local tiny coffee shop, probably the last of its kind, they pay little attention to the sough of incoming shelling.

A young man, also with a home guard armlet, cycles to the crowd at an insane speed. 'Good god, it's just a complete nightmare,' he jumps off his bicycle, breathing heavily. He is shocked, his eyes goggled. 'We need to speed up the civilian evacuation.'

According to messages coming from their local authorities, the cities have been badly damaged in the fighting, with hundreds, if not thousands, of civilians, trapped in basements not able to flee.

Despite numerous calls, Russia has not agreed to provide safe civilian passages.

In Irpin, thousands of women and children gathered at the city railway station, in an attempt to take an evacuation train. On 5 March, Russia bombed a railway track leading to Kyiv, effectively cutting the way out off.

Meanwhile, the Ukrainian emergency service personnel continued evacuating civilians to the destroyed bridge at the city's southern outskirt as Russia seized most of Irpin.

By the afternoon of 6 March, at least 200 civilians, including 50 children, have been taken to a safe place outside the city.

Nonetheless, even the passage through the Irpin bridge, turned into a nightmare as Russian forces came closer.

On 6 March at noon, Russians shelled the passage while it was full of civilians. According to reports from the ground, a family of four, including two children, was killed. In total, at least eight civilians were killed in Irpin on 6 March alone, according to Mayor Oleksandr Markushyn.

8 March 2022

Death of volunteers helping starving animals

Anna Myroniuk

At noon on 4 March, an SUV drove through the streets of Bucha, formerly a cozy green town near Kyiv, now a hotspot of Russia's war against Ukraine.

Three people were in the car: Serhiy Ustymenko, 25, a co-founder of a car repair shop, Maxym Kuzmenko, 28, a hookah server, and Anastasia Yalanska, 26, a lead recruiter at an IT company.

Bucha was a dangerous place, largely controlled by Russian forces. The three young Ukrainians were there on an important mission.

They had just delivered dog food to a dog shelter that had run out of it and were on their way back to pick up Ustymenko's parents. They had just nearly made it home. As the car was approaching their house, there was a deafening sound. A Russian vehicle – witnesses identify it as either a tank or an infantry fighting vehicle – opened fire on the car.

When the shooting stopped, Valeriy Ustymenko, the father of Serhiy, ran to the car. Everyone inside was already dead. He dragged out the three bodies and took them to his basement, where he has been hiding from the constant shelling, like most people in Bucha.

Three days later, the bodies are still there. Due to shelling, they can't be buried. Their friends and families can't say goodbye to their loved ones. Ustymenko's father is still in the basement, with the bodies of his son and his son's two friends.

There was no way that Russians didn't know they were shooting at civilians, the victims' friends say. 'The car was [obviously] civilian,' said Dmytro Zubkov, a friend of Maxym Kuzmenko. 'Maxym was wearing a hat with a pom pom. They didn't look like the military at all.'

Ustymenko turned 25 in December. Despite his young age, he had managed to achieve a lot. He co-founded a car repair shop in Kyiv and united a big crowd of friends around it, said his friend Ivan Soloviy. 'He was the best driver of, well,' Soloviy paused, 'all of Kyiv.'

Ustymenko was a member of several automobile clubs and groups, Soloviy said. 'His service station was always open for us. Recently, we would only get together there.'

Friends remember Ustymenko as 'the soul of any company', but also a kind and reliable friend. 'He was a friend,' Soloviy said, sobbing, 'that would never betray you.'

Maxym Kuzmenko, 28, a hookah server in a Kyiv bar, is also remembered warmly by his friends. 'He was always there for those who needed him,' said Kateryna Zhvalyuk, his employer and friend.

During the coronavirus lockdown in Kyiv, Kuzmenko volunteered as a driver. He returned to volunteer work when Russia launched its full-scale invasion of Ukraine in late February. When the invasion started, Zhvalyuk's bar started helping the Ukrainian army and hospitals with food. Kuzmenko ran deliveries.

When the bar ran out of food, Kuzmenko decided to keep volunteering with his other friends, delivering essential goods to people across Kyiv Oblast. Zubkov, a co-founder of a pizza restaurant chain, was one of those friends. He cooked meals that Kuzmenko delivered. 'We cooked for everyone who needed it,' he said. 'More often we helped the elderly and children's cancer hospitals.'

'He always did more than was expected from him. You give him a task and he does more,' said Zhvalyuk. 'I used to ask him: "Why are you doing more when it's good enough already?" He would answer: "I must get better than I am now."'

Anastasia Yalanska, 26, was a talented IT recruiter. She started her new job just three weeks ago. The team was happy to have her join them, her colleagues said. 'I asked her if she wanted to grow and run HR for a large company ... how high she wanted to reach ... she said: "Yes, I can do it",' said Jeremy Achin, her boss. 'She was very ambitious, she was not scared.'

Achin thought that with the right guidance Yalanska could achieve great heights in her field. 'But now we will never see that future,' he said, bursting into tears.

Andriy Piddubny, Yalanska's former colleague, remembers her warmly. He said she was 'professional, honest, and straightforward'. 'She always spoke her mind,' he said. 'She was very dedicated and upbeat, everyone loved her.'

Yalanska's best friend Anastasiya Hryshchenko said that her family and friends were concerned for her safety and asked her to stay away from places of heavy shelling. 'She always helped those in need,' said Yalanska's husband Eugen Yalanskiy. 'Until her last breath. She was the best of all people.'

9 March 2022

Ukraine's biggest children's hospital treats people wounded by Russians

Igor Kossov

When surgeon Oleh Godik woke up on 24 February, he knew that life had changed fundamentally.

A day later, when he had to operate on a boy who'd been critically wounded in the neck by shrapnel from Russian forces, he knew he had been right. Despite his best attempts to save the boy, the wound was too severe. The child died not long after.

Godik works at Ohmatdyt, Ukraine's biggest children's hospital, whose name is an acronym for Ohrana Materynstva y Dytynstva (Protection of Motherhood and Childhood).

'After we finished operating, we understood that this is not war but terrorism,' Godik said in an 8 March interview, in the hospital's new surgery center, securely on the ground floor in its sturdiest building. 'The Russian soldiers were shooting the civilian population even then – [the child's] entire family was shot and killed.'

Since the first day of Russia's invasion, this prestigious and storied institution was forced to grapple with the challenge of defending its hundreds of patients not just from cancer and other serious ailments but from the bullets and missiles outside.

In the opening days of the war, firefights between Ukrainian forces and Russian advance reconnaissance teams took place near the hospital's walls. Several rounds struck the original surgery center, breaking windows. While the Russian saboteurs were swept from the city, the hospital is still in danger. A few days ago, a Russian cruise missile was destroyed by Kyiv's air defenses just overhead.

The Kyiv-based hospital's hundreds of staffers scrambled to rearrange the interior to ensure the safety of the staff and their patients. As Russian forces pushed towards Kyiv, Ohmatdyt began to evacuate patients to the relative safety of western Ukraine or to other countries.

By 8 March, the hospital evacuated all the patients it could, Godik said. There are a few critical patients that cannot be moved and remain in Ohmatdyt's care. I watched one of the last of the evacuation buses, plastered with handwritten signs saying 'Children', fill up with patients, their family members and several staffers on 8 March, amid heavy flurries of snow. A doctor and a spokesperson embraced tightly at the hospital entrance as they said goodbye.

The remainder of the staff, about 300 people, has hunkered down, many moving in to live in the hospital full-time. When the war began, they'd set up an underground bomb shelter and a secure surgery ward and prepared themselves to receive children and adults wounded by Russian forces, who have been blasting civilians every day since the invasion began.

They hadn't had to wait long for the casualties to arrive.

'When a Russian tank column goes in [to a populated area], it shoots left and right at the residential houses,' pediatric surgeon and professor Anatoliy Levitskiy told me. 'A mother is killed, a grandmother's legs are torn off. A father brings in a child – the father has a light wound.'

The little girl he was talking about also got off relatively easily – the flesh on the bottom of her foot was stripped away by Russian fire and the hospital closed the wound on 8 March, using the latest in modern equipment.

That's just one example. Ever since the first boy was brought in on 25 February – and died – the hospital has treated over 15 serious casualties, half of them children. Many suffered wounds to their extremities or worse.

The hospital also treated many other casualties, whose injuries were less serious and are now able to recover relatively quickly.

In the first few days, there were more people with bullet wounds. Later on, as Russia's blitz failed and it reverted to its doctrinal terror tactics of shelling civilians, more people were brought in with fragmentation wounds, largely from mortars, Levitskiy said.

In a 5 March interview with the *Current Time* news outlet, Ohmatdyt director Volodymyr Zhovnyr described treating an 11-year-old who had been hit by a mortar fragment in the jaw. The child's family members also took wounds to the arms and legs in the same incident – Russian forces fired on their location as they tried to escape.

The wounds aren't just physical. Lidiia Dmytrashko, the hospital's press attaché, described the psychological scars of young and adult patients. 'There are children whose mothers were blown up before their eyes,' said

Dmytrashko. 'Of course there are children who arrived in a horrible psychological state. One boy couldn't unclench his hands. One girl is drawing pictures for her [late] mother ... Some have panic attacks. Everyone's taking it differently.'

The hospital has a team of psychologists working with every patient, most of whom remain under extreme stress.

As a surgeon, Godik is able to compartmentalize his stress and set it aside. 'It's professionalism,' he said. 'We know that this is our job.'

'I can quote an old film of the occupiers, *The Officers*,' he said. 'There was a phrase in it: "the profession to defend the homeland." I've thought about taking an assault rifle to go kill and defend but, when I started operating, I decided that my hands are needed more here.'

People who need his hands are largely trickling in from the outskirts of Kyiv, particularly the battlegrounds of Irpin and Bucha, two suburban towns that have been mauled and partly occupied by Russian forces.

According to multiple accounts, Russian forces have indiscriminately fired on civilian targets such as buildings and vehicles, destroying and wounding an unknown number of people with direct-fire guns and indirect-fire shells, mortars and rockets.

The Russians have also blocked a significant portion of the population from leaving, either by turning them away or by firing on their escape routes. On 6 March, Russian mortar teams deliberately targeted a refugee evacuation column trying to cross Irpin River into Kyiv by walking across planks under the destroyed bridge.

Multiple journalists saw the Russian mortarmen bracket their shots, walking their fire closer and closer to the fleeing civilians until they killed eight people, including one family – a mother, two children and a family friend.

Those who are blocked in or too afraid to leave Irpin and Bucha have it just as bad. They've been disconnected from electricity and many have suffered interruptions to their food and gas supply. Many of them are sick or injured and unable to leave, as supplies dwindle to a critical level.

Ombudsman Lyudmyla Denisova had reported on 6 March that two injured children in Bucha died due to their inability to receive medical care. Medic Viktoria Kramarenko, who helps people fleeing from the area, confirmed that the hospitals in Irpin have wounded people and small children, who are blocked from leaving by Russian forces.

Ohmatdyt knows this all too well. While the doctors here live in relative comfort, thanks to Kyiv's abundant supplies and the tireless work of volunteers, things are much worse outside the city. 'In Irpin, there's an army hospital with lots of civilians but they can't evacuate,' said Godik. 'Many wounded people from the villages are also there who can't be transported here.'

The other day, he said, a mother and her young son who managed to escape the area had been brought in to Ohmatdyt. The boy had been wounded in the hip and the mother, who has diabetes, was left devoid of insulin, as they sheltered in a basement for five days. The mother has been placed on life support and her condition has stabilized.

'We're waiting for the green corridors from Bucha, Irpin and Hostomel, then we'll expect to get a flow of patients,' he said. 'We are focusing our attention on organizing more beds.'

Things are bad north of Kyiv as well. One traumatology colleague is caught in occupied territory, tending to 11 civilian wounded – the only surgeon in the town of Dymer, according to Godik. 'He has no anesthesiologist, nothing,' the surgeon said. 'He's already lost one patient.'

Russian troops in the area are becoming increasingly ferocious by the day, he added, a statement confirmed almost verbatim by *The Kyiv Independent*'s source in the neighboring village of Kozarovichi.

In spite of these horrors, Ohmatdyt staff is doggedly determined to believe in the best. Colleagues and companies from all over the world, including Israel, the US and Switzerland, have offered support – money, equipment and other aid, helping keep up spirits and the faith that Ukrainian victory is coming.

'"Before the war" and "during the war" – things have completely changed,' said Levitskiy. 'I hope there will be an "after the war".'

11 March 2022

Trendy restaurants in Kyiv switch to cook for army, hospitals, elderly amid war

Anna Myroniuk

Editor's note: The Kyiv Independent *isn't sharing the names of the restaurants in this story for security reasons.*

Before the war, this restaurant in central Kyiv was always packed, no matter the time of the day. It was a popular spot among creative youth and foreigners.

In usual times, it served beef bourguignon and Kyiv mule cocktails, but the war made changes to the menu. Now the restaurant bakes bread for hospitals and cooks chicken soup for defenders of the city.

This restaurant is among dozens in Kyiv that shut down for customers but opened their kitchens to volunteers to help the country amid war.

The place is hardly recognizable from its days of partying. The decorations are gone, and the windows are covered with black fabric.

But just like before the war, the restaurant is a magnet for young people. Volunteers come here to cook for those in need. Helping the country in the company of like-minded people helps them cope with the tragedy of war.

As volunteers pack meals for delivery, a reminder of the restaurant's normal life comes through: the techno music playing from the speakers.

A ladle instead of machine gun

Pavlo Khrobust, 25, used to work at a restaurant as a cook but quit not long ago. The war brought him back to the familiar kitchen – now, as a volunteer.

'At first, I wanted to join the Territorial Defense Forces,' Khrobust said. 'But I realized that I am useless there. I started thinking what use I could be of and figured – it's cooking.'

'Instead of a machine gun I grabbed a ladle and a knife,' he went on.

The quality of army food is far from restaurant dishes, Khrobust said. He wanted to change that and provide soldiers with healthy and tasty meals. 'Considering the intensity of physical activities of the soldiers, they require food different from what they have in the army, something more delicious,' he said.

'Good food keeps the spirit high,' Khrobust said. 'The soldiers do everything so we can sleep at night and we do everything for them to be well-fed.'

He came up with a balanced menu, which includes vegetables, porridges, soups and sometimes, fruit.

Oleksiy Bilyk, 21, gives it a final touch – freshly baked bread. 'Someone said they can bring a lot of flour if we can make something out of it. I thought of a huge pizza oven we have in our second restaurant and realized we can use it to bake bread,' said Bilyk, a waiter.

He taught himself to bake taking lessons on the internet. At first, he did not have baking forms, so he used plates and pots instead – the bread was of various shapes.

'We delivered it to the hospitals and to lonely seniors. We would pack a few small buns,' he said. Now Bilyk bakes around 80 loaves a day, something he could not have imagined a few weeks ago. He had never baked before the war started.

He was unable to join the army due to an issue with his documents, so he was happy to be able to help in another way. 'I learned something new. I did something to help. And I feel relieved that I can be useful,' he said.

Olga Romanchuk, 23, also had to learn new things. A land specialist in an international company building windmills, she now helps out in the kitchen.

'I felt that I wanted to help, but I couldn't bear arms,' Romanchuk said. 'So, I thought I can cut potatoes, everyone can.'

Teaching volunteers to cook was the biggest challenge, said Khrobust. 'There are IT specialists here, there is a girl who is a chemist in a laboratory,' the chief cook said. 'We had to teach them, so it was a lot of work at first.'

But a couple of days later, they were already a team.

Restaurants uniting in a bid to help

The restaurant is among a dozen eateries in central Kyiv that joined efforts to help Ukrainian civilians and the military amid the war. Together they produce around 20,000 lunches daily. And that is just one group of restaurants in one neighborhood.

'During this tough time, we all managed to unite. It's such a Ukrainian thing, our strong side is to unite,' Vlada Herasimchuk, 25, said.

Herasimchuk is a waiter and now a coordinator of the volunteer movement of the area. 'There are many open kitchens in the center,' she said. 'Many people took on roles of coordinators. We collect inquiries all over the city and pass them along to one another to make logistics more convenient.'

The restaurants also share groceries with each other. 'We also have volunteers who have cars and who are ready to help [with deliveries],' Herasimchuk said.

Despite the threat of shelling, the volunteers have been coming to the restaurants to cook meals for those in need for over a week now. 'There is a very interesting thing I just realized,' Herasimchuk said. 'Ukrainians are very hardworking people. All people here, it's necessary for them to be doing something.'

12 March 2022

Evacuees risk their lives as they flee to Kyiv

Igor Kossov

While Ukrainian forces have, so far, successfully held off the Russian troops from taking Kyiv, the towns around the capital have become some of the most intense battlegrounds of the ongoing war.

Russia seized the outlying suburban towns with vehicles and infantry, setting up checkpoints and, in many cases, cutting off access to utilities, phone and internet access, and food.

The local civilians bore the brunt of the damage. Many remained trapped, in most cases for over a week, either because Russian forces wouldn't let them leave or they were afraid of being cut down by Russian fire if they tried to flee to the safety of Kyiv.

Scenes of Russian troops firing at civilians trying to flee, with bodies piling on the streets of Kyiv's northwest suburbs, have now become a horrific image of what Russia's war brought to Ukraine.

As of 9 March, the United Nations Office for Human Rights had recorded 1,424 civilian casualties, 516 killed, including 37 children, and 908 injured after Russia invaded Ukraine on 24 February. The organization believes that the actual figures are 'considerably higher, especially in government-controlled areas'.

The past week has seen numerous attempts to move civilians out of surrounded or occupied areas through 'green corridors' all over the country, the towns and villages around Kyiv being no exception.

But, as in many other parts of the country, Russian forces have selectively violated these corridors, either firing on the evacuees with indirect-fire weapons or shooting them point-blank.

For many, the road to safety was taxing, because of the trials along the way and the pain of what they had to leave behind.

The Kyiv Independent has gathered stories from people who fled the various towns and villages towards the safety of Kyiv.

Demydiv

The northern village of Demydiv of some 3,700 people sits near the edge of the reservoir, widely known as the Kyiv Sea. Valentyna Bilan was trapped there with her family from the first days of the war and until 9 March, when they got out.

'We saw a lot of tanks coming from Belarus,' she told me by phone after successfully escaping into Kyiv with her husband and dog. 'Then battles began in our village. The center was destroyed, houses were demolished. We didn't have a phone connection, food or water all this time.'

The Russians climbed a nearby water tower and set up weapons on it, giving them a vantage point to shoot targets in the area. They also started going around houses, forcing the gates open and inspecting basements to see who was hiding there, according to Bilan.

All this made her and her husband decide that it was time to go.

An evacuation corridor was supposed to be in effect on 9 March. They linked up with a group of about 20 people that decided to ford the nearby length of the Irpin River and into the northern outskirts of Kyiv.

As soon as they departed, they ran into a young Russian soldier, who said with a smirk: 'So you actually think you'll make it?'

Bilan expressed confidence that they would. It was then that the soldier made a call to somebody.

When they got to the river, they saw it wasn't going to be easy. Ukrainian forces had blown a nearby dam and pumping station connecting the river to the reservoir, causing the water level to rise. To cross, the evacuees, including children and the elderly, would have to plunge into waist-high water, while the temperature outside was three degrees below freezing.

All they had to hand were a few styrofoam floats for the kids.

As soon as they began to cross, Russian helicopters arrived and began to strafe them with machine-gun fire, Bilan said.

'And then they started to shoot at us from the helicopters,' she told me, beginning to cry. 'At the children, at us, right where we were crossing ... I saw the "splash splash splash" of bullets on the water.'

'My neighbor went underwater and her child on the styrofoam was screaming. She came out again and they survived,' Bilan recalled through her tears. 'One paralyzed old woman was being helped by the guys. One guy is a hero, he went a dozen times into the water and pulled us out. After that, his legs were all purple from the cold.'

'I don't remember how I made it across – we had a dog and I apparently dragged her with me. I have a sick husband – I don't remember how we came out of it.'

Not everyone made it. Two of the men helping people cross were wounded by the machine gun fire, Bilan said. One was killed.

After they forded the river, they had to walk eight kilometers with all their stuff, while soaked, in sub-zero temperatures, until they could be picked up and taken to Kyiv.

There, Bilan and her husband were reunited with their children. She still has a high fever from walking in the cold while wet.

'I went through the EuroMaidan [the 2013 wave of civil unrest in Ukraine], I've seen worse,' she said. 'I miraculously survived then too. Maybe I was preserved for something greater. My son is defending Kyiv, which is why I'm meant to be here.'

Bucha

The town of Bucha has been the site of many horror stories, of people trapped, unable to reach their families or simply being gunned down in the streets.

The Kyiv Independent's source in the medical field in Bucha reported digging mass graves over the past two days.

Dmytro Tkachuk, a Bucha resident, posted a tale of his family's escape from the town on Facebook on 8 March. 'In the beginning of March, we went out to get drinking water from the pump, came to the end of the street and ran into enemy armor, marked with the letter V,' he wrote. 'We turned around and went home. Fear paralyzed the mind but the body still moved.'

Airstrikes had ripped through the town, demolishing and igniting buildings, forcing the family to relocate to the basement, which had a temperature of 5–7 degrees Celsius. Eventually, a Russian tank drove onto their street and fired directly into the second house over from theirs, according to Tkachuk. The tank then struck the cupola of a church just down the street.

'The sound was like all the bell towers in the world ringing at the same time,' Tkachuk wrote.

When he saw Russian squads walking around peeking into people's windows, he realized there was no sense in waiting around any longer. The neighbors joined his family when they saw them leaving. As locals, they knew all the small paths and side streets, letting them avoid the Russian checkpoint.

After resting up in an Irpin church, they had to move across a field to get to the river crossing. Soldiers told them that as soon as they heard a whistling sound, they had mere seconds to dive to the ground.

The advice came in handy almost immediately. As they moved across the field, numerous rounds came hurtling in, throwing up explosions and demolishing buildings on both sides of the bridge. The family was fleeing with their two grandmothers. On the way to the crossing, one of the grandmothers' legs gave out, forcing Tkachuk and his sister to carry her, while lugging around a suitcase with his valuables.

'The granny was screaming for us to leave her and run for the bridge,' he wrote. 'If that's not hell, what is?'

They huddled under the bridge with the other frightened people – moving forward was too dangerous while shells were flying. Eventually, a Ukrainian soldier cleared them to advance.

A soldier on the other side screamed for Tkachuk to run but with the weight of his grandmother and his belongings, he couldn't run. As he was crossing the open space, he was thinking: 'Just not a shell, just not a shell, please.'

'When we entered Kyiv, I cried,' he wrote.

Vorzel

When the war began, Elena Slivinskaya, her husband and two daughters aged 4 and 8 were in Kyiv.

They thought that maybe it'd be safer to wait out the hostilities at their house in Vorzel, near Bucha. That proved to be a mistake.

In the opening hours of the war, the Russians bombed the neighboring town of Hostomel, where a military airfield is based, before dropping airborne troops on top of it. While these troops were quickly eliminated by Ukraine, the bombing continued.

One bomb destroyed the garage of Slivinskaya's next-door neighbor in Vorzel.

'The bombing and the shooting was constant,' she said. 'We constantly spent time with the children in the basement.'

The earliest explosions terrified the little girls, who started screaming. They constantly wanted to go down to the basement. But staying in the cold, damp basement too long was also dangerous, as one of the girls was sick and running a very high fever.

The Russian troops that moved through Vorzel found no signs of resistance among the locals. But that didn't stop them from firing at the houses' second floors, possibly to make sure people didn't peek out at them, Slivinskaya said. She was told that at least one of her neighbors had been shot dead by a Russian soldier while walking outside.

Even though there was no connection, some SMS (State Migration Service) still managed to get through once in a while. One of these stated there would be an evacuation on 9 March.

'There was a mass of people, they said they were only evacuating women and children,' she said. 'But we also saw that there were cars waiting. I told my husband, he jumped in our car and we joined the column.'

What followed was a 14-hour stint behind the wheel. The vehicular queue was enormous, hundreds of cars barely creeping along, passing Ukrainian checkpoints through the night, towards the Zhytomyr Highway and into Kyiv. Vorzel is just 10 kilometers west of Kyiv.

Slivinskaya recalled how eerie it felt, being a sitting target out in the open, with numerous headlights in the middle of the night. Trapped between cars ahead and behind, there would be nowhere to floor it if things got bad. Continuous explosions could be heard on all sides, any one of which seemed like it could hit the convoy at any moment.

'But we finally broke through,' and made it into Kyiv, Slivinskaya said.

Stoyanka

Some people manage to escape the war zone only after they've drawn their final breath.

In early March, two old friends in the village of Stoyanka-2, east of Kyiv and just south of Irpin, went on a supply run.

'They went to pick up some diesel fuel and medicine for civilian use,' said Oleksandr, the nephew of one of the two men. 'They had no weapons. When they were returning to Stoyanka, two Russian APCs stood in their way. They ran into a temporary Russian checkpoint.'

The friends raised their hands and the Russian commanding officer waved them through. But all of a sudden, Russian soldiers behind him opened fire.

'They were shooting to kill,' Oleksandr said.

One of the friends was killed outright. But Oleksandr's uncle, wounded in the arm and side, managed to crawl away and survive. A neighbor picked him up, bound his wounds and took him to Stoyanka-2.

Miraculously, one of their neighbors had a guest, a visiting surgeon who was there because of the war. He had his tools and painkillers with him and managed to save the uncle, who was well enough to stand and move around on his own several days later.

His friend Arkady continued to lie in the road for four days until Oleksandr could pick up his body and drive it towards Kyiv. Along the way, he picked up another slain man and his wife, who had been wounded in the leg and was beside herself with grief.

The two bodies were brought across the Irpin River crossing to the other side and sent to Kyiv for burial.

Yet even after his brush with death, Oleksandr's uncle refuses to leave his home in Stoyanka, vowing to defend it to the last.

13 March 2022

Covid-19 patients face dilemma of infecting others while hiding in bomb shelters

Thaisa Semenova

Editor's Note: The Kyiv Independent *hasn't published Oleksandr's full name for security reasons: he still goes into Russian-controlled territory.*

In late February, Kyiv resident Serhii Fokin had a tough decision to make: walk into a bomb shelter during an air raid and risk infecting those around him, or stay at home, risking being killed by a Russian missile.

Fokin chose the second option, staying in his apartment's corridor near a bearing wall, known to resist blasts better than others.

Medical masks and social distancing have become a thing of the past in Ukraine ever since Russia launched its all-out war against the country on 24 February. The precautionary measures recommended during the pandemic have largely been neglected by Ukrainians, who are now focused on saving their lives from constant shelling and other attacks.

But the virus hasn't disappeared.

By the time the further Russian offensive began, only 38% of Ukrainians had been fully vaccinated, according to the Health Ministry, and over 646,000 active coronavirus cases were reported as Russian troops rolled into Ukraine.

Only a day before the invasion, on 23 February, over 25,000 new Covid-19 cases were registered in Ukraine.

According to the World Health Organization (WHO), Ukraine is coming off one of its worst waves of coronavirus since the pandemic began. Like many other countries, Ukraine experienced a surge in the number of cases due to the spread of the Omicron variant. The latest peak was in early February.

By mid-February, 60% of Covid-19 tests conducted in the country were positive.

Fokin learned about his positive result on 24 February, the first day of Russia's all-out war. Kyiv was already being bombed, but laboratories were still operating and offered testing.

Fokin did not inform his family physician that he was sick because he thought there was no need to take sick leave during the war. Besides, 'the doctor already had a lot on his plate,' he says.

Still, Fokin was afraid in case he did need medical assistance, that it would be impossible to get it. 'There were no complications, but I was very afraid there would be in this situation,' he said.

On the second night of the offensive, Fokin heard multiple explosions in Kyiv. He saw his neighbors running to the bomb shelter, visibly panicking. However, no matter how scared he was, joining them wasn't an option for Fokin. He says that at the moment he had a persistent cough, and the risk of infecting everyone in the shelter was too high.

Fokin was also worried that he would not be able to sleep on the floor in the shelter, which would be too much stress for his already weakened body. 'Dying from bombing is just a possibility,' he says, while not sleeping well could also add to his deteriorating health.

WHO experts say that war creates favorable conditions for infectious diseases to spread, as shelters are densely crowded, and access to hospitals is limited, since war-related injuries become a priority.

As of 6 March, 34 Ukrainian hospitals have been damaged or destroyed by Russia's war, according to Health Minister Viktor Lyashko. The Health Ministry also reported attacks on cars with oxygen for Covid-19 patients.

Though some laboratories and hospitals are out of operation, on the 15th day of the war, 10 March, the Health Ministry registered 6,700 new Covid-19 cases. Some 5,700 patients were hospitalized on the same day.

Another Kyiv resident Kateryna Ilchenko got infected in a bomb shelter during the first days of the full-scale invasion. There were about 30 people hiding from shelling in one space. 'The space was quite large, but there was almost no ventilation,' Ilchenko told *The Kyiv Independent*.

After getting infected, she continued going to the shelter following air raid alerts, but says she was constantly wearing a mask.

Ilchenko didn't do much to treat the virus, just drank more hot liquids than usual. 'To be honest, Covid-19 was not my biggest concern,' she says. As her mother was stuck in Irpin, a satellite city outside of Kyiv that has been a hot spot of Russia's war, Ilchenko couldn't focus on taking care of herself while being worried about her mother, whose whole life was in danger.

Though the spread of Covid-19 in Ukraine amid Russia's war might seem like a local problem, it could affect the pace of the pandemic way beyond Ukraine's borders.

16 March 2022

300,000 people trapped in besieged Mariupol face living hell

Asami Terajima

When Mariupol journalist Artem Popov speaks about his hometown, it sounds like he has a lump in his throat.

The southeastern city of Mariupol has turned into a front line of Russia's brutal war against Ukraine. It's dangerous to move around the city because Russian warplanes are flying over Mariupol every day, constantly shelling residential areas where civilians live, Popov says. 'Tears do not stop in Mariupol,' he told me. 'Tears of fear and pain are what every resident of our city goes through [every day].'

The 30-year-old lived his whole life in the southeastern city of Mariupol before fleeing on 8 March. Once a bustling port city offering many tourist attractions from a famous mosque to beaches, today it resembles a place from an apocalyptic movie, Popov says, because 'almost all the neighborhoods of the city have been destroyed'.

Watching it has been a horror.

'My neighbors, my friends, my relatives, my acquaintances, and places where I've made the best memories of my life are being shelled,' he said.

The besieged Mariupol has endured some of Ukraine's worst misery since Russia unleashed its full-scale invasion of its neighbor on 24 February. The city has been subject to heavy Russian bombardment since Moscow's troops effectively encircled it on 2 March.

The pre-war population of Mariupol was over 400,000 people. About 300,000 civilians were still left in the besieged city as of 14 March, according to Deputy Prime Minister Iryna Vereshchuk.

This includes around 3,000 newborn babies, lacking medicine and food, according to Foreign Minister Dmytro Kuleba.

An improvement came on 14–15 March, when over 20,000 people were able to evacuate Mariupol, according to Vereshchuk.

Others remain stuck in the city, cut off from electricity, water and gas. The city's internet and mobile networks have shut down since the siege began over two weeks ago. News from the city comes from sporadic contacts and a few international photographers who remain in Mariupol.

The siege has left people hungry, dehydrated and stuck in freezing basements to avoid indiscriminate Russian shelling.

Russia has continuously broken agreed-upon ceasefires to evacuate civilians out of Mariupol and bring relief goods into the city. Critical supplies are becoming dangerously scarce. As of one week ago, grocery stores and pharmacies either ran out of stock or were looted.

The International Committee of the Red Cross (ICRC) warned that Mariupol residents will face a 'worst-case scenario' if their immediate safety and access to humanitarian aid isn't are ensured.

More than 2,500 people, including children, have been killed in Mariupol since the beginning of Russia's all-out war, according to Ukrainian presidential office advisor Oleksiy Arestovych. The real number may be higher since the true count is impossible to measure under constant Russian bombardment.

'The Russians are wiping out the city,' Arestovych said on 14 March.

Living hell

Motionless bodies are left on the streets of Mariupol. With the heavy bombardment, it's difficult for the emergency services to collect the bodies of those killed. Those collected are hastily and unceremoniously buried in mass graves.

Running dangerously short of food and water, Mariupol residents have been chopping wood to cook and keep warm in sub-zero temperatures, local authorities reported. Those living in the worst-hit parts of the city have been reduced to tapping the now-defunct radiators in their homes, or melting snow.

Some walk and search through the debris of destroyed homes to find something edible.

Mariupol resident Maksym Svetlov, who left the city shortly before Russia's all-out war started but still has relatives in the city, said, 'The situation is getting worse with every hour of shelling.'

Russian forces are continuously shelling various parts of the city, including the central walkway in the heart of Mariupol, he said. Shelling happens almost every 30 minutes, making it dangerous for civilians to leave shelters. 'People can't even go out somewhere to get water, they can't even go because they are afraid that they won't come back,' Svetlov told *The Kyiv Independent*.

Many families are running out of basic supplies and small children are particularly vulnerable to deteriorating health conditions, according to Doctors Without Borders, an international organization monitoring Mariupol closely.

Children's bodies cannot withstand wide fluctuations in food and water intake unlike adults, leaving them at high risk of dehydration. Zelensky said that a 6-year-old girl died of dehydration in Mariupol on 8 March. She took her last breath alone because her mother was killed by shelling earlier, according to Donetsk Oblast Governor Pavlo Kyrylenko.

Doctors Without Borders said Mariupol residents are also dying from a lack of medication. Dispatches from the city say that there are no more medications in Mariupol, especially for diabetes and cancer patients.

Why Mariupol?

Mariupol is strategically important for Russia as it lies along the Azov Sea coast between the annexed Crimean Peninsula and the Russian-occupied parts of eastern Ukraine.

If Russia seizes Mariupol and connects the two territories, it will cut Ukraine off from the Azov Sea.

On 14 March, Russian state media claimed that a land corridor was established between Donbas and Crimea, citing pro-Kremlin leadership in the annexed peninsula. This has not yet been confirmed.

The situation in Mariupol is typical of Russian siege warfare tactics, which will likely spread as the war moves into a new phase, according to Rita Konaev, the associate director of analysis at Georgetown University's Center for Security and Emerging Technology.

The Kremlin forces have begun imposing brutal siege tactics as they launch attacks on Ukraine's major cities, using cluster munitions and the bombing of civilian infrastructure. The tactics resemble Russian dictator Vladimir Putin's ruthless military campaigns in Syria and Chechnya, where his army reduced cities to rubble.

Volnovakha, a city of 21,000 people in Donetsk Oblast located just 60 kilometers north of Mariupol, has suffered days of bombardment and is largely destroyed. Russian forces captured Volnovakha on 12 March, a strategic point on their advance towards Mariupol.

Donetsk Oblast governor Kyrylenko said on 15 March that Russian troops entered a hospital on the outskirts of Mariupol and took patients and medical staff hostage. 'Russians drove 400 people from neighboring houses to the hospital and they can't leave,' he described.

The grim strategy from Putin's playbook is to break morale by severely damaging cities' infrastructure and causing high levels of displacement from the cities, Konaev told *Vox* earlier this month.

Survivor's guilt

Mariupol resident Diana Berg feels guilt for leaving her home in Mariupol. 'It's the guilt of a survivor,' the 41-year-old told *The Kyiv Independent*.

Though originally from Donetsk, occupied by Russia since 2014, Berg felt at home in Mariupol, and that's why they had stayed there until 3 March, she said.

But as days of 'hell' continued in encircled Mariupol, the activist, who's been helping locals, started to look for an escape route with her husband so that they could bring their relatives and friends to safety. She said many people would have left the city if they knew what was going to happen, but the situation worsened unexpectedly.

Because of shelling, that plan never pulled through, and the couple was forced to leave on their own. They left everything behind to escape, crossing Russian military columns and Moscow-controlled checkpoints.

Many of her loved ones, including her older relatives and close friends, are still trapped in Mariupol. She said the last time she heard from them was almost a week ago and she has no idea how they are doing. Like many others in the city, Berg's family was only able to say a few words to her at the time because they were trying to save their phone battery.

Berg said she is 'very desperate' to hear back from her family.

Search for relatives

Every day is also a pain for those whose relatives or friends are still stuck in Mariupol. 'Mariupol! Please let me know anything about my relatives,' a woman writes in a Facebook group dedicated to locating missing relatives in Mariupol. 'My son Yan Ivanovich Leliv, grandson Nazar Pozhidaev (10-year-old) and his mother Ksenia Pozhidaeva,' she wrote, describing the attached photo.

Online groups created for family members or friends looking for information about their loved ones trapped in affected areas are receiving hundreds of requests a day. A Facebook group called 'Group of Mariupol City' is one of the many that helps people look for any pieces of information about their loved ones.

Though it's unlikely that they will find out how their relatives are doing through this group, some may be comforted by comments saying that the locations of their loved ones haven't been attacked. Those who manage to connect with their relatives thanks to sporadically appearing mobile connection post updates.

Some comments read, 'my relative told me that they are cooking food outside,' while others inform that 'the street that you asked about doesn't exist anymore, sorry'.

Poltava resident Natasha Yaremenko is one of those looking for relatives in Mariupol. The last time she heard from her sister was almost two weeks ago. She was told then that 'there was no light, water, or heat' and her sister has not responded since then.

'I just want to hear something – that she's alive and well,' Yaremenko told *The Kyiv Independent*.

18 March 2022

Russian soldiers kill mother of two as she drives family to safety

Anna Myroniuk

In the early morning of 1 March, Svitlana Zhulina was driving her family away from war-torn Kyiv Oblast. Her husband, Andriy Vilson, was sitting next to her, their two sons of 8 and 10 in the back seat.

They were driving along Zhytomyr Highway, a westbound road very familiar to Kyivans. In peacetime, people would use it to get to the Ukrainian 'western capital' of Lviv. Now, it was the road to safety.

Suddenly, Andriy heard a loud explosion and his wife's head fell against him. A sniper's bullet had hit her.

He stopped the car and rushed to save the rest of his family.

'It was a horror for the kids. The bullet hit the windshield and their mother who was there just a moment ago is gone,' Andriy said.

The doors were blocked, so he got out through the window and started taking his kids out of the car.

'I took Artem first,' Andriy said of his older son, 'and they shot me in the right leg. I hid Artem behind the car hood so they could not reach him.'

Andriy then returned for Myroslav, his youngest.

'Myroslav lingered. He looked at my leg, saw a big hole in it, and said: "Dad, there's a hole." And right then those bastards shot him in the leg,' he said.

As he was hiding the wounded Myroslav, the Russian soldiers shot his left leg. He fell.

The beginning of the end

Five days prior, Russia had declared a full-scale war on Ukraine. Svitlana, 46, and her brother Oleksii Kurach, 37, decided to take their families out of Kyiv to Berezivka, a nearby village where their parents live.

They wanted to wait it out in Berezivka and see how the events unfolded. For a few days, this plan worked well. It remained quiet in their village, even while Kyiv was being heavily shelled.

On 26 February, the building in which Svitlana and Andriy had purchased an apartment in Kyiv was hit by a Russian missile. Six people were injured.

'We were just about to move in there. We had renovated the apartment. It was close to the lyceum, so the kids wouldn't have had to walk a long distance,' said Andriy. 'Thank God we did not move in,' he had thought when the building was hit.

It felt as though they had managed to escape the danger. Despite the village having been cut off from electricity, water, and cell connection, they thought they were safe in Berezivka. That was before they saw Russian tanks moving past their windows.

It was time to leave, said Inga Kurach, Oleksii's wife and mother of their young daughter. 'After the Russian column passed our house, we started to hear loud explosions,' she said. 'We spent the afternoon in the basement, crying. We all agreed that we needed to leave.'

The next morning, the two families got in their cars to flee the war to western Ukraine. The Kurach family took the lead, while Svitlana, Andriy, and their two sons followed suit.

They drove slowly, as the debris from shells was scattered across the road. After two kilometers of driving along the highway, they saw a tank on the other side of the road. The 'V' sign painted on it indicated that it was Russian.

'I shouted at my husband: "Tank! Turn around!"' Inga said. 'I was scared.'

As Oleksii was turning around, Russian bullets hit their car. 'The window next to me and my daughter broke first, and then all the others did, too. We bowed our heads. Apparently, it saved us,' Inga said.

They realized that the Svitlana's car was being shelled at and stopped. 'I told my husband: "Step on it! They will kill us all now."'

Saving the kids

Andriy and his two sons were lying on the ground next to their car. 'The Russians kept shooting at the car,' he said. 'They wanted to get to the kids.'

He then saw a Russian military convoy moving towards them and told his kids to play dead. 'When I imagine what it's like for a child to be told to lie like you're dead, and your mother is now dead,' Andriy said, struggling to find words. 'It's just ...'

When the Russian tanks passed them, the Russian soldiers started a 'mopping-up' operation. There was no point in playing dead anymore. 'When the Russian soldiers saw the severity of the [kids'] wounds, they were shocked,' Andriy said.

They then started checking Andriy's smartphone to see whether he had informed the Ukrainian military about the movement of Russian troops. They found nothing, he said, and then started discussing what to do with him. 'I was bleeding heavily. They realized that they needed to do something,' he said.

They tried to call up their medical officers, but no one came. Eventually, they put tourniquets on his legs. 'They told me: "You have two kids to take care of." I replied: "Thanks to your snipers",' Andriy recalled.

'They then said: "Still, do not die." I answered: "I will try. Let me save my kids."'

Russian soldiers allowed him to call his wife's parents, so that they could come and pick them up. The soldiers promised they wouldn't touch them.

When his parents-in-law arrived, Andriy was feeling dizzy due to serious blood loss, and the Russians helped put him into their car. They did not let them take his wife's body.

Later that day, Svitlana's parents returned to pick up their daughter's body anyway.

'Grandma and grandpa are heroes,' Andriy said. 'They took a wheelbarrow and went there on foot. They opened the car door in front of the Russians, got their child, put her on the wheelbarrow, took some things that were there, and came back.'

Long way to recovery

After the attack, both families had to go back to the village house in Berezivka. Andriy and his youngest son Myroslav urgently needed medical treatment. His friends found a former military doctor in the village. 'He came every day, despite shelling,' Inga said. 'A very brave person.'

'If it weren't for him, we would have certainly had gangrene,' Andriy said. 'He stuffed medicine into my wounds with his fingers. He said: "Otherwise it will rot."'

Still, Andriy and his son required inpatient treatment. After six days, they decided to give it another try and get out of the village.

'The doctor called us and said that there was information about a Russian checkpoint that had started letting through cars with white flags,' Inga said. 'We decided to take the risk,' she continued. 'With what had happened to us, we felt three times more scared than before.'

Inga and Oleksii grabbed the children, placed the wounded ones in the back seat, and started driving towards the Russian checkpoint. They were asked to stop.

'I was sitting next to my husband in the front seat, holding my daughter close and tilting her head down so they would not hurt her,' Inga recalled. 'I was weeping,' she went on. 'The Russians saw it and said: "We won't hurt you."'

They let them go.

Oleksii drove his brother-in-law and nephew all the way to the hospital in Khmelnytskyi, a city in western Ukraine hours away from Kyiv.

Andriy's younger son, Myroslav, underwent surgery and had Ilizarov apparatus, a metal fixator placed on his leg. His recovery will take up to eight months.

The kids are holding up, but the horror of seeing their mother shot dead by a sniper had a devastating effect on them, Andriy said. 'They were shocked when they saw her. "Mom, mom" they screamed. She did not respond.'

19 March 2022

Russia throws untrained civilians from occupied Donbas into hot spots of its war in Ukraine

Thaisa Semenova

Editor's Note: The Kyiv Independent *isn't revealing last names of the people from the Russian-occupied parts of Ukraine interviewed for this story for safety reasons.*

Nearly every man that Oleksii, a 24-year-old resident of Russian-occupied Khrestivka in Donetsk Oblast, knows – friends, school classmates, and former colleagues from a coal mine – has been illegally conscripted by Russian-controlled proxies.

None of them have served in the military before, he says. Yet many of them have been thrown into the hottest spots of Russia's war against Ukraine.

'These people have never even held a machine gun in their hands,' Oleksii told *The Kyiv Independent.*

In the weeks following Russia's all-out war that began on 24 February, Russian-controlled militants escalated hostilities in Donbas, the partially occupied region in eastern Ukraine in Donetsk and Luhansk oblasts that was invaded by Russia in 2014.

Russia's proxies wrongfully accused Ukraine's armed forces of escalation, announced a demonstrative evacuation of women and children from Donbas to Russia and launched a mobilization campaign conscripting all men under 55.

Oleksii himself has managed to avoid mobilization by luck. When the campaign started, he was in Vinnytsia, a regional capital in central Ukraine. He arrived there to take exams at his school, Donetsk National University, where he is pursuing a Master's degree in computer sciences. The university relocated from Donetsk after Russia occupied it in 2014.

His former colleagues from the Komsomolets Donbasu coal mine, however, have faced a different fate. Oleksii says that they were abducted by Russian-backed militants right from their workplaces and deployed to the southern front in Mariupol, a city in Donetsk Oblast that has seen some of the heaviest fighting since 24 February.

The only friend of Oleksii who hasn't yet been forcefully conscripted to the Russian army is 27-year-old Serhii. The Komsomolets Donbasu coal mine listed him as an 'essential worker' and provided him with exemption from mobilization. The exemption expires in April, and Serhii isn't certain whether the coal mine will extend it.

When asked through Oleksii to speak on the record, Serhii declined. 'I won't speak to a journalist. No offence, mate. Today I'm at home, tomorrow they can take me away, and my mom and girlfriend will stay in Khrestivka and face issues,' he wrote in a text message to Oleksii, which *The Kyiv Independent* has seen.

Many locals are afraid of talking with Ukrainian or Western media. Many think that the Russian Federal Security Service will access their correspondence on social media platforms or listen in on their phone calls.

In a conversation with Oleksii, Serhii confirmed that many of his coworkers from the coal mine, civilians with no previous military experience, were forcefully mobilized to the Russian army, and the majority of them are engaged in combat in Ukraine alongside Russian troops.

Seed of doubt

Oleksii provided me with access to his account on the Russian social network VK, where the Komsomolets Donbasu coal mine workers and their family members chat in a closed group.

We saw dozens of posts where the wives of illegally mobilized Donbas residents were discussing their plans on how to find their husbands: some suggested going to Russian-occupied Donetsk for a protest near the Russian proxy headquarters; others shared that they wrote letters to Russian President Vladimir Putin asking for help but got no response.

'We have to do something! My husband called me yesterday and said they are at the forefront of combat, and it's terrible,' Iryna wrote in a closed group.

Men in the comments were asking if there was any way to avoid mobilization or leave the occupied parts of Donbas. The group members agreed that the chances are low.

The Kyiv Independent reached one of the men who hadn't left his house for two weeks, hiding from Russian-controlled forces. Ivan, a 25-year-old miner, said in a voice message that militants stop men everywhere, simply on their way to grocery stores, and ask for an ID. If a man doesn't have an ID, militants take him to a 'police station' for identification and, after that, send him directly to a mobilization point.

'They [militants] walk around, knock on all the apartments' doors, looking for men,' Ivan said. They send conscripts to what they assure is a 3–7-day military exercise but when they arrive they are deployed to fight Ukraine, according to Ivan.

He hasn't heard from his mobilized friends for a week. At some point, Ivan stopped answering *The Kyiv Independent's* questions and later deleted the chat.

Several women in the closed Komsomolets Donbasu coal mine VK group said that someone they know has already been notified that their sons, about 18 years old, were killed in combat. After that, they write, they began to doubt news on Russian state TV and started to watch Ukrainian TV channels on YouTube.

'Why is it rattling so terribly? Why is everything in Volnovakha and Mariupol so different from what they say on TV? What will happen to our men? Why don't they talk about our men dying?' Natalia wondered in a post.

According to the intelligence unit of Ukraine's Defense Ministry, the vast majority of mobilized Donbas residents are sent to the hottest spots without special training 'to clear obstacles and dig trenches'. The losses among new recruits reach 70–80%, the ministry said.

It also reported that Russia uses the Donetsk Metallurgical Plant to burn the corpses of residents killed in battle to hide the actual number of casualties.

No escape

In mid-February, Yevhen, another employee of the Komsomolets Donbasu coal mine, was discussing the prospective mobilization with his boss. The boss told him that mobilization would be mandatory but assured it would not happen anytime soon.

But at midnight on 21 February, Yevhen, 27, was told to pack his stuff and come to the mobilization point.

His wife Anastasia tried to persuade him not to go, as he had not received an official invitation. The family has two daughters, 5 and 3 years old.

But Yevhen told her that 'nobody could weasel their way out'.

After enlistment, he has been moved between at least five settlements before Anastasia lost touch with her husband. The last time they talked, he was somewhere near Mariupol. 'We haven't gotten in touch for five days,' she told me in a phone call.

Anastasia says that conscripts from Donbas were transported in a military truck with no roof for 14 hours, amid the freezing winter weather. She also said that the recruits didn't have food and water for three days. 'They witnessed things one doesn't even see in movies,' she said.

According to Anastasia, civilians from Donbas are forced to be at front-line positions. Otherwise, Russian forces threaten to shoot them.

Many of the Donbas conscripts are seriously wounded, or have been killed, Anastasia said. 'And I still don't know what happened to my husband,' she added.

21 March 2022

How Ukraine swaps living soldiers for dead Russians

Illia Ponomarenko

Ukrainian emergency response workers dig into the fresh soil by a riverbank.

'Careful,' they tell each other. 'Just like that. Remove the upper layer bit by bit.'

Every strike of the spade unearths new items in the moist dirt. Parts of cloth tatters, boot bottoms, traces of clotted blood.

Then, blackened hands appear. The workers endure the subtle smell of death rising from underneath the soil.

'Alright, get those stretchers and lashings. We got another one almost ready.'

It's an unmarked communal grave, one of many begotten by the brutal mayhem of Russia's war in Ukraine.

Inside that pit near the town of Rusaniv east of Kyiv, several Russian soldiers were given an improvised burial courtesy of the local townsfolk, saving their bodies from animals and decomposing in the open.

A fierce clash with Ukrainian forces defending the capital spelled their quick and bitter end. But in a twist of dark irony, the invading army's dead soldiers will redeem themselves in death – and help save the living.

Six of them will be exchanged for two Ukrainian soldiers taken as prisoners of war in a rare instance of an unofficial swap between the opposing armies on the battlefield.

And unlike so many other Russian dead, these were taken from their unmarked grave in the Ukrainian meadows to eventually find a final resting place back in their homeland ...

Dying nameless

The destroyed Russian BMPs contain many things left behind by their killed former operators: standard 'Army of Russia' ration packs, toilet paper, parts of medical kits, toothbrushes, pieces of Russian dark-green camouflage fatigues.

Russian crews practically lived inside their vehicles, keeping all personal effects close at hand.

They also didn't seem thrilled with the Russian military rations, which have gained notoriety during the war. Many Russian prisoners of war said the MRE ('meals ready to eat') kits allocated to them were long expired, due to severe food-supply issues in the Russian military. The infantrymen killed near Rusaniv seem to have shared this opinion: their rations were left largely intact. Instead, they had a large stock of Russian-made snacks, as well as cheap canned fish products from Ukrainian supermarkets.

None of the assault's participants had any identification documents with them. 'They simply take the IDs away from them before the attack,' Ukrainian soldiers say. 'No service cards, no dog tags, nothing. We don't get it – did their commanders believe they would fight harder if left to die nameless?'

Some of their names are recovered anyway.

Among the rubbish falling off the destroyed BMPs, one can find a couple of Russian bank cards bearing their owner's name: 'Aleksandr Gagarin.' It is impossible to know which of the nameless bodies used to respond to that name in life.

Another piece of evidence is a name tape, knifed off a killed soldier's fatigues: 'Lubsandabayev B.N.' A simple search of Russian social networks indicates that a man named Bair Nikolaevich Lubsandabayev, an ethnic Buryat, was most likely 24 years old, born in the town of Tsagatui between Lake Baikal and the Mongolian border. His mother Ariuna is an elementary school teacher in Tsagatui, and he has a sister named Ayana.

In his school years, he was fond of futsal and nature studies, as mentioned in local newspapers. A Russian military publication says in December 2018 he graduated from Far Eastern Higher Combined Arms Command School in the city of Blagoveschensk and later served with 'a motor rifle brigade in the Orenburg Oblast' – that is, the 21st Guards Motor Rifle Brigade. By all appearances, he was killed in that attack near Rusaniv – 5,000 kilometers away from his hometown in Buryatia.

The rest of Lubsandabayev's comrades in arms remained nameless to the Ukrainian troops.

'They won't bite'

Ukrainian soldiers hurry the emergency service workers along and bring more spades to help them out.

The Russian forces are still only about three kilometers away. The Ukrainian military does not want to take chances and hopes to leave the exposed terrain as soon as possible.

The deal is simple: six Russian bodies for two living Ukrainian soldiers held captive following the latest fighting in the area.

Emergency workers hastily load up the blackened cadavers on stretches and drag them to the riverbank.

An inflatable boat will transport them one by one to the other side, where a pickup truck is waiting.

Through negotiations via unsecured communication lines, with the help of civilian mediators, the exchange will take place soon, as agreed upon by officers from both sides.

'Don't you worry, they won't bite,' Ukrainian soldiers smile as they watch civilian volunteers cautiously looking at decaying bodies laid on the road next to the car.

'They're not dangerous anymore. They are now helping us get our guys back.'

22 March 2022

My day with volunteers saving lives in war zones outside Kyiv

Igor Kossov

A clear, frigid day rises over Irpin. The bright sun overhead provides only mild comfort. The icy breeze penetrates to the bone.

'It's gonna be an interesting one today, Igor,' Oleksandr says to me, upbeat.

I met this guy earlier in the war, when I was monitoring refugee evacuations at the Irpin River crossing, in case the Russians decided to casually drop some mortars and slaughter some families again, like they do.

He spilled out of his old silver van in front of me on the shattered bridge and asked me to go get a medic. One of his passengers was wounded in the leg. The other two were beyond the need for medics.

I helped him carry one of the bodies, his uncle's friend, gunned down by the Russians in the village of Stoyanka for no reason; we got to talking. He's a civilian volunteer, placed by Territorial Defense on a waiting list. Waiting is against his nature. Oleksandr couldn't wait.

For weeks, Oleksandr and his friend Andrii have been driving into the war zones outside Kyiv, running critical supplies in and getting people out. Oleksandr reckons they've evacuated over 250 civilians and I believe it. In the one day I spent with them, they evacuated seven.

They also help deliver power banks, food and medicine, help rescue left-behind pets or, when it's too late to save someone, bring out bodies to get a proper burial in Kyiv and hopefully serve as evidence in some future court of human rights against Russia.

'When people sit for over a week without light, internet or news, they come out and ask us "Is Kyiv still ours?"' Oleksandr says. 'We reassure them, yes, Kyiv is ours, everything is good there. Here, we brought you some bread.'

Today, they let me tag along on one of their daily missions. While Oleksandr gave me permission to share, I've kept both their last names hidden for security purposes, as they don't plan to stop sticking their necks out any time soon.

'It's gonna be an interesting one today.' In a war zone, that can mean a number of things, like that Chinese epigram, 'May you live in interesting times.' The remnant of a smoke pillar from an artillery shell that struck a nearby field a few minutes ago is still drifting skyward. Thicker smoke is rising from the direction of Bucha, a hell unending I'm not sure I'm ready to see.

No time to overthink it. We jump into the van with a woman named Iryna who needs to evacuate her dogs from Irpin's woodside outskirts.

Animals

It's amazing how many dogs you see when war breaks out. The dogs are everywhere. Many aren't even haggard mutts but handsome permutations of stately breeds: healthy, alert and well-fed. Sometimes, the beginning of a dog fight takes snarling shape, only to dissolve again moments later.

I don't know how many are with the military and how many have been left behind and are now doing their best to survive like the rest of us.

Pets are a major calculus for people deciding to stay or leave. After figuring out what to do with their families, the hardest question many here grapple with is what to do with their pets.

In a few days, I've met half a dozen locals who couldn't bring themselves to leave because of their animals. I saw a middle-aged woman sobbing like a child because she had to leave her dog and cats behind. Later this day, we'd meet a man, whose dogs were the main anchor holding him to the village where the Russians almost killed him.

'When people ask us "should I leave the dog," I say why?' Oleksandr says. 'Take it with you ... We don't leave anyone behind.'

Iryna, who already evacuated the rest of her canine friends, is also determined not to leave any behind. When she unlocks her door, though, I can see why several trips were needed, as two Spanish mastiffs the size of young grizzly bears barely squeeze their bulk through the frame. One of them has intensely bloodshot eyes. It's frightening. You can saddle that thing up and ride down the Russians like the Cossacks of old.

I mention this aloud and they love it. My companions talk about finding some cavalry sabers to complete the effect. Alas, the mastiffs are show dogs: big, friendly softies, wholly untrained in the ways of war. They are, however, completely uncontrollable unless their mom is nearby. If one wants to go somewhere, a grown man's grip on the leash will not even slow it down.

Iryna's back a few minutes later, with three bags of dog food half the size of my body. They're crammed into the van, along with bundles of frozen meat. She loads the last of her hellhounds in the back and we zoom off towards the crossing.

Fear and risk

'We are here on our own fear and risk,' Oleksandr would say to me as we discussed my ride-along.

The phrase is a Russian saying, which means taking full responsibility for your own safety. In the battlegrounds outside Kyiv, it sounds especially poignant, even when translated.

But the dynamic duo's risks are rarely uncalculated. They always check available intelligence in advance. And there's always someone to ask. During the course of their volunteer service, they appear to have made friends with half the troops rotating through Irpin, from the uniformed regulars to the wild Cossack-looking character with the huge, decorative earring and the drooping mustache, looking like he'd been plucked from Stenka Razin's rebellion of 1670 and handed an assault rifle.

Sometimes, Oleksandr said, their silver van even ferried sniper and mortar teams to specific locations, becoming a well-memed 'taxi service'.

Most troops and locals are willing to share tidbits of information on what they know of the Russians' movements, where it's safe to go and where it isn't, in exchange for a lusty 'Glory to Ukraine'. They're helpful but they're not always right. 'They might say "don't go there lads, it's scary there, they're killing people there," even though we just came from there and no one's killing anyone,' Oleksandr says. 'We always check with certain people who haven't let us down. Then we analyze and decide. But it always comes with a big dose of risk.'

He's not kidding. Bullets and mortars can and do come out of nowhere. The friends often had to take cover to wait out a barrage. As their forces face heavy resistance, Russians in the area may be edgy. And they've made it abundantly clear they won't bother sparing civilians.

As I chew on this information, we run into two Ukrainian soldiers with covered faces, who stop us and demand to see our documents. 'Alright boys, on the ground with your faces down,' gently says the older of the two. As quizzical looks creep into the volunteers' faces, he takes the wrap down from over his grinning mouth.

'You can change your Pampers now,' he says. They crack up laughing. He's a friend of theirs, just giving us a scare. He lets us go with an update and a hearty 'good luck'.

Can't sit still

Oleksandr, an IT entrepreneur, first became a volunteer in 2014, when Russia invaded Luhansk and Donetsk oblasts and annexed Crimea.

In February, he was sucked back into the life when he got the news from Hostomel on the third day of the war. His ex-wife had been shot and wounded, trapped in the city with her friend and her child from her second husband.

'No one could gather the courage to come get them, including her father and her second husband,' said Oleksandr. 'We went to the bridge by car, then crossed on foot … We carried them out.'

He hadn't talked to his ex-wife in a long time over some personal disagreements but all of that fell by the wayside when life was on the line. Risking his life for her awoke a whole spectrum of emotions. Being the only man who came to get her has pushed their relationship into new, more complicated territory.

'I was really afraid but didn't want to lose her a second time,' he said. After being rescued, she's gone to Italy, where Oleksandr's sister and nephews are staying.

The experience realigned his value system. 'I understood then that I can't just sit in one place,' he said to me on the phone. To Oleksandr, 'sitting around, checking Facebook is worse than coming under fire'.

His friend Andrii, whom he met playing geocaching games, has a travel agency and has traveled all over the world. The friends would often meet time and again after not seeing each other for years. When they last reconnected, they became partners in what they consider their most important undertaking.

Andrii seems the brasher of the duo while Oleksandr is a bit more measured. With the calm detachment of combat medics, the lackadaisical quips of Marvel protagonists and their big hearts, the friends perfectly complement one another.

'Not too many people are ready to risk their lives for people they don't know,' says Oleksandr.

But you can't always get to everyone in time. Since they started working, the friends have evacuated over 30 bodies.

'I'm not much of a believer but I believe [funerals have] to be done the Christian way,' Oleksandr says. 'The body has to be checked in, the cause of death established ... these are people and they deserve not to be buried in some mound like a dog.'

Unfortunately, the friends' next mission is to go into the possibly occupied urban village of Stoyanka-2 and recover some of the deceased ...

Chekhov and Dostoevsky

At the bridge, we get a call about two groups of people needing evac, a few from Chekhov Street and one from Dostoevsky Street. We decided to hit Chekhov first, not for any literary merit, it just seemed closer.

The nearer we get to the address, the clearer it becomes that the area is still in the Russians' grasp. The road slopes up ominously, a sniper's paradise. Andrii serpentines his way in and out of the side streets as we go uphill. We pause on the edge of one intersection. Oleksandr has a bad feeling, reason enough not to go.

All of a sudden, Andrii 'wants to try something'.

Before anyone can stop him, he guns the van forward, swerves left onto Chekhov Street, then almost immediately swerves right onto another side street behind a tall apartment building and stops the van. Not a minute later, we hear the incoming whine, followed by a blast somewhere nearby.

'Oh, mortars,' Oleksandr opines. 'Haven't heard those in a while.'

There's a second incoming whistle, followed by a third. 'Are they aiming at us?' I wonder aloud. It's hard to say. One thing's for goddamned sure, the folks on Chekhov Street are going to have to wait a little longer for their rescue.

After waiting a little while ourselves, we jump back in the vehicle and swerve back onto our only way out. Simultaneously, the van door slides open, dumping two metallic racks onto the road. Andrii brings the van to a halt.

'Leave them,' Oleksandr says. 'Just leave them.'

But Andrii's already picking them up. 'They're not ours, is the thing. If they were mine ...' He shoves them through the window to us.

'Can we go now please?' Oleksandr says.

'Look, I see something,' says Andrii, jumping out of the van once more.

'You've got to be f*cking kidding me,' I say. 'Is he doing it on purpose?'

Andrii jumps back inside. 'I found some chocolates!' He throws a sealed package of some gourmet snacks on the dashboard.

'Dude.'

Andrii floors it and we race down the street, before any mortars or snipers can zero in on our position. It's time to try Dostoevsky's abode.

This author's not as angry, although he does make us pass through a circuitous labyrinth trying to find the right address. Very true to form, I must say. We pick up a woman with golden teeth and her gorgeously fluffy rabbit. Thankfully, this one has a pet carrier.

Back to safety

As sunset bathes Irpin in apricot light, there's one more rescue I can join the two friends for. An old woman had a stroke and now she can't stand up. Thankfully, we drove over to her place without much incident.

She lies in the back room, rolled towards the wall. The interior is as frigid as the street outside. All the family members are clad in winter clothing.

They try to gently roll her on her back, as she makes a heartbreaking moan. As they lay out a sturdy blanket to load her up on, her reedy voice pipes up. 'Don't break!' she shouts. 'Don't break!'

It takes four of us to carry her out, each securely grasping one corner of the blanket. A thin white cushion laid over some wooden pallets in the van makes for a poor mattress but it's the best we've got. Her adult daughter joins her, bags already packed for Kyiv.

Ukrainian soldiers stand at the bridge, olive drab stretchers at the ready. The stroke victim will be fine. They carry her off, with her daughter in tow. Unfortunately, the evacuation ends on a sour note, as I end up ripping the handle of the bag I was helping the daughter carry. She's understandably pissed at me. I know I would be.

With curfew approaching in several hours and deadlines piling up, it's time for me to go. I shake Oleksandr's hand, thanking him for letting me come on this journey. He smiles and says he'll see me later.

And crossing the river and jumping into a refugee vehicle, I head back into fortress Kyiv.

War is always a showcase of the worst that humanity has to offer. The devastation of Kharkiv and Mariupol, the slaughter in Bucha, Irpin and Hostomel, all showed what the Russian army is capable of, especially when commanded by a man with glacial poison flowing in his veins, who would crown himself Emperor of the Rus or order tens of thousands of men to die trying.

But around the broad red strokes of violence and sadism, one can see the little brushstrokes filling the negative space. Strokes of kindness and self-sacrifice, of heroism and defiance, of quiet grace and nobility in the face of annihilation. The best that humanity has to offer.

As I ride back to my apartment in Kyiv, it gives me some measure of comfort to have examined this canvas up close. Because it reminds me that through this great sea of blackness, a lit pathway stretches, for most of us to pass through to the other side. And I'm reminded that there will always be people like Oleksandr and Andrii tending to those lights.

24 March 2022

Fearless Kyiv utility workers keep the city running under Russia's shelling

Anna Myroniuk

As Russian bombs and rockets land on Kyiv's residential buildings, the city's utility services' workers drudge overtime to clear the streets of the damage, debris and garbage left behind in the wake of Russia's attacks.

As many as 4,000 homes across Ukraine have been damaged by Russia's military since the full-scale war broke out on 24 February, according to the latest estimate by the State Emergency Service.

Russia's scorched earth tactic in Ukraine aimed at destroying everything that stands in its way has provided a lot of extra work to street cleaners, garbage collectors and heating network repairmen.

I talked to three brave utility service workers who are doing what they can to keep a city clean that is under frequent shelling.

Each of them said: 'If not us, then who?'

'We do not want Icelandic geysers on the streets'

Roman Kryvokhatko, 31, is a heating network repairman. At first, he wanted to sign up for the Territorial Defense, but his district unit was packed with volunteers. Eventually, he decided that the best way of helping Ukraine amid the war would be by simply doing his job.

'We need to keep the networks in decent condition. Otherwise, in two to three weeks geysers will be everywhere. We do not want that,' he said.

He now takes on extra shifts since many of his coworkers joined the military or Territorial Defense Force and there is a shortage of hands. 'Honestly, at times I am scared,' he said standing next to a shell crater, 'but the work must be done.'

This was exactly his approach when he rushed to inspect a pipe on 18 March following a shelling. That morning Kryvokhatko was cycling to work when he heard a loud pop. He fell to the ground. The sound was of pieces of a Russian rocket hitting the ground two kilometers away from him killing one and injuring 19 people.

As it turned out, rocket parts hit the ground near a residential building, heavily damaging it and a heating pipe nearby. The pipe was deep underground, so Kryvokhatko and his colleagues started digging down the shell crater to find the pipe and contain the damage. Part of the pipe hit was beyond repair so they substituted it with a new one. They worked for two hours, late into Kyiv's curfew, in order to get the work done.

'If we hadn't patched it on time, there would have been a fountain of hot water and people would have gotten burnt and welted,' he said.

Wake up shell

Inna Kuchynska, 49, is a street cleaner. Almost every morning since the war broke out, she has been waking up to Russia's shelling at 5 a.m. sharp. 'I open my eyes and say: "Good morning to you, too",' Kuchynska said.

The morning of 17 March was no different. This time, however, Russia's rocket hit close to her home. The shockwave blew open her window. 'It scared me ... I even saw the flash in the sky,' she said.

She immediately got dressed and headed to the site of the shelling. 'I did not need my boss to call me and say to go there. It goes without saying. That's our job,' Kuchynska said.

Parts of Russia's rocket hit one building, but the shock shattered the windows of almost a dozen buildings. This meant a lot of work for Kuchynska. 'Window frames, glass, bricks. It was awful,' she said. 'Residents came out and helped us clean ... They picked up brooms and came to sweep the ground.'

Five days after the attack, Kuchynska and her colleagues were still cleaning up the debris.

'War or no war, we keep working. That's it,' she said. Speaking of her job as a street cleaner, Kuchynska said: 'My mission is to bring joy to people.'

'Some fight with Russians, others with litter'

Igor Oveshkov, 53, is a garbage truck driver. As his huge vehicle deftly avoided anti-tank hedgehogs down Kyiv's narrow streets, he said, jokingly: 'Slalom driving.'

'I do not remember turning the steering wheel around this much, even at driving school,' he went on.

Since the war started, he has had just two days off, but he doesn't complain. 'It needs to be done,' Oveshkov said. 'What keeps me going is responsibility, I guess.'

On the first day of Russia's war on 24 February, he went on his regular route. Soon after, the first siren sounded. 'Boss called me and said: "Come back." I replied: "No, if it gets me, it gets me, whether I am here or there. Now I can at least drive away",' he recalled.

On that day Oveshkov completed his route. Ever since he has been driving his truck no matter what.

The first days of the war were the most intense. The paradox, he said, is that people left but the amount of garbage multiplied. He, however, found an explanation: 'People panicked. They started throwing everything away, all the perishable products.'

'When we arrived, there were, say, three full containers and next to them a hill of garbage that would fit into three more containers,' Oveshkov went on.

Now it is easier, he said, but there is no time to relax. This job likes consistency.

'Some fight on the frontline while others fight with litter,' Oveshkov said. 'It is a tough fight. One day of delays and the garbage wins.'

He stopped to check his to-do list, and told his colleague: 'This one, if no one picks it up, we will.'

'If not us, then who?' he replied.

24 March 2022

Inside massacre of civilian evacuees outside Kyiv

Igor Kossov

In the village of Stoyanka-2 outside Kyiv, a half-dozen cars line the road, riddled with holes, their bodywork mangled by bullets and an explosion.

Their windows, bearing handwritten Ukrainian signs saying 'Children' are perforated or shattered. The suitcases inside the vehicles appear to have been searched. The bodies have been recovered by volunteers or removed by Russian soldiers or locals.

This is what remains of the quarter of a 20-car civilian evacuation convoy that tried to escape the suburban town of Irpin on the morning of 6 March. As the convoy entered Stoyanka-2, Russian forces opened fire, most likely from a nearby building, killing at least four people in the first five cars and wounding several more. The rest managed to back up, turn around and flee.

Oleksandr Syrtsov saw it happen directly in front of him. 'I saw with my own eyes how my loved ones were being shot to death ... like cannon fodder,' he told *The Kyiv Independent* over the phone from Kyiv. 'In 30 seconds, I lost my friend, my cousin, all my things, my documents, my car ... all I kept was my life.'

The scene, however lurid, drowns in the scores of similar scenes happening around the country. Russian forces throughout Ukraine have fired on fleeing civilians time and again, killing and wounding an unknown amount of evacuees.

On 23 March, the Office of the UN High Commissioner for Human Rights (UNHCR) reported 977 civilians killed and another 1,594 wounded since Russia invaded on 24 February. UNHCR warned that the actual number is most likely 'considerably higher'.

On the same day as the ambush in Stoyanka-2, Russian forces shelled and mortared evacuees trying to cross the Irpin River several kilometers away, killing eight people.

Trapped in Irpin

A native of Donetsk Oblast, Syrtsov had lived in Irpin, a town just outside Kyiv, for the past two years.

When the war began early in the morning on 24 February, Russian forces surged towards the capital and its outlying towns, blasting them with missiles and helicopters and landing troops. The town of Hostomel on Kyiv's north-western border, which contained an important airfield, was one of the Russians' first targets. Soon, the devastation spread to the nearby towns of Bucha and Irpin as well.

Syrtsov was trapped in his high-rise apartment building, along with the rest of its occupants and his friend, also named Oleksandr. The friend was visiting for work reasons on 23 February and decided to spend the night. The decision would seal his fate.

As shells and missiles slammed into Irpin, the residents of the entire building took shelter in the underground parking garage, which at one point was filled with 200 people. Even though it was perpetually cold down there, the first few days weren't so bad. The building had electricity and amenities. Later, access to utilities was severed. People were left in the dark, with no gas, no mobile internet connection and dwindling supplies.

People kept leaving every day but many were too worried to go and remained behind. Eventually, they realized they couldn't keep it up any longer.

'On the evening of 5 March, everyone prepared for it, knowing they would leave the next morning because staying was becoming untenable,' said Syrtsov. 'There was no electricity or water, our complex got shelled many times, the situation was critical, food was running out. There were small children.'

The kill zone

The convoy of 20 cars set out on their journey at 7.30 a.m. on 5 March. As the direct bridge to Kyiv had been blown earlier, they would have to go the long way around, through the villages of Stoyanka and Stoyanka-2. They passed a Ukrainian checkpoint, where the troops cleared them to proceed after checking everybody's documents.

'No one among the Ukrainian troops guessed that there might be an ambush waiting,' said Syrtsov.

He was driving one of the cars, a BMW, with a married couple as passengers. His friend Oleksandr was driving an Audi, with Syrtsov's cousin Artyom Podkopayev in the front passenger seat, and Podkopayev's wife and 4-year-old son in the back.

The morning was dead silent, eerily so, as the vehicles slowly drove around the remnants of a Russian combat vehicle in the road and approached Stoyanka-2, stopping within 200 meters. Everybody was nervous to proceed. Eventually, Syrtsov's friend stepped out of the car and asked who would go first.

The group hesitated, with several people saying that they have children. Eventually 'my friend waved his hand, got in the car and went first', said Syrtsov.

With Oleksandr in the lead, the first five vehicles slowly accelerated to about 15 kilometers per hour, crawling past several tall buildings to the left of the road. Syrtsov, in vehicle number six, began to follow.

The thump of automatic fire shattered the morning stillness.

The impacts seemed like firecrackers being thrown at and under the cars, Syrtsov said. He didn't know who was shooting. He guessed the fire probably came from one of the buildings to the left. However, when later examined, the struck vehicles also showed indentations on their right side. Syrtsov's car was also hit but not as hard as the first five.

'The first five cars went forward and I was in the sixth, I hit reverse,' he said. 'I paused for three seconds, ducked down, saw with my own eyes how the cars were being shot apart and reversed about 70 meters.' He hit some other vehicle, loaded with bread, that was pointed in the opposite direction.

'It happened so quickly,' he said. 'In that moment, my fear was very intense, but there was an understanding that my life might end here. I didn't scream or freak out, I just did everything automatically to try to save my life.'

Going in reverse saved him. The remaining evacuees' vehicles began to turn around to head back to Irpin and they picked him up. Though Syrtsov had spent over a week with no mobile connection, his phone caught a signal in the kill zone. Fifteen seconds later, he got a call from Iryna Podkopayeva, the wife of his cousin Artyom, who was in the lead car.

'She tells me Artyom is killed, Sasha is killed, I'm in the car, what do I do?' said Syrtsov. 'She called me right from the car. I told her to come out and head this way. If it's your fate, you will live. Or something like that.'

Inside the first car

Podkopayeva recalled that moment in a phone call with *The Kyiv Independent*. 'It sounded like many petards, a sort of "tuktuktuktuk",' when the shooting started, she said. 'And then it seemed to me like the car just crashed – I later found out that it was a grenade exploding on the driver's side. Then there was shooting. Last thing I remember is that the guys raised their hands to surrender.'

Her husband yelled to her to hide the kid, whom she grabbed and crushed to her body with all her strength. Terrified by the explosions, the boy began screaming and crying.

The window shattered, sending fragments skipping across her face and ear. Then the gunfire abruptly stopped. The car was filled with smoke.

'I opened my eyes to see what was happening. The driver was ... that's it.'

The driver was slumped over, the nose missing from his face.

'My husband was lying on the ground, covered in blood. He was convulsing.'

Iryna struggled to remember how to move the seat forward in the small coupe, before managing to grab the purse with her documents and come outside with her son. Wrapping him in a blanket, she wandered forward in a state of shock, going in the opposite direction from Irpin.

Soon, she blundered into a Russian checkpoint, where Russian soldiers took her and her child into a nearby building and got them some water.

'I hadn't even realized that they were the ones who were shooting at first but then I pieced it together,' she said.

Twenty minutes later, she was placed in a random car with some other survivors – a man and his two children, whose wife had been killed in the shootout – and they were sent on their way. Eventually she ran into some Ukrainians, who helped her and her son make it into Kyiv. She has since evacuated the country.

Death toll
Syrtsov is aware of at least four people who have been killed and several others who were wounded in the shootout.

He and the occupants of the rear 15 cars went back to their parking garage. The only other way out for them was to leave their cars behind and cross the Irpin River under the demolished bridge, across some wooden planks and pallets the Ukrainian forces laid down.

But that route was not an option on 6 March. As many civilians tried to get out that way, the crossing came under intense Russian mortar fire, putting evacuation on hold and killing eight people.

One shell killed an entire family, including a mother, two children, and a family friend, according to multiple journalists on site, who saw it happen. Eyewitnesses told *The Kyiv Independent* that the barrage of the crossing was very heavy that day.

Several volunteers who operate in Irpin made contact with Syrtsov after seeing his family's story on Instagram and volunteered to evacuate the bodies of Oleksandr and Podkopayev from Stoyanka-2.

Their bodies, recovered from next to the stricken Audi, were sent to Dnipropetrovsk Oblast, where Syrtsov's friend Oleksandr is from. The funeral was held on 20 March.

'It's a tragedy. They were so young, they could have lived and lived,' said Syrtsov.

26 March 2022

Ukraine reaches breaking point in Russia's war

Illia Ponomarenko

Russia's all-out war in Ukraine has subverted a lot of prophecies – doomsday omens and bright hopes alike.

It has now been a month of this new reality since Russia's attacks began early in the morning on 24 February 2022.

Yes, the Kremlin really did launch a World War II-level military offensive against Ukraine. Their invasion is full of war crimes and barbarities, and lacks an obvious voice of reason.

No, Ukraine didn't turn out to be frail and didn't kneel before the invading army.

Instead, after a month of hostilities, tangible results indicate that Ukraine has sustained the war's first major blow. It defeated the Kremlin's initial, most dangerous plan of a quick, shock-and-awe invasion.

Now, the war is entering a new phase – a grueling longer-term war of attrition, and a new, difficult test for the Ukrainian military and the nation.

But thanks to important early victories, as well as broad international support, this new phase opens a wide window of opportunity for inflicting a full-fledged military defeat upon Russia.

No breakthrough

As of 25 March, Russia still had no strategic success with any of its five key axes of the Ukraine campaign: Kyiv, Kharkiv, Donbas, Mariupol, Mykolaiv. Except for Donbas and Mariupol, where the invaders are making very limited, slow, and painful gains, all major Russian advancement has been halted for more than two weeks.

Throughout the initial, very active phase of advances, Russia managed to secure broad territorial gains in Ukraine's north (near Kyiv and Chernihiv), northeast (near Kharkiv), and south (Kherson, Berdiansk, Mariupol).

The 'operational pause', as dubbed by the Ukrainian defense community, unfolded throughout the country after 8–11 March.

It was believed that Russia took this short breathing spell to possibly regroup its forces and improve its logistics which had caused massive troubles in terms of food and fuel supplies. However, the lull continues. International monitors do not indicate Russia successfully making major improvements in its logistics or reorganizing its forces that have demonstrated unexpectedly low performance so far.

Moreover, in many areas, such as west of Kyiv, Russian forces have been seen entrenched in urban battlefields, going on the defensive to possibly hold on to what they gained in the earliest days.

Numerous and fierce attempts to advance have resulted in little to no progress in almost each of the principal axes. West or east of Kyiv, there have been almost no territorial gains for nearly two weeks, be it the Irpin–Hostomel–Bucha triangle or the vast areas east of Brovary.

In Mykolaiv, numerous frontal attacks from occupied Kherson also resulted in nothing but severe Russian casualties. By 22–23 March, Russians effectively halted their attempts to advance toward the city. Attempts to bypass Mykolaiv and toward the city of Voznesensk or threaten Kryvyi Rih have also not proven successful.

As a result, in the south, Russia is not even close to threatening Odesa by land, despite enjoying full supremacy at sea. It is not even attempting to attack Odesa by way of the beach with an amphibious landing force, since it would be a guaranteed failure given the circumstances.

In the northeast, despite hard isolation and a horrific humanitarian situation, Sumy, Kharkiv, and Chernihiv are successfully withstanding Russian assaults. In many ways, when it comes to Sumy and Chernihiv, this fierce and unending resistance relieves a lot of pressure from the areas east of Kyiv.

And again, Russia has made no principal gains in those axes over the last two weeks. When it comes to Chernihiv and Sumy oblasts it still has very infirm control of the long supply lines running along the E95 and H07 highways between the Russian border and the area east of Kyiv.

In the south, Russia has managed to gain footholds in Kherson, Nova Kakhovka, Melitopol, Enerhodar, and Berdiansk, where it met little resistance in the earliest days. But even there, it has been making little to no progress for days and weeks.

Russia is also making attempts at two axes of attack – one trying to advance north from Zaporizhzhia Oblast and one trying to advance south in Kharkiv Oblast – to meet each other somewhere in the middle.

Such a rendezvous would isolate a large Ukrainian military grouping of forces in central Donbas (Sloviansk, Kramatorsk, Sievierodonetsk, Lysychansk), where Ukraine holds most of its combat-potent units. But to do so, the advancing Russian axes would have to endure a total of at least 250 kilometers of roads amid fierce Ukrainian resistance at every strong point on the way.

The northern Russian group in this theater is not even close to being ready to advance further south. It has been stuck in extremely hard fighting in the city of Izium in Kharkiv Oblast for weeks and still faces numerous obstacles in its way. In Donetsk and Luhansk oblasts, there also have been no major territorial gains since mid-March.

The Ukrainian military opted to retreat to the vicinity of the region's key cities, such as Sievierodonetsk and Lysychansk, turning these areas into giant urban fortresses, where Russian air supremacy loses the upper hand.

In this region, Russia's few territorial gains came at extreme costs. Having seized Volnovakha between Donetsk and Mariupol in a series of extremely costly attacks, Russian-led militants have barely made any new advances, getting stopped in intense fighting near the small town of Ugledar just northwest.

Even from these current positions, after a month of fighting, the enemy still faces several heavily fortified Ukrainian points, such as Kurakhove, Mariinka, or Avdiivka, not to mention large key cities.

Reports on the ground indicate numerous frontal attacks against Avdiivka and Mariinka north and southwest of Donetsk, respectively, in which Russian-mobilized militants sustained extreme losses for weeks, with no results.

Poor results amid severe casualties stir resentment among many Russian observers, even such as Igor Girkin, the infamous warlord of the early days of the Donbas campaign in 2014. In his numerous interviews with pro-Kremlin media outlets, the former high-ranking terrorist says at such a pace the Donbas militants, much of the Russian force in the region, will shortly run out of manpower for any further offensive operations.

Mariupol, in this picture, remains the worst hellscape. The city's garrison, despite the full blockade and relentless Russian bombardment, has continued waging block-by-block warfare for over 20 days, making Russian advances extremely slow, hard, and costly.

Even if Russia, having paid a high price, finally seizes the city in the coming weeks, it will effectively end up conquering nothing but barely habitable heaps of ruins, similar to Volnovakha, which was also razed to the ground.

Mariupol's giant industrial cluster has been destroyed, along with its housing stock and vital infrastructure. Since Russia seized the northwestern coast of the Azov Sea, the besieged Mariupol has barely had any clear or immediate significance for Russia other than a symbol of a stubborn Ukrainian fortress.

In fact, with Mariupol blocked and the south of Donetsk Oblast seized, Moscow has already established its fabled 'land corridor between Russia and Crimea'.

But Russia's obstinate attempts to take the city by assault at any price, despite extreme casualties, indicate nothing but Vladimir Putin's utter desire to put his own emotional, political objectives over military necessity – not a good foundation for the whole campaign.

26 March 2022

'Iconic' Saint Javelin helps fundraise over $1 million for Ukraine
Alexander Query

'Saint Javelin' became a rallying sign of Ukraine's resistance since Russia invaded on 24 February.

An Orthodox Madonna clad in green and cradling a Javelin anti-tank missile, the viral meme found a new use in the hands of Christian Borys, a Toronto marketer who was a journalist in Ukraine in 2014–2019.

Days before the war started, Borys created a $10 sticker out of the viral meme to help Ukrainian orphans in what he thought would be a modest contribution to Ukraine's support relief. He also created SaintJavelin.com to sell those stickers online.

'The sticker was a fluke,' Borys told *The Kyiv Independent*.

He had initially set up a $30,000 goal for his charity. A month in, Borys raised over $1 million, an unexpected success for the entrepreneur turned charity worker. 'It's just very overwhelming,' Borys said.

Overwhelming success

The initial fundraising goal was aimed at providing scholarships to children who lost their parents in the war in Donbas that Russia started in 2014 – a personal topic for Borys.

'One of the stories I worked on when I was in Ukraine was about families who had lost mostly fathers in the war,' Borys said. He interviewed widowed mothers, listening to their stories of grief and losses. 'It's one of those things that stick with you forever,' he said.

Borys collaborated with a Canadian charity HelpUsHelp. He went from hundreds of $10 stickers to over 6,000 items sold in 60 countries. 'It became a full-time job,' he said. 'It's so overwhelming, we're trying to scale back a bit.'

To keep the operation running, Borys had to solve customer support, logistics and operational issues. Each of his bank accounts was temporarily frozen because there was so much cash flowing through them that the banks thought he was laundering money, he told the *Toronto Life*, a Canadian local newspaper.

With that much money coming in, he rethought the purpose of the aid. 'We changed it from all of this money going towards orphans to all of this money will go to victims of violence,' he said.

Aside from working with HelpUsHelp, Borys began working with the 2402 Fund created by Ukrainian journalists to help equip reporters and newsrooms with the necessary equipment, vehicles and protective gear.

Apart from his Saint Javelin merch project, Borys works with the Ukrainian World Congress, which represents the Ukrainian diaspora all over the world. Borys helped the organization set up a logistics chain for aid flowing into Ukraine, including first aid kits, tourniquets, bulletproof vests, kevlar helmets.

Borys said transparency is key in such a large-scale charity operation. 'My goal is to show everything because nobody's gonna trust somebody who's hiding anything,' he said.

Art for charity

The Saint Javelin design was not an original creation of Borys. Ukrainian graphic designer Evgeniy Shalashov, based in Lviv and employed by Borys, slightly adapted a 2012 painting by US artist Chris Shaw that was already a hit.

In mid-February, Shaw 'woke up to find an image of "Saint Javelin" going viral all over the internet as a meme', a digital alteration of his 2012 painting, 'Madonna Kalashnikov'.

Shaw painted the 'Madonna Kalashnikov', a feminine religious icon holding a gold-leafed AK-47, in 2012, in the aftermath of the Arab Spring that shook the Middle East in the early 2010s.

In 2015, Madonna Kalashnikov was conscripted by the Ukrainian Army and became a morale patch for Ukraine's military.

'The experience of Saint Javelin, simply, has been amazing, humbling, incredible, and also leaves me with mixed feelings,' Shaw told *The Kyiv Independent*. 'Of course, nobody asked me if my art could be used or sold,' he said. 'However, after seeing the image used successfully to raise money for Ukraine I felt better that at least some of the profits made would be used for good purposes.'

'For Saint Javelin to become an image helping to aid relief and show solidarity with Ukraine is amazing. Now that she is everywhere, I want her to do good,' he added.

Saint Javelin isn't the only Madonna art associated with the war in Ukraine now. Ukrainian illustrator Anta Frirean, based in Germany, recently published on her Instagram a religious adaptation of a viral picture of a mother from Kyiv breastfeeding her baby, her body reeling from shattered glass wounds. Frirean's Instagram links to a webpage listing numerous charities and foundations to donate and help support Ukraine against Russia.

Meanwhile, Russia's war rages and hits close to home for the Saint Javelin team.

The Ukrainian members of Borys' marketing agency 'Black Hawk', who lived in Kharkiv, Ukraine's second-largest city, had to leave because the city had been destroyed, Borys said. They are now hiding in smaller towns and villages in Ukraine, searching for apartments in Poland for their wives and children.

Shalashov, who adapted the Saint Javelin graphic, has been forced into bomb shelters so many times that he chose to flee to a village near his city, Lviv. When he first answered *The Kyiv Independent*, he apologized for the delay because of his lack of sleep due to the raid sirens in western Ukraine. 'I think the success of our campaign is all about the good people, who want to help Ukraine, who want peace in the world,' Shalashov later said. 'Design is the last thing here.'

28 March 2022

Crack down in occupied Kherson

Igor Kossov

Editor's Note: The Kyiv Independent *used false names for all sources who spoke from Kherson Oblast for this story, for the sake of security.*

Life is getting worse in the city of Kherson, which has been occupied by Russian forces for nearly a month.

The near-total absence of critical drugs for chronic diseases like diabetes and high blood pressure has left people who depend on them in a critical state. Food remains scarce and expensive, while the ability to buy it is limited and takes up the majority of the locals' day.

'In general, life ends at 3 p.m.,' said Yulia, a local resident. 'The stores work until 3. Thankfully, transportation works. People go to the markets, stand in line and come back home. City services are operational but they also have shortened workdays.'

Kherson, a regional capital in southern Ukraine, is the only major city that the Russians managed to take control of. But the resistance inside Kherson hasn't died with occupation.

As the Russian forces grow increasingly impatient and frustrated with constant pro-Ukrainian protests, their ferocity has greatly increased over the past week. Violent crackdowns and abductions are on the rise as yet-unconfirmed threats of mass deportations loom.

Journalists, once left alone, have shifted into working underground to avoid drawing attention from the Russian forces. As fighting continues near Kherson and multiple Ukrainian cities face devastation, locals fear that they may be subjected to the same atrocities.

Battles are reportedly ongoing near Kherson. News sources including AFP and *New York Times* cited a Pentagon official on 25 March, who said that Russians are losing control of the city and that it's once again 'contested'. Local residents denied this, saying Russian forces still patrol the streets in force. However, residents have reported hearing loud explosions happening not far from the city at night.

'The battles are ongoing between Chornobaivka and Mykolaiv,' said Valentyn, who lives in Chornobaivka, a village outside Kherson, where Ukrainian forces have counterattacked a nearby airfield 11 times since 24 February, according to the President's Office. 'But it's getting closer and closer to us. Evidently, our forces are advancing because we hear the fighting more and more.'

Supply shortages

Igor, an entrepreneur who helps operate a chain of bakeries in Kherson, says that his supply chain has been in a sorry state since the occupation. Bakery employees have had to drive around villages and towns throughout the area, as well as scour the internet to look for basic goods like flour, butter and sugar, often finding none.

'It's getting harder and harder since no one has any left,' Igor said. 'Prices have gone up by three to five times. This reflects on the price of bread.'

Shortages in the city have been partly alleviated by deliveries of vegetables and other goods from local villages according to Kostiantyn, a broadcast journalist in Kherson. These goods are delivered mainly to marketplaces, as stores and supermarkets have largely shut down, amid looting by Russians. 'The Russian army seizes stuff from the supermarkets on a daily basis,' Kostiantyn said. 'We saw them carrying out appliances, microwaves and such, loading them up and sending them all somewhere. Now all the big stores are completely looted and they [Russians] have turned to looting the smaller ones.'

The lines at outdoor markets are extremely long and going there to buy food is often an all-day affair, sources told *The Kyiv Independent*.

According to a BBC report from 22 March, a poultry farm outside the nearby village of Chornobaivka was left without sufficient feed for its 3 million birds and started handing them out so local residents could at least make use of them. Volunteers delivered chickens into the city, across residences, hospitals and children's shelters.

Igor pointed out that not only are the prices high, the sellers often insist on being paid in cash, which isn't easy to come by. People can begin to line up at ATMs at 5 a.m., just to wait for hours to be able to withdraw a maximum of Hr 1,000 ($34).

Valentyn said the sellers want cash because they say they can't pay for the food they bring in otherwise. Recently, he said, more have started accepting electronic payments in his village.

Food shortages are just part of the problem. The other part is the lack of fuel. Because it's so hard to come by, the range of delivery trucks is extremely limited, meaning they can't go out very far to try to find supplies.

The bigger problem is with medicine. 'The biggest deficit is for medicines for people with chronic diseases, such as diabetes, there's almost no insulin,' said Yulia.

The Guardian quoted locals as saying that more people are dying from lack of medication than from bullets. Others have corroborated this claim. Medications that people depend on to treat cardiac conditions or high blood pressure are virtually absent and there have been absolutely no deliveries since the occupation began. The Russian forces have not let any humanitarian convoys through, locals said.

According to Yulia, hospitals are still equipped with medication and if a person ends up in a hospital, there's a higher chance that they can get the drugs they need. In pharmacies, however, it's virtually impossible to get any painkillers or even something as basic as valerian root.

Volunteers are trying their best to relieve these shortages but their options are limited.

Journalism crackdown

The work of journalists, especially broadcasters, has changed tremendously, according to Kostiantyn. Those who are identifiable as the media now have a target on their back. 'We're TV people and the presence of a microphone or camera used to be a defense,' he said. 'Now, to appear with a camera or a mic is practically impossible – it immediately attracts attention. The scariest thing that has begun in Kherson is the repressions, including against journalists.'

The Russians shut down local channels in the earliest days of the occupation, switching them over to Russian broadcasts, he said. Cable TV held out for a week longer until it was simply shut off. Now, tuning into cable just displays dead air.

Kostiantyn's team, which used to work exclusively in the video medium, using conspicuous equipment, has had to adapt. Good equipment is now only used to shoot video packages indoors, in secure locations, producing stories about life in shelters or the work of volunteers. All shooting and audio recording on the street is done with easily concealable phones or voice recorders.

The news format switched away from video and towards text, with many more longreads being posted, as people being stuck at home are reading more. Almost all work is done remotely.

Even so, journalists continue to face interference. Sites have been hit with distributed denial of service attacks. 'They won't let us work,' said Kostiantyn.

Journalists have also received threats, including Kostiantyn's colleagues. 'This includes calls and letters and social media messages saying "watch what you write, this will be Russia, why do you need the trouble? Stop your activity." And then various insults.'

It hasn't stopped there. Journalists have also been abducted and interrogated, like Oleh Baturin, a journalist for the *Novy Den* newspaper in Kherson Oblast, who was seized from the city of Kakhovka on 12 March.

Over the course of his ordeal, he said the Russians interrogated him, trying to find supposed figureheads behind the daily protests that enveloped Kherson since the occupation began. He was released on 20 March.

Growing hostility

The local sources confirmed that the Russians have made it their top priority to try to hunt down the supposed organizers of the daily protests against occupation that have been held in the center of the city since early March.

'I get the impression that they can't understand who is the "main instigator" of these demonstrations, so they started to intensely abduct activists and well-known people in the city,' said Yulia. 'A few days ago, they abducted the director of a drama theater.'

The media reported that the director, city deputy and opinion leader, Oleksandr Kniga, was seized and questioned about the supposed organizers of the rallies before being released, which he confirmed.

Yulia said that some of the Russian forces really appeared to think that they were liberators and really believed that there was some mastermind out there, pushing locals to protest. They weren't able to consider the possibility that people who care about freedom, democracy and self-determination are self-organizing.

'They need to have some kind of shepherd to control them and they can't understand why we come out – they have this idea that we're being forced and coordinated centrally,' she said. 'It's funny and sad at the same time.'

Even though people like Yulia are able to find humor in the Russians' mentality, the crackdowns are deadly serious. Previously, Russians have let the protests run their course or tried to drown them out by blasting audio from old Soviet cartoons, Kostiantyn said. Now, as soon as they see any gathering taking place in the city center, they bring out a convoy of paddy wagons and deploy large formations of armor-wearing, assault rifle-wielding forces, able to arrest hundreds of people.

Last week, Russians deployed tear gas and flashbang grenades against the protesters and even opened fire with live rounds, wounding at least one local resident, locals told *The Kyiv Independent*. For all of these reasons, demonstrations have shrunk dramatically from thousands of people to less than a hundred.

'In the past week, these meetings were dispersed by force – with flashbangs, tear gas, clubs, arrests and beatings,' said Kostiantyn. 'Everyone has breathed in some tear gas by now.'

Igor, who was part of the EuroMaidan protests in 2014, added that many people, including himself, have had armed Russians come to their houses to conduct a search and ask questions. The men would then leave with a threat of 'serious problems' if the resident ever caught their attention again.

'There's no rule of law, it's not like you can call a lawyer. They just do what they want,' Igor said. 'They can break down your door, seize you, take you to an unknown location, interrogate you. Here, people are completely undefended.'

'When seven armed men show up to your house at 6 a.m and tell you that the next time they see you at a protest, they'll simply take you somewhere and lose you, then of course it forms an impression,' he added.

Asked if he's seen any run-ins with the Russians, Valentyn described how two young local men, who were probably drinking alcohol on the street in Chornobaivka, were shot by Russian forces who may have thought they were preparing Molotov cocktails in the bottles. The Russians also fired on a civilian car that was driving through the village.

British publication *The Times* reported that the Russians' patience has run out in Kherson and they were considering large-scale terror against the locals, including the possibility of mass deportations. Most sources who spoke to *The Kyiv Independent* find this plausible, in light of the reports that Russians have forcibly deported thousands of people from Mariupol, a besieged seaport in southern Ukraine, into Russia.

Kostiantyn reported a heavy presence of black-clad Russian National Guard personnel in the city, who are deployed in force every time people gather to demonstrate.

30 March 2022

Ukrainian designers swap fashion week collections for army apparel
Elina-Alem Kent

While international designers may be busy doing shows at Milan and Paris fashion weeks, Ukrainian designers are making clothes for war.

After Russia launched its full-scale invasion of Ukraine on 24 February, Ukrainian designers have decided to use their sewing skills to support the Ukrainian army. Instead of fashionable shoes and stylish outerwear, they are now making camouflage nets, combat boots, and even armored vests.

The Kyiv Independent spoke to Ukrainian designers helping the country amid war.

From menswear to camouflage
Ukrainian designer Serge Smolin, whose brand Idol makes designer suits, used to help men stand out. Now he's making sure that men blend in, providing the Ukrainian army with camouflage nets.

After escaping Kyiv, which has been targeted by Russian artillery and missiles, Smolin arrived at his parents' home in western Ukraine.

The designer immediately went to the nearest military checkpoint to see what was needed. They needed someone to weave camouflage nets. Smolin's newly formed team, which included his family and artist Serge Payet, found rolls of cloth at home and got to work. 'We joke that we are making "macrame" for our new collection,' Smolin told *The Kyiv Independent*.

They are using the local school's large gym for weaving. The camouflage nets were later routed to hotspots around Ukraine, including Kyiv's suburbs.

From high heels to combat boots
The popular shoe brand Kachorovska is known for its comfortable, stylish, and affordable shoes.

The brand prides itself in keeping its designs beautiful without sacrificing comfort, Maria Slenzak, Kachorovska's brand manager, told *The Kyiv Independent*.

But since the start of Russia's full-scale invasion, the brand has repurposed its production from trendy footwear to combat boots. Kachorovska is now collaborating with three different factories, each providing soles, leather, and employees for the production of boots for the Armed Forces and Territorial Defense.

The first 500 pairs were sewn by Kachorovska's team on their own funds. Later, they turned to the public for support and have started accepting donations to cover supplies. The brand doesn't have access to tactical cloth, so they use leather instead. 'All pairs were sewn under constant sirens with the threat of airstrikes, with the bombing of cities where the combat boots are made,' Slenzak says. 'It takes courage for our team to work in such conditions.'

People can donate to Kachorovska's charity fund used to purchase supplies on their Instagram @kachorovska_atelier. The brand turns off the donation link when they gather enough funds needed to sew the next batch.

The production and delivery of the boots are done under extreme circumstances and stress, but the feedback from soldiers has kept the Kachorovska team motivated. 'They are very satisfied,' Slenzak says.

From outerwear and couture to military vests

Several fashion brands, such as Nebesite and Frolov, have turned to making bulletproof vests in order to support the Armed Forces and Territorial Defense.

Nebesite, previously an outerwear brand, was preparing to celebrate its fourth birthday with its new spring collection. Within 48 hours of the first attacks, the team was already looking and contacting experts on how to use their skills to help the military.

The brand found a manufacturer of metal plates for bulletproof vests and was able to partner up with them, designing a simplified version of the vests. The brand was able to provide the first 250 vests free of charge. 'At our own expense, the brand's budget, which we had prepared for the spring and the next winter collection,' Tanya Mogila, Nebesite's designer, told *The Kyiv Independent*. The body armor was distributed to people in Irpin, Kyiv and at the Zhytomyr highway checkpoint.

Prices of materials have gone up since the start of the war, with the cost of making a vest jumping to around $190. The money is spent on the fabric, metal plates, and salaries for the seamstresses who are making the vests under shelling.

Meanwhile, a popular brand Frolov is using its platform to fundraise for military vests. Their aim is to find money to buy the steel needed for the vests in Europe, as it has become increasingly difficult to source it in Ukraine. For that, Frolov's brand has already raised over 20,000 euros abroad. The brand has donated several of their sewing machines to volunteers, while some of Frolov's employees stayed to sew the vests. The vests made so far are already in the possession of the Ukrainian army.

1 April 2022

Ukraine's railway keeps the country running amid war

Anna Myroniuk

From the early days of the war, Ukrainian Railways, or Ukrzaliznytsya, has become central to the country's life and defense.

Ukrzaliznytsia has been helping the army by producing anti-tank hedgehogs and transporting the uncollected bodies of Russian soldiers killed on the front lines. Its role in helping civilians is even greater. Trains have been running back and forth, taking people out of war hotspots, and bringing humanitarian aid in. In a little over a month, Ukrzaliznytsia has delivered over 8,000 tons of aid and evacuated over 3 million people to safety.

To do so, railway workers have been risking their lives.

Natalya Babicheva, 48, was a train attendant who took people from Ukraine's war-torn east to the relatively safe west.

The evacuation train she worked on was on its way to pick up children from the Donbas when it came under fire. This happened shortly before the train's arrival at the station in the town of Lyman late on 12 March.

Shrapnel hit Babicheva's neck. She died of blood loss in the hands of her husband, who worked with her.

'She loved life so much,' said her friend and colleague Iryna Haidai, sobbing.

Haidai is a train crew instructor who formed the team for this evacuation train. She said that Babicheva could not stand aside and watch as people suffered. 'She told me that she was inclined to take this job because, as she told me: "It is the only way I could help people",' Haidai said, recalling a conversation she had with Babicheva.

Her husband Andriy now wants to continue his wife's legacy and get back to evacuating people from war hotspots, Haidai said.

Andriy buried Natalya in their hometown of Krasnohorivka, which lies on the Donbas front line. 'Her husband told me it was a very quick funeral due to the heavy shelling,' Haidai said.

Babicheva is among the 71 railway employees who have been killed in Ukraine since the full-scale war broke out in late February. The count includes Ukrzaliznytsia employees killed by Russian attacks both while working and off-duty.

'She loved her work very much. She hadn't achieved her full potential. She was a train attendant. I always said that she should have been at least a train administrator,' Haidai said. 'She just wasn't given enough time.'

Fitting everyone in

Oleksandr Besarab, 32, a train administrator, has been on the front line of Ukrzaliznytsia's evacuation efforts since the very start of the war.

Instead of the usual six days his shift has already lasted for a month with no days off. 'We are lucky to have never come under shelling, even though we have been working non-stop for these past four weeks,' Besarab said.

He and his team of 20 railway workers ended up living on the train for the entire month. They had to apply additional security measures: shut the lights off at night and draw the curtains so as not to attract unwanted attention.

Not only their routine but their route also changed.

On the day the war started, Besarab's train was on its way from the western city of Rakhiv to the southern city of Mykolaiv, his hometown. The train never made it to its point of arrival. 'Our train route went through Kherson and the occupiers were already there,' he said. 'I was very anxious. My family was in Mykolaiv, which was being shelled.'

Going to Kherson was dangerous so the train got stuck in the city of Kryvyi Rih, which eventually became its final stop. Ever since then, the train has been making evacuation trips between the central city and the west.

The biggest challenge for Besarab has been curbing panic. 'The first days were hot,' he said, 'I mean there were so many passengers ... People were sitting on one another.'

'Imagine, normally you have 30 passengers in the carriage, but now you have 200,' Besarab went on. 'We closed the train car's doors and then realized that the people standing in the airlock couldn't even move.'

It was difficult for people both mentally and physically, he said. Some had chest pains, others panic attacks. Besarab would walk along the train car calming the passengers down. 'It was tough,' Besarab recalls having a short break now. 'I think it is morally wrong to leave people behind, especially in wartime,' he said, preparing for his next shift.

Cut off

Some workers of the railway found themselves in the epicenter of combat immediately after the war broke out. They were unable to help the others. They sought help themselves.

Olena Francuzova, 53, is head of Mariupol railway station. Her peaceful city on the shore of the Azov Sea in the Donbas turned into a war hotspot overnight. 'It was very difficult. We were constantly in the basement under shelling,' she said.

Mariupol railway station had managed to keep working until 27 February. Then the Russian army destroyed the nearby station in Volnovakha and cut Mariupol off.

'The only way out was through Volnovakha,' Francuzova said. She managed to escape the besieged Mariupol after three weeks. Many of her colleagues have yet to leave. 'We are in touch with all the railway workers,' she said. 'The people who have stayed in the occupied territory, they also want to get out of there and get to a part of the country that is like where they lived and worked, and which they love.'

Ukrzaliznytsia not only evacuates passengers from east to west, but also helps its staff from war hotspots to relocate to safety. 'I was offered a job at the rail station of Uzhhorod, where I am about to go any time now with my family,' she said.

Francuzova said she is proud of Ukrainian Railways' response to the crises and is happy to be a part of the team. In any capacity. 'I can do anything. I started my career at the railroad as a ticket clerk. Then I worked at the help desk, in the luggage room, and as a station operator,' she said. 'There is plenty of work at the country's rail stations since they've turned into hubs for humanitarian aid.'

Humanitarian aid hubs

Railway stations across Ukraine have turned into help centers for everyone in need. They offer food, shelter, clothes, everything an evacuee coming from a war hotspot might need.

Darya Kochukh, a marketer turned volunteer, is responsible for feeding all comers at Kyiv railway station. 'Some people say they have not had warm food for two weeks, others say they have not even seen a slice of bread,' she said. 'What calms me down is to see that these people are safe now and I helped them,' she goes on.

When the war broke Kochukh realized she needed to do something to help her country. 'Here at the railway station, there are always a lot of people, life is booming. You see how many people help and how many people seek help. This atmosphere pushes you to help more and more,' she said.

While Kochukh's job is to ensure everyone has a bite of food, Anna Crocus's focus is on helping the kids.

An owner of the tourism agency, Crocus organized her friends to bring clothes, medicine, and baby carriages to the railway station for children arriving from the frontlines. 'There were kids from Irpin and Bucha,' referring to war hotspots near Kyiv, 'a girl was fully wet as she had to walk through the water to the evacuation bus.'

'There was a little boy of six or seven, Vanichka … He said: "Mom was killed yesterday." It was a horror here in the first days,' she went on.

'I think I must have learned to cry inside. As you do not want to show people that you are upset. You want to cheer them up somehow,' Crocus said.

Soon, aid started arriving from all over the globe. There was so much of it that the volunteers started sending aid to the frontlines. 'In the first days we had 10–20 tons of aid coming every day from local people and from abroad. From Poland, Italy,' Petro Stetsiuk, head of Kyiv railway station said.

The railway repurposed its halls, turning some into baby care rooms, others into storage for humanitarian aid. 'Often passengers help to unload trains carrying aid,' Stetsiuk said, highlighting how Ukrainians have stepped up to help each other in a time of crisis.

1 April 2022

Inside a hospital in occupied town near Kyiv

Anastasiia Lapatina

When the war began, Anton Dovgopol, the 36-year-old director of the Irpin City Polyclinic, got a phone call early in the morning. He learned that Ivankiv, a little village some 80 kilometers northwest of Kyiv, was under a Russian attack. He told his wife to get their go-bag ready, reached out to the mayor's office, calling for an urgent meeting, and immediately went to work.

Irpin, Bucha, Vorzel, and Hostomel, developing suburbs on the outskirts of Kyiv, quickly became hot spots when Russia launched its full-scale assault on Ukraine on 24 February. Advancing through those towns was key for the Russian military to reach the nation's capital. Irpin City Polyclinic, with branches in Bucha and Vorzel, found itself in the middle of war and occupation.

Dovgopol spoke with *The Kyiv Independent* about what it took the hospital to continue functioning through the battles that followed, until it no longer could. 'It looked like we would be in the epicenter [of fighting],' Dovgopol said during an interview over the phone, as he was taking his wife and two little sons into safety in western Ukraine. 'It was just my intuition.'

When the war came, Dovgopol's priority was to make each of the three branches of Irpin's hospital autonomous. All had to be ready to carry out surgeries, deliver babies, and operate around the clock, in case transport lines or communication between them was disrupted.

It didn't take long for that to happen. Only 24 hours later, food deliveries stopped. Electricity went off the day after, and eventually, so did the water and gas. The hospital secured extra generators and food, and continued operating. Dovgopol appointed members of his staff as supervisors in Irpin and Vorzel, and went to the nearby Bucha – a town that would soon become a hot spot of Russia's war.

Just five kilometers away from Bucha was Antonov International Airport, which came under shelling and air attacks hours after Russia declared war. Russian forces badly needed the airport to disembark its airborne units close to Kyiv. After one day of heavy fighting, the first wounded Russian soldiers started coming into Dovgopol's hospital in Bucha.

Two wounded and one dead, the soldiers were from Kemerovo, a Siberian city in Russia. One of them, a former police officer, told Dovgopol that they were supposed to be holding the ground after Kyiv was captured. The soldier was surprised that Ukrainians didn't meet them as liberators.

When wounded Ukrainian soldiers came in, the hospital staff put them in civilian clothes, gave them fake name tags, and hid their IDs so they wouldn't become targets if Russians burst in.

A week into Russia's war, logistics within Bucha and between cities were mostly shut – Russian checkpoints spread around the city, while roads and bridges were either destroyed or too dangerous.

In Vorzel, a neighboring town, locals were running out of food. Trying to prevent a humanitarian catastrophe, Dovgopol made a decision to use an ambulance to get supplies to the town.

'This was when I first encountered the Russians,' he told *The Kyiv Independent*. 'I got lucky – slowly, with my hands in the air, I drove up to the three soldiers who pointed their guns at me, and told them I was transporting food for pregnant women.' They let him pass.

The hospital's branch in Vorzel had 10 pregnant women who were expected to give birth soon, and six women that had babies during the war. Dovgopol dropped off supplies that were enough for four days and went back to Bucha.

What ensued was sheer madness, he says.

On 3 March, the Ukrainian government announced that Bucha was liberated – a video of soldiers proudly putting up a Ukrainian flag circulated online. But that same night, Russian forces violently broke into Bucha and occupied the entire city, Dovgopol says. The fighting was constant, and reached the hospital's territory.

'We put police members that guarded the hospital into white robes, otherwise they could be shot to death,' Dovgopol says. 'Same with the Territorial Defense guys – we dressed them into civilian clothes and hid their weapons.'

Territorial defense units told the hospital's staff that Russian forces were planning to seize the hospital and take their men who were injured. Russians raided the clinic a few days later.

They looked for their compatriots, but in vain – Dovgopol's team gave all injured Russians to the SBU, and evacuated all Ukrainian soldiers to a military hospital nearby. After checking people's documents, Russian soldiers left.

As enemy attacks intensified, dead bodies began appearing on Bucha's streets, and continued shelling made it impossible to clear them out. 'We just had to start burying the bodies, as risky as it was, because it just became unbearable. There were bodies everywhere, dogs eating them ...' Dovgopol recalls.

Reaching the cemetery was impossible, as the area was full of snipers. So on 10 March, Dovgopol and his colleagues dug out a mass grave near a local church, burying 67 people. They took photos and assigned numbers to every person, passing this information to the police. The hospital managed to identify 35 bodies, including three Ukrainian soldiers. The names of 32 people remained unknown.

For the few days that followed, Dovgopol and his colleagues drove around Bucha with whatever food they had left, letting people know of upcoming evacuations. Russian forces in the city didn't threaten their ambulance, but controlled their movement. Two Russian military vehicles followed them everywhere they went.

On 11 March, Russian soldiers burst into the hospital and demanded to see its leaders. 'There is no government here,' Russians told Dovgopol.

Yet some local officials remained in the city, wearing white uniforms under the cover of hospital staff to avoid being a target.

'We want to collaborate with you,' Russian soldiers told Dovgopol. 'And we want you to head the local interim administration. If you want to continue working here, you have to cooperate with us. If you try to leave, you will regret it.'

They promised to come back at 11 a.m. the next day. The morning came, but the Russians never showed up.

The hospital's team agreed to evacuate as soon as possible. There was no evacuation corridor. But as the fighting reignited in Bucha, it became clear that there may not be another chance to get out. Five hospital workers refused to leave – some had nowhere to go, some had old parents to look after.

Dovgopol and his team packed their most expensive medical equipment into vehicles and carefully left the hospital.

As a dozen cars moved through the city, headed by Dovgopol in an ambulance, around 200 civilian cars joined them. The column moved via the route the hospital's director remembered from a few days ago, when the Red Cross escorted him to Kyiv to pick up extra supplies.

The roads were crowded with shot cars, and bodies of killed civilians in them. Hours later, Dovgopol's column slowly reached the Ukraine-controlled outskirts of Kyiv, and civilian cars dispersed.

The remaining staff members soon abandoned the hospital, which Russian forces now occupy, Dovgopol said. 'If we stayed, they'd make us slaves of the Russian world,' he added.

Personal note from Asami Terajima, reporter

My name is Asami Terajima, and I'm one of the founding members of *The Kyiv Independent.* I previously worked as a business reporter at the *Kyiv Post,* covering the country's economy, energy, and investment — but never war.

Everything changed when Russia began its full-scale invasion of Ukraine. I discovered a part of myself that I'd never known before. I never knew that journalism was all I wanted to do in life, how much it meant to me — and how much I loved reporting. That hunger to find something new, that thirst for breaking stories that hopefully matter to the world. That sense of obligation — and privilege — to keep the world informed on what's happening in the country I've grown to love so much. And most importantly, I never knew that conflict reporting would be something I aspire to pursue in the future, even after the war in Ukraine ends one day, hopefully in the Middle East. (Before the invasion, I dreamt of working in the United Nations.)

But none of it was easy, of course. It took time to get used to the endless sound of explosions on the first days of the full-scale invasion and not let panic inside me affect my reporting of the war. After all, I never thought I would one day live in a city under attack. Even though I grew up in Ukraine, the years-long war in the eastern Donbas region felt far away. I never thought the war would reach Kyiv, Lviv, Odesa, and other cities I've been to with my family.

The first few weeks were especially rough. I was separated from my family and my close friends in Kyiv, and the only human interaction I had was going to the grocery store to buy some food. It was difficult not being able to discuss what I felt with my loved ones in person. Alone, I was always working when I was awake, and went to sleep thinking about the civilians — especially children — stuck in Mariupol, and elsewhere in Ukraine that suffered the most during the first stage of the all-out war.

As time passed, I realized I had this extreme privilege to test myself. The test is to see if I can prove to be a good journalist, and do my best to tell the stories that the war is yet to bring. I am still working on it, every day and really hard — and hopefully, I will get there one day.

Another thing I learned about myself during the war is how close I feel to Kyiv. Growing up as a third-culture kid, I never really knew where my home was — or whether I belonged anywhere. I left my motherland Japan at the age of six, moved to Moscow, then came to Kyiv when I was 10 and have lived here ever since. Even though I don't consider myself Ukrainian, and I never thought I'd settle in Kyiv for so long, I can't imagine leaving it now. My friends are here, and this place feels like home to me — a feeling I never understood in my 22 years of living until the full-scale invasion of Ukraine began.

2 April 2022

My rescue mission to flee Russia's war with three kids

Natalia Datskevych

An endless feeling of fear that seems to never go away. Every loud sound, every sudden spark in the sky, causes panic.

My life, together with the lives of millions of Ukrainians, turned into hell when Russia launched a full-scale invasion of Ukraine.

This is the story of how I was trapped near the Russian border with my husband and my three daughters and how we were able to finally escape.

Hours after the war began and the Hostomel Airport, northwest of Kyiv, turned into a warzone, we decided to flee the capital. We left for our family home in a village in the northern Chernihiv Oblast, not far from the Russian border. In the beginning of the war, many chose to leave big cities for rural areas, thinking that they will remain quiet. So did we.

Soon we understood that this was a mistake.

As we got settled in our new place – formally a town, but looking more like a village – the situation began to look dire.

The nearby Chernihiv, Kyiv, and Sumy were bombarded day and night. So was Kharkiv to the east. Cities hundreds of kilometers south – Kherson, Mykolaiv, and Mariupol – had come under deadly attacks as well. Soon, Mariupol would become the site of a horrendous tragedy, with thousands of civilians, including women and children, killed by Russian shelling.

A particular video from a morgue in Mariupol, where the doctor showed journalists the lifeless body of a one-month-old baby, will stay in my memory forever.

In our village, people were on the verge of panic. The locals told me that we are surrounded by Russian tanks and soldiers. 'It's too dangerous to leave now,' they said. 'You'd better think twice before you try to leave, you have three children.'

The fear grew as I read the news that Belarusian soldiers were about to cross the border into Ukraine and join the war. This would have cut our village off from Kyiv.

Russians had been shelling a nearby village. During the shelling, we would go down to the basement. I remember how, during one of those times in the basement, I was holding my crying one-year-old daughter in my arms, and trembling myself, knowing that my family is in grave danger and help isn't coming.

But on the warm sunny morning of 21 March, a slim hope appeared.

My husband went out to find some milk. Ten minutes later he called back.

'Pack our stuff, we have an hour. One man agreed to take us to Kyiv,' he said briefly over the phone.

The escape that could have cost us our lives had begun. Leaving was terrifying: we saw in the news many reports of Russians attacking and killing civilians driving to safety, including families with children.

Our family of five got into the car and followed a minibus that was heading to Kyiv to get bread for our village.

We've been told to prepare all the documents, including children's birth certificates, to show at every checkpoint along the way.

The kids were quiet as never before.

Leaving our village, we saw the first checkpoint within a few minutes. Thank God it was a Ukrainian checkpoint. After looking thoroughly at our documents, a Ukrainian soldier wished us a safe journey to Kyiv.

There were more than twenty checkpoints on our way. I never considered myself a religious person but I prayed every time we drove past a checkpoint.

Passing by another one, somewhere deep in the forest, I saw a soldier who looked no older than my eldest daughter. He looked like he was 15 or 16 years old. He was tightly gripping an assault rifle.

'He is probably very brave,' said my middle daughter, a six-year-old.

'He is,' I whispered back.

We drove for five hours, through an unfamiliar forest. Before the war, the drive to Kyiv would take an hour and a half.

Burned cars lying on the side of the road, checkpoints, and mines – everything pointed to the new Ukrainian reality.

Finally, we reached the city.

In Kyiv, we passed a memorable place damaged by Russian missiles – a TV tower and the nearby Babyn Yar Holocaust memorial site, where five people were killed by a missile strike on 1 March.

Nearly every street we passed was partly blocked with anti-tank hedgehogs.

The numbing, incredibly strong fear didn't leave my body, as missiles and shells continued to strike near Kyiv. The fighting in Kyiv's northwest suburbs of Irpin, Bucha and Hostomel was heard from our Kyiv apartment.

We kept thinking about Kharkiv and Mariupol, and the thousands of innocent people slaughtered by Russia. We knew that we might be next.

So we decided to go to the central train station and try to flee.

After passing several checkpoints, I heard the long-awaited announcement: 'Boarding for the evacuation train from Kyiv to Lviv.'

There were a lot of empty seats on the train, which contrasted sharply with the first two weeks of the war when people had to stand or lay down on the train floor, holding their loved ones, children, and pets.

Eight hours later, our family finally got to Lviv late at night, amid curfew.

After sleeping on the floor of the train station for several hours, side by side with dozens of exhausted children and their mothers, we continued our journey.

We decided to leave the country.

The train from Lviv to the Polish city of Przemysl was so packed with refugees that even the famous Tokyo Metro System, during rush hour, would be jealous of the crowd.

By that time we heard that 3.5 million Ukrainians fled the country, escaping the war. I recalled it as I was watching thousands of refugees cramming into the train to Poland, about to join the grim statistics.

The trip from Lviv to Przemysl usually takes slightly over an hour. Ours took seven hours. All I could think about is how much I wanted to breathe in some fresh air.

As we arrived, we had to wait for 40 minutes before the doors opened. Many had lost their nerve. Older women began to cry to be let out, the children sobbed, and someone simply stayed silent.

But as soon as our feet touched the platform, I felt that my mission to save my children from the war was completed.

Moments later, a question from my eldest daughter caught me off guard.

'Mom, can we get back on this train and return to Lviv?' she asked me with tears in her eyes.

'When the war is over we will, we will,' I responded, sobbing.

6 April 2022

New phase in war opens up as Ukraine defeats Russia in Battle of Kyiv
Illia Ponomarenko

The Battle of Kyiv is over, with Ukraine as its victor. After nearly 40 days of fierce hostilities, by 1 April Russian forces had withdrawn from battlefields in northern Ukraine within just days. Despite a massive effort, Russia failed to encircle the Ukrainian capital and install a blockade. After sustaining heavy losses and accomplishing none of their key goals, Russian forces retreated, but not before inflicting devastating damage to Ukrainian towns and cities and committing numerous war crimes.

The political decision to give up on Kyiv reverberated around the country. Along with Kyiv Oblast, Russian forces in early April also left Chernihiv and Sumy oblasts.

These moves amounted to the first significant Russian defeat in its all-out war against Ukraine. But it also opened the war's new phase, in which Russia will attempt to regroup to achieve narrower goals in Ukraine's east and south.

The Battle of Kyiv may be over, but what comes next is the even more decisive and difficult Battle of Donbas. This fight is likely to define the war's outcome.

Humiliating setback

The outcome of the operation to surround Kyiv became very clear in late March.

Following nearly two weeks of a protracted operational pause, Russian forces stationed west and northwest of Kyiv had yet to resolve serious logistical issues, particularly regarding food and fuel supplies.

By mid-March, Russia was still in control of all key transport points to the northwest, including the Bucha–Irpin–Hostomel triangle, as well as Borodyanka and Ivankiv. This afforded Russian forces an unchallenged long supply line between Belarus by way of the area around the Chornobyl nuclear power plant.

Russia also controlled parts of the E40 highway, effectively severing key communications channels running west. The goal was clear: to envelop Kyiv from the west.

But attempts to go further south of the E40 since mid-March made virtually no progress.

East of Kyiv, Russia also continued with fierce attempts to advance along the E95 and H07 highways running from Chernihiv and Sumy, respectively. But over the first month of the war, it also failed to seize any of the two cities, despite brutal fighting and heavy bombardment.

It also failed to secure firm control of its long supply lines, suffering from devastating Ukrainian attacks along highways near Ukraine's northwestern woods. Ukrainian military and paramilitary units practicing hit-and-run tactics masterfully targeted hostile armored power and supply convoys, effectively wreaking havoc among Russian ranks.

West of Kyiv, the Russian military was eventually bogged down in close-quarter combat in dense urban terrain, where Russian air and artillery power lost its efficacy.

The advancement, slow and painful, stalled, as Russian forces continued to sustain losses and supply shortages. Attempts to use the operative lull to regroup and reassess its campaign near Kyiv, it appears, also resulted in nothing.

Manpower shortage was also obvious: according to data collected by Ukraine, Russia had deployed nearly 20 battalion tactical groups to attack Kyiv, a well-defended city of at least 3.5 million.

Beginning on 20 March, Ukrainian forces both east and west of the city launched a series of counter-offensive moves that started to bring new, but limited results. On 22 March, Ukrainian forces liberated and gained a foothold in the town of Makariv, west of Kyiv along the Zhytomyr Highway.

In the following, Russian positions weakened along the highway as well as in the Irpin–Hostomel–Bucha triangle. Social media posts began circulating in Ukraine about a potential pocket in the triangle, an act of fierce revenge for the ill-fated Ukrainian defeats of 2014.

According to the British Defence Ministry, after 25 March, Russian forces east of Kyiv were sustaining losses and running out of supplies. The Ukrainian military, in a series of counter-attacks, also continued regaining towns and villages along the Sumy highway.

The Ukrainian victory in Irpin, the full liberation of which was publicly declared on 28 March, was very likely a loud wake-up call for Russia.

The full withdrawal started shortly following the Russian Defense Ministry announcing a 'drastic decrease in military activity in the Kyiv and Chernihiv directions' on 29 March.

Contrary to expectations, units with Russia's 29th, 35th, and 36th combined arms armies did not leave at least some of its forces entrenched for a long static war at key points. In late March, official statements from the British Defence Ministry still expected a new battle in the suburbs of Kyiv.

But it never came. The Russian military presence in Kyiv Oblast effectively evaporated within nearly 48 hours.

The Russian command simply backed away from many local military gains it had fought for weeks, having secured nothing.

It left Hostomel and Bucha, with multiple pieces of evidence of mass executions, torture, and rape revealed as the Ukrainian military retook the cities. It also left Borodyanka and Ivankiv, vital transportation points. It left scores of dead bodies and many documented instances of mass pillaging, which says a lot about the invading army's morale and discipline.

As shortly as 2 April, Ukraine's military raised the Ukrainian flag above the Chornobyl Nuclear Power Plant, which had been seized by Russia in the earliest hours of Russia's all-out invasion.

The whole of Kyiv Oblast was declared free of Russian forces later that day. Russia's decision was far-reaching – within the next few days, Ukrainian forces also regained control of the Chernihiv Oblast, and on 4 April, according to local authorities, there were no longer any cities occupied by Russia in Sumy Oblast either.

The Russian withdrawal from the north was also precipitated by successful Ukrainian counterattacks, like the one near the city of Trostianets in Sumy Oblast on 26 March.

Two major cities are no longer suffering from Russian attempts to isolate them. In many ways, their stubborn resistance relieved a lot of pressure from Kyiv and helped the capital city prepare for effective defense.

All told, the Kremlin has given up on nearly 40% of the territories it seized after 24 February.

This humiliating defeat for the Russian military has very likely put more strain on morale among its troops.

New phase

According to international monitors, Russian units withdrawing from northern Ukraine have sustained serious losses or have even been rendered combat ineffective.

Many of them are likely to require 'significant re-equipping and refurbishment' if they can be thrown into battle again, according to British military intelligence from 5 April.

According to the Institute for the Study of War (ISW), a US-based think tank, the main body of Russian forces near Kyiv completed an organized retreat covered by artillery. But Russian retrograde has been so disorderly that some pockets of Russian forces were left behind.

In Sumy and Chernihiv oblasts, reports from local authorities also suggest that many of the remaining Russian pockets were cleaned up by advancing Ukrainian forces.

'The disorder of the Russian withdrawal suggests that at least some of the units now reconcentrating in Belarus and western Russia will remain combat ineffective for a protracted period,' the ISW said on 3 April.

'Russian troops attempting to refit after pulling back from around Kyiv will likely have to reconsolidate into their units, identify which soldiers are still present, sort out their equipment and assess its combat readiness, and generally reconstitute before they can even begin to receive replacements and new equipment and prepare for further combat operations.'

According to Ukraine's figures, as of 2 April, up to 75 Russian battalion tactical groups were still operational. Meanwhile, up to 34 battalion tactical groups were being restored in Russia and Belarus, while 16 others were destroyed in combat. At the beginning of the all-out invasion, Russia was believed to have deployed nearly 120–125 battalion tactical groups against Ukraine.

A significant part of Russian forces is exhausted – and requires a lot of time and resources, including manpower, to return to action. But upon all estimates, Russia is still scrambling to amass more skilled manpower to compensate for losses, let alone amplify its power.

The Kremlin has not yet decided to declare partial or general mobilization for its so-called 'special military operation' against Ukraine.

There are few doubts that Russia will redeploy those forces to Donbas, as well as to the Izium axe in Kharkiv Oblast to exert pressure against the largest Ukrainian military group in eastern Ukraine.

All signs point to this being the new pivotal epicenter of the war.

A successful breakthrough from Izium farther south will allow Russia to encircle Ukrainian forces in key cities of Donbas and then potentially defeat them, which would be a devastating blow to Ukraine.

To do so, the ISW believes, Russia would have to take Sloviansk and then move toward occupied Donetsk and Horlivka to the south to get a significant portion of the Ukrainian military surrounded.

'If Russian forces are unable to take Sloviansk at all, Russian frontal assaults in Donbas are unlikely to independently break through Ukrainian defenses, and Russia's campaign to capture the entirety of Luhansk and Donetsk oblasts will likely fail,' the ISW said on 4 April.

Additionally, Russian reinforcements from northeastern Ukraine to Donbas are 'highly unlikely to meaningfully change the balance of forces'.

'Russian forces withdrawn from the Kyiv axis are highly unlikely to be effectively deployed elsewhere in Ukraine and are likely a spent force,' the think tank said.

Meanwhile, the latest independent studies say Russia is nonetheless planning to immediately redeploy forces from the Kyiv Oblast to the Kharkiv axe.

Conflict Intelligence Team (CIT), an online investigative project, said on 4 April that a train carrying troops had been spotted in Belarus on 2 April likely carrying BMD-2 vehicles of Russia's 76th, 98th, and 31st airborne brigades that had been engaged in combat in Kyiv Oblast.

According to the CIT, the train was heading to Novy Oskol in Russia's Belgorod Oblast close to Valuiki, a key military point of concentration for the Kharkiv axe of attack.

T-73B3 tanks likely coming from Russia's Smolensk Oblast were also spotted on 3 April being transported to Valuyki.

'The new arriving hardware will likely proceed south via to Kupiansk and Izium (in Ukraine), which was recently seized by the Russian military, towards Sloviansk,' the ISW said. 'The redeployment of the withdrawn and possibly unused vehicles means that the Russian command is set on and the battle of Donbas is going to heat up in the coming days.'

6 April 2022

As Ukraine regains control of Borodyanka area, more Russians' atrocities come to light

Anna Myroniuk

Burned and shattered, high-rise residential buildings in the center of Borodyanka, a town 40 kilometers northwest of Kyiv, hide even more horror underneath.

Around 200 people have been buried alive in the basements when Russian bombs destroyed the buildings, local authorities estimate.

'Hope dies last,' said Anatoliy Rudnichenko, an adviser to the mayor of Borodyanka, speaking of whether any of these civilians could have survived. He then sighed heavily and whispered: 'You and I both understand that none of them are alive.'

In early March, Russian planes dropped 500-kilogram bombs on the town, demolishing around 10 high-rise houses. Their residents had been hiding in the basements at the time of the attack.

'Borodyanka is the first town in our country where Russians bombed civilians,' Rudnichenko said. *The Kyiv Independent* hasn't been able to confirm it.

'We have no military bases, nothing,' he said, emphasizing that what Russia did to his town is, he believes, a war crime. Since the start of the invasion, the Russian government has been falsely claiming that the Russian forces are targeting only military infrastructure.

Home to 12,000 people, Borodyanka and the nearby villages returned under Ukraine's control on 1 April, when Russian troops withdrew from Kyiv Oblast after weeks of intense fighting around Kyiv.

Since then, the Ukrainian forces have been demining the area. On 5 April alone, they have picked up enough unexploded shells to fill in three cars.

After the demining was over, on 6 April, the rescuers started clearing the rubble and looking for bodies. The day before, trucks were already lining up nearby, ready to take the bodies.

Borodyanka has possibly seen more civilian casualties than any other place in the region, according to Prosecutor General Iryna Venediktova.

This comes just days after Ukraine and the world were shocked by the revelations of the mass murder of civilians committed by Russian forces in Bucha, another town near Kyiv.

Borodyanka is different: here, locals were killed by air bombs, not tortured and shot in the streets, like in Bucha. But the number of victims can be even higher.

Sharing the last

The gym of Borodyanka's lyceum now serves as a humanitarian aid hub, where volunteers sort food and hygiene products and put them into boxes.

The volunteers are residents of Borodyanka and nearby villages who have first sought help themselves and now help others.

Lyubov Paliura is from the village of Berestyanka, located about 10 kilometers northeast of the town.

A Russian shell hit her house on the day of her marriage anniversary on 19 March. She was out, but her husband was at home at the moment of the attack. He was lucky to survive, she said.

Still, Paliura believes her family was lucky to not have suffered during the occupation much. 'People from Borodyanka come and you see that they barely hold up. Such families are often with four, five, six kids,' Paliura said. 'They are so pale that it is clear that they starved.'

Humanitarian aid started arriving in the area just a few weeks ago. Thousands of people had lived with no electricity, gas, and mobile network for about a month.

Among them is Tetyana Shklyarska, a family doctor from Fenevychi, a village located 30 kilometers to the north from Borodyanka.

'We did not have a stock of food, but we shared the last bits we had with others,' Shklyarska said. 'Everyone tried to help one another.'

When her family started running out of food, they decided to find a way to bake bread for themselves. They had no flour but had wheat and an old manual coffee grinder.

At first, they were using it to grind wheat into flour. Later, they reworked a feed chopper into a handmade wheat grinding machine.

'We had no bread and we wanted it so much,' Shklyarska said. 'Kids told me, "Mom, we had never realized what the taste of bread really is. Now we know."'

Food has just started arriving in her village. Aid comes both from large organizations and from fellow Ukrainians. It's the latter that Shklyarska remembers most warmly.

'We open these packages and see things for kids, a handful of grain, even a jar of jam that has been started already,' she said. 'This is so touching.'

Shklyarska says her heart warms seeing how people help one another. Back in 2014, when Russia unleashed a war in the Donbas, she was among those sending humanitarian aid to locals in eastern Ukraine. Now she herself receives it from other Ukrainians.

Taking everything away

Russian soldiers have been looting houses of people across the villages in the Borodyanka area taking away everything, valuable and not.

'Paintings, chairs, baby carriages, and even Easter baskets – they took everything,' said Zoya Chkheidze, a resident of Leonivka, a village 25 kilometers to the north of Borodyanka.

According to her, the Russians covered their tanks with stolen rugs.

'They even took teapots, shovels, axes,' she went on.

'The Russians walked around the yards, took away the phones. They punctured the wheels in our cars and told us to be quiet and sit at home,' said Valentyna Klymenko, a local.

'They took away everything from our cellars, linens ... They took away TVs. It was like they saw TVs for the first time,' she went on.

'They simply looted the entire village. They took everything from us,' Klymenko said, crying.

According to the locals, Russian soldiers only let people flee the village in exchange for money.

'We paid. My two nephews did,' Klymenko said. 'The fee was $1,000 per car. They took dollars only. They did not want hryvnias.'

Many people were shot dead by the Russians, and many went missing, according to people living in the villages of Andriivka, Shybene, and Katyzhanka.

On the first day of the war, Russian soldiers shot at a car that was trying to flee Katyzhanka with a white flag.

The car caught fire. Three passengers were killed. The only survivor was Anna Pomanets, 14.

'She somehow managed to jump out of the car,' local resident Tetiana, who was reluctant to share her last name, told *The Kyiv Independent*. Her neighbors confirmed her account.

'As she was running, the Russians shot at this child,' Tetiana said.

According to the villagers, a local couple and a bishop provided first aid and took the girl to the hospital the next day. She had a bullet in her hand and needed surgery.

'To see the car with her father and other people explode in front of her eyes ...' Tetiana said. 'It will be a lifelong trauma for this child.'

7 April 2022

Bucha massacre survivors: 'Why do Russians hate us so much?'
Illia Ponomarenko and Igor Kossov

Just a bit over a month ago, Bucha was a comfortable, cozy, and rapidly growing suburb just northwest of Kyiv.

The town was a place of middle-class apartment complexes and houses, surrounded by woods.

Today, Bucha is a synonym of horror known worldwide.

Russia's defeat in the Battle of Kyiv and its rapid subsequent withdrawal in late March has unearthed things no sane mind would want to witness. Bucha is now the scene of the worst massacre committed on the European continent in the 21st century.

The Bucha massacre contains what seems like a bottomless trove of personalized evidence.

In the almost six weeks spent under Russian occupation, residents of Bucha said they were subjected to searches, robbery, torture and summary execution.

Over 410 bodies have been collected from Kyiv Oblast and submitted for forensic analysis as of 3 April, according to Prosecutor General Iryna Venediktova.

A worker in Bucha who helped recover bodies and introduced himself as Serhiy, told *The Kyiv Independent* on 5 April that he had seen over 300. Bucha officials added that there may be dozens more in local residences and in the woods.

Many were shot at Russian checkpoints. Some were found with bound hands and fatal bullet wounds. Pictures coming out of Bucha on the first days after Ukraine's Armed Forces went in showed people strewn across the roads, left to lie where they fell.

Some were buried by locals, while others were dragged into piles and set on fire, likely by the Russians.

The city is known to contain at least one mass grave.

'Why do they hate us so much?' cried Halyna Opalat, standing near a housing complex in Bucha, looking at the ruins across the street. 'Why? Because we're a nation? This used to be such a beautiful city. Now it's frightening to look at. My soul hurts.'

The Ukrainian military liberated Bucha on 1 April, as the Russians were withdrawing from Kyiv Oblast. While former residents are pouring into Bucha to see if their homes survived, danger lurks all throughout the city.

Over the course of a single day, 5,000 explosive hazards were discovered in Kyiv Oblast, according to Interior Minister Denys Monastyrsky. These include mines, unexploded ordnance such as shells, missiles and bombs, as well as booby traps. Officials said that buildings in the area have been trapped with explosives, such as grenades, by the retreating Russian troops.

'The demining in Kyiv Oblast will serve as a model for the rest of the country,' Monastyrsky said.

Month-long massacre

A brief conversation with any of the Bucha survivors unleashes a torrent of revelations of what the Russian military did to the city.

'There are lots of improvised burial places, here and there, in backyards, in dead ends,' said Vladyslava Lyubarets, a 51-year-old professor standing in a long breadline to receive newly arrived Ukrainian humanitarian aid.

'Lots and lots of people just went missing. Here in Bucha, Russians would take food, jewelry, and people would give it all up just to stay alive,' she said.

'Phones were the first thing they used to take away from us. They made people kill their poultry, and if they refused, Russians would simply shoot the hens and take the carcasses with them. For many elderly women here, that poultry was their only hope to survive.'

'Many people here had almost no food for two weeks. I will never forget the day when a senior kissed a neighbor's hands just because she brought a boiled egg and some fresh water.'

Other Buchans also mentioned Russian soldiers bursting into their homes and seizing food, such as grains or canned goods. But that was far from the worst of what the invaders did.

Venediktova announced that Ukraine is investigating thousands of possible war crimes. It now has over 200 suspects, with material evidence of their alleged involvement.

Civilians reported that how they were treated depended on the Russian soldiers they ran into. Some didn't touch the civilians. Others were liable to shoot on sight.

'The Kadyrovites' checkpoint was the scariest,' said Lyubarets referring to Chechen forces loyal to Chechnya leader Ramzan Kadyrov, which Russia had deployed in the area.

'They could shoot to kill without asking questions, without checking documents. In that area, there were a lot of corpses that have now been buried on the territory of the church. Kadyrovites killed everyone – women, men, children, the age didn't matter.'

'There were checkpoints that killed only men, ages 18–65. They checked their documents and killed them,' she continued. 'There were [checkpoints] that shot some people and let others through, with no explanation.'

Lyubarets said she saw a man get shot at a checkpoint. She also relayed the story of a 14-year-old boy who ran to the shelter where her family was staying – he said his father was killed on the street.

The teen had three bullet wounds, which Lyubarets and her husband bandaged with clothing and women's sanitary products. Several men from the shelter risked their lives to creep out, drag the body away and bury it in the yard.

For local men potentially fit for military service, things were particularly hard.

'They got me out for an execution,' said Yuriy Snegiriov, 57. 'This is what they told us: "We've been commissioned to deprive you of allowance." By saying that, they meant killing. We know they had an order to do that. But in my case, they eventually let me be.'

Rumors spread quickly that some Russian units were hunting for men. So in many cases, the only way to stay alive was to keep a low profile for as long as possible.

'I survived just because I hid in basements all the time, keeping out of their sight,' says Oleksandr Paitsun, a younger man, also waiting in a breadline for humanitarian assistance.

'Bucha was divided into sectors. And in my sector, Russians most of the time were too busy to look more carefully. In my sector, there was a Rosgvardia

(Russian National Guard) unit, like really young guys, they might let one go. But the military would not.'

'They were very ferocious,' said resident Lyudmila Khoda, 79, who said her neighbors used to come back with frequent stories that someone they knew had been killed.

Some human remains have been burnt. The National Police showed journalists a pile of unidentified, charred bodies in Bucha on 5 April, near a small playground.

Four of the bodies belonged to women and two to men. One of the female bodies was very small and may have been a child, said the head of the National Police in Kyiv Oblast Andrii Nebytov.

He said Russian troops most likely found the victims in a basement where they may have taken shelter, before gunning them down, then gathering the remains into a pile and setting them on fire.

'We have only started searching,' Nebytov said on 5 April when asked if there are many sites where bodies were burnt in this manner. He expects more bodies will be found in parks and forests throughout the area.

Yegor Firsov, a former Ukrainian lawmaker and now a member of the Territorial Defense force, would agree. After visiting Bucha, he said that the final death toll will be even higher than estimated: Many bodies are in people's backyards and have yet to be found.

Serhiy, who helped recover and transport bodies, said that he's seen bodies with bullet holes in their arms and legs, which he believes to be evidence of torture. Nebytov said on 5 April that earlier, five people were found shot to death, with bound hands, in a basement in Bucha.

In March, Anton Dovgopol, a director of the Irpin City Polyclinic, told *The Kyiv Independent* that he was involved in digging a mass grave on church territory and burying 67 people there.

Satellite imagery by Maxar Technologies taken on 31 March showed a trench dug into the grounds near the Church of Saint Andrew in Bucha.

Lyubarets also said that abuse and muggings were rampant. Soldiers would stop people on the street and strip them of articles of clothing they liked. Refusing would get you shot. But it didn't always end there.

'Sometimes they would make people strip down naked and lie on the ground, then bind their hands. They would then lie there until neighbors came to check out if they were still alive and untied them,' she said, describing a practice a different source confirmed seeing.

Forcibly visiting apartments to search them was common, multiple people told *The Kyiv Independent*. If a civilian didn't leave their door unlocked or let the Russians in, they would break down the door and start shooting.

Mykola Mosyarevych, was one of the local young men who managed to survive the massacre.

He spent the whole month of Russian occupation in a basement at the Continent apartment complex, one of the best-known living quarters in Bucha. Just thanks to his neighbors, and some negligence among Russian soldiers, who once allowed them to get some food from a destroyed supermarket nearby, he also managed to survive.

Mosyarevych walks past what used to be a fancy residential complex, now heavily damaged skeletons of buildings and heaps of garbage and empty ammunition boxes. Russian paratrooper units used to occupy the complex and delivered artillery fire from among the civilian buildings.

'I just don't get why they were doing this,' he said, slipping into tears as he walked among liberated ruins in the cold wind.

He spent much of the past month without seeing the daylight.

'I just don't understand. Don't understand why they would want to do this to us.'

8 April 2022

Inside joint effort to provide Ukrainians with healthcare amid war
Igor Kossov

With her husband's dependence on cancer treatments, the war is the worst thing that could have happened to Bucha resident Halyna Opalat.

'He needs to be on an IV, but we weren't able to make it to Kyiv,' said the 69-year-old, whose travel was blocked by Russians, then by temporary restrictions after Ukrainian victory here. 'The nurse used to give him injections, but she escaped and now there's no one left.'

Opalat's husband is one of countless Ukrainians whose healthcare was thrown into chaos. With Russian attack axes cutting supply lines or trapping civilians, many Ukrainians with chronic conditions were left without critical drugs for weeks. Others were forced into unhygienic cramped shelters, in the cold, without enough food, in the middle of a Covid wave.

'This war has a huge impact on the health of people,' said World Health Organization (WHO) country representative Jarno Habicht.

However, thanks to the work of international organizations, volunteers on the ground and the health ministry all working together, access to care is improving across much of Ukraine.

Habicht spoke to *The Kyiv Independent* in the afternoon on 1 April, an hour after an aid convoy entered the embattled city of Sumy, with the WHO's support.

The convoy contained multiple trauma kits. Each one has enough supplies to operate on 150 people. It also contained several interagency kits, each having enough medication and supplies to provide primary care to 15,000 people.

More recently, on 5 April, a UN convoy has reached the city of Sievierodonetsk, where intense fighting has left residents without access to electricity, gas or clean water, as well as other basic necessities. The convoy brought food rations, flour, plastic sheeting and blankets for some 17,000 people, as well as four electricity generators for use by the local hospital.

Previously, aid convoys also reached Kherson, Kharkiv and Chernihiv, Habicht said. However, the besieged and largely destroyed city of Mariupol remains beyond the reach of aid convoys for now.

Habicht said coordinating the aid and trying to ensure it's allowed through is a 'round-the-clock process that never stops. Russian forces often block humanitarian convoys or make it too dangerous for them to travel by shelling areas.

'We've brought some of the best brains of the WHO to Ukraine in past weeks, from Afghanistan and from the [WHO] headquarters to support Ukraine and to ensure supplies can reach hospitals,' said Habicht.

Convoys are put together by many different organizations and depend on the work of volunteers.

'The volunteer drivers who deliver supplies are real heroes,' said Inna Ivanenko, director of the health NGO Patients of Ukraine that organizes humanitarian aid.

Russia's war substantially rewrote the reality of Ukraine's healthcare infrastructure.

According to the Health Ministry's comments to *The Kyiv Independent*, Russian forces damaged 279 medical institutions, fully destroying 19 of them. They are known to be specifically targeting hospitals, like in Mariupol, where Russian air forces bombed a maternity hospital on 9 March, killing four people, including one pregnant woman with her unborn child.

Russian forces also shot 70 ambulances and seized another 104. They also besieged and occupied cities and towns, destroyed infrastructure and cut off transportation.

According to Habicht, about half of Ukraine's 22,000 pharmacies closed due to the invasion, although the Health Ministry said this week that 80% of pharmacies in the country are now open again.

Fighting, shelling, internal displacement and Russian checkpoints disrupted people's ability to pick up drugs, see their doctors and visit clinics and hospitals, many of which continue to operate around the clock, with doctors, nurses and other staff sacrificing their time and safety to provide treatments.

The war also created shortages of non-infectious and chronic care medicines, Habicht said. Conditions that require regular care include diabetes, cancer, hypertension and others.

'In the first weeks of the war, there was a very drastic situation with insulin,' said Ivanenko, 'This also affected two hormonal drugs for treating the thyroid.'

'But volunteers helped and a lot of humanitarian insulin came ... and now the situation with insulin is more or less normal,' she said. 'There were gaps but the situation is improving.'

'The anti-retroviral situation is also improving,' Habicht added. 'Anti-tetanus vaccines have been delivered to the public health authorities in the past week. So from that angle, even if there were gaps, they are gradually getting filled.'

The bigger problem is oncology care, said Ivanenko. While many oncology drugs have been procured and are sitting in warehouses, moving them to where people need them is a challenge, leading to shortages.

The Health Ministry wrote that it's taking 'maximum effort' to ensure children with cancer are able to get treatment in safer parts of Ukraine or continue treatment abroad, in the EU. Over 400 children are now getting free oncology care in other countries.

But communicable diseases are a risk as well, especially with so many people fleeing for their lives – Habicht said it's going to be an 'enormous stress test' for the health system.

Tuberculosis has been a constant problem in Ukraine and it may get worse. While Ivanenko said there wasn't a disruption in access to TB drugs because they had been procured and delivered, a new outbreak of the respiratory disease may be coming.

'People spent a lot of time in cold basements in unsanitary conditions,' she said. 'We predict there will be a new spark of TB and maybe multi-drug resistant TB.'

The other major respiratory illness is Covid. The Health Ministry reported that on 5 April, 2,161 new daily infections were recorded, down from a peak of 39,620 confirmed cases on 3 February, according to the WHO.

Habicht said that before the war, Ukraine saw a plateau in its omicron variant wave. Since then, the number of cases has decreased.

'But we must realize that the monitoring system is currently also disrupted,' he said. 'Many private labs are not doing Covid tests and public labs are also testing for other needs, not just Covid. So when we see 2,000–3,000 new cases every day, I would say it is underreported.'

Health officials, Ukrainian nonprofits, volunteers and international organizations are doing their best to both deliver supplies to areas where they're needed, as well as parts of Ukraine that saw an influx of displaced evacuees.

'Displaced people may have left home with one bag and no medicines, so in western and central Ukraine, it's very important to ensure care can continue and medications are available,' Habicht said.

The Health Ministry said it's doing 'everything possible and impossible' to ensure treatment is available and that patients needing consultation 'should turn to medical institutions in the safer regions of the country.'

The ministry collected over 3,189 tons of drugs, equipment and medical supplies worth Hr 3.2 billion. This week, 13 tons of medication for chronic diseases worth $20 million was delivered thanks to the Heart to Heart Initiative and HOPE Worldwide.

The ministry is also boosting support for pharmacies while trying to ensure drug prices do not spike at a critical time.

Still, the far reaching health impacts of the war will require a lot more work to mitigate.

'What we see is actually people have lots more conditions,' said Habicht. 'Many have delayed their care. Also, because of being on the move, they have malnutrition and we are seeing the impacts of that. Many women are delivering early.'

'Because it's only five weeks, [the full impact of the war] is difficult to describe. We potentially have impacts for years and a [psychological] impact for generations.'

9 April 2022

Volunteers create coordination platform for foreigners who want to help Ukraine

Thaisa Semenova

After Russia began its full-scale invasion of Ukraine on 24 February, businessman Vasyl Yabryk rushed to help temporarily displaced Ukrainians with housing and humanitarian aid.

But soon he learned that it takes more than a desire to help to be an effective volunteer.

Yabryk says that the more experienced volunteers, who have been helping displaced people from the occupied Donbas since 2014, were providing the much-needed aid faster than him.

At the same time, he kept receiving multiple messages from foreigners asking how they could help Ukrainians affected by war.

So he decided to create a one-stop shop for new volunteers and everyone who wants to support Ukraine as it defends itself from the Russian aggression.

That's when Yabryk, the owner of a group of companies in Uzhhorod, a regional capital in western Ukraine, teamed up with two other businessmen and created a coordination platform Ukraine Helpers.

The website lists organizations that needs donations, shows how people from abroad can offer shelter to Ukrainian refugees, and has information on how to join Ukraine's foreign legion.

It also features an interactive map with humanitarian warehouses abroad. People who want to donate medicine, goods for children, food, or other humanitarian aid can find suitable warehouses that are closest to them.

'Today the battle is ongoing not only at the front, but also in the rear. The front won't survive either if the rear loses,' Yabryk told *The Kyiv Independent*.

Since Russia unleashed its all-out war against Ukraine, more than 4.2 million people have fled the country, while another 6.5 million have been internally displaced, according to the United Nations. As they were escaping Russian fire and bombardment, many refugees left in a rush with few essentials, if any, and now need support.

Meanwhile, thousands of Ukrainians remain trapped in the hotspots of Russia's war without food and medicine supplies. Their survival often relies on humanitarian aid delivered by the Ukrainian government and non-profit efforts.

According to Yabryk, all the organizations featured on the Ukraine Helpers website pass verification by both the volunteers and Ukraine's government. When foreign foundations apply to be featured, the team of Ukraine Helpers contacts the local Ukrainian Embassy to make sure they are trustworthy.

'That way foreigners can be confident Ukrainians will receive the help in the shortest time possible,' he said.

According to Yabryk, the website has more than 1,000 daily visitors from 80 countries. Most of them come from the United States and Germany.

The platform also plans to add an option for people to support Ukrainian businesses. The idea is to introduce Ukrainian companies whose goods and services can be bought to support them amid crisis.

The business community has suffered greatly during the war.

According to the Ministry of Economy, over 1,400 Ukrainian companies have applied for relocation to safer regions as of 5 April.

One of the most prominent Ukrainian e-commerce platforms Rozetka fired most of the team because the company's monthly turnover fell from Hr 4 billion ($137 million) to Hr 23 million ($786,000).

Large Ukrainian supermarket chain Silpo was forced to close 68 stores, of which 23 had been destroyed. About 9,000 people used to work at the Silpo stores that are now closed.

The co-founders of Ukraine Helpers have themselves felt the blow of Russia's war on the businesses, as they all had to put their enterprises on hold.

Yabryk is one of them. His Yabryk Management Group includes a chain of pizza restaurants, a pub, fitness centers, an ice rink and other businesses. Many of them are now on pause.

By buying Ukrainian goods and services, people will actually not only support local business, but the whole of the Ukrainian economy.

Prime Minister Denys Shmygal repeatedly said that all businesses that are able to operate should do so to contribute to the Ukrainian economy amid the war.

Shmyhal estimates that Ukraine's total losses from war will exceed $1 trillion, of which the destruction of infrastructure amounts to $120 billion. The European Bank for Reconstruction and Development forecasted that Ukraine's economy could shrink by a fifth this year.

'The economy must work, as many jobs must be kept as possible, and as few people as possible should leave the country because all these factors affect the success of our resistance,' Yabryk said.

12 April 2022

Russian airstrike survivors: 'We came home, and there was no house'
Anna Myroniuk and Oleksiy Sorokin

Chernihiv Oblast – After Russian troops have withdrawn from Ukraine's northmost region, an expected, yet no less horrific, destruction was uncovered.

Russian airstrikes targeted both high-rise buildings in Chernihiv and small houses in nearby villages, leaving many people in the regional capital and its suburbs dead, injured, and without a home.

According to local authorities, 700 people including 200 civilians have been killed in the regional capital alone. The death toll in neighboring villages is impossible to count as many are still left under the rubble.

The house of Natalya Solomennyk, a nurse, was hit three times. First, an artillery shell landed, then a bomb, and a mine.

She and her family survived thanks to an old bomb shelter in their village just outside Chernihiv, Novoselivka.

'This bomb shelter was built in 1941. Villagers were hiding there during World War II,' said Solomennyk.

'Now, during this war, it was our turn to hide there,' she went on.

Nothing left but hope
Novoselivka, a village that was home to 800 people, is practically gone. It seems that every house has been damaged or destroyed.

Local residents say that they spent 21 days hiding – either in their small basements or in the Soviet-made bomb shelters last used 80 years ago.

Electricity and gas have been out since late February. Yet, many stayed put, having nowhere to run.

Among them was Solomennyk with her husband and son, who survived the Russian bombardment and shelling in a local bomb shelter.

The bomb shelter fit 15 people, including children, the elderly, and a pregnant woman. All of them survived while many of their neighbors were killed.

Some bodies are still under the rubble of their houses, villagers and local authorities said.

'There were people in the nearby dormitory when it was bombed. We don't know what happened to them,' Solomennyk told *The Kyiv Independent*.

Three days later, a bomb landed next to her house and the entire lane caught fire.

The house where she lived for 36 years was gone.

'I gave birth to my kids there, I raised them there, my grandchildren were born there,' Solomennyk said, bursting into tears.

'I managed to untie the cow to save it. Frankly, I have no idea where it is. I feel sorry for it, of course,' she added.

When their house was hit, the family decided it was time to flee.

They walked four kilometers to the nearby village, where Solomennyk's mother lives. They carried nothing – they had nothing left to take with them.

'I borrowed underwear from a friend. I was left with nothing,' she said. 'I feel crushed.'

Solomennyk's neighbors suffered a similar loss.

The family of Larysa Chuhay put all their money into their house that now lies in rubble.

Chuhay told *The Kyiv Independent* that she, her husband and their two children decided to flee the village when the first bombs landed nearby.

After sleeping at her husband's workplace in Chernihiv, they returned on 8 March to check on their house and take additional clothes.

'We came and there was no house,' she said.

Now that Russians have withdrawn from Chernihiv Oblast, many villagers come back to Novoselivka to clean up the debris left from what used to be their homes and try to recover at least some of their belongings.

Some stay in the empty houses in nearby villages.

'I fled to Voznesenske,' Raisa Kirusha, who works as a guard, said of a village several kilometers east of Novoselivka.

'People hosted me, many thanks to them,' she went on.

Kirusha is back home now to work in the garden, or what is left of it.

'It's sowing time,' Kirusha said. She is hoping to grow a harvest on the scorched soil.

Bombing the city

While the outskirts of Chernihiv are in ruins, the regional capital of 285,000 people is also heavily damaged.

Russian air strikes have destroyed apartment buildings, a local stadium, a kindergarten, several medical facilities, grocery stores and even a library located in a 19th-century building.

'The building of the library is historical. It survived World War II, but did not make it through Russian aggression,' said Chernihiv Oblast Governor Vyacheslav Chaus.

'They only attacked civilian facilities,' he went on.

According to Chaus, hundreds of residential buildings have been destroyed in the city, hundreds of civilians killed and even more injured.

The attacks have been clearly targeting civilians. On 16 March, shelling killed 14 people who were queuing to buy bread, including a US citizen.

One of the darkest days in Chernihiv was 3 March when Russian planes dropped bombs on several buildings, killing 47 people at once.

'We heard two planes,' recalled a local citizen Vyacheslav Kuts, who lives near the bombed site. 'The shock wave threw me together with the door into the entryway.'

'I grabbed my kids and carried them to the basement amid the air strikes,' Kuts said, pointing to the entrance to the shelter that has been hit with bomb fragments.

The explosion was so massive that the glass broke in all the windows in the entire neighborhood. Since then, the neighborhood has had no gas or electricity.

'When it was minus 13 degrees outside, it was minus 2 degrees in my apartment,' Kuts recalled.

Together with neighbors, Kuts covered the windows with wood and metal to keep warm.

Until a few days ago, when the electricity got fixed, they cooked on a gas burner.

Soon after the 3 March attack, both planes bombing Chernihiv have been shot down by the Ukrainian forces. One pilot, Alexander Krasnoyartsev, was captured and acknowledged that Russian planes have deliberately bombed residential areas.

'I understand it's war, but to bomb in such a way ...' Kuts goes on swearing at the Russian army.

Like others in Chernihiv, he understands that the lull may be temporary and new air strikes can happen.

'We are all scared,' Kuts said of potential attacks. 'But we keep smiling. Because we are alive.'

17 April 2022

One onslaught, one family, one lucky chance: Surviving the Mariupol theater bombing

Asami Terajima

Viktoria Dubovitskaya, 24, and her two children survived the Russian bombing of the Mariupol Drama Theater by pure luck.

Like hundreds of Mariupol residents, Dubovitskaya's family was sheltering near the theater's main stage.

But on 16 March, her two-year-old daughter Anastasia got sick, and the family was offered a place on the second floor.

On the same day, Russians dropped a massive bomb on the theater. The stage area was the epicenter of the explosion. The building crashed and hundreds were killed.

'We stepped over [bodies] and ran out,' Dubovitskaya told *The Kyiv Independent.*

The exact death toll of Russia's 16 March strike on the Mariupol Drama Theater is yet unknown. According to the Human Rights Watch, the theater was used as a shelter by over 600 people, most of whom were women, children, and the elderly. The word 'children' was written in Russian on both sides of the building, to warn Russians against bombing it.

Ombudsman Lyudmyla Denisova said that only 130 people were able to escape the theater.

The Mariupol City Council reported that, 'according to eyewitnesses', around 300 people had been killed in the theater in what appears to be the single deadliest Russian assault to date.

Dubovitskaya said no one was able to get inside the theater after the bombing to rescue the civilians trapped inside, as Russia never stopped shelling and bombing Mariupol.

The city has been heavily bombarded since 24 February when Russia launched its all-out war against Ukraine and has been besieged since early March.

According to Ukrainian authorities, Russian forces killed at least 3,000 Mariupol residents, and 90% of all buildings in Mariupol were damaged or destroyed.

Local authorities, however, said as many as 22,000 civilians may have been killed in Mariupol.

City under siege

Mariupol's humanitarian crisis escalated so quickly that it was too late for people to leave the city when they realized the severity of the situation.

Despite the city being under attack since 24 February, Dubovitskaya didn't think she needed to flee. After all, she remembered that Mariupol had withstood a brief Russian occupation in 2014, during Russia's initial push to occupy eastern Ukraine.

She couldn't have imagined the atrocities that would be waiting for her and the rest of those who chose to stay in the city with a pre-war population of 450,000.

The day when the war's deadliest attack on civilians took place in Mariupol's theater, there were some 300,000 people still trapped in the city. Encircled by Russian troops and cut off communications since 2 March, efforts to deliver humanitarian aid into the city have repeatedly been blocked by the Russian forces.

Russia's siege has left Mariupol residents hungry, dehydrated and stuck in cold basements to avoid indiscriminate Russian shelling. Electricity, gas and water have been cut off, and the city's internet and mobile networks have not been working since early March.

Photos of workers hastily burying dead bodies in mass graves under steady bombardment have been published worldwide.

Since the city is under siege, it is impossible for the authorities to record and count all casualties.

Donetsk Oblast Governor Pavlo Kyrylenko has so far given the gloomiest estimates saying that between 20,000 to 22,000 civilians may have been killed in Mariupol.

Ukrainian intelligence has recorded 13 mobile crematoriums used by Russian troops to 'cover up the traces of their war crimes.'

Russian occupiers have begun exhuming the bodies and each courtyard has its own guard to prevent residents burying the bodies, the Mariupol City Council reported. 'Why the exhumation is being carried out and where the bodies will be sent is unknown,' the statement said.

Sheltering in theater

Dubovitskaya first came to the theater-turned-shelter on 5 March. Her apartment building had been shelled at least four times.

Dubovitskaya said there were around 1,500 people inside the theater at the time. She had to beg to get in because it was already full. Dubovitskaya and her kids spent most nights sleeping on the floor.

Her family was given a bowl of soup once a day. There was only enough food to feed the children, so adults would eat the leftovers, Dubovitskaya said.

As more people left in attempts to flee the city, Dubovitskaya said there was eventually enough food for adults to receive one meal each day as well. People mostly sat quietly, looking out the windows to see what was going on outside.

Dubovitskaya took some videos in Mariupol, but she had to delete them all when passing through Russian-controlled checkpoints on her way out of the city. As expected, the Russians asked the people fleeing the city to show their phones and documents.

'It was scary because they could have forced us out [of the vehicle], and we would have been left there,' she said.

Surviving airstrike

Dubovitskaya remembers that the morning of 16 March was quieter than usual.

After Mariupol's department store and the road that leads to the theater were bombed at around 5 a.m, hours of silence followed.

'It was strange,' Dubovitskaya said.

Not knowing what was ahead, she joked around with those sheltering that the Russians were suspiciously silent and something even more horrifying might happen soon.

It turned out to be true.

The explosion suddenly hit when Dubovitskaya was walking into her room on the second floor. Air raid sirens hadn't been working for days.

The blast was so powerful that it threw her at the wall. She hit her face and injured her back, but says she didn't feel the pain at that moment.

All she could think about was her kids. Dubovitskaya could neither see nor breathe after the explosion because of all the dust in the air. She heard her son Artem screaming not far from her, but the younger Anastasia was nowhere to be seen.

She began looking for her daughter. It took her about 20 minutes to find Anastasia, who was covered in dust and was hard to identify at first.

Dubovitskaya ran back upstairs to grab her documents before fleeing the theater.

With them she took a young boy named Nazar, whom she found alone in the building while looking for her daughter Anastasia.

She saw many people lying on the floor. She doesn't know whether they were alive or not.

As soon as they stepped out of the ruined theater, the four of them ran as fast as they could. Dubovitskaya was afraid to stop because Russians continued to shell the city.

Leaving Nazar with the few rescue officers that were present near the site, Dubovitskaya and her two children took shelter at a school nearby.

After spending a week there, a woman she met at the shelter agreed to take Dubovitskaya's family to Nikolske in Donetsk Oblast. There, Dubrovitskaya reunited with her husband, who was working in Poland when the war started.

They soon moved to Lviv, a regional capital in western Ukraine that welcomed many internally displaced people.

Though she spoke with a calm tone throughout the interview, Dubovitskaya was visibly in pain when talking about Russia's destruction of her hometown.

'Why did they particularly choose to bombard Mariupol?' she heightened her tone as she asked the question, and immediately offered an answer: 'It was entertainment for them.'

Though born in Crimea, a Ukrainian peninsula occupied by Russia since 2014, she had lived the majority of her life in Mariupol. This was where she met her husband and got married, had kids and made many memories.

Dubovitskaya's children haven't been able to sleep normally since surviving the attack in Mariupol.

What happened on 16 March was a shock for two-year-old Anastasia, who was injured during the explosion, Dubovitskaya said. It took her daughter days to start talking again.

Seeing blood-covered bodies was a shock to her six-year-old son Artem as well.

For Dubovitskaya, wrapping her head around Russia's cruelty was no easier. 'I just cried and couldn't understand how this all happened,' she said.

18 April 2022

Kharkiv Oblast resident forcibly deported to Russia: 'It's not a country, it's a prison'

Daria Shulzhenko

Editor's Note: The Kyiv Independent *isn't revealing last name of the person interviewed for this story and the name of his native village for safety reasons.*

Ukrainian farmer Ihor escaped the 'living hell' of Russia's ongoing war in Ukraine in late March after he had spent a month in his occupied village in Kharkiv Oblast.

But instead of being evacuated to a safe place, he was brought to yet another 'nightmare' – Russia itself.

Ihor, along with 60 other residents of his native village, was forcibly deported to the Russian city of Belgorod on 17 March. They haven't been able to return to Ukraine since.

'We were confronted with a fact – you are going to Russia,' Ihor says. 'No one even asked us whether we wanted it or not.'

Tetiana Lomakina, who coordinates humanitarian issues at the President's Office, says they estimate that around 45,000 Ukrainians have been illegally deported to Russia from the temporarily occupied territories of Ukraine.

It's not just weapons that Russian occupiers use to force people to flee to Russia, but the unbearable living conditions they create in the occupied cities and villages, while at the same time not allowing locals to evacuate to Ukrainian-controlled areas.

'It's a violation of the rules and regulations of war. Forcing people to cross the border of their country is a war crime,' Lomakina says.

A month of horror
Russian shelling cut off power lines in Ihor's village just an hour after Moscow launched its full-scale invasion of Ukraine on 24 February. Since then, the power supply hasn't been restored.

Russian forces soon entered his village. Ihor says he was terrified to see dozens of Russian tanks and armored vehicles near his home.

'You understand that there is nothing you can do, and you no longer control your life,' he says.

Local grocery stores opened later that morning, allowing residents to take goods for free to prevent looting and destruction of their buildings and equipment. Butchers from the local farm gave away pork to civilians as they could no longer store meat in coolers without electricity.

That was the last time people in the village received fresh food.

Russian forces occupied the village so quickly that only a few residents managed to escape. Most residents remained in their homes, living with no power, heating, and mobile network, as well as no supplies of medicine, food, or hygiene products.

Ihor says he was lucky to have had some food stocked. He also had a dairy cow, whose milk he was giving to a neighboring family with small kids that were starving.

Soon, Russian soldiers started wandering around the village, demanding that the locals give them their food. People were too afraid to disobey.

Ihor was told that one of his fellow villagers refused to follow the order, yelling at the occupiers and telling them to leave the yard of his house.

'He got shot immediately,' Ihor says.

After Russian forces found documents listing the names of local veterans who had fought against Russia in the Donbas in the village's administration, they launched a hunt for them. Ihor says they were breaking into houses and destroying everything on their way.

Ihor knows of only two veterans who managed to escape. The fate of others found by the Russian military is unknown yet. Ihor believes they were killed.

He says that despite all the horrors, his village didn't witness the same level of Russians' atrocities as in Bucha, Irpin and Borodyanka. He assumes that was because many soldiers occupying his village were recruited from Russian-occupied parts of Donetsk and Luhansk oblasts.

He heard some of them saying they were forced to fight.

A man in his 50s from a Russian-occupied city in Donbas told Ihor that his daughter and son-in-law had just bought an apartment in Kharkiv and he was 'sent to fight against them'.

'He said, "they are there now and I'm here, shelling them,"' Ihor recalls.

The village is still under occupation and the number of casualties there is yet to be revealed.

In early March, Ihor was told about 20 new graves that had been dug for the dead locals. Several days after that, heavy shelling killed a couple he knew, along with their pregnant daughter and her little son.

No choice

With mobile and internet connection cut off, the village's residents had no access to news about Russia's war since the first day of the full-scale invasion. Not knowing how it was going added to the fear they lived in, Ihor says.

Russians knew exactly how to use that.

'[Russian] soldiers have been spreading rumors that Kharkiv surrendered and Kyiv was about to be taken as well,' Ihor says. 'They kept saying that 70% of Ukraine was taken by Russia.'

Ihor says he almost believed in it until he found an old radio and listened to Ukrainian news. He was relieved to learn that it wasn't true.

Just like many other residents, Ihor wanted to escape the occupied village. The surrounding area was mined, so locals have repeatedly asked Russian soldiers to allow evacuation to Ukrainian-controlled Kharkiv. Their response was always the same.

'They kept telling us "go to Russia. You must go to Russia",' Ihor recalls.

He asked the soldiers whether he could walk to Kharkiv. He could try, they said, but 'if he got shot on the way, that was his problem'.

When Ihor was told that the Russians started illegally conscripting local men to fight on their side, he was terrified. He was convinced that refusal would get him killed.

But eventually, he was forced to be deported to Russia.

Dozens of locals gathered near a bus heading to Russia that day. The 'severe' overnight shelling made them come, Ihor says. Only a few residents were deported before that.

Lomakina says Russia shelled occupied territories, including those in Kharkiv Oblast, to intimidate people and not let them escape on their own.

'Russian forces try to break Ukrainians' will, destroy everything human in them and create impossible living conditions,' she says, so that they have no choice but to flee to Russia.

Lomakina says it's a brutal violation of the Geneva Conventions that prohibit deportation of people from 'the occupied territory to the territory of the occupying power or to that of any other country'.

According to Ihor, when the bus to Belgorod took off, passengers were shedding tears. Devastated to leave their homes, they had no idea what to expect upon arrival.

Escaping prison

At the Russian border outpost in Belgorod, Ihor was questioned by a man who introduced himself as an FSB (Federal Security Service) officer. He says the interaction was very humiliating and oppressing.

Their first stop in Russia was a filtration camp set up in the middle of a field.

Lomakina says Ukraine doesn't have much information about these camps. She assumes these places often have no internet and mobile connection, and the staff is constantly watching people there. Some also have their documents taken away by the Russian forces.

Many Ukrainians are often sent to distant regions of Russia. Lomakina says they know of Ukrainians who have been deported to Samara, Kursk, Tula, Cheboksary, and other impoverished Russian cities.

Lomakina says that the Kremlin's next step could be to bring Russians to the occupied territories of Ukraine instead. 'That way, they would be able to better control the situation in the territories they are trying to seize.'

Ihor says no one from his village agreed to stay in the filtration camp. Some even lied they had places to stay overnight. So the bus just dropped them all off at a local train station.

Ihor had no money and no plan on how to escape Russia, so he headed to his relatives in Moscow. On his way to the capital, he saw multiple Russian cities – neglected and shabby – and heard people on the train discussing Russia's war in Ukraine. Many were saying that Ukrainians deserved the war.

He saw Moscow with multiple foreign stores closed, short on various goods as a result of sanctions, and people fighting to buy some sugar at grocery stores. Ihor says that no cashless payments are allowed, and neither is exchanging money.

'In Russia, if you are against Putin, you are against Russia,' Ihor says. 'It's not a country, it's a prison.'

He desperately wanted to escape Russia. Three days after he came to Moscow, Ihor reached out to a woman from his village who was still in Belgorod. She needed a driver to help her flee the country. He agreed immediately. Other Ukrainians he contacted were too afraid to try to leave.

The two decided to head to Belarus and then to Poland. When trying to cross one of Russia's border checkpoints, they were locked in a small room with no food and water. Russian border guards didn't explain why and how long they had to stay there.

They spent seven hours locked up before Russian officers let them go. Ihor still doesn't know the true purpose behind their 'detention'.

After crossing into Belarus, Ihor felt relieved. Although they saw dozens of Russian tanks there, the country 'felt nothing like Russia'. People were kind and welcoming, he says, asking Ukrainians 'to tell them the truth about the war'.

Now Ihor is safe in Poland, though he fears for those who are still trapped in his native village.

Ihor hopes it was the last time he encountered 'the Russian world'.

'It felt like an escape from prison,' he says.

20 April 2022

'Hide the girls': How Russian soldiers rape and torture Ukrainians
Anna Myroniuk, with Igor Kossov

Bucha, Kyiv Oblast – A week before she would have turned 23, Karina Yershova was killed by Russian soldiers in Bucha, a town outside Kyiv.

They tortured her and most likely raped her, Karina's stepfather Andriy Dereko told *The Kyiv Independent*. Then, they shot her in the head.

'It was clear that they [police] know she was raped as she was tortured, but the detective would not tell us this up front. She said: "I have no moral right to tell you" ... But hinted at [rape],' Dereko said.

According to Dereko, his stepdaughter was a petite woman who worked as a manager at a local sushi bar and didn't pose any threat to anyone.

The police did not show Karina's body to her parents, saying it would be too shocking to see. She was buried in a closed coffin on 13 April in Bila Tserkva in Kyiv Oblast, a day after being identified.

Since the Russian soldiers withdrew from Kyiv Oblast in early April, authorities have been collecting and exhuming the bodies of civilians slaughtered by Russians during the one-month occupation. In Bucha only, they have discovered over 400 bodies of murdered civilians. Russians killed every fifth resident who remained in the city, according to Bucha Mayor Anatoliy Fedoruk.

The exhumations and the testimonies of surviving locals have shed light on another Russian atrocity: mass rape of Ukrainians, including women, men, and children.

Multiple cases of rape in Bucha have been reported by lawyers, psychotherapists, and authorities. According to Ombudsman Lyudmila Denisova, 25 girls and women aged 14–24 were held captive in one basement in Bucha and were repeatedly raped by a group of Russian soldiers.

Dereko asked the detectives to at least let him see the photos of his step-daughter's dead body. He was shown Karina's upper body only. What he saw was terrifying.

'There were cuts and lacerations, there was also a piece of flesh torn off from her ribs,' he said. 'It's obvious they tortured her.'

The police told Dereko that Karina's leg had also been shot. She apparently tried to stop the bleeding with a tourniquet.

He suspects Karina tried to defend herself, which only further angered the perpetrators.

'Half of her nails were torn off,' Dereko said.

Police told him where his stepdaughter was killed and found: at a house just 1.5 kilometers away from Karina's place, in the same part of Bucha.

Bucha resident Mykola lives nearby. He told *The Kyiv Independent* that he knows how Karina died. He asked to be identified by his first name only for safety reasons.

According to him, on 16 March, Russian soldiers brought the already wounded Karina to the house of his neighbors, an elderly couple, Viktor and Natalya Mazokha.

'They brought a wounded girl to them. I don't know what happened next, but a soldier unleashed a volley of machine gunfire at the ground, then an officer came and shot all three of them,' Mykola told *The Kyiv Independent*.

'Three days later a Russian soldier came [to us] and said: "There are corpses there."'

Mykola was unable to immediately bury the dead as snipers were shooting at anyone who was outside.

After a week or two had passed, Russian soldiers returned to Mykola's home to tell him they had two hours to bury the bodies.

The Kyiv Independent has reconstructed the events leading up to the killing of Karina Yershova.

Haunted by war

Russia's war first intruded into Karina's life when she was a teenager.

In 2014, when Russia invaded Ukraine in the east, Karina fled her native Donetsk with her family. They managed to escape and resettled in the quiet suburbs of Kyiv.

Eight years later, Russian troops came there, too. Karina's parents fled right away. She lived separately and refused to join them.

'We tried to talk her into leaving throughout the entire day on 24 February,' Dereko said, recalling the first day of Russia's full-scale invasion.

She underestimated the risks, Dereko believes: 'I can understand her. Who would have thought that those beasts would slaughter regular people?'

Wars are not fought against civilians, but for territories, he thought.

'Here they fought for fridges, for goods, with ordinary people,' Dereko said, referring to Russian soldiers mass looting the homes of Ukrainians.

Russian soldiers destroyed and looted their family's apartment in Irpin, a city neighboring Bucha, where Karina used to live before moving out and going to Bucha.

They took his stepdaughter's old iPhone 6, Dereko said.

'If they told me, I would have bought a bag full of those iPhones, only to make sure she stayed alive.'

She used this phone to call her stepdad on 10 March, the last time they spoke.

'When we talked for the last time, the Russians warned her against using her phone. They thought she was filming them. She told them: "I'm talking to my mom."'

They made her hang up. Then she called back and said she was alright, Dereko recalls. By then Russian tanks had already been parked near her apartment building, Karina told her stepdad.

Soon Karina stopped replying.

The last time she was seen at home was early March, said Vyacheslav Chumak, her neighbor.

He found her sitting in the stairwell. Karina said she couldn't enter her apartment as she had no keys. Chumak invited her home.

He and his wife fed Karina and asked her what happened. She told them that Russian soldiers had stopped her on the street during curfew and detained her. She had to stay overnight in their barracks.

'She told us that they had gotten drunk. One of the soldiers had his leg shot near his ass, the other one was run over by a tank or an infantry vehicle, she said,' Karina's neighbor went on.

In the morning they let her go but took away her phone, Karina told Chumak.

After speaking with her neighbors, Karina fell asleep in their armchair for 10 or 20 minutes, Chumak said, and soon left. She managed to get into her apartment, he said.

In a day or two, a light blue car with the letter 'V' – one of the symbols Russian troops put on vehicles in their war against Ukraine – arrived to pick up Karina.

According to Chumak, the driver was an acquaintance of the owner of the apartment Karina rented.

'She packed her bags into this car and waved my wife goodbye,' Chumak said. 'We never saw her again.'

Girls in danger

Across the entire Kyiv Oblast, including Bucha, women were warned to lie low, sometimes by Russian soldiers themselves, to avoid being raped.

'A Russian soldier came and said: "Do not let the young one out", pointing at me,' Tetiana Aleksandrova, 38, a resident of Bucha, told *The Kyiv Independent*. She was hiding in a shelter in a kindergarten with her husband and other locals.

She would perpetually put on multiple jackets to appear bulky, and the woman who ran the shelter said she coated Tetiana with soot when Russian soldiers came by.

Women in nearby villages tell similar stories.

'Russians told my husband: "Hide the girls". I overheard them saying it,' said Inga Odinokova, the mother of a 25-year-old daughter. They are both residents of Velykyi Lis, a tiny village in Kyiv Oblast, 35 kilometers northwest from Bucha.

Russian soldiers told Odinokova that the kadyrovites, members of a paramilitary organization from Chechnya named so for their leader Ramzan Kadyrov, settled in a nearby village of Shybene and that they were rapists. Multiple women in Shybene confirmed Odinokova's account.

In another place in Kyiv Oblast, a 34-year-old woman witnessed kadyrovites raping and killing her neighbours. She is a client of Vilena Kit, a psychologist from Lviv who is helping victims of Russia's war to overcome trauma.

Kit does not disclose her client's name citing ethics. She, however, received permission from one woman to tell her story to *The Kyiv Independent*.

'When this woman came, she was speechless, she could not say anything. When she started talking, it would become hard for her to breathe,' Kit said.

She saw a girl and a woman she knew her entire life being raped and hanged. The youngest was 16, the oldest was 48, Kit said.

'She was not raped, but the secondary trauma she received is very intense,' the psychologist added.

Most reports about sexual violence are coming from Kyiv Oblast, said Julia Anosova, a lawyer with La Strada, a human rights non-profit.

Since the full-scale war broke out, their hotline for psychological aid has recorded nine cases of rape involving 13 victims, including children.

Russian soldiers often gang-raped Ukrainians, Anosova said.

The lawyer believes that Russian soldiers now use sexual violence as a weapon of war against Ukrainians.

'From what we see now, including how numerous such cases are, and how often multiple victims are involved at once, I assume that rape has now become a weapon of war,' Anosova said.

The lawyer believes that this makes the issue different to what Ukraine experienced in 2014–2015 during the hottest phase of the war in Donbas.

'Back then, there were cases of rape, but in detention facilities. It is a very specific type of crime. Now rape happens in private households of the victims,' she said.

Sexual violence is recognized as a war crime by the Geneva Conventions and a breach of international humanitarian law.

The Prosecutor General's Office has been collecting evidence of rape since the first cases were reported. On 22 March, the first Russian soldier was charged with repeated rape of a woman in Kyiv Oblast, Prosecutor General Iryna Venediktova said.

Prosecutors, however, have not revealed the total number of rape cases against Russian soldiers that are under currently investigation. The Office has not responded to *The Kyiv Independent*'s request for comment by publication time.

The Security Service of Ukraine (SBU) intercepted phone calls and published what they say are conversations between Russian soldiers and their girlfriends and wives. Many of them share stories of how Russian soldiers commit sex crimes.

'Here three tankers raped a girl,' a man is heard saying in Russian on one of the recordings published by the SBU. 'Who?' a woman asks. 'Three tankers. A 16-year-old girl,' the soldier replies.

On another recording released by the SBU, a woman is heard encouraging her husband to rape Ukrainian women.

'You go ahead, rape Ukrainian women and do not tell me anything,' a woman is saying, giggling. 'Alright,' her husband replies.

Journalists of Radio Free Europe/Radio Liberty identified the couple whose conversation was recorded. They are Roman Bykovsky and Olga Bykovskaya, a soldier and his wife from the Russian city of Orel, who moved to Crimea after the Russian occupation. Roman was among the Russian soldiers invading Ukraine's south, according to the investigation.

Dereko, the stepfather of Karina, allegedly raped and killed in Bucha, is in the south now, too.

Russian soldiers like Bykovsky made him first flee Donetsk, then Irpin, then relocate to a village near Odesa.

He was deprived of everything he had, including the most precious, his stepdaughter.

'The one who shot her is to blame, as well as the one who took the murderer there on a tank, as well as the one who ordered them to break through the border with Ukraine. That one, who hides in a bunker, and decided to invade is also responsible,' said Dereko, referring to Russian dictator Vladimir Putin.

'Those wives who are happily supporting this, they are to blame, too,' he went on.

'Our family will never forgive this. We will hate them forever.'

22 April 2022

Uncovering the scope of the Bucha massacre

Igor Kossov

Bucha, Kyiv Oblast – As Ukraine recaptured the town of Bucha, the world saw the extent of the violence Russian soldiers inflicted on the civilian population.

Since the Russian forces were driven out of Kyiv Oblast, 412 bodies have been found in the town's streets, buildings and mass graves as of 19 April, according to Bucha Mayor Anatoliy Fedoruk. Over 600 bodies were reported in Bucha District as of 15 April, Human Rights Watch reported, citing the chief regional prosecutor.

Over the past three weeks, rescuers, volunteers and journalists have been combing through the evidence and survivors' testimonies to establish what happened here over the six weeks of occupation.

It all came down to one clear fact: Russians had a citywide shooting spree in Bucha. According to Fedoruk, over 80% of the bodies have bullet wounds, largely in the head and torso.

'If in Irpin [a city next to Bucha] people died from fragments caused by shelling and mortars, in addition to being shot, then in Bucha people were mainly just shot,' Taras Vyazovchenko, a city council member, told *The Kyiv Independent*. 'There are practically no accidental hits among the victims.'

According to interviews with local officials and over two dozen residents, Russian troops killed people both randomly and systematically. They sought some people out, like local officials, activists or sometimes just men of military age. They killed others on the street for various reasons and sometimes no reason at all.

'There are shootings of peaceful citizens that can't be explained in any way,' Anatoliy Kotesh, a deputy police chief for the Buchanskyi District, told *The Kyiv Independent*.

While local officials couldn't give exact figures on how many people were found on the streets and how many were found in homes and basements, they said the amounts are comparable.

The Russians split the city into four sections, Fedoruk said. They were variously held by units largely composed either of ethnic Russians, ethnic Siberians such as Buryats, or the Chechen military, often referred to as Kadyrovites after their leader Ramzan Kadyrov.

The killings hit the Yablonska, Sklozavodska and Lisova Bucha parts of the city especially hard, according to the mayor. The area around Yablunska and Vokzalna streets saw some of the worst of the carnage.

'It got to the point where if people were walking to those micro-neighborhoods, the Russians told them not to go,' said Bucha volunteer Denys, who declined to give his last name for safety reasons.

Other than being killed outright, some locals were tormented by Russian troops, who threatened people with death or forced them to obey humiliating orders. Others were reportedly abducted to local villages to be tortured there, according to Vyazovchenko.

Hunting people down

The invaders conducted large-scale searches for local threats throughout the city.

'Since the occupation of the city, every house, every apartment, every institution and business was broken into, opened by Russian occupiers,' said Fedoruk. 'Doors, windows, gates, all were broken and they went in to clear.'

The Russians went around, hunting specific people and types of people.

'They had printed lists,' Fedoruk said. The lists must have been printed out before the war, he believes. People on the lists included political leaders, members of the city and regional government.

Other sources confirmed that there were lists. Vyazovchenko said apartments belonging to officials were searched more thoroughly or frequently compared to their neighboring flats. According to Vyazovchenko, the Russians also looked for activists.

BBC Ukraine reported that jailed Kremlin critic Alexei Navalny's second cousin Ilya Navalny was found in a mass grave in Bucha, possibly killed for his relation to the Russian dissident or even simply for sharing the same last name.

Andrii, a Territorial Defense member who's currently operating in Bucha, Irpin and the nearby villages, told *The Kyiv Independent* that all military service members, people who fought Russian proxies in Donbas, and Territorial Defense joinees were persons of interest. Some of them were found murdered, with their hands tied behind their backs.

Multiple survivors who stayed in Bucha throughout the occupation told *The Kyiv Independent* that Russian troops were killing men of military age. When they didn't kill them, they threatened to kill them.

'Yes, they searched the homes ... sometimes if they saw men of military age, they took them away and they weren't heard from again,' said Tamara Hryhorieva, a custodian at School 3 in Bucha. 'I have an acquaintance [in Lisova Bucha]. They came to her home, took away her husband, her brother-in-law and her son.'

The father of her granddaughter, 28-year-old Territorial Defense member Vitaliy Karpenko, was also shot in this area on 4 March and his body laid on the ground throughout the entire month-long occupation until it could be picked up, identified and buried.

Andrii from Territorial Defense said the Russians employed some local informants who rode along in their armored personnel carriers, pointing out the homes of the people Russians wanted to hunt down. He declined to give his last name because he is helping the Security Service of Ukraine find and arrest such people.

Oleksandr Omelyanenko, the chief of police in the Buchanskyi District, confirmed to *The Kyiv Independent* that there were cases of collaboration that are being investigated.

Kotesh, his deputy, said that it's unclear how much of this happened under duress.

Shot in their homes and shelters

Other times, Russians killed people in homes and shelters for reasons that are still unknown.

'We can't explain the logic of Russian occupiers – they killed people over any suspicions,' said Kotesh. '[They might have assumed] that he works with the Ukrainian military or another reason they most likely invented for themselves.'

Tetyana, a young woman who lives near the infamous Yablunska Street, where many bodies of civilians were discovered after the liberation of Bucha, told *The Kyiv Independent* that the Russians came into her apartment and shot her husband to death for an unknown reason while she was sheltering in the basement.

She declined to give her last name or any more details, saying the memory was too painful.

People who spoke to *The Kyiv Independent* also said that Russians fired and threw grenades into basements where people were hiding.

Tetiana Oleksandrova was forced to take shelter under School No. 3, after her apartment was shelled, concussing her. The school basement contained mostly elderly women, as well as four people in their 30s – Oleksandrova, her husband Andrii Fotchenko, another man, and a disturbed woman named Yulia who claimed to have seen her family torn apart by a shell.

Eventually, the Russians came, intending to use the school as a base. A Kadyrovite 'with jackal eyes' appeared at the top of the basement stairs with an assault rifle and opened fire, Oleksandrova said.

The bullets grazed Fotchenko's rib, hit the other man in the leg and would have struck Oleksandrova if she hadn't pushed someone away and bounced off towards the wall. She realized whom she pushed away when she saw Yulia's brains on the basement floor. 'That bullet was for me,' she said in retrospect.

The Russians then threw four flashbangs into the basement, giving Oleksandrova and her cat their second set of concussions. The elderly women piped up, telling the Russians that they're grandmothers and begging them not to attack. The remaining 30-somethings claimed to be the seniors' caretakers. 'Without them, we'd have been killed,' Oleksandrova said.

Another example could be found on Tarasivska Street, amid a group of three-storey residences. Local residents told *The Kyiv Independent* of three people who were shot to death inside an apartment. A neighbor, Mykola, said that on 16 March, Russian soldiers brought a wounded girl to the home of an older couple, Viktor and Natalya Mazokha. The young woman was identified as 23-year-old Karina Yershova, who was likely raped and tortured by the Russian troops.

'I don't know what happened next but the soldier fired a volley at the ground, an officer came in and shot all three of them,' Mykola told *The Kyiv Independent*. Three days later, Mykola and the other neighbors were told that there were bodies in the apartment. Over a week later, the neighbors were told they had two hours to bury them.

The three were buried together, along with a man who had been shot down by a sniper elsewhere in the immediate area. The four graves were later exhumed and the bodies taken away to be medically examined and given a proper burial.

Gunned down on the street
Still others were killed either randomly or because they happened to be outside and the Russians decided to open fire for whatever reason.

Multiple residents of a cluster of nine-storey residential buildings on Tarasivska Street said that Russian snipers covered the entire area and being on the street for any reason was liable to get you shot.

Six people from the cluster were killed. Another two died from health complications because the Russian kill zones prevented medical aid from reaching them.

But more random killings seem to have happened around Yablunska Street, where local survivor Nadiia saw a man riding a bike randomly shot to death. She declined to provide her last name for security.

Several minutes away stands another nine-storey building where three residents were killed by Russians. A dark bloodstain on the pavement marks the spot where a man named Oleh fell. He was gunned down for walking around a corner, within view of an adjacent building where a high-ranking Russian officer was staying, his neighbor, Liudmyla Sulema told *The Kyiv Independent*.

Another building resident named Artyom descended to the building's garage in the middle of the day. Russian soldiers walked over, opened the garage and shot him to death, Sulema said. According to Human Rights Watch, Artyom was getting food. Before the invasion, he reportedly worked on a military base painting vehicles for the Ukrainian military.

Many people were shot either when they were forced to go outside to scrounge for food and water, bury bodies or escape from the occupied city.

Denys, the volunteer in Bucha, says that some of his friends and neighbors have been killed.

'My classmate was shot in his car when he was trying to get out,' he told *The Kyiv Independent*.

'My neighbor in a different neighborhood went out searching for food with his friend,' he continued. 'The neighbor was killed and the friend was given a wheelbarrow to take him away and bury him somewhere.'

Even being indoors was no guarantee that you wouldn't be shot from outside. A woman from Artyom and Oleh's building, also named Tetiana, showed *The Kyiv Independent* bullet holes in the glass of her 9th floor balcony. Human Rights Watch reported that elsewhere in Bucha, a man was critically wounded when bullets came flying through his balcony window.

Killings, threats and humiliation for fun

Oleksandrova, who took shelter at School No. 3 and later at Yablunka kindergarten near the housing complex of the same name, said she heard a few Russian soldiers admit to taking potshots at people out of boredom.

'They would say "we're bored",' she told *The Kyiv Independent*. 'He said, "sometimes we like how you dance to avoid the bullets."' Oleksandrova's husband, Fotchenko, quoted a Russian soldier as saying, 'Yes, we're shooting chaotically.'

Others have said that these kinds of attitudes were widespread.

Vasyl Kozabovsky and his entire family had to face death when Russians ordered them out of their shelter and lined them up against the wall of their house on Suvorova Street, saying, 'now we're going to shoot you all. Our orders are to kill everyone.'

His wife fell to her knees as Kozabovsky pleaded for the Russians to at least spare their kids, including his underage son and pregnant daughter, who stared directly into the eyes of one of the invaders. 'Fine, we won't shoot you,' the Russians eventually said.

Survivors said Russians sometimes forced people to strip in the cold or put sacks on their heads and fired guns next to them.

As Buchans were killed, others would try to bury them, which was extremely dangerous. According to Fotchenko, one young man was shot in the leg while burying a body; in the absence of good medical care, the leg had to be amputated.

Vyazovchenko said that in one instance, when two men were killed, their relatives were only allowed to bury one. Russians booby-trapped the other body with an explosive.

He added that some people were abducted from Bucha and taken to nearby villages, where they were tortured by the Russians.

Laura Hvorostyna, who ran the Yablunka kindergarten where many survivors took shelter, came up with a phrase for the occupied Bucha experience.

'It was Auschwitz lite,' she said.

23 April 2022

Ukrainian couples celebrate love amid war

Daria Shulzhenko

It was a beautiful wedding ceremony at the St. Michael's monastery in Kyiv downtown.

Lit with dozens of candles, the usually crowded church was almost empty when Sviatoslav Fursin and Yaryna Arieva, both dressed in traditional Ukrainian vyshyvanka embroidered shirts, were pronounced husband and wife.

But there were no wedding bells and no celebration to follow.

The couple left the church amid the loud and terrifying air raid sirens and headed directly to the nearest bomb shelter.

It was the first day of Russia's full-scale invasion of Ukraine.

'We decided that if we die, we die together,' Fursin says.

Fursin and Arieva are among the many couples who tied the knot during Russia's war. According to the Justice Ministry's recent report, over 30,000 couples have gotten married in Ukraine since 24 February.

Some couples were planning their weddings before Russia's bombings hit Ukraine and decided that the war shouldn't stop them. Others – especially those in war zones – rushed to get married after realizing that their lives could end at any moment.

As losing loved ones is now a daily possibility in Ukraine, celebrating love brings hope and joy in the country's darkest hour.

'War is not an obstacle to love,' Fursin says.

Applause in bomb shelter

They met at a rally over two years ago. United by their love for Ukraine, Kyiv-based students Fursin, 24, and Arieva, 21, spent hours talking about politics, school work and life. Soon they started dating.

'It's easier to list our differences than what we have in common,' Fursin says.

On 24 February, exactly one year before the war, Fursin proposed.

'It was quite a weird proposal,' he recalls. 'We were lying at home after work, talking about different things and I offered her to marry me.'

'She said yes.'

Since the proposal was spontaneous, he didn't have a ring at that moment. Fursin and Arieva tied red threads on each other's hands instead, as a symbol of their engagement.

Fursin says Arieva's somewhat conservative parents were against the couple moving in together before getting married. Arieva's father is Volodymyr Ariev, a member of parliament representing the European Solidarity party. In 2020, Arieva was elected to the Kyiv City Council as a member of the same party.

They had a wedding planned for 6 May. But in late 2021, as the threat of a further Russian invasion was looming over the country, the two decided to get married as soon as possible, and in case Russia does invade Ukraine, they can 'live together and protect each other'.

Russia started the offensive before they were able to tie the knot. But it still didn't change their plan.

As thousands of Kyiv residents were rushing to escape the city on 24 February, after Russia launched the first strikes at the capital, Fursin was running around the city trying to organize their spontaneous wedding.

A priest at St. Michael's monastery agreed to marry them.

Although they didn't agree on it beforehand, the two showed up wearing vyshyvankas, traditional Ukrainian embroidered shirts.

It was a small ceremony with only their family members and a close friend present. But it was beautiful and special, Fursin says.

They left the church under the air raid sirens and were surprised to hear everyone at the bomb shelter applauding them upon arrival.

Just like they wanted, Fursin and Arieva soon moved in together. But instead of a nicely-furnished apartment, the couple lives in a small room at a Territorial Defense unit where Fursin currently serves as a volunteer.

'It's not marriage but the war that changed us,' Fursin says. 'It made our relationship stronger, but it also made her worry about me more.'

No time to hesitate

Kyiv resident Yaroslava Fedorash says she and her partner Yevhen have always been quite a 'socially active couple'. Former journalist Fedorash, 28, met her future husband at a rally in Kyiv in 2020.

They started dating shortly and soon moved in together. In December, during their trip to Greece, Yevhen proposed.

They were standing by the seaside during the sunset when he pulled out a ring.

'It was all so sincere,' Fedorash recalls.

There and then, without a doubt, she said yes.

Fedorash and her future husband planned to tie the knot on 29 April, the day his grandparents got married. Their 50th wedding anniversary was coming, and the two couples wanted to combine the celebrations. But the plan was shattered on 24 February.

Yevhen joined the Territorial Defense Forces soon after the war started, while Fedorash was volunteering for the military. She says she was crying 'out of pride and worry' when he joined the force.

'I will not be ashamed to tell our kids what their parents were doing in February 2022,' she says.

Despite the new reality, the two kept wondering whether it would be possible to register their marriage during the war. One day, Fedorash accidentally found out that one registry office in Kyiv's outskirts was still operating.

She then texted Yevhen, asking about his plans for the next day, and if he could take some time off the service.

'He replied, "Yes, why?" And I said that we were going to get married,' Fedorash recalls, saying that she was slightly worried waiting on his reply.

But he only asked where and at what time he should be.

They got married on 3 March.

Fedorash, who wanted to get married in an elegant wedding gown, was dressed in her friend's black vyshyvanka dress. She put on red lipstick right before the ceremony to look a bit more festive. Her fiancé was wearing his military uniform.

'Now I understand that this was all so apropos,' Fedorash says. 'It emphasized what we do and our views.'

Fedorash says there are many reasons for people to marry during the war. The saddest one is that a wife has more legal rights than a girlfriend when it comes to visiting hospitals, or the worst, identifying a body in the morgue.

But even thoughts about that are terrifying, she says.

Instead of focusing on the worst case scenarios, the two have started planning their shared future in the peaceful times, talking about having children soon after Ukraine's victory.

'We don't want to celebrate our wedding as much as we want to celebrate our victory in this war,' she says.

Returning home to get married

Police officer Dmytro Kruchay from the city of Kryvyi Rih, which is now near the front line, ran into his future wife Anastasia in a local grocery store over a year ago.

The two have been inseparable since.

Kruchay, 32, says they were talking about marriage long before the war. He bought her a nice ring and proposed in October. Anastasia, 30, said yes.

But they couldn't set a date since Kruchay was almost constantly busy doing his job. And then Russia's full-scale war began.

He was frightened after finding out about the beginning of the war. Not for himself, but for his beloved fiancée.

Anastasia's employer helped her relocate to Poland to escape the war. But she spent less than a week abroad.

One day, she called Kruchay saying she was coming back home, that she would rather be there with him, 'handing him bullets,' so that they could die together 'if that was meant to be.'

Soon after her return, Kruchay heard of a special simplified procedure for the military and police officers to register marriages during the war. He called Anastasia to ask if she still would want to do it and was thrilled to hear her 'yes'.

On 29 March, at a police unit in their native Kryvyi Rih, the head of Kruchay's police detachment married them.

Kruchay says he didn't want to make a big deal out of it, but his colleagues still gathered to celebrate the love of their fellow officer and invited a photographer. He was happy with how it went, and so was Anastasia.

'When you go to protect your country, it is so important to know that you have someone to return to,' he says. 'A small family and a place you call home.'

Postponed celebration

26 February was supposed to be one of the happiest days for Kyiv emergency service worker Oleksandr Kravchuk and his fiancée Inna.

The two were planning a small wedding for 20 guests at a restaurant in Kyiv. They had already paid for it, along with a limo, and a photographer. But in the early morning of 24 February, Kravchuk was urgently called to work.

Kravchuk, 27, says he was still hoping to hold their small ceremony and postponed calling it off until the last moment. Most of the guests they invited had already left Kyiv by that time.

Instead of getting married, Kravchuk spent the day with his team, extinguishing a fires that broke out in Kyiv after Russian shelling.

The couple was quite upset about the canceled celebration, but Kravchuk says he was more worried about taking Inna and her parents – who arrived in Kyiv from western Ukraine on 24 February for their daughter's wedding – out of the capital.

Around two weeks into Russia's war, when Inna was safe in her home town of Uzhhorod, Kravchuk says that the wedding was back on his mind.

'War is war, but if we decided to get married, I figured that we should do it,' he says.

Kravchuk says the management of his department helped arrange the ceremony for him and Inna, as well as two other couples from his unit. Just like Kravchuk's family, two other couples planned to get married before the war broke out.

At lunchtime on 23 March, at a local registry office in Kyiv, Kravchuk and Inna were pronounced husband and wife.

The newlyweds, along with some of Kravchuk's colleagues, celebrated the weddings by eating a chocolate cake at their unit. They got back to work soon after that.

For safety reasons, Kravchuk had to bring Inna back to her parents' home in Uzhhorod the next day.

He promised her an actual celebration after the war. 'But we have to win first,' he says.

24 April 2022

Kharkiv residents under fire: 'I hear some shelling every hour'
Asami Terajima

Even after a Russian missile blew up Kharkiv's city hall and the central square on 1 March, Oleksandr Zuiev didn't want to leave his hometown.

Zuiev, 46, didn't believe Russian forces would target civilians and never expected his own apartment to come under fire.

'I was wrong,' he says now.

Zuiev was outside with his dog on 18 March, when he saw a plane fly over his head and heard a powerful explosion blast into the courtyard.

A few seconds after, he saw a large mass of iron fall, followed by a large explosion destroying an institutional building approximately 300 meters away.

Zuiev sprinted to the ninth floor of his family's apartment, where his wife and their one-year-old were at the moment of the attack.

'I'm bleeding!' he heard his wife shouting as he ran up the stairs.

He could barely see anything with all the dust from the explosion but spotted his wife holding their son, her face covered with blood. Miraculously, the child didn't have a scratch despite sitting next to the window.

His wife had to get a total of 25 stitches on her face and her arms. The stitches have now been removed but left permanent scars.

'The war has left its mark on [our] whole life,' Zuiev told *The Kyiv Independent*. Kharkiv resident Oleksandr Zuiev, 46, holds his one-year-old son in his arms. There are countless stories like that happening in Kharkiv every day.

Located just 40 kilometers from the eastern border with Russia, Kharkiv was an early strategic target in Moscow's advance.

The city has been battered by weeks of heavy Russian bombardment. Bombs, shells and rockets have smashed Kharkiv's historic center and residential areas, killing hundreds of civilians in perhaps the most intense assaults outside the besieged southeastern port city of Mariupol.

Kharkiv, a regional capital in eastern Ukraine and the country's second-largest metropolis with a pre-war population of 1.4 million people, is now largely emptied and littered with rubble, mangled cars and twisted steel.

'It's still hard to believe that this is happening in the 21st century,' Zuiev said.

According to Kharkiv Oblast emergency service, at least 500 civilians have been killed as of 16 March but the true number is likely higher.

Indiscriminate shelling in heavily populated areas destroyed 2,055 buildings, most of which can't be restored, according to Kharkiv Mayor Ihor Terekhov.

As Russia now concentrates its military force in eastern Ukraine, attacks on Kharkiv have intensified and their geography has broadened, Terekhov said.

Since the first days of Russia's war, thousands of people have been hiding in Kharkiv's metro stations from endless shelling and bombing.

Staying in isolation

Kharkiv resident Yevhen Ivanenko, 30, wanted to leave the city on 24 February, the first day of the war. But he kept postponing it.

As days passed by, Ivanenko felt like he needed to stay for some reason, though he still can't pinpoint what it was. He hoped that he could be 'useful' in Kharkiv but it could have also been that he didn't want to leave again. He has lived in Kharkiv since fleeing his home in Crimea in 2014, after Russian occupation.

Until recently, he lived by himself, occasionally going to the bomb shelter when he felt lonely. The basement that served as bomb shelter was cold and dark, so he said it was difficult to stay there for many days, and despite the heavy shelling he gets out.

'I hear some shelling every hour,' he told *The Kyiv Independent*. 'It feels like something is always happening.'

In early April, his residential area became more targeted and a neighboring building was hit and caught on fire. Though his apartment was not attacked, he began to have difficulty sleeping because of loud explosions that seemed to have occurred close by.

He has now moved into his friend's apartment, in a quieter district of Kharkiv. He doesn't intend on leaving the city anytime soon.

As his city stands in ruins, he's trying to be 'useful' by at least helping to clean up debris from sites of explosion.

It's 'very sad' to see familiar buildings get destroyed, Ivanenko said. But 'the most important thing is for people to be alive'.

Keeping the city running

Kharkiv resident Oleksandr Khorosho, 38, started helping his community in the very first days of the war.

He transformed his spacious basement into a bomb shelter and took in as many people as he could, most of whom he met for the first time.

A total of about 1,000 people came on the first days, he says, but now it's down to 60 because many fled the city.

He works with organizations providing humanitarian aid to distribute food and other needs among the residents of his bomb shelter. Many families who stayed in the shelter before going abroad are now helping him by sending warm clothes back to Kharkiv.

Although the basement is a bit cold and needs repairs, Khorosho says he tries to make it as comfortable as he can. After living together for more than a month, the shelter's residents feel like relatives to him, he adds.

'It's as if we live in a big dorm,' he told *The Kyiv Independent*.

Khorosho can still hear the sounds of explosions very well in the shelter. He remembers how he heard a series of loud explosions one day and the walls were trembling as if there was an earthquake. He said he ran down the stairs of the shelter thinking that they would crumble.

'I'm a grown-up man,' he said. 'And I was very scared.'

Besides offering shelter to fellow residents, Khorosho also delivers food and other essentials to people in several Kharkiv districts and in the suburbs. To collect requests for help on one platfrom, he set up a Telegram channel. They often come from people who had to leave their elderly members of the family in Kharkiv, asking Khorosho to deliver critical medicines or just check in on them.

He said that many of the elderly people left in the neighborhoods live in fear, often alone by themselves. Many are also cut off from electricity and gas, so he brings them something warm, whether it be a home-cooked meal or tea.

'Despite the fear, I decided to help people, because I understand that they are probably more scared than me,' he said.

Cut off from electricity, the elderly often don't know what's happening in the country, he said.

In addition to delivering them the necessary goods and talking with them in-person so they feel less lonely, he also tries to look for some good news to share during his visits. It could be anything like the Ukrainian forces defeating a Russian column, he said.

'I never say "no" to anyone, I like [helping people],' he explained. 'It's like I get a boost of energy from it, and it's a difficult time.'

Khorosho initially wanted to join the Territorial Defense Force, a volunteer military formation, but there were too many volunteers and those with combat experience were prioritized. So he continues to help in the way he can.

'You still want to help the country, and the people here in Kharkiv,' he said. 'My mind will go crazy if I sit in the bomb shelter all day. That's why I want to help and I will help our people until our victory.'

25 April 2022

Ukrainian law enforcers search for collaborators who helped Russians

Igor Kossov

The Russian soldiers that occupied settlements in Kyiv Oblast killed over a thousand civilians.

Many people were hunted down systematically for being local political leaders, Donbas combat veterans, Territorial Defense joinees or other people of interest to the Russians.

To find them, Russian forces carried lists with people's names and addresses. But they also made use of local informants. These collaborators helped Russian forces either track down targets, locate wealthy homes to loot or get information about Ukrainian military positions.

Now, a hunt for alleged collaborators is underway in recaptured parts of the country. The Security Service of Ukraine (SBU) is working with the national and local police, Territorial Defense units and the State Emergency Service to find suspected collaborators and prosecute them for treason.

'These facts do exist and we are working on them,' Oleksandr Omelyanenko, the chief of police in the Kyiv Oblast's Buchanskyi District told *The Kyiv Independent*.

On 7 April, SBU spokesman Artyom Dehtyarenko announced that 33 alleged collaborators have been identified in Kyiv Oblast. On 15 April, he said that over 300 alleged collaborators were arrested in total. The SBU has since announced more arrests.

'It's unknown how many of them were under duress,' Anatoliy Kotesh, a deputy police chief for the Buchanskyi District, pointed out to *The Kyiv Independent*.

The Kyiv Independent spoke with three Territorial Defense members and a source with the SBU about the search for collaborators. They declined to be identified by full name due to the nature of their work. Local residents and survivors of the occupation of Bucha and battle of Irpin also spoke of informants.

'How widespread was this phenomenon? Not very,' Andriy, a Territorial Defense member whose current job is to help the SBU find and arrest collaborators, told *The Kyiv Independent.*

But some of the people who were found killed with their hands tied were in Territorial Defense or other branches of service, Andriy says, raising suspicions that they were pointed at by locals.

Fear and sympathy

Andriy said that many of those who worked with the Russians were doing so for protection, trying to guarantee survival for themselves or their families.

There were also people who were ideologically aligned with the Russians, including those who moved to the area from Donetsk and Luhansk oblasts that have been partially occupied by Russia since 2014, Andrii said.

But many from this second category were later released because there was no sufficient evidence of them working with the Russians in a way that breaks the law. The most recent law on collaboration with Russia was signed on 15 March. It criminalizes cooperation with Russian forces and occupation authorities.

'In other words, they are in solidarity with, they sympathize with the Russian army and even waited for it but didn't take any actions against people,' said Andriy.

During the occupation, these sympathies had earned some of them the right to move about and use resources like power generators in areas where electricity was cut off, with less fear of being shot by the invaders.

'These people continue to live there, their neighbors are giving them the stink-eye but that's how it is,' Andriy said.

Freedom of movement through occupied areas is one of the signs locals and law enforcers look at to try to identify potential collaborators. They also look at apartments that have been left untouched in buildings where the remaining units have been broken into or looted.

'People aren't stupid, they can see who gets shot at and who can walk around freely,' said Viktor, another member of Territorial Defense who has helped officials with trying to track people down in Bucha and Irpin, two satellite towns northwest of Kyiv. He, too, declined to have his full name publicized due to the nature of his work.

He said that a couple that had moved to Bucha's Lermontova Street from Luhansk Oblast in the fall was recently arrested. The locals became suspicious of the couple's seemingly limitless freedom to move through Bucha when it was occupied.

'I was called in the morning. They told me here's this family, the information on them is 100% and there are witnesses ready to confirm,' said Viktor.

When he got there, 'a crowd of people formed. I asked them to not do anything until the SBU came.'

Asked if moments like these ever led to mob justice, Viktor replied that taking the law into one's own hands is a 'taboo' for locals.

In fact, it's rare for people to stick their necks out and become formal witnesses, Andriy said. While people will tell police that their neighbor rode along with the Russians pointing out where the veterans lived, they clam up when it's time to go on the record.

'Everyone's afraid. Even if they saw something, neighbors prefer to stay silent because they don't know how things will turn out,' Andriy said.

This makes the work of discovering collaborators slow and frustrating for the SBU, he said.

Searches and arrests

Still, Ukrainian security forces can boast of some progress.

They already got their hands on the biggest Russia collaborator in the country on 12 April when the SBU nabbed Viktor Medvedchuk, co-founder of a pro-Kremlin party and family friend of Russian President Vladimir Putin.

Medvedchuk has promoted Russia's interests in Ukraine for decades and made big money on it. He was charged with high treason in May and October but fled house arrest when Russia invaded. On 12 April, he was recaptured, wearing a set of Ukrainian Armed Forces camouflage fatigues.

Others soon followed. On 14 April, the National Police announced that a 62-year-old Kryvyi Rih native who was visiting Bucha was arrested, accused of helping the Russian forces patrol the city, threaten, beat or kill local residents and provide the positions of Ukrainian forces.

On 21 April, the Buchanskyi District Prosecutor's Office charged three Kyiv Oblast residents with treason for allegedly helping the Russians move through the village of Mykhailivka-Rubezhivka with weapons to round up locals, providing food and supplies to the Russians and accompanying the Russians on their vehicles to help them bypass Ukrainian positions.

More suspects were found among the ranks of the national rail operator Ukrzaliznytsia. The SBU arrested one of the heads of a division of the Donetsk Railway who had allegedly been recruited by the Russians to collect data on the Armed Forces' movement and the locations of checkpoints.

Another employee from the central office was accused of mass emailing his colleagues, calling on them to support the Russian forces. Two other men were accused of helping Russians navigate the Irpin, Bucha and Vorzel areas.

Locals in Kyiv Oblast are using social media to out people they suspect of working with the invaders.

A volunteer in Bucha named Denys, who declined to give his last name for security, told *The Kyiv Independent* that he once personally knew a man whom the locals recently accused of collaborating with the Russians on social media.

'When I saw his picture being passed around with the information that he's helping the occupiers, going to loot with them, showing them which houses are the richest and which ones are empty, I was surprised and began to check on it,' said Denys. 'That same day, three mutual acquaintances sent me verified information, which points to it being the truth.'

Denys said this man reportedly worked with a woman when helping Russians. He said she managed to escape from Kyiv Oblast and is reported to be heading to Poland as a refugee. A different Bucha resident named Tamara Hryhorieva also said that she saw photos of a woman of that description being shared online for Territorial Defense units throughout the country.

On 20 April, Facebook group Volunteers of Bucha posted a photo of a man and a woman, saying the SBU is searching for them for alleged collaboration. The man's first name and apparent age matches Denys' description.

The mayor of Bucha, Anatoliy Fedoruk, has not escaped some of his residents' suspicion. In their conversations with *The Kyiv Independent*, a handful of Buchans and Territorial Defense members all but accused Fedoruk of collaborating with Russians, saying that nobody knew where he was during the occupation. On the contrary, several other Buchans pointed out that no evidence of wrongdoing has been presented.

A journalist confronted Fedoruk with the question of where he was during the occupation at an 12 April press briefing, alluding to the public suspicions about his allegiance. Fedoruk denied the allegations, saying he was in Bucha throughout the occupation and claiming to have had a close call with a Russian soldier in mid-March.

2 May 2022

Families mourn fallen defenders of Ukraine

Daria Shulzhenko

Early in the morning on 9 March, Rostyslav Kotenko dialed the number of his father, Ukraine's Armed Forces Colonel Serhii Kotenko.

The two hadn't spoken since Kotenko's father left to fight Russian forces in the war's hot spots, near Kherson and Zaporizhzhia.

The long-awaited but brief conversation ended with Kotenko saying the most important yet rarely spoken words between them.

'Dad, I love you,' he said.

Those words turned out to be Kotenko's last to his father. In a couple of hours that same day, a Russian artillery attack killed Serhii. He was 54.

On 16 March, President Volodymyr Zelensky awarded Colonel Kotenko the Hero of Ukraine title posthumously. Kotenko says he is beyond proud to be the son of such a great man who was and always will be his hero.

'He always wanted to be at the frontline. He felt more useful there,' Kotenko says.

'He was a true patriot, a true hero.'

Russia's war has already killed up to 3,000 Ukrainian soldiers, Zelensky estimated in an interview with CNN on 15 April. Around 10,000 Ukrainian troops have been injured, and it's 'hard to say how many will survive,' he said.

Behind every number in these statistics, there is a Ukrainian hero who sacrificed their life fighting for the country's freedom, as well as a grieving family endeavoring to overcome the heartbreaking tragedy of losing a loved one.

Serhii Kotenko, 54

Rostyslav says his father was 'a man among men'.

Born in the town of Haisyn, Vinnytsia Oblast, Kotenko joined the military shortly after finishing school and soon became a local platoon commander. He got married in his early 20s and had two sons, to whom he was an 'example and a good friend'.

Kotenko retired after 20 years in the military. But his proactive personality didn't let him enjoy his retirement: He spent several years working at different enterprises in his hometown where he was valued for 'bringing discipline and order,' his son says.

In 2014, Kotenko even became the head of the Haisyn regional administration. But Russia's war in Ukraine's Donbas changed his life.

He gave up his job and joined the military again in 2015.

As commander of the Ninth Battalion of the Ground Forces' 59th Motorized Brigade, Kotenko protected Ukraine ever since.

Rostyslav says his father was a brave man who 'led people and always tried to be the first at the frontline'.

Kotenko's battalion defended multiple towns and villages in Ukraine's hottest spots near the Russian-occupied Luhansk and Donetsk, including Popasna, a city 100 kilometers to the west of Russian-occupied Luhansk, and Vodiane village in Donetsk Oblast.

For his courage and personal merits in protecting Ukraine, Kotenko was awarded the Bohdan Khmelnytsky Order in 2019.

On 24 February, when Russia started its all-out invasion of Ukraine, Serhii's battalion was located somewhere in Kherson Oblast, not far from the Russian-occupied Crimean peninsula.

Rostyslav says his father fearlessly fought the Russian army in Kherson and Zaporizhzhia regions, taking out dozens of Russian military equipment and multiple troops. The fighting was so intense in those regions that Serhii even called his wife one night to say goodbye to her. She was relieved when he called her back in a couple of hours saying they had 'repulsed the attack and broke out of Russia's encirclement.'

Rostyslav says his father was always 'extremely worried about his soldiers' and painfully handled the loss of his fellow officers.

He even told his brother Oleksandr, who at one point was volunteering for the Ukrainian military, not to sign a contract with the army to save his life. Oleksandr, however, didn't follow his brother's advice and joined the military.

Russian shelling killed him on 7 March not far from Mykolaiv. He was 51.

'It was very difficult for him to handle the loss of his brother,' Rostyslav says.

He admired and loved his father a lot, and even named his son after him. But as an adult, Rostyslav says, he rarely told his father that he loved him, saying that he was proud of him instead.

That morning, when Rostyslav finally reached out to his dad, the words just flew out of his mouth – his last words.

After lunch, Serhii went to the positions to check on his soldiers there. Moments later, Russia's artillery shelling started. It killed Serhii and injured many soldiers from his battalion.

Rostyslav says their last phone call eases his pain a little. But his life will never be the same without his father.

'I would want him to be injured, to lose his legs or arms. I would look after him if only he was alive,' he says.

Colonel Kotenko was buried next to his brother in their hometown of Haisyn on 11 March.

Rostyslav says he will always remember how joyful his father was, and how courageously he fought for a free Ukraine.

'A true hero ...'

Tymofiy Rudiak, 43

Liudmyla Rudiak met her future husband Tymofiy at a local library in her native Latkivtsi village in Ternopil Oblast. She was 14.

Sixteen-year-old Tymofiy, who came to the village for the summer holidays, using any excuse to see Liudmyla, would come by her house to ask for books. That summer, the two started dating.

They were inseparable, she says. She waited for him to return from the army and four years after they met, the couple tied the knot.

It was a traditional three-day Ukrainian wedding for over 300 guests. A year later, when Tymofiy was serving at a military unit in Kamianets-Podilskyi, their son Denys was born.

They soon moved to Tymofiy's native town of Fastiv in Kyiv Oblast and nested there, having two more children.

They were happy together, Liudmyla says. United not only by their love for each other and their children but also by their love for Ukraine. So when Russia started the war in Ukraine's Donbas, Tymofiy joined the military without a doubt.

Liudmyla says she had a hard time accepting his decision: She was afraid to lose Tymofiy, and wanted their children – the youngest son was two years old back then – to grow up having a father.

'He told me "If you and I are patriots, who would I be if I stayed at home and watched it all happening there?"' she recalls. 'I couldn't find the words to object.'

Rudiak voluntarily joined the military in 2014 and served three and a half years. He took part in the defense of Donetsk Airport, which is one of the most tragic, yet legendary episodes of Russia's war in Donbas, as well as other hot spots.

Liudmyla says the war traumatized Tymofiy. Every time he came home for a short vacation, the family noticed how anxious and stressed he was.

'He would wake up at night screaming, start walking and hit the wall or fall on the ground covering his head with his hands when there were fireworks or firecracker explosions,' she says.

The family tried to help and support him as much as possible. But they had less than five years to do so and finally enjoy their life together until Tymofiy had to return to the frontline again.

On 24 February, the two woke up to the sound of explosions. After they took the kids to a safe place, Tymofiy headed to the local military recruitment office. Shortly after, he came to Liudmyla's workplace to say goodbye.

'He said he loved me,' she recalls. 'And then we were just standing there hugging, in silence.'

'But I didn't have enough of that,' she says crying. 'We didn't have enough time together.'

It was the last time she saw her husband: Tymofiy joined the 95th Airborne Brigade that day and was stationed in Kyiv Oblast.

All Liudmyla knows is that Tymofiy was in Makariv, a town in Kyiv Oblast, the last time he called her on 3 March. She first thought he didn't have a chance to charge his phone. After a week, Liudmyla realized her husband would have found a chance to contact her.

On 11 March, Tymofiy's friends identified his body in a morgue in Zhytomyr Oblast.

Based on the damage to his body, Liudmyla assumes that it was a Russian missile that killed him. The morgue staff returned her a fragment of a silver chain that she gave him. It was covered in her husband's blood.

Shocked and heartbroken, she doesn't remember the funeral.

Even though Tymofiy's death certificate says he died on 3 March, when they lost connection with him, Liudmyla believes it happened between 4 and 5 March, when she woke up in the middle of the night with her heart fluttering like mad as if 'feeling that the love of her life was gone.'

'27 years together,' she says.

'I can't imagine ... I don't know how to live without him.'

Serhii Vorobiov, 57

Ukrainian gymnast Oleksandr Vorobiov, who won the bronze medal at the 2008 Summer Olympics in Beijing, says he wouldn't have achieved anything if not for his father.

Serhii Vorobiov encouraged his son to go into sports and always supported him.

'Even when I didn't believe in myself,' Oleksandr says.

Before 2014, Vorobiov spent most of his time at his family's farm in a village near Kamianske, a town in Dnipropetrovsk Oblast. Oleksandr says his father 'adored' that farm and supported dozens of village residents by employing them.

The war, however, changed his priorities, putting Ukraine's freedom first.

Oleksandr doesn't know much about where his father had been fighting since 2014. Serhii didn't talk about it very much, to avoid worrying his wife. At first, he didn't even mention going to the frontline but told the family that he was out for meetings with the Svoboda political party that he joined in 2014.

Yet Serhii's wife wasn't surprised when she found out. She knew how he loved and rooted for Ukraine. He even switched to the Ukrainian language, after spending his whole life speaking Russian.

Oleksandr says his father expected Russia to start the all-out invasion of Ukraine. So when that happened, Serhii was ready.

As a member of the volunteer battalion 'Carpathian Sich', Vorobiov headed to defend Kyiv and its neighboring settlements. Oleksandr says he only talked with his father twice during that time but heard about the horrors his father witnessed there.

'He saw dead bodies, beheaded,' Oleksandr says. 'He was shocked.'

Serhii spent about a month fighting in Kyiv Oblast, later clearing the area from Russian mines, rescuing locals, and removing corpses from the streets.

He came home for one day, to attend the funeral of his fellow soldier, then headed to defend Kharkiv.

The last time Serhii called his wife was on 10 April. He was very upset that two soldiers from his battalion had been killed that day.

A couple of hours after that call, she received a message from Serhii: 'Yulia, goodbye, I love you.'

Serhii, along with fellow soldiers, were in a car when a Russian tank attacked them. His legs were torn off after the strike, but he managed to escape the car and died on the ground near it. Oleksandr believes his father sent that message a moment before he died on 11 April.

Oleksandr says he still can't believe his father is gone.

'He has always been my hero,' Oleksandr says. 'But now ... He is even more than that.'

5 May 2022

Russia's war may half Ukraine's economy, increasing budget deficit by billions

Natalia Datskevych

After Ukraine ended 2021 with a historically high gross domestic product (GDP) of $195 billion, top officials issued optimistic forecasts for the coming year.

Then the war began, killing all of the country's economic plans.

As of late April, the Russian military has destroyed 30% of Ukraine's infrastructure, causing $100 billion worth of damage.

Total losses to the economy, both direct and indirect, have already reached over $560 billion, according to the head of President Volodymyr Zelensky's office, Andriy Yermak.

Russia's full-scale invasion has forced more than five million people to flee Ukraine. Around 60% of small- and medium-sized businesses are currently closed or suspended.

According to World Bank estimates, Ukraine's economy will contract by 45% in 2022.

'This is already terrifying,' said Deputy Director at the Center for Economic Strategy Maria Repko. 'This means that we no longer have a third of our economy.'

According to Ukraine's State Statistics Service, inflation in Ukraine may quadruple to 15–20% by the end of the year.

The blocked ports of the Azov and Black seas killed maritime shipping and cut half of the country's exports, as well as 90% of grain trade with foreign countries.

As of early May, around 4.5 million tons of grain were stuck at Ukrainian ports, according to Martin Frick, the World Food Programme director in Germany.

'[Logistics] were ruined. Old supply chains through the ports are not working and won't resume operation in the nearest future,' said Repko.

In March, Ukraine exported just 5.97 million tons of goods worth $2.7 billion. Imports fell by two-thirds to 1.6 million tons worth $1.8 billion due to an unprecedented decline in consumer demand.

Russia's invasion is already 'sending shockwaves throughout the globe,' according to Kristalina Georgieva, managing director of the International Monetary Fund.

'The economic consequences from the war spread fast and far, to neighbors and beyond,' Georgieva said during her curtain-raiser speech to the IMF–World Bank Spring Meetings.

Russia's war will be among the top reasons for the decline in global growth this year and the next, she said. The Fund will downgrade their forecasts for 143 economies, which account for 86% of global GDP.

Budget deficit

Fending off the war has cost big bucks for Ukraine.

According to Danylo Hetmantsev, the head of the Ukrainian parliament's finance and taxation committee, budgetary spending has quadrupled compared to that of peacetime. The monthly budget deficit currently ranges from $5–7 billion, most of which goes to the military and social support.

At the same time, the state's main sources of income are in trouble. Total budget revenues have fallen by 75%.

Dividends paid by state-owned enterprises, which previously covered 30% of all revenues, are going down. Other forms of income are also expected to decline. Before the war started, Ukraine's Finance Ministry planned to collect $18 billion of taxes on imported goods, $14 billion in value added tax, and $2.6 billion in excise taxes in 2022.

After one month of all-out war, the country's customs managed to collect only a fifth of the planned revenues – $240 million instead of the expected $1.3 billion.

In addition, the government has allowed businesses to switch to a simplified taxation system, allowing them to pay 2% of turnover instead of all other taxes, including income tax and VAT, among others.

In mid-March, the government dropped fuel VAT from 20% to 7% tax so farmers could buy enough for the season's sowing campaign and to enable the delivery of critical supplies like food and medicine.

The government is already planning to restore some taxes. A bill has been registered in the Verkhovna Rada proposing to raise VAT.

Personal note from Anna Myroniuk, head of investigations

It is challenging to report on a war in your own country while being affected by it on a daily basis. You cannot just request a rotation and go home as foreign correspondents do. This is your home. Under attack.

On 24 February 2022, I woke up to explosions. Around 5 a.m., a Russian rocket landed just across the street from my home in the Kyiv outskirts. Walls shook; I ran to the balcony and saw a grey mushroom-shaped cloud. 'Evidently, time to leave,' I thought, grabbing my backpack.

I walked to the closest gas station. While waiting for a colleague to pick me up, I was writing news for our website.

Soon my mother found herself trapped in Bucha, a city just outside Kyiv. Once known for its parks and forests, it is now infamous for the Russian soldiers' massacre of local residents during the occupation.

My mother moved to Bucha in 2014, fleeing Russia's war in our native city of Donetsk.

The war has followed her. Eight years later, her new home became the front line, too.

My mother spent about two weeks in the basement of her residential building in Bucha with no electricity, gas, or mobile connection, short on food and water.

While she was hiding from the Russian artillery and troops in her basement, I was reporting on one of the first cases of Russian atrocities happening in the city: the murder of Ukrainian volunteers delivering food for stray animals in the local shelter in the first days of the invasion. A Russian infantry vehicle shot at their civilian car. For some time, I couldn't help but think that my mom could be in the next car the Russians opened fire at.

She was lucky to get out in one piece by car through the 'green corridor' set up for evacuation on 10 March 2022.

Some of my relatives are still stuck in Russian-occupied territories. One male relative, like other men in the occupied territories, faces the risk of being conscripted into the army in Russian-occupied Donetsk, where he lives.

On 4 May 2022, my ex-boyfriend of two years, who I had known for almost a decade, was killed on the front line near Izium in the Kharkiv Oblast.

We had broken up a year and a half before his death. I live in an apartment that we once shared, which at times brings back a lot of memories.

When I learned the news, I was devastated. I wasn't able to work for about a week and spent most of this time with our common friends. We were talking and crying on one another's shoulders.

My colleagues at *The Kyiv Independent* were a giant support throughout this tough period. Our chief editor Olga Rudenko accompanied me at my ex-boyfriend's funeral, while editor Oleksiy Sorokin was there for me when I was at my lowest, worrying about my mom in Bucha.

Together we went through a lot. First, we were sacked from the *Kyiv Post* for defending editorial independence, then navigated news coverage while hiding from Russian missiles in the underground in the first days of the invasion, and now we light one another's candles to keep working during blackouts.

The war clearly affected every member of our team. It hasn't always been smooth between us, but we have stuck together despite everything – the common values that we share made us a real team.

7 May 2022

Russia's offensive in Donbas bogs down

Illia Ponomarenko

The Battle of Donbas is raging high, but it's not going the way Russia wanted it to.

Almost 20 days in, the much-anticipated and feared grand offensive falls short of expectations.

It is still not even close to achieving its ultimate goal – the encircling and crippling of the core Ukrainian military group in the region.

Amid fierce hostilities, Russia has only managed to achieve limited territorial gains at significant cost.

Slow and painful, the offensive has gradually stalled amid weak Russian reserves and strong Ukrainian defenses.

The assault appears destined to fall short of the symbolic success that Russia likely wished to achieve prior to Victory Day on 9 May, the day on which Russia commemorates its role in the defeat of Nazi Germany in World War II.

Broken axis

Prior to the beginning of the Donbas offensive in early April, Russia, according to estimates, concentrated a total of somewhere between 76 and 87 battalion tactical grounds (BTGs) in Ukraine – a total of around 70,000–80,000 troops.

According to the US Department of Defense, over 22 BTGs were positioned in Russia's Belgorod Oblast, likely to be replenished and remain in reserve.

These units essentially constituted the entire combat-capable force and reserve that Russia could dedicate to the campaign.

The failed blitzkrieg that followed, upon estimates by the United Kingdom's Ministry of Defense, rendered nearly a quarter of Russia's 120–125 BTGs incapable of any major operations.

What stood against Russia's offensive, according to Ukraine's President Volodymyr Zelensky, was a Ukrainian force of nearly 44,000 troops concentrated in heavily fortified, urban areas in central Donbas – the cities of Sloviansk, Kramatorsk, Sievierodonetsk, Lysychansk, and the northern parts of Russian-occupied Donetsk.

In this new operation, Russia was to eliminate the Ukrainian salient with two massive strikes from the north (along the Izium–Sloviansk highway) and from the south of the Zaporizhzhia and Donetsk oblasts.

The two key axes were to meet up in between, effectively cutting the Ukrainian force off from supplies and the rest of the country.

A critical axis was also to surround the Sievierodonetsk–Lysychansk area, bisecting the Ukrainian salient.

The start of Russia's key offensive in Donbas was confirmed by Zelensky on 18 April. Hostilities in the region never died down from day one of the big invasion but, in mid-April, Russian forces partially regrouped and focused on Donbas as the central prize

However, as of early May, mere days before the 9 May deadline by which the Kremlin appears to have wanted to display some sort of 'victory,' Russian forces have managed to achieve little.

Over two weeks of intense fighting, Russia has advanced by no more than 20–30 kilometers in either of the two axes, within a salient of nearly 14,000 square kilometers – roughly the size of the US state of Connecticut.

The Russian military has made some limited gains south of Izium in Kharkiv Oblast, having advanced toward Barvinkove. But, as of early May, it has not managed to gain access to Izium or gain a foothold along the Barvinkove–Sloviansk road, which would allow it to approach Sloviansk from the west.

Russia currently has 25 BTGs attempting to advance in this direction, according to the British Ministry of Defense.

On the other axis, Russian forces since mid-April have managed to begin outflanking the Sievierodonetsk–Lysychansk area in Luhansk Oblast, having entered the town of Kreminna and moved some 30 kilometers west towards the towns of Yarova and Lyman, where continue to face resilient Ukrainian defenses.

This advancement constitutes Russia's biggest progress thus far after nearly three weeks of intense fighting.

On 25 April, Russian forces also seized the town of Novotoshkivske in Luhansk Oblast, which had been razed to the ground amid hostilities and abandoned by civilians.

No significant progress has been achieved by Russia since then.

It is critical to note that, according to Western intelligence, the Kremlin likely counted on a decisive victory, including the complete seizure of Mariupol, by early May.

On the southern axis, parts of Russia's 58th Combined Arms Army have also failed to demonstrate any significant gains in the recent weeks.

Ukrainian units continue to successfully defend key points of Huliaipole, Velyka Novosilka, and Vuhledar in Zaporizhzhia and Donetsk oblasts since mid-March, preventing the Russian axis from moving north.

According to the Pentagon, the southern deadlock appeared to have been so tight that Russia decided to withdraw at least two BTGs from Mariupol (despite ongoing attempts to take the Azovstal steel plant by storm) and likely redeploy them to Donbas.

The Battle of Donbas' map looks virtually the same since the Russian withdrawal from the north in late March.

'Due to strong Ukrainian resistance, Russian territorial gains have been limited and achieved at significant costs to Russian forces,' the UK Ministry of Defense stated on 29 April.

Moreover, according to British intelligence, following the battles of Kyiv, Sumy, and Chernihiv, the Kremlin had limited time to re-equip and reorganize its forces before the Donbas Offensive. Therefore, this reality, alongside poor morale, has hindered Russia's combat effectiveness and the offensive's momentum.

By early May, Russian attempts to advance stalled on all axes.

Mobile defense

Since the end of the Battle of Kyiv, Russia appears to have learned some lessons.

Rather than head-on, frontal pushes, Putin's forces have been methodically probing Ukrainian defenses and trying to hit where it hurts, enjoying quantitative superiority in terms of artillery power.

Meanwhile, Ukrainian forces are sticking to mobile defense tactics that have succeeded in undermining the Russian blitzkrieg in the north.

Instead of taking a hard and static defense against a technically superior enemy, the Ukrainian military maneuvers and rotates reserves, taking advantage of local terrain and exhausting Russian forces.

As such, Ukraine's military retreated from Kreminna on 18 April, a town northwest of Sievierodonetsk, to avoid being overwhelmed and to continue exhausting Russian forces for more suitable defense lines.

April's rainy forecast, alongside the rugged, forested terrain of central Donbas also played in Ukraine's favor.

Ukrainian forces have also continued to outmatch Russia in terms of unmanned aerial vehicles surveilling battlefields. The abundance of Western-provided, man-portable anti-aircraft weapons (particularly advanced British-made Martlet MANPADs) has also helped the Ukrainian military limit the Russian artillery's situational awareness as scores of Orlan-10s and other UAVs were downed.

Notably, as of 6 May, Russia has not managed to overwhelm or surround any of Ukraine's heavily fortified strongpoints and has also failed to merge their attack axes coming from Izium and Rubizhne in central Donbas.

Since the very beginning of the full-scale war, it has also failed to break through the old Donbas frontline in its best-defended sections, particularly near Donetsk and parts of Luhansk Oblast.

Even when it comes to overtaking the highway running southeast between Izium and Sloviansk, or the open steppe of Zaporizhzhia Oblast, Russian forces have found it costly to move on.

What lies ahead of Russia in the Battle of Donbas is a range of heavily fortified strongpoints, prepared for a long-lasting and fierce defense, including Sloviansk, Sievierodonetsk, Kurakhove, and Avdiivka.

At the same time, Ukraine's rear appears to have motivated and experienced reserves at its disposal, particularly the 3rd and the 4th Tank Brigade units deployed to the Sloviansk–Kramatorsk area.

Nonetheless, Russia has not ceased its attempts to gnaw through Ukrainian defenses, even though its main forces have been in hard combat for more than 14 days.

As of 6 May, local authorities report fierce fighting near Sievierodonetsk, with Russian forces trying to attack the city from multiple directions.

Counter-offensive

In addition, Russia appears to have a rather scarce reserve for a large-scale operation that is the territorial size of the 1943 Battle of Kursk.

North of Kharkiv Oblast, Russia still deploys parts of the 6th Combined Arms Army, particularly the 200th Brigade, which is known to have sustained heavy losses near Kharkiv and withdrew for recovery.

Following nearly three weeks of the Battle of Donbas, the expert community is increasingly doubtful about any prospects of Russian success in the operation.

'Further Russian reinforcements to the Izium axis are unlikely to enable stalled Russian forces to achieve substantial advances,' the Institute of the Study of War (ISW), a Washington DC-based think tank, said on 30 April.

'Russian forces appear increasingly unlikely to achieve any major advances in eastern Ukraine, and Ukrainian forces may be able to conduct wider counterattacks in the coming days.'

And indeed, on 5 May, Ukraine's Commander-in-Chief Valerii Zaluzhnyi announced in a conversation with the US Joint Chiefs of Staff chairman Mark Milley that Ukrainian forces launched 'counter-offensive actions' near Kharkiv and Izium.

Even before that, Ukraine's military and US intelligence both said that Ukrainian forces have managed to advance 40 kilometers near Kharkiv, mainly in areas northeast of the city.

On 6 May, the Ukrainian military reported the liberation of a number of towns some 30 kilometers northeast of the city, having pushed the Russian forces farther north to the state border.

Ukraine's activity in the region will likely be of secondary, auxiliary nature to divert parts of the main Russian forces in Donbas.

'The Ukrainian counteroffensive out of Kharkiv city may disrupt Russian forces northeast of Kharkiv and will likely force Russian forces to decide whether to reinforce positions near Kharkiv or risk losing most or all of their positions within artillery range of the city,' the ISW wrote on 5 May.

'Russian forces made few advances in continued attacks in eastern Ukraine, and Ukrainian forces may be able to build their ongoing counterattacks and repulse Russian attacks along the Izyum axis into a wider counter offensive to retake Russian-occupied territory in Kharkiv Oblast.'

8 May 2022

Zelensky gives powerful address on Victory Day
The Kyiv Independent News Desk

'Decades after World War II, the darkness has returned to Ukraine,' President Volodymyr Zelensky said in a pre-recorded speech. 'Evil has returned. In a different form, under different slogans, but with the same purpose ... We did not last even a century. Our "never again" was enough for 77 years.'

14 May 2022

Azovstal garrison: 'We'll keep fighting as long as we're alive'
Illia Ponomarenko

Those are the things that spell the days of soldiers at Azovstal, the last Ukrainian fortress in the Russian-besieged city of Mariupol.

After almost 80 days of fierce fighting, over 1,000 Ukrainian combatants, hundreds among them injured, are still holding out at the giant steel factory.

For days and weeks, Russia's military have been pouring the full of its firepower upon the industrial ruins, in a bid to gain a symbolic victory over what used to be a key Azov Sea port city of 500,000, at any price.

With the rest of the city occupied, Azovstal remains the last area under Ukrainian control.

Yet, after weeks in close combat, remnants of Ukraine's National Guard, marines, the police, and Territorial Defense units – all those still able to hold a gun – keep fighting as they stand back against the sea.

The time is running short.

The last standing in Mariupol is in dire straits. The fighters are growing bitter and desperate about their high command in Kyiv and the whole world that they say are doing too little to help them.

Having secured the evacuation of hundreds of civilians from Azovstal, the soldiers are ready to go on until the bitter end.

Surrender is not an option, they say.

But hope is still glimmering – that the world will force the Kremlin into letting the embattled garrison go, with dignity.

They hope for a miracle.

But, despite broad international involvement, Russia keeps denying evacuation of the encircled Ukrainian forces.

Russian dictator Vladimir Putin has personally ordered to 'fully blockade' the plant.

The Azovstal was one of Mariupol's two giant metallurgical enterprises, along with Illich Steel and Iron Works.

A giant industrial complex of 11 square kilometers in area (nearly 7% of the city territory), it was established in the early 1930s as part of the Soviet government's massive industrialization campaign.

This 'city inside the city', dotted with blast furnaces and chimney shafts, towers over Mariupol as one of its symbols. It used to employ nearly 10,000 workers as part of Ukraine's richest man Rinat Akhmetov's industrial empire.

The Azovstal plant is washed by the Azov Sea from the south and belted by the Kalmius River that divides Mariupol in two halves. The area of the plant remains the last bit of the Azov Sea shore controlled by Ukraine.

Since the start of Russia's all-out war on Ukraine on 24 February, the Russian blitzkrieg was facing little resistance in Ukraine's south.

Russian battalions went north from the occupied Crimea, rushed toward Kherson and seized it as soon as 2 March. Key cities of Ukraine's south, Berdiansk and Melitopol, were taken without a fight within days.

Russian forces moved along the Azov Sea coastline and approached Mariupol, their main target in the region. Russian forces failed to invade the city in 2014 and 2015.

Yet another axis pushed west from the old front line of Donetsk Oblast. In late February, Russia approached and devastated the city of Volnovakha, a key transportation point north of Mariupol.

Mariupol was getting surrounded and cut off from the rest of the country.

What happened next was possibly the worst devastation of a European city since World War II. At least 20,000 dead, nearly 300,000 fled in terror, and nearly 95% of buildings and structures were ruined, according to local Ukrainian authorities.

The 3,500-strong Ukrainian garrison, mainly the National Guards' Azov Regiment and the 36th Marine Brigade, was facing nearly 14,000 Russian regular forces and Donbas collaborationists.

Insane house-to-house fighting and massive Russian bombardment turned Mariupol into a giant cemetery of debris and improvised graves in parks and backyards. A once thriving city became a landfill of destroyed Russian armor.

But slowly and steadily, by mid-April, amid immense bloodshed, the Ukrainian garrison got locked up at the Azovstal – the last main fortress prepared for long defense.

According to the garrison's estimation, in the period between 24 February and 15 April, the Azov Regiment alone killed 2,500 Russian manpower in the city, wounded more 5,000, and also destroyed over 60 and damaged over 30 tanks. That's not including fatalities scored by other Ukrainian formations.

According to the Ukrainian command, this continuing resistance forced Russia into keeping at least 10 battalion tactical groups away from other critical axes of attack against Ukraine – nearly 10% of the whole Russian force invading Ukraine.

Russia has already been too quick to declare a full victory in Mariupol on 21 April, even though the Azovstal was still standing and repelling attacks. The Kremlin then failed to take over Azovstal in time for 9 May, the symbolic WWII victory day, the cornerstone of Russian war propaganda.

Putin on 21 April claimed Russia would halt active hostilities and would instead lay siege to the steel factory. But the dictator's patience was short – Russia almost immediately resumed bombing the Azovstal and throwing in its most-capable assault groups.

Yet, as of mid-May, the Azovstal is still standing, isolated by at least 100 kilometers of Russian-controlled territory.

Into the fire

The old Soviet industrial monster is a maze of tens of kilometers of catacombs, workshops, railways, and underground passages running at least eight meters below the ground.

Many consider it an ideal defensive ground.

But in reality, as the garrison soldiers say, this improvised fortress is far more vulnerable than many expect it to be. Those old walls of concrete just can't sustain Russia's weeks-long bombardment.

Civilians, medics, and the military have been dying every day as Russian bombers and warships methodically grind the Azovstal premises into dust.

As days go by, the fortress dives deeper into the hell of gore and destruction.

'The worst inferno, the worst nightmare one can just imagine,' says Captain Svyatoslav Palamar, a deputy commander with the Azov Regiment going by the call-name Kalyna.

'Stalingrad doubled down. This is just what it is.'

At the Avozstal, days are the same and seem to be a bad dream that never ends.

In one of his poignant Facebook posts written amid clashes, the Marines leader Sergiy Volynskiy (Volyna) called it 'a hellish reality show where we ... use every chance of salvation while the world is just following an exciting plot.'

Exhausted soldiers have overgrown beards and haven't had a chance to bathe for a long time. In the half-dark of dungeons, they sleep on cardboard boxes or heaps of torn clothes. Some manage to erect makeshift tents and pretend to be having a cozy shelter.

Sometimes one can get a couple of hours of sleep in underground shelters. And many try and take a nap outside, right at their firing positions in the ruins.

They still have the remnants of standard military rations and grits found elsewhere, from which they cook thin soups and porridge on campfires. Some younger soldiers grew thin and weigh as little as 59 kilograms, as a result of what they ironically call 'the Azovstal diet'. 'On Easter, we even managed to find some flour and bake a sort of flatbread,' Palamar says.

Soldiers have to drink technical water from the factory.

As the warm season comes, multiple dead bodies scattered all over the place spread contamination and the smell of death.

Fires, explosions, and soot make it hard to breathe.

Sometimes, Russia does nearly 150 bombing sorties a day, including with the use of Tupolev Tu-22M strategic bombers.

Weak internet connection ensured by communication specialists risking their lives is the last solace – and also a window into the outer world that follows the battle's every second. Pictures and videos sent from the Azovstal show the misery of the wounded.

On 28 April, Russian bombers destroyed an improvised hospital established in the dungeons of Azovstal.

The situation became beyond critical.

'We run low on bandaging materials, medicine, antibiotic drugs. We have almost no instruments. The wounded die every single day as they can't get timely treatment,' Palamar says. Now, the Azovstal has nearly 600 wounded. And with every day, this number grows.

Some have to endure surgery with no anesthesia. In this battle, getting badly wounded likely means slowly dying in pain.

What gives them some comfort is that likely all civilians have been evacuated from the Azovstal, following intense talks involving the United Nations and the Red Cross.

On 7 May, Ukraine's Deputy Prime Minister Iryna Vereshchuk confirmed that all 'women, children and the elderly' have been finally taken to safe places in a series of efforts, after two months at the Azovstal shelters.

'They did not live just next to us, as many would think,' Palamar says. 'We did not share the same premises to avoid putting them in jeopardy. We used to come to see them from time to time. When there were airstrikes, we used to come to clear debris. We would share food and medicine. If we were just by their side, this would mean we used them as a living shield and this would give a sort of justification behind what Putin's forces are doing.'

The Mariupol garrison has lost three fighters killed and six wounded to ensure the civilian evacuation – Russian forces never hesitated to open fire during the pre-agreed ceasefire, while international organizations members never entered the Azovstal territory to meet the evacuees.

Keep holding on

But that's just civilians.

The Mariupol garrison keeps asking that the dying combatants be recovered as well.

The situation is growing desperate with every day.

On 4 May, Russian forces managed to break into the Azovstal premises, entering fierce close-quarter combat with the Ukrainian defenders. Nearly 2,000 Russian stormtroopers try to overwhelm the resistance while Russian aviation razes all around to ashes.

Yet, the Ukrainian flag is still flapping over the ruined factory.

But desperation and bitterness also grow. The Azovstal has a lot of questions about why Russian forces need just four days to make it to the Mariupol outskirts from Crimea, facing no resistance.

And why the surrounded garrison has had to fight for 80 days all alone, waiting for a Ukrainian offensive to help it break through the Russian blockade.

In March, President Volodymyr Zelensky, in a direct conversation with commanders, suggested that the garrison tries to battle its way out of the city by itself. But without an auxiliary strike upon Russians by main Ukrainian forces, that would be just suicidal, as the Mariupol force decided. 'We told the president we can't go as our wounded need to be evacuated first,' Palamar said. 'We just couldn't do that, leaving the wounded behind, leaving civilians unprotected.'

Many weeks after, Ukraine's top command still says a direct military strike to save the dying garrison is still not possible due to the overwhelming Russian force in the region.

But the country's leadership, according to Zelensky, does everything possible to find a diplomatic solution.

'All this time, we hear it from the command: Guys, hold on until a certain day in March,' Palamar says. 'We keep holding on. What's next? Nothing happens. Then hold on until a day in April. And we do. No one's helping us. Hold on until 1 May, 5 May, 6 May. We keep holding on but nothing is happening, no military action is being done to unblock us.'

They still have just one order from Kyiv: to keep holding on.

They have repeatedly declined Russian demands to surrender.

To members of the Azov Regiment, which had previously gained a controversial reputation for harboring far-right combatants and using neo-Nazi insignia, surrendering means death from torture in captivity, as they believe.

'We're going to keep fighting as long as we are alive,' Palamar says. 'No one has broken our spirit ... We're fighting for the sake of the Ukrainian people and the whole civilized world. We all understand that if we do not prevail here, Putin will go further. The front line of war and all things will be very different.'

But still, they have a hope of leaving this hell alive and free.

Almost every day, the Azovstal defense leaders keep making last-ditch addresses to the world's movers and shakers. Recep Tayyip Erdoğan of Turkey, the Pope, and even Elon Musk, all asked dearly to help evacuate the garrison.

As Crimean Tatar leader Mustafa Dzhemilev announced on 12 May, Russia directly declined Turkey's repeated initiatives to extract the Ukrainian military from the Azovstal by the sea and ensure their presence in Turkey until the end of the war.

Russia also declined to let the Mariupol garrison go in exchange for all Russian prisoners of war held in Ukraine.

Now the Azovstal soldiers are waiting for a miracle.

'We give the top priority to the things that we do for this country, not to our lives,' Palamar says. 'But as a deputy commander, I ask that the world, its politicians and opinion leaders, intervene and render pressure upon Putin via international organizations regarding the evacuation of the Mariupol garrison. This must be done in the nearest time.

'We're talking about days and hours.'

16 May 2022

Mariupol evacuees: 'People just dying, city in chaos'

Asami Terajima

A large white tent in a shopping center parking lot in Zaporizhzhia welcomes hundreds of evacuees who left everything behind after Russian forces destroyed peace in their hometowns.

Under the marquee, displaced people sit at long communal tables and silently gulp down warm meals prepared by volunteers.

Still in shock from what they saw after Russian troops stormed their cities, some are barely holding back tears and are still visibly shaking. They are given clothes and medicine, as they figure out a plan to get to regions less exposed to attacks.

Further along the tent, a noticeboard is filled with photos of missing relatives and announcements offering to transport evacuees westwards.

While evacuees are mainly arriving from temporarily Russian-occupied cities in Zaporizhzhia Oblast, some also come from Mariupol, Donetsk Oblast, a besieged city in southeastern Ukraine that has experienced the most aggressive Russian bombardment.

Evacuating from Mariupol has remained a gamble for months now, as Russian forces encircled the bombed-out port city on 2 March.

Only a handful of Ukrainian evacuation buses have been able to reach Mariupol thus far, leaving civilians with few options: to rely on their personal vehicles or to flee on foot.

But neither option guarantees safe escape.

Some Mariupol survivors, as though by a miracle, have arrived in damaged vehicles with their windows shattered, after having gone through almost 20 Russian-controlled checkpoints.

Mariupol City Council volunteers stationed at the evacuee reception center in Zaporizhzhia told *The Kyiv Independent* in late April that families fleeing Mariupol usually arrive after having spent days, or even weeks, in the temporarily Russian-occupied city of Berdiansk.

In total, 120,000 Mariupol residents have arrived in Zaporizhzhia, Regional Governor Oleksandr Starukh said during a briefing on 16 May. He added that over 6,000 have decided to stay in Zaporizhzhia, while others fled elsewhere.

According to Starukh, the number of evacuees arriving in Zaporizhzhia has decreased in recent weeks and there are currently about 1,000 people a day, with 200–300 coming from Mariupol.

For instance, the governor said 238 Mariupol evacuees have arrived in Zaporizhzhia on 15 May.

With no means of communication or access to electricity, heating, and water, Mariupol residents have spent weeks in basements hiding from indiscriminate Russian bombardment.

According to Mariupol Mayor Vadym Boichenko, around 20,000 of the city's residents may have already been killed by Russia's war, but the exact number of victims may never be discovered.

Since early April, Russia's military has been using mobile crematoriums in an attempt to erase the evidence of their war crimes by burning dead bodies, Ukraine's intelligence said.

Ukrainian officials have also identified mass graves in the outskirts of Mariupol, where Russian forces are disposing of the bodies of thousands of civilians left out on the streets.

Many evacuees are in tears while recounting the brutality of the Russian siege, filled with fear about what may happen to their friends and relatives who are still there.

Mariupol City Council said on 11 May that as many as 170,000 civilians remain trapped in the city.

Leaving father behind

Many of the survivors describe apocalyptic scenes from the once-bustling port city of Mariupol with a pre-war population of 450,000, now reduced to ashes.

'They [Russian occupiers] were just shooting at residential buildings,' Mariupol resident Svitlana Mayorova told *The Kyiv Independent*. 'There were many Russian soldiers and a lot of Russian military equipment around the houses.'

Although the 24-year-old initially fled Mariupol on foot on 22 March, she returned in mid-April once she was able to get in touch with her mother, who was hiding in another part of the city.

Once they managed to reunite, the two headed eastwards through the neighboring settlement of Sartana, Donetsk Oblast, bypassing Mariupol to finally get to Yalta. From there, Mayorova and her mother hired a private driver and escaped to Zaporizhzhia with another family through Berdiansk.

Recounting the horrors of watching her hometown turn into a giant grave-yard, Mayorova said she was especially frightened when Russian planes were flying overhead. 'A bomb fell on a neighboring house, and the house was just gone,' she said. 'About 16 people were killed.'

Mayorova survived nearly two months of the siege in a bomb shelter in Mariupol's hard-hit Livoberezhnyi (Left-bank) district, the neighborhood from which the Russians began forcibly moving a large number of residents into Russian-controlled territory in March.

Russian forces would warn civilians that there would be intense shelling, so 'it was either you die at home, or be "evacuated" to Russia,' Mayorova said. As Russia intensified attacks on civilian infrastructure each day, it became a question of life and death. For many, going to Russia was the only escape out of bombarded Mariupol, she said.

By 28 April, the Kremlin claimed to have forcibly deported over a million Ukrainians to Russia from its occupied territories in Ukraine.

Luckily, Mayorova had left the district before Russian forces made their way to the bomb shelter where she had been staying. After she finally heard back from her 58-year-old mother, she jumped in a car with her father to pick her up.

Her mother, Olga, had been hiding in the basement of her apartment in the Tsentralnyi (Central) District, where heavy fighting had also been taking place.

Olga told *The Kyiv Independent* that the Russian tanks had stood just five meters away from her windows and the building would shake every time shots were fired. 'It was really scary, [and the Russian occupiers] were shoot-ing very loudly,' Olga said, recalling the intense fear she had felt.

On their way out of the besieged city, both daughter and mother recall one street covered with dead bodies. Unlike other streets, Russian forces had not yet removed the bodies of dead civilians from the road, the evacu-ees said.

Mayorova's father stayed behind because of a disability and it would be difficult for him to evacuate from Mariupol.

Constant fear

Serhiy Kostiantynov, who left Mariupol in late March, said Russian evacuation buses only took civilians to Russia or to Russian-occupied territories back then. He himself hopped onto one of the buses after his apartment was shelled and eventually burned down.

His only car had already been destroyed in the early days of Russia's war and Kostiantynov was desperate to get out of this 'hell', he said. He said he had to evacuate his wife and their five-month-old baby by any means.

The 35-year-old was terrified to the extent that he could not think straight, especially while battling 'constant hunger'. The shelling was so intense that it could have literally killed anybody and the bombing was incessant. It was turning into a real-life Russian roulette.

'You live in constant fear,' he told *The Kyiv Independent*. 'People were just dying. The city is in chaos.'

Up until they left, his family only went to the basement when it was absolutely necessary. He said it was freezing down there, especially for his newborn baby who was always crying.

Not knowing whether he would be able to make it back home alive, Kostiantynov had to leave his home regularly to get water and to cook over an open fire so that his child could have a hot meal. Trips outside were laden with danger; he said many neighbors never came back.

Kostiantynov remembers leaving his apartment one day and passing by a man sitting on a bench, smoking. On his way back, he found the man dead on the exact same spot, with half of his head missing.

He also remembers watching an entire family, from a small child to its grandparents, being buried in a courtyard, after they were hit suddenly by intense shelling while standing near an open fire.

Many courtyards have been turned into graveyards, Kostiantynov said. He himself has buried about 40 dead bodies.

Once Kostiantynov's family made the decision to leave Mariupol, a Russian bus took them, as well as many others, to another Russian-occupied settlement nearby.

Evacuees were then forced to pick between the three destinations: Russian-occupied Donetsk or two cities in Russia, Taganrog or Rostov-on-Don. Russian soldiers forbade evacuees to return to Ukrainian-controlled territory, Kostiantynov said.

Luckily, he was able to strike a secret deal with a local in Nikolske, Donetsk Oblast, who agreed to help the family get to Zaporizhzhia Oblast.

Almost all others on the buses were taken to Russia, many of them against their will.

Kostiantynov's parents are still in Mariupol and he has yet to hear back from them.

Born in siege

Mariupol resident Anna Vilkova, 26, was about to give birth to her second child when Russia unleashed its full-scale invasion of Ukraine on 24 February. Her family decided to stay in Mariupol, hoping that the hostilities would eventually die down.

On 1 March, her father rushed her to a local maternity hospital and she gave birth as soon as they arrived. It was the last day that the hospital still had access to electricity, so doctors were able to perform an operation to deliver her child.

Her father and husband remained in their apartments until both of their homes were destroyed in mid-March. Vilkova's two-year-old son Illia stayed with her parents. She said that she was especially frightened because she would not have been able to run if the hospital was attacked due to her stitches.

Her 57-year-old father also recounted the terror of the weeks prior to when they were all able to flee their hometown.

He saw dead bodies on the streets everywhere he went, one of them his acquaintance. He said a bomb had fallen on his acquantaince, decapitating him and leaving the rest of his body strewn across the street.

Vilkova's father said he would constantly hear warplanes flying outside and that it was like 'suicide' to go anywhere. He buried many people that he knew. 'God knows how many people were killed near a bonfire when an air bomb fell on them,' he said.

'It's just corpses lying outside, no one can keep up to bury them,' Vilkova told *The Kyiv Independent*.

The rest of her family soon joined her in the basement of the hospital and stayed there for a week. While the basement was not very deep, there were many families hiding inside.

Even though everyone was terrified, people supported each other and even sang Ukrainian songs once in a while, Vilkova said.

Thankfully, Vilkova's husband had just bought a car in February and it still had fuel, so they eventually made their way out of the city. The routes going westwards were mined, so their only option was to head eastwards toward Russian-occupied territory, her husband said.

Weeks later, they arrived in Zaporizhzhia just before their newborn baby Ivan turned two months old.

Only memory left

At present, after two and a half months of heavy fighting, the city of Mariupol is effectively under Russian control.

The remaining defenders of Mariupol are holding out against concerted Russian attacks on the Azovstal steel plant, Ukraine's last stronghold in the city.

There was not a day that smoke would not billow into the air, 14-year-old Mariupol escapee Alina Ishchenko told *The Kyiv Independent*.

Even before her family fled their hometown in late March, they remember seeing Russian forces opening fire at Azovstal.

A month after their escape, Ishchenko still holds on to a picture of her dead friend Veronika's body and wonders whether she was buried. Russian forces dropped a bomb on her classmate's house in mid-March and wiped out nearly her entire family.

Ishchenko's house was also destroyed due to the attack, so she was forced to live in a nearby basement. There was not enough space underground for adults, so Ishchenko's parents lived outside, behind the walls of a destroyed house, hoping that another bomb would not fall on them.

'For the first days, we would yell "aviation, everyone hide,"' Ishchenko's mother said. 'But then we understood that if it [a bomb] falls, it falls. And if it falls, there is no point to hide.'

Ishchenko was told by a friend that bodies still lay on the ruins of their destroyed house. Pointing to the picture that her mother took before they left Mariupol of the dead bodies in the ruins, she said, 'this is how the entire city looks.'

The smell of dead bodies is something still fresh in Ishchenko's mind.

'All that's left of Mariupol is its name and the people who remember and love the city the way it once used to be,' she said, holding back tears.

19 May 2022

Daughter mourns loved ones killed in Kyiv Oblast: 'Humans can't do what they did to my family'

Daria Shulzhenko

On 23 March, Kyiv resident Olena Sukhenko got the most terrifying phone call of her life. 'Russians came to our house,' her younger brother told her. 'They took our mother. Our father went with her.'

She felt the ground slipping out from beneath her feet.

Olena asked her brother to leave the house immediately and hide in a safer place but he refused. Hours after Russian troops kidnapped her parents from their home in the then-occupied village of Motyzhyn in Kyiv Oblast, they returned and took her brother as well.

All three had stayed in Motyzhyn to help fellow residents survive the occupation. They provided fellow villagers with food and medicine and helped them flee. Olena's mother Olha also served as Motyzhyn's mayor.

Their work was cut short when the family was abducted. Olena lost the ability to talk to her loved ones but she didn't lose hope. Day after day, she sent supportive messages to her family, hoping to rescue them from Russian captivity.

But her faith broke after Ukrainian forces liberated Kyiv Oblast. A grave with four dead bodies was found in the forest around Motyzhyn on 2 April.

Three of them were her family members, found shot dead, with their hands tied behind their backs and signs of torture on their bodies.

'And for what?' Olena asks, trying to hold back tears. 'For being Ukrainians.'

In Kyiv Oblast alone, Russian forces killed at least 1,200 civilians during a month of occupation. After the region was liberated, the extent of Russian soldiers' violence against civilians was laid bare. New graves are still being discovered.

'Not only Putin's hands are covered with their blood,' says Olena. 'But everyone who is silent, everyone who stands aside.'

Stolen life

Olena said her family was full of love, understanding, mutual support and care for one another. They also cared deeply about their fellow residents of Motyzhyn.

Her mother has been Motyzhyn's mayor since 2006. Olena says she was deeply loved and respected in the village.

According to Olena, thanks to her mother, Motyzhyn had paved roads, street lights, and other improvements. She was also praised for arranging village celebrations and supporting local war veterans and the elderly. For that, Olena says, she was called the 'soul of the village'.

185

'Everybody loved her,' Olena said. 'The elderly would come to her office just to chat ... She has been helping everyone and never refused.'

Her father, Ihor, owned two grocery stores in the village and did a lot of electrical work for the locals. Olena says they jokingly called him a 'husband of the village's council' since he helped his wife a great deal. They had a wonderful life together, Olena said.

Olena's family house in Motyzhyn was filled with joy and laughter every time the family got together. Along with her husband and their little daughter, Olena visited almost every weekend. So did her younger brother Oleksandr, who was 25 at the time he was killed.

Olena said she was beyond close with her brother and spoke to him every day. They both lived in Kyiv, Olena with her family and Oleksandr with his girlfriend. 'He was a part of me,' she says. 'I loved him very much.'

Oleksandr worked as a manager at a local construction company. He was also a local football star, having played with several Ukrainian football clubs. Olena said he was a true patriot of Ukraine and was very much in love with his girlfriend Daria, whom he had dated for seven years. 'They were delaying getting married, expecting to have a long life together,' Olena says.

Shortly before the war, she recalled him saying that he had only now started living his life to the fullest, having a 'good job, friends and many plans for the future'.

It didn't last long.

Until the end

The possibility of Russia's all-out invasion of Ukraine had been discussed in Olena's family for months.

They even came up with an eventuality: Olena and Oleksandr, with their loved ones, would come to Motyzhyn in case something happened in Kyiv.

'We believed that it would be safer to stay in a smaller town,' Olena said.

They came to Motyzhyn the day Russia attacked Ukraine on 24 February. They were not the only ones who fled Kyiv to the neighboring villages: Olena says Motyzhyn's population of 1,000 residents increased fourfold at the beginning of the war.

Her mother immediately took an active role in coordinating the village's life during the war. Olena's father and brother soon joined the local Territorial Defense unit.

Even though they heard explosions nearby, they never expected something so horrible would take place in their hometown.

On 27 Febuary, however, Russian tanks entered the village. 'I saw them from the balcony of our house,' she says. 'I can't even describe the feeling ... The earth was buzzing.'

Then she heard about the village's first victim. A man, who was crossing the road in front of Russian occupiers, was shot and wounded. A local doctor volunteered to take him to the hospital outside Motyzhyn. But Russian soldiers shelled the car, killing both men.

'Then I realized I had to save my baby,' Olena says.

Although she did not want to leave her parents behind, the stories of slain civilians made her flee the village on 4 March. Olena's father drove in front of her car to give her a chance to save herself in case of shelling. He escorted her to the nearest Ukrainian-controlled village.

'I pressed my hand to the window to say goodbye to him, and that was it,' Olena recalls.

Her family members hadn't even considered leaving Motyzhyn because there were so many people depending on them, says Olena.

At the very start of the war, Olena's father gave away all the goods from his stores to the locals, while her mother delivered milk from a local plant to women with children. Risking their lives, they visited Motyzhyn residents every day, trying to provide people in need with food, medicine and other support.

They also helped people escape the village by car and hosted the family of a local Territorial Defense commander, whose house was destroyed by a missile.

'They decided that they would stay in the village with their people until the end,' she says.

Abduction, torture, murder

On the morning of 23 March, Olena called her mother as usual. Her brother picked up.

'He told me that Russian soldiers came to their house and searched it,' she says. 'They took his car and left.'

Terrified, Olena asked her family to leave the house and find a safe place. 'He told me "why would they come back here if they had already taken the car?"' she recalls. 'It was so stupid but hopeful to believe that they would not come back.'

But they did. Several hours after the search, Russian forces returned and took Olha. Her husband did not want to leave his wife and went together with her.

Olena called her brother and again urged him to leave the house. In response, Oleksandr told her he would wait for their parents at home since he 'reached an agreement with Russians that they will bring them back alive'.

'He decided that those ... beasts could be trusted,' Olena says.

She would soon receive a message from him saying that 'everything was fine with them, but he has to turn the phone off'. Even though Olena wanted to believe him, she knew they were not fine.

'He couldn't go anywhere because he thought they would do something to our parents if he left,' Olena says. 'I think that if I stayed there, I would sit and wait for my parents just like he did.'

Eventually, Russian occupiers returned and abducted Oleksandr.

Olena and Oleksandr's girlfriend spent the next few days searching for Olena's family, reaching out to locals and authorities, as well as spreading information about them on social media.

Olena says she texted them every day, hoping they would read her messages. More than anything, she wanted to save them.

On 2 April, after Kyiv Oblast was liberated from Russian occupiers, Ukrainian troops found freshly disturbed ground in a forest around Motyzhyn.

There they were, the people she loved, buried in a shallow grave in the woods.

Her mother had been shot in the head several times. Her brother and father had been violently tortured: Oleksandr had some punctures on his neck and her father's face was heavily damaged. Both were also shot multiple times and had their hands tied behind their backs.

'Humans can't do what they did to my family,' she says.

Other details of the abduction and murder are yet to be established. Though Olena wants the case to be investigated in the European Court of Human Rights, she knows nothing would ever bring her family back or ease her pain. 'In one moment, I became not a daughter and sister, but just an adult without a family.'

They were buried in Motyzhyn on 7 April. Olena says, up to 400 people came to say goodbye to them.

Now, she doesn't know how to enter that empty house that only weeks earlier was filled with the laughter of the people she loved most. 'Maybe, our nation is built on such people. Our history is written thanks to such people, and wars end in victories for us thanks to such people,' Olena says. 'Heroes ... I will remember them as heroes.'

23 May 2022

Russian soldier jailed for life for killing civilian in Ukraine, lawyer prepares appeal

Anna Myroniuk

A Kyiv court sentenced Russian soldier Vadim Shishimarin, 21, to life in prison for killing a civilian in Sumy Oblast during the Russian troops' retreat on 28 February.

Shishimarin pleaded guilty to fatally shooting his victim, adding that he didn't want to kill him. While the defense asked for the soldier's acquittal, the judges on 23 May ruled that he is guilty of a war crime and deserves the harshest available punishment.

'Even though the defendant said he did not intend to kill, the court does not trust these claims and believes there was an intent,' said judge Serhiy Ahafonov.

Shishimarin is the first Russian soldier convicted of a war crime in Ukraine.

As of 23 May, the Prosecutor General's Office said it was investigating 12,909 alleged Russian war crimes.

Prosecutor General Iryna Venediktova said on 23 May that 4,600 civilians, including 232 children, have been killed in Ukraine since Russia began its all-out war on 24 February. According to the United Nations, at least 2,345 civilians have been killed in Ukraine.

Shishimarin shot 62-year-old Oleksandr Shelipov in the head in the village of Chupakhivka. He said he was following a fellow soldier's order.

The order constitutes a war crime, as it violates the Geneva Convention, which protects the civilian population during war, Ahafonov said. Moreover, the order came from a soldier who was not Shishimarin's commanding officer and whom he did not know.

'He was not obligated to carry out that order,' Ahafonov said.

Shishimarin's lawyer, Viktor Ovsyannikov, who asked the court to acquit his defendant despite him pleading guilty, said he would appeal.

'The actions of my defendant have been judged incorrectly,' Ovsyannikov said. The lawyer believes Shishimarin did not commit a war crime but didn't say what kind of crime he believes the soldier committed.

The court said that it also chose the harshest punishment for Shishimarin because he breached the territorial integrity of Ukraine by participating in the Russian invasion and killed a noncombatant senior citizen.

27 May 2022

Domestic violence victims struggle to get help amid war: 'If Russians don't kill me – he might'

Thaisa Semenova

After three missed calls, Kristina picks up the phone and says, barely above a whisper: 'I can't talk now. I'm not alone.' When calling back, she turns on the tub in the bathroom so her husband can't hear her.

For several months, she had been gathering the strength to leave her husband, who was inflicting psychological and physical abuse on her. Days before Russia began its full-scale invasion on 24 February, she had finally made up her mind, agreeing with her mother to move into her place in a village near

Mykolaiv, a regional capital in the south of Ukraine. But her mother got sick with Covid-19 and they decided to wait until she recovered.

Now she's trapped with her husband in their apartment in Mykolaiv, leaving it only to go for groceries or to the bomb shelter.

'Sometimes, I don't want to leave the bomb shelter, even when there's no air raid alert. At least he won't beat me when we are surrounded by other people. I feel like if the Russians don't kill me, he might,' Kristina, whose last name we don't publish for security reasons, told *The Kyiv Independent*.

She says her husband has become even more violent than usual during the war. Once, he hit her in the stomach because he thought she was flirting with a neighbor while hiding in the bomb shelter. 'He said I smiled too friendly and then started to hit me,' she recalls.

According to psychotherapist Maria Fabrycheva, the aggression of a domestic tyrant is usually a manifestation of helplessness when a person is afraid, so expectedly in times of war abusers may snap at their victim more often. 'Abusers cannot express a normal feeling of fear healthily,' she said.

Intimate partner violence is the most common form of violence against women in both conflict and non-conflict settings, according to the World Bank. Armed conflict, regardless of its character or sides involved, exacerbates existing inequalities and places women at a heightened risk of violence, the United Nations Committee on the Elimination of Discrimination against Women said in a report.

Kateryna Pavlichenko, deputy interior minister, reported that about 326,000 domestic violence cases were registered in Ukraine last year. Getting an accurate count of cases is difficult now, as many victims don't turn to the police or simply don't have the opportunity to do so due to active hostilities.

Struggle to seek help
'Unfortunately, hostilities have become a catalyst for the exacerbation of domestic violence in families where these facts existed before the war,' said Alyona Krivulyak, one of the leaders of La Strada Ukraine, a non-governmental organization that runs a national hotline for the prevention of domestic violence, human trafficking and gender discrimination.

Law enforcement agencies, especially in places where active hostilities are ongoing, often can't respond to calls, further exacerbating the problem, Krivulyak said. The police also have an increased workload due to war-related issues.

Marta Chumalo, a co-founder of the Women's Perspectives nonprofit in Lviv, said the war has made it more difficult to access help even in cities where there is no active fighting as the police departments have to prioritize preparations for possible attacks.

'We know of cases when a woman wanted to file a complaint against an offender or get an update on her case but was told to come back later and that there were more pressing issues,' Chumalo said. 'Another victim called the police, and they responded: "It's an air raid, we can't come, we can talk to him on the phone." How can a physical threat be solved over the phone?'

Of course, it is not always the case that the police don't respond to domestic violence calls, she said, but seeking help has for sure become more challenging.

In the event it's not possible to contact the police, for example, in temporarily occupied territories, women can get help at medical institutions, Krivulyak suggested. She added that doctors are obliged not only to provide assistance to domestic violence victims but also to document such cases. This will help to hold abusers accountable in the future.

'Victims can also turn to Territorial Defense forces. No, they don't have the power to prosecute, but they can enforce the order.'

Before the war, the police could issue an urgent injunction requiring the offender to leave the premises within 10 days. This is now only possible in safer regions, where the security situation allows for it.

'Despite a common understanding that this is very wrong, the police cannot force the abuser to leave the premises due to the fighting. They can't throw a person out during rocket fire. The court cannot do that now either,' said Krivulyak.

Psychotherapist Fabrycheva said if there's an opportunity to leave the abuser and ask for help from family or close friends, the victim should do so. But the victims often don't see the benefit of leaving, hoping that 'tomorrow everything will be fine, he will change', or even blame themselves for the violence and pity the abuser.

'One should ask oneself: "Do I want to continue my life with someone who never, even in a critical situation such as war, not only can't protect but also attacks me?"' she said.

The victim's family and friends should understand that a person in such a difficult physiological state is unlikely to make a decision of leaving on their own, so an intervention may be needed, Fabrycheva stressed. 'All over the country, we see the consequences of a tyrant's actions. The domestic tyrant is the same, only on a small scale. Too often, women find reasons to stay. But they have to pass the Rubicon and say: "Enough. I choose myself."'

Fleeing abroad

Some victims of domestic violence who couldn't find help in Ukraine have turned to local police and social services abroad.

Chumalo said that quite a few women who have suffered from domestic violence have fled abroad, taking advantage of the fact that martial law imposed during the war allows women to take their children abroad without official permission from the other parent.

'I can say that they probably didn't flee from bombardments in Lviv since the situation is relatively safe, but from domestic violence. And now they can finally feel safe,' Chumalo said.

She added that abuse victims shouldn't be afraid to ask for help from local support centers as there is a well-established procedure in the European Union countries.

Mariia Goubernik, a 22-year-old from Donetsk, and her younger sisters Taisiia and Oleksandra have suffered their father's abuse their entire lives. Their mother silently ignored the abuse, according to Taisiia. The eldest daughter never turned to the police in Ukraine, afraid that they wouldn't react appropriately, and her sisters, who live with parents, unlike her, would have to come back home to an even worse situation.

'I know how often domestic violence cases don't even end up in court, no proceedings are opened,' she said.

In mid-March, when the family came to a refugee shelter in Calpe in southern Spain, their father hit the youngest daughter, nine-year-old Oleksandra, on the head. Mariia and Taisiia found her sitting in the corner of the shelter sobbing in hysterics, repeatedly saying: 'I'm scared. I'm scared. I'm scared ...'

The situation had reached a point of no return, Mariia thought, and it was time to hold their father accountable. The sisters agreed that after having to flee home twice – first moving to Kyiv in 2014 after Russian proxies took control over the eastern city of Donetsk, then going abroad on 24 February – they truly deserved a calm life. That evening they googled the nearest police station and went there on foot from the shelter for more than an hour.

They were taken immediately to an emergency women's shelter. Two days later, the Spanish court issued a preliminary decision prohibiting her father from approaching his children in just two days.

After the court hearing, Taisiia recalls, her mother blamed her children for the destruction of the family. 'Mom wants and can bring our father back. But if he tries to come here to our hotel, it is solved very simply– we'll call the police as he would violate the court's decision,' Mariia Goubernik said.

Gourbernik said the fear still remains that the next court decision may overturn the first one as the Spanish court can only consider cases that took place in Spain, and her father didn't commit severe bodily assault there. However, she believes there's no going back to the previous ways. 'Domestic violence cases are taken very seriously here,' she said.

Personal note from Alexander Query, reporter

After more than two months of war, nobody panics any more in Kyiv when the sirens blare out.

It's May and warm enough outside to leave the windows open, bringing in the smell of spring's return as the city comes back to life.

We finally take the time to enjoy a cigarette on the balcony while trying to blot out the horrors outside. We can't forget, but the mind does need at least a semblance of normality to face the madness of a man hidden in a Russian bunker.

I was lucky. I feel guilty because I'd been lucky. Unlike a lot of Ukrainians, I escaped the worst and, in comparison, we have been spared the horrors that Russia has forced on Ukraine. *The Kyiv Independent* is still there, as is Ukraine. Some friends are dead; others are wounded, both physically and psychologically. One gets used to everything, even war. My girlfriend and I have adopted a dog. And yet, I was far from playing it cool on the fateful morning of 24 February.

Last drink before the end of the world
On the evening of 23 February, while my girlfriend was away in the country for a few days near Kyiv, I decided to relax a bit between two articles. A thought crossed my mind while I headed towards the Alchemist, a local bar where I have my habits. 'It's the last drink before the end of the world,' I thought to myself with a vague smile – a toast I regularly repeated that evening. Little did we know.

The strikes started the following morning. With my mind all hazy, the deadened shock of the missiles and the black smoke over the town caught me off-guard at first. Then reality settled. It was the beginning of a waking nightmare.

In a flash, I remembered the infernal sequence that had led to this disaster, trying to focus despite those sirens which were to become the soundtrack of my life from now on.

Declarations of 'independence' from territories now occupied by Russia, Putin's mouth twisted with hate, puffy with rage and still confident in a quick victory. Armchair experts had already pronounced Kyiv dead and Ukraine taken by the horde, while millions of existences shattered that day because of one man's madness. The future would prove them wrong.

I had come to cover the war in 2016 and had found myself at home in Ukraine. History was in the making in this land, and I wanted to be there to witness it first-hand. I had started on the front line, and the front line was now kicking at my door. Leave or stay? Put my fiancée in safety and come back to

work in the besieged capital? We had spent weeks before the invasion arguing about this subject. She had made fun of me when we went to the local
supermarket, a few days earlier, to stock up on provisions in case of a siege.
She was now caught in the traffic jams a few kilometers from Kyiv trying to
get back to the capital through the chaos of evacuations.

Fear. What will the Russians do if they take Kyiv? What is my life worth
when confronted with the urgency of doing my job, compared to what I owe
Ukraine? But the fear disappeared, diluting itself within the sense of duty. My
great declarations would be of no use if I left now. More than ever, Ukraine
needed journalists. I had to stay, even if it meant learning how to live under
the bombs.

Once my girlfriend had got back, we rearranged our flat as a bunker. The
mattresses were placed in the corridor, with drinking water, the plugs nearby.
Taping over the windows, keeping away from them, regretting buying an
apartment with such high ceilings.

Taking small, quiet steps, as if the Russians were already here. The sirens
continued — why not try to go to the underground in case there's another
attack? We had studied the maps of Kyiv, to know if we were near a building
that could be attacked. We didn't know it yet, but the maps the Russians were
using dated back to the 1980s. It would prove fatal for them at Chornobyl,
where they would dig in to protect themselves from the Ukrainian artillery. We rejoiced in their slow death and burnt-out Z-marked tanks. I could
now eat breakfast while watching pictures of dead Russian soldiers without
a flinch.

We took our over-heavy bags and headed for the underground. Groups
of people were gathering to listen to Zelensky's speech. I tried to work but
without plugs, my batteries didn't last long. I had to make a choice: stay up
above ground and work, or protect myself in a shelter which could become
a fatal trap if the bombs block it.

Boredom, waiting, faces marked by anguish. Back to the flat, trying to cozy
up as well as we can while waiting for the next missile to hit the city. The first
night of total war is us waiting in the dark.

Missiles strike at dawn
The air was contaminated when we came up out of the underground. The
town was grey, the atmosphere stern. The bitter smell of the apocalypse
floated in the air. Locals' shadowy figures were running from one point to
another, with their bags and their animals. The underground was full as we
left it. The Russians' strategy was simple: wear Kyivians down. The missiles
struck at dawn, when everybody managed at last to get some shuteye for
a few hours of precious sleep; and during all that time, we worked. The *Kyiv*

Post team, which sacked us all, had deserted its post – their editor-in-chief is in Barcelona, proclaiming his patriotism on the social networks.

Olga [*The Kyiv Independent*'s editor-in-chief] was very clear on our work chat: SAFETY ABOVE EVERYTHING ELSE, in all caps. Safety above everything else – but with the duty in mind. At *The Kyiv Independent,* our mission is to inform the world about what is happening in Ukraine and the sense of duty was overwhelming.

I had suddenly become the go-to guy for a few French media in need of reports on the ground, hour after hour. This monotonous work was taking a toll on the hours I owed to *The Kyiv Independent,* making me frustrated and moody. Time to wake up and accept the situation.

I'm not a war correspondent; I am a journalist in a war zone. With one difference compared with the international journalists who come to cover the conflict for a few weeks: I live here. Every decision I take could put my family in danger if the Russians take Kyiv.

The Russian invasion progresses, as do the saboteurs. After nightfall you can hear the shots. We are not far from the center, not far from the presidential administration. The Battle of Kyiv had started before the Russian troops had even reached the borders of the oblast. We keep ourselves up to date about where we are and what we are doing. We spent the first weekend of the war under a curfew with my girlfriend, Igor, Asami and a friend in our apartment. An illusion of protection. Maintaining the link, in the dark, of what constitutes our humanity when confronting the animals that are so determined to destroy Ukraine. We learned to spot the sounds of the missiles. We were not ready. When we came back from the underground we repacked our bags – they were too heavy. We don't need all those clothes, no need for that book, or so many notebooks. If we flee, it won't be a trip which will allow us the luxury of keeping all that we want. Only the strict minimum. If we leave ...

Stress adds up to panic. Rumors are running around that the center of Kyiv could be hit. And still the same nagging question: where is the border between courage and foolhardiness? A new life is opening up, regulated by the expected explosions from outside. Our personal rhythm adapts to curfews. I will have to re-learn how to live in the deserted capital.

Igor and I came out of the flat after two days of curfew, with bulletproof vests on our backs and helmets on our heads, dressed up as if the Russians were already here. I felt particularly stupid, all geared up in deserted Kreshchatyk Street, passing in front of people queuing for food in the rare open stores. I decided I wouldn't wear my bulletproof vest in Kyiv any more. Those pictures of other reporters, wanting to add exoticism to the situation by wearing their protective gear in the capital, start to get on my nerves. The very idea of filming oneself on the balcony of a hotel with a bulletproof jacket makes my eyes roll. Bitterness takes over.

And the 'and ifs' – 'and if I had a car ... and if I had a cameraman ... I could do all this'. I'm not a special war correspondent: I am a correspondent. I will have to get used to this slightly indefinite status that comes with the fact of living in Kyiv.

My colleagues at *The Kyiv Independent* are exemplary. When one of them drops from fatigue, another replaces them to keep feeding the stream of news, which is going to become one of the newspaper's hallmarks for success. I don't know if they ask themselves as many questions as I do. We try to avoid talking about our emotions. It's too early, we have too much work to do. What I see is the urgency to write, to tell, to describe history, to be a part of it.

They are not the only ones. A growing number of Ukrainian journalists have to face the grueling ordeal of seeing their very own country being carved up every day, forced to maintain a certain detachment to talk about Ukraine's wounds despite the pain, like an amputee who forces their eyes to stay open during the operation long enough to designate the culprit.

28 May 2022

'Welcome to hell': Ukrainian airborne fighting Russia in Donbas woods

Illia Ponomarenko and Kostyantyn Chernichkin

The battlefield stretches through the dense forest on the banks of the Siversky Donets River.

Soldiers with Ukraine's 79th Airborne Brigade crawl out of sandy trenches, preparing their 40 mm under-barrel rounds.

Barrels up, they aim at an imperceptible enemy line running some 300 meters away, hidden behind a wall of tall pines.

'Three, four, fire!'

The ensuing whistle and blast merge with the never-ending thunder of artillery barrage on either side.

'Those f*cks should know we're still here and ready,' the paratroopers say as they lay down their weapons to rest and seek cover.

Here, as in many other parts of Donbas, Ukrainian fighters rarely see their enemies' faces.

The largest and bloodiest battle in Europe since World War II is, in many ways, a cutthroat duel between Russian and Ukrainian artillery. Russia has a clear numerical advantage in this fight, gradually securing its gains by eliminating the Ukrainian lines that stand in its way.

The decisive battle has been going on for nearly 40 days. Russia is slowly and painfully pressing through Ukrainian defenses, turning villages to ashes in its wake.

Now, amid recent progress by Russia, the situation in the region is reaching a critical point.

Despite heavy losses, Ukraine's military continues to fight hard, trying to wear out Russian forces. Surprisingly, given the circumstances, morale remains high among Ukrainian troops.

The river war

The 79th Airborne Brigade is holding the line in terrain that is quite localized within Donbas – the densely forested pine woods of northern Donetsk Oblast.

The area was once very popular for its numerous holiday resorts and summer getaways. These days, children's summer camps harbor weary troops between battles and cottages once frequented by vacationers are used as frontline strongholds.

The 79th fire support company has dug its trenches in the deep forests south of Lyman, a key city that has been hit hard by Russia's war.

Little villages within several kilometers of the front line have since been abandoned.

The zone of action welcomes those who venture near with the phrase 'WELCOME TO HELL' written in large Russian script by Ukrainian soldiers across a shrapnel-riddled metal fence. Scores of Uragan missile tails peeking up from the ground get the mood across.

In late May, the fierce battle waged in Donbas turned grim as Russia managed to deploy fresh reserves and amp up the pressure on already-depleted Ukrainian forces.

Russia has, over the past few weeks, largely abandoned its axis near the city of Izium, Kharkiv Oblast, and concentrated on areas at the border of Donetsk and Luhansk oblasts, as well as on the northern bank of the Siversky Donets River.

Rather than trying to encircle the entirety of Ukraine's military in the east, Russia was forced to suppress its appetite by instead isolating and destroying smaller pockets of troops.

After over a month of stalled offensives, Russian forces have finally managed to make steady progress in the southeast near the ruined community of Popasna, Luhansk Oblast. Russian forces have compromised the key T1302 highway (nicknamed 'the road of life'), which connects the twin cities of Sievierodonetsk and Lysychansk in Luhansk Oblast with Donetsk Oblast.

Russia now keeps the principal Ukrainian supply line under fire control and threatens to cut it off completely.

A continuous onslaught of Russian forces from the north has also pushed weary Ukrainian defenses towards the banks of the Siversky Donets River. Following Russian airstrikes and a massive artillery barrage on Lyman, Ukrainian forces have had to retreat south again.

Continuous attempts by Russia to cross the river and merge with the Popasna axis raise fears of a large Ukrainian group getting cut off in Sievierodonetsk–Lysychansk.

However, the latest developments indicate that the Ukrainian command decided to reinforce the Sievierodonetsk garrison, rather than withdraw. Russia has to get through over 20 kilometers of fighting to close the pocket.

Large Ukrainian forces, including the 79th Airborne units, are maintaining the defense in the forests of Siversky Donets that comprise the Holy Mountains National Nature Park, fighting hard to prevent Russian forces from crossing the river.

Burning skies
The 79th's anti-tank unit's trenches have an extensive arsenal of western-provided anti-tank weapons.

Swedish-made 84 mm AT4s, American M141s (SMAW-Ds), widespread British NLAWs, and rarer RGW-90 MATADORs, all lean against the earthen trench walls next to machine guns pointed against the deep forest.

'Our big regards to taxpayers giving us these toys,' the paratroopers laugh. 'This forest has a lot of destroyed Russian vehicles if someone wants an illustrated cost performance report.'

9 May, the day on which Russia commemorates the Allied victory of World War II, was believed to have been Russia's deadline for its success in Donbas and the company witnessed the most savage Russian assault in weeks.

A large Russian party led by a BTR-80 personnel carrier appeared from behind the cover of trees and engaged in a frontal attack on the 79th's trenches.

'That was a sort of their weird way to celebrate the 9 May,' says Ukrainian soldier Maksym Chuprun. 'We thought we'd be done here. But some of us here, including myself, started running here and there all the time behind the machine guns and opening fire all the time. We were just trying to make an impression of a far larger force standing here.'

'And it worked! We were hearing them shouting on their comms: "Shit, there are 60 of them here!" But in reality, there were just a handful of paratroopers.'

The Russian attack failed: the 79th's airborne damaged the Russian BTR with a SMAW-D (which is not supposed to be used as an anti-tank weapon in the first place) and some 70 meters away a couple of RPG-18 Mukha shots finished off the vehicle.

After having sustained losses, the Russian infantry retreated into the woods under crossfire.

This incident is just one of many treacherous moments during the war. What lies ahead is an even more brutal fight, as Russia has done everything possible to squeeze Ukrainian forces from the river banks toward Sloviansk and Kramatorsk, the region's main fortresses.

Artillery barrage on the flanks, meanwhile, never stops.

Once every 10 to 15 minutes, the thunder of artillery fire gets so intense that even the most battle-hardened troops are on alert. Russian BM-21 Gran missile systems splutter constantly, barraging distant Ukrainian lines.

'That's just nothing,' the soldiers say. 'In the night, the sky is shining bright here sometimes because of artillery.'

Blood on the truck

Luckily, the distant strikes do not get any closer.

Time moves slowly. Every four-hour combat shift takes place behind machine guns with cigarettes in hand, silent, straining endlessly to catch a glimpse of potential enemies hidden in the distance.

Reprieve is granted as a new set of heavily geared paratroopers carrying anti-tank tubes on their shoulder emerge from the forest – it's shift change.

Troops off shift can finally return to the abandoned basements where they have been sheltering for some cheap coffee, canned meat, and hopefully a few hours of sleep on a mattress in a dark corner with a pair of earphones in.

The comms are buzzing at all times in the semi-darkness, issuing warnings about Russian drones scanning their sector.

'Orlan-10 has been spotted, disguising mode on,' a radio set buzzes.

'Plus,' soldiers say, giving the standard reply.

'You know, when Russians ask for a peace treaty, we should make it one of the conditions that they replace the word "*orel*" ["eagle"] with the word "*kozel*" ["goat"],' says a paratrooper, spreading canned meat on a slice of bread with a knife. 'So they will have to call their drones not Orlan but Kozlan. I just hate those things.'

In these parts, Orlans are the grim messengers of Russian artillery.

Even in the rear shelters, soldiers keep their rifles close at hand, sometimes even hugging them to their chest as they take a nap.

'You could see those huge rusty stains on the bottom of my Ford pickup truck,' says a battalion deputy leader, sipping hot Nescafé from a plastic cup and mixing it with cigarette smoke in the dark. 'Well it's not rust. It's the blood of a Russian soldier. We took him the other day when a Russian squad tried to attack us here in the night. They thought we were an Alpha Spetznaz group or something and got out. They left this young dude behind, injured.'

'We tried to talk to him. He was 20, maybe 21. He only managed to say that his name was Vadim, he served with the 15th Guards Motorized Rifle Brigade, and that his unit's main mission in the area was to just get entrenched and wait.'

'But that was it – he kicked the bucket in my truck as I was trying to evacuate him.'

1 June 2022

Russia destroys Ukraine's historic heritage, steals rare collections from museums

Natalia Datskevych

In 1937, Pablo Picasso, widely acknowledged as one of the greatest painters in history, said after visiting an exhibition in Paris: 'I bow down before the artistic miracle of this brilliant Ukrainian.' He was talking about the folk painter Maria Prymachenko and her paintings in the 'naive art' genre.

Eighty-five years later, on 26 February, a collection of 25 of her works almost burned up when the Russian military fired on a museum in the village of Ivankovo in Kyiv Oblast. The museum's other exhibits, such as works of the Ukrainian embroiderer Hanna Veres, did not survive the fire. 'Putin wants to destroy European heritage and culture, wipe them off the face of the earth,' Ukraine's Culture Minister Oleksandr Tkachenko said in early March.

Almost 100 days into the Kremlin's large-scale invasion of Ukraine, hundreds of cultural heritage sites in the country have been destroyed and thousands of rare historical artifacts have been stolen.

As of 27 May, the Culture Ministry has documented 367 war crimes against Ukraine's cultural heritage, including the destruction of 29 museums, 133 churches, 66 theaters and libraries, and even a century-old Jewish cemetery. This cemetery in Hlukhiv, Sumy Oblast, which is a site of pilgrimage for Jews, was hit by two Russian missiles on 8 May.

'Russians have the precise aim of destroying our culture as part of our identity, something that distinguishes Ukraine from Russia,' Bloomberg quoted Olha Honchar, co-founder of Ukraine's Museum Crisis Center, as saying. 'It has become quite clear now for the whole world that Russia bombs museums, archives, and theaters not by accident.'

Wave of destruction

The destruction of the museum in Ivankovo was just the beginning. Russia's barbaric bombing barrage has wrecked many iconic artifacts of the nation's storied past.

In three months of the all-out war, Kharkiv Oblast, which borders Russia, saw the most damage to art and landmarks. By mid-May, every fourth crime against Ukraine's cultural heritage was recorded there.

Most of these crimes in the region, 79 cases, took place in Kharkiv itself, the regional capital and Ukraine's second-largest city. In early March, a Russian fire smashed the windows of the Kharkiv Art Museum, which housed 25,000 masterpieces by Ukrainian and world artists.

A version of the famous painting 'Cossacks Write a Letter to the Turkish Sultan' by Ukrainian-born artist Ilya Repin was evacuated from the museum, according to Marina Filatova, the head of the foreign art department. The main version of the painting is in a museum in Russia, like many artworks created by Ukrainians during the Russian Empire times.

However, the state of many other rare and old paintings displayed in the museum can only be assessed after the war. Museum workers had to remove them from the walls in a rush.

On the night of 7 May, Russian missiles hit the museum and historic home of Ukraine's famous poet and philosopher Hryhoriy Skovoroda, located in the village of Skovorodynivka in Kharkiv Oblast. The building was severely damaged, and a number of valuable exhibits were buried under the rubble.

'Not every terrorist will even think about targeted missile strikes on museums,' President Volodymyr Zelensky said in response to the destruction. 'And this is the kind of army that is fighting against us.'

Some of the worst of the devastation hit the city of Mariupol in Donetsk Oblast. It lost 53 historic sites, including its drama theater, built in the late 1880s. This theater was destroyed on 16 March by a bomb dropped by a Russian aircraft, which reportedly killed at least 600 civilians that were taking shelter there.

A month later, the city council reported that Russian occupiers had looted a unique 700-piece collection of coins and medals from a local museum in Mariupol. They allegedly transported the collection to the Russian-occupied part of Donetsk Oblast.

An art museum named after Arkhip Kuindzhi, a famous Mariupol-born landscape painter of Pontic Greek descent, was robbed as well.

On 27 April, invaders took all valuable exhibits from the museum, including three Kuindzhi paintings and 'Near the Shores of the Caucasus', an original painting by famed marine artist Ivan Aivazovsky.

The looted Kuindzhi piece called 'Red Sunset', painted over 115 years ago, alone costs more than $700,000, according to Tatyana Buli, the head of the museum, who evacuated the city and is now in Kyiv.

'What I hid [in the basement of the museum], it survived,' Buli told the BBC. 'But you see, everything was handed over to the occupiers.'

Russian media reported that more than 2,000 exhibits were taken out of Mariupol museums for 'temporary storage' in occupied Donetsk.

In four other Ukrainian oblasts – Kyiv, Chernihiv, Sumy, and Luhansk – the ministry recorded almost 160 war crime cases against historical heritage.

In the 1,300-year-old city of Chernihiv, the Russian military destroyed the former museum of Ukrainian antiquities, a 19th-century building built in the Gothic Revival style, most recently serving as a youth library.

'The building survived shelling by the Bolsheviks in 1918 and 1919 and World War II under the bombs of the German Nazis,' wrote Serhiy Laevsky, the director of the history museum in Chernihiv. 'The Moscow Nazi horde came and ruined a monument of local history.'

In late April, Ivan Fedorov, the mayor of the occupied city of Melitopol in Zaporizhzhia Oblast, reported another shocking news: Russian invaders stole a 'unique and priceless' collection of 2,300-years-old Scythian gold from the local history museum in Melitopol.

Gold artifacts were discovered in massive burial mounds, known as kurgans, by archaeologists in the 1950s. In all, the occupiers stole 198 items, including floral ornaments and breastplates, according to the Crimean Tatar Resource Center.

They also took non-Scythian exhibits, like 48 pieces of historical weaponry from the 17th through the 20th centuries, as well as 76 items made at least 1,500 years ago.

'This is one of the largest and most expensive collections in Ukraine,' said Fedorov.

Poor preparation

While Russian forces are to blame for the destruction of so much of Ukraine's cultural heritage, some Ukrainian experts believe the country hasn't done enough to protect its art and history before the escalation.

Eight days before Russia's invasion of Ukraine, art historian Konstantin Akinsha was horrified at what might happen to museums if war broke out.

Most museums were not prepared.

'In a full-scale Russian invasion, practically all significant museum collections would be in danger,' Akinsha wrote in his column for the *Wall Street Journal*.

'The majority of museums have miserable budgets and would not even be able to afford the necessary crates,' he said. Underfunding has made the notion of evacuating exhibits to safer facilities under guard even hazier.

Moreover, the Culture Ministry had not prepared any plans for the centralized evacuation of museum exhibits or instructions on how to act during a war, according to Tetyana Rud, chief curator of the Kharkiv Literary Museum.

The decision to save the collections fell on the shoulders of each museum separately.

'Most of the buildings have basements, where many directors heroically spent the first two weeks of the war,' said Yana Barinova, the head of Kyiv City Council's cultural department.

The highest levels of government made no other publicly known efforts to preserve the museum collections in the days leading up to the war. Barinova believes the protection of museum collections was not a top priority for the government.

It was 'part of President Volodymyr Zelensky's efforts to prevent panic', Akinsha believes.

3 June 2022

100 days of Russia's war: What our staff learned about their country, the world, and themselves

The Kyiv Independent staff

Editor's Note: As 3 June marks 100 days of Russia's all-out war, The Kyiv Independent *publishes its staff's takes on what they have learned or understood over this time.*

Olga Rudenko, editor-in-chief

100 days. When Russia started its invasion in February, it was impossible to imagine this catastrophe would be on for 100 days with still no end in sight.

100 days may sound vague, but each day represents thousands of tragedies: lives lost, people tortured and raped, homes destroyed.

But it's not all a pure nightmare, it's also a time of revelations. People show their true colors, ideas get shaped, and societal trends manifest themselves.

I used to be reasonably skeptical when I heard that we, Ukrainians, were of an entirely different nature compared to our Russian neighbors. Yes, I thought, we are freedom-loving and have had three revolutions in less than 30 years, while Russians have allowed themselves to be dragged back into the swamp of authoritarianism without putting up a fight. But surely it must be a combination of factors from recent history that led to that? I thought, all people are vulnerable to succumb to the craziest of propaganda.

But this invasion completely changed the way I think about the differences between the Ukrainian and Russian people.

Russians aren't a normal nation who got lost and turned the wrong way, or got unlucky that an authoritarian ruler came to power. No, they turned the wrong way many times, impossible to know how long ago, until finally the country became what it is: a fascist state – no, a fascist society, a mix of aggressors and their apathetic accomplices. The way they have swallowed up the murderous war against their neighbors and cheer on the killings and rapes is an indictment not of the Russian state, but of Russians as a group. Their state will be defeated and they will have to reinvent themselves as a nation.

Ukrainians, on the other hand, aren't a group that got 'lucky' for getting Viktor Yanukovych instead of Vladimir Putin. There is a reason for why there hasn't been a Putin in Ukraine, and that reason is that the Ukrainian people would never tolerate Putin. In Ukraine, there is no societal demand for a violent strongman in power. The Ukrainian people's strength is in themselves. They don't need a 'strong hand' – their own hands are strong enough, and they feel it. We saw it in the early days of the invasion, when regular people confronted armed Russian soldiers, and we see it today, with people protesting Russians in occupied Kherson, and with the Ukrainian military fighting fiercely at the front lines.

I'm not a social historian, and I can't explain what exactly led to this utter difference between the two people who have a shared past. But what this invasion made absolutely clear is that they don't have any shared future. Ukraine defeated Russia on the first day of the invasion, when it didn't surrender, and there is no changing that.

Igor Kossov, *investigative reporter*

Last independence day found me on the twilit summer streets of Kyiv that I've come to love so much.

I walked along Khreshchatyk Street, looking at all the families with blue and yellow ribbons, laughing couples and children with balloons. And I pictured Russia in the distance, coiled to strike.

And a thought popped into my head, fully formed, about how weird it is that as a Russian-Ukrainian (born in Kyiv and raised in New York), 'half of me came from this and half came from that which wants to destroy this'.

I didn't know how correct that phrasing would turn out to be. Because five months later, Russians forced their way in from all sides, destroying cities and murdering thousands.

Some of those fathers I saw on Khreshchatyk would be crouched in the trees, firing rocket launchers at Russian tanks or shot in the head with their arms bound. Some of those mothers and children would be torn apart by shells or driven into exile. Some would be tortured or raped.

My brain was trying to tell me something then, because I stupidly, irresponsibly underestimated Russia until the end. I hadn't fully realized how much it wanted to destroy Ukraine.

Russia doesn't just want the land. It doesn't just want the geopolitical dominance. It literally wants to annihilate what it means to be Ukrainian, as Putin, his cronies, his TV stations and loyal subjects have repeatedly stated. The fact that they haven't succeeded in most regions was not for lack of trying. They may as well have said '*Ukraine delenda est*'.

I bring this up because I'm not the only one who underestimated Russia's desire to destroy Ukraine. Many Western leaders and people were shocked at what they saw, when it should have been blindingly obvious to any of us if we had bothered to look.

And some of them still don't get it. Some still believe in treating the Kremlin as an honorable adversary at the negotiating table. Some of them are leaders.

If there's one thing we should have all realized is goddamn certain: Putin's Russia cannot be negotiated with. Only stopped. This thankless task falls on Ukraine's shoulders but it can't do it alone.

Daria Shulzhenko, reporter

This war made me realize how fragile a human life is. One moment you stand at a train station, expecting to evacuate from a town once beautiful and lively but so dreadfully mutilated by a brutal war, leaving everything behind to save the most valuable – life. A split second later comes a terrifying shrieking sound followed by a loud blast. It takes away everything – all dreams, plans, and hopes. And just like that, dozens of lives are taken away.

Such terror has been happening all over Ukraine for 100 days now. Ferociously and villainously, Russia kills innocent Ukrainians every day.

Right now, somewhere out there, a Ukrainian mother is crying over her killed child. She wants to recall her baby's laughter. Instead, her memory brings out the horrifying image of the dead body torn apart by a Russian missile. There is a grieving father who has lost his whole family and does not know how to keep on living, or a sister who mourns her brother tortured to death by Russian troops, by Russia itself.

Even though Russia has been abusing Ukraine not only for the past 100 days or eight years, but for decades and centuries, I have never fully realized how badly it wanted to wipe out my country.

Now I see that as long as Russia exists, as long as its imperialism is thriving, my life and the lives of all Ukrainians are under threat. Even this very moment could be my last moment just because I am Ukrainian. Just because Russia wants it that way.

And it's not only our task now but the world's task as well to never let Russia get what it wants. Because what it wants equals the end of Ukraine and the free world.

Asami Terajima, reporter

When I was a child, words like 'war' and 'missiles' sounded so foreign to me.

My young self assumed that there is unbreakable peace in the world and children no longer had to see their parents head to war – something that I only read about in textbooks. Never had I known how much of a privilege it was to enjoy that carefree childhood. To not know what air raid sirens and shelling sound like. To not know what the aftermath of a missile attack looks like. To not know what dead bodies smell like.

It's a privilege that Russia took away from millions of children across Ukraine.

Ever since Russia launched its full-scale invasion, more than half of the nation's children have had to flee their homes. As Moscow continues to wage war in Ukraine, more and more children are being exposed to unimaginable horrors.

There are kids who had to watch Russian soldiers torture and kill their parents. Russia's war did not just take away their youth, but also stopped the hearts of an unknown number of Ukrainian children. They never got the chance to grow up, go on a first date, and maybe even get in trouble in school and laugh about it years afterwards.

I still think about the 14-year-old survivor of the Mariupol siege whom I met weeks after her family barely escaped the bombed-out city. She showed me photos of her completely destroyed house and how the corpses of her classmate's family just laid there because no one could bury them due to relentless Russian bombardment. She still holds on to the photos, wondering whether her friend was buried.

I think about what I was doing at her age, and my heart aches. But it also made me realize how vital it is that we continue reporting – we need to make sure that the world is witnessing the toll of Russia's eight-year-war.

Toma Istomina, *deputy editor-in-chief*

Just minutes into the war, I learned that your own apartment can feel like the least safe place on earth. And that keeping busy with work can help you stay sane when your life is in danger. And that no matter how prepared you think you are, when your country is invaded from all fronts, as missiles rain down on your city, it turns your world upside down.

Weeks into the war, I learned that saving a single human life can push some people to sacrifice their own and that for others, thousands of lives are merely means that justify the ends. And that you can publish news about your hometown under fire with your family at risk and still be professional, as tears are running down your cheeks. And that the flowers you receive during a war easily beat any other bouquet you have ever held in your hands.

Months into the war, I learned that you can get used to death, to the overwhelming death that you hear and learn about every single day. And yet after a certain number of lives lost, you become numb to it because your mind can only take so much. I learned that you can work for months without proper time off and still be productive (though your boss may disagree on this one). And that you can paradoxically experience the most beautiful feeling during the darkest of times. Though enjoying it to the fullest is a challenge that you might not dare to take up. I learned that an act of bravery is the easiest thing to do when courage is part of your nature and that it's also absolutely unattainable for those who come short of it. Even 100 days into the war. Even after so many examples.

Alexander Query, *reporter*

100 days of war, and Ukraine is still standing. I already knew about the extraordinary strength and the Ukrainians' faith in their land but this war confirmed that these are not just words.

Ukrainians taught me a sense of duty I look up to and adopt in my daily routine. We, journalists, owe it to the soldiers defending Ukraine's sovereignty. We owe it to the countless victims of the war that Russia started against Ukraine eight years ago to erase a country whose only fault was to dream of its own future.

I've learned not to shy away from tragedies. Ukraine has 40 million stories to tell, and the world needs to listen.

There's always room for hope, and I've learned to cherish the friendships I've built here, hardened by the steel of war. There's no more room for self-pity, or fear. They dissolved in anger toward Russia.

I've learned to live with the knowledge that we may be hit by a Russian missile tomorrow. It means acting today without yielding to fear.

The center of Europe is now in Eastern Europe and the Baltics, where countries that know Russia too well won't back down in front of Vladimir Putin's madness. They know that fear is Putin's favorite weapon.

Fear shapes the moral compass of Western diplomacy. History books won't be kind to Germany, and France, where I'm from. I'm ashamed of my home-land's spineless excuses to hide cowardice in the face of a colossus with feet of clay.

Oleg Sukhov, reporter

Russia's full-scale invasion of Ukraine was not surprising to me. It is the logical culmination and (probably) the endgame of Putin's semi-totalitarian regime. Putin had been preparing for this invasion for years, and his regime had been evolving towards a more totalitarian and more war-mongering stage for decades.

As someone who used to live in Russia, I was not surprised that most of the Russian population either backed the aggression or didn't speak out against it due to conformism. This slavish and aggressive attitude was instilled during the seven decades of Soviet totalitarianism and the two decades of Putin's dictatorship. If Russia were a small country, this problem would not be as bad because Russia would not be able to harm anyone and would have to solve its domestic problems without launching aggressive wars. But the fact that Russia claims to be a great power poisons this attitude with insane imperial-ism, which will eventually kill the Russian state.

Putin's invasion of Ukraine has already cut off all cultural, political and eco-nomic ties that Russia could have had with Ukraine and ensured that Ukraine will never be part of Russia's sphere of influence. It is the death knell of the Russian empire. Eventually, this neo-Soviet behemoth is likely to collapse like Nazi Germany in 1945, while Ukraine has the chance of becoming a full-fledged constitutional republic with rule of law and joining NATO and the EU.

Anna Myroniuk, head of investigations

The war made me once again realize how fragile our regular day-to-day lives are and how valuable are simple things like a call from your mom or a hug from a friend.

The war has also taught me that however difficult it is we must carry on with our lives because that is something our soldiers are fighting for, too. We must continue to stroll the parks and squares of our cities, to laugh, and to love.

I have never been more proud of Ukrainians, both military and civilians. Never have I felt so honored to be a Ukrainian myself.

This war made me reconsider love. Out of love for their country and each other Ukrainians bravely fight to protect their future. The way our people self-organized and helped one another during crises is inspiring. The way people across the European Union supported Ukraine is touching. I was moved watching Lithuanians chipping in to raise money to buy a Bayraktar drone for Ukraine, and then once again when Turkey decided to give it for free.

I recently went abroad for work for the first time since the full-scale war broke out. Having arrived in Poland late at night, I went to a café to grab a bite while I was waiting for a bus. It was raining heavily, and I was wet, cold, and hungry. They usually don't serve food that late, but when they heard that I was from Ukraine, they did. Their chef brought me some soup for free. I burst into tears.

I wish this unconditional support we feel from common people across Europe was mirrored in the EU's support for Ukraine on the official level.

Lili Bivings, contributing editor

Since the war started I've learned just how deep the belief in Russia's 'greatness' and 'strength' runs in political circles, newsrooms, and through the halls of academia– all over the world. While these actors spent decades marveling at Russia, they tragically disregarded Ukraine and Ukrainian history.

As a master's student at an American university, I was shocked to learn just how far people were ready to go to defend Russia, Russian culture, and Russian society, even as Russian bombs rained down on Ukrainian cities and report after report of Russian atrocities came to light. Those who defended Ukraine were at times labeled as 'emotional' or 'biased' because of personal connections to the country.

At the same time, we've seen to what extent Russia has underestimated Ukraine – its love for its country, willingness to fight, and desire to be free and independent from Russia's malign influence.

It's precisely these combining forces of dismissing Ukraine, of refusing to heed its warnings, that have led to the horrifying consequences Ukrainians have to live through with each day that Russia's war continues. Consequences that include some children being forced to live the rest of their lives without their parents.

What we should all take from this tragic moment in history is that the voices of the oppressed have much more to teach us about the oppressor, and that if we are to move forward, we must learn to listen to those that suffer.

Oleksiy Sorokin, senior editor

It's been 100 days of unimaginable pain and suffering for myself, my family, friends, and every person I know. The worst part is that it feels like we are now used to this pain, and I don't know how we will be able to get out of this state even when this brutal, unprovoked, and unjust war is over.

We are accustomed to sitting in bomb shelters, hearing air raid sirens, to knowing that thousands of people are killed, injured, raped, and tortured day and night. We are used to not having days off and feeling guilty for not doing more.

We are also accustomed to many people in the West being tired of war, tired of us dying, not giving up, and not willing to sacrifice our lives and our country for the comfort of their homes. We are constantly asking people not to become numb to war crimes, but in a sense, I feel that we are moving in this direction ourselves.

We see destroyed cities, lives shattered, and families torn apart, and we understand that this is the new normal we live in. It's heartbreaking that we are now accustomed to death, to losing people that would otherwise have lived, who would have been loving parents, caring friends, and wonderful people.

Yet, we are also used to the notion that we cannot lose. This is a war of conquest, a war of colonization, and a deliberate genocide in the making. We are familiar with the fact that this war will end with either the fascist Russian regime falling or us dying.

And to be honest, we're not planning on dying anytime soon.

Anastasiia Lapatina, reporter

Before the war, I really assumed that I knew what that word meant.

I closely followed events in other conflict zones around the world, I was friends with people who grew up and lived through wars, I listened to their stories and tried my hardest to deepen my understanding of their experiences. But when I heard my mother's terrified voice as she was clinging to a mattress pushed against a window – an illusion of safety in a house that had no basement – with artillery going off just hundreds of meters away from our home, I realized that I truly knew nothing about war.

Three months in, I feel I know a lot.

I know a lot about destruction – not in the abstract, but in the most literal sense of the word, when entire cities essentially disappear, with only rubble, dead bodies, and terrified survivors of Russian occupation left behind. I know about suffering – the unimaginable and all-encompassing kind, when a little boy stands near his mother's grave, a man loses his entire family to a Russian airstrike, or a mother watches her young daughter being raped by Russian soldiers.

I also know a lot about privilege – the absurd kind, because none of the things described above apply to me or my family, and that is a privilege. We're all alive, our house is mainly intact, none of us is injured.

But more importantly, I know a whole lot about love – the kind you never thought people were capable of, yet they are. In these 100 days, Ukrainians have shown to the world the true meaning of bravery, resilience, and love – the love we have for every centimeter of our land, our language, our culture, our democratic values, all things Russia has so persistently tried to destroy. But I am genuinely convinced that love will always defeat hate. It has to. And it is precisely because of this love that we will win.

Olena Goncharova, Canadian correspondent

I remember day one of the war as clear as if it was yesterday. I'm sitting in my office, thousands of kilometers away from home, I'm on a night news shift knowing that something terrible will happen tonight. I want to pray, but I feel I can't find the words. And then I see the avalanche of messages – from friends and family, most of them almost identical, with just two words that sent chills down my spine: 'It started.' It's almost 5 a.m. in Ukraine and nobody sleeps. I'm watching a video of a missile hitting the city I love more than words can describe, my hometown, my Kyiv. I'm wailing, I can barely pull myself together, I'm nothing but heartfelt grief at that moment. It's the day I want to erase from my memory, yet I know – just like millions of fellow Ukrainians – I will never be able to forget it.

Fast forward to day 100. It's been over three months since the war seemed far away, and you understand that the problems you used to care about are not problems at all. The perspective has changed now that your relative's house was destroyed by a missile. Now that you've seen a child who used to excel at dance competitions with their legs amputated. It is hard to silence that guilt inside of you that never goes away because you happened to stay alive and thousands of others were not as lucky. So you do what you can to help. And no matter how small and insignificant your contribution may seem, it matters and gets you closer to the moment you can send an avalanche of messages to your loved ones, saying just two words: 'We won!'

Thaisa Semenova, reporter

In the early days of the war, I interviewed Anastasiia, 25, my university peer. She fled Ukraine with her two-year-old son, spending hours in line at the Polish border and then walking 13 kilometers on her feet. She couldn't even hug her husband goodbye as people in the crowd pushed him away. Shortly after our conversation, I learned he died in combat in Kyiv Oblast, and she became a widow at 25. The love of her life was gone, just like that.

Since then, I can't stop thinking about how a war can take away everything – the people we love and our own time on Earth. I am among the lucky ones who haven't lost loved ones to war. It's scary even to write this as if thinking about losing someone could somehow bring the tragedy closer.

In those 100 days, my mornings have started the same way: A minute after waking up, I'd grab my phone and text my loved ones. I would ask, 'how are you?' but would actually mean so much more than that – 'I love you,' 'I care about you,' 'I hope you're safe,' 'Please be alive and text me back'.

As cheesy as it may sound, during the war I've learned that love is what matters the most in life. Not a career, ambitions, or money.

I left Ukraine two days after the invasion. That's probably why I haven't had nightmares about explosions or shelling. My dreams are about the pre-war life that I've lost – holding hands with someone that I'd just met at some bar, drunk laughing with friends, hugging my mom. Being in exile, I only hope one day I get to have it all back.

Sergiy Slipchenko, reporter

In the winter of 2013, I closely followed the events unfolding throughout Ukraine, as a peaceful demonstration turned into a bloody revolution known as the Revolution of Dignity or EuroMaidan.

Despite being thousands of kilometers away, in Toronto, I felt a strange, unbreakable connection with those strangers in the streets.

Watching my countrymen stand up for what they believe in, and die for the future of our nation, I experienced great pride in being Ukrainian.

All of a sudden, for once in my life my peers knew about Ukraine, where it was located, and the strength and spirit of the people living there. It felt like a rediscovery and resurgence of Ukraine and its culture.

Shortly after the revolution, Russia tried to squander that victory and chain Ukraine up through a fabricated conflict. However, Ukrainians fought back and despite an ongoing war, the country continued to prosper.

In 2021, I moved to Kyiv, wanting to come back to my homeland, with my wife and kids. Those short few months were without a doubt the best time in my life. I had the job of my dreams, our own place to call home, and a beautiful city to explore. That perfect life was ripped away from my family and me, and yet I know I am one of the lucky that managed to flee the war unscathed.

Others, those much less fortunate than myself, have to endure unimaginable horrors due to the whims of a tyrant. Yet, I know that at the end of this nightmare Ukraine and its people will remain free, their spirit unbroken, unyielding.

7 June 2022

Portrait of the invader: Understanding the Russian soldier

Igor Kossov

One hundred days of all-out war has been plenty of time to get acquainted with the Russian troops.

Their lackluster combat performance, artillery barrages against cities, treatment of civilians, intercepted messages home, and interviews with dozens of civilians around Ukraine allow one to put together a mosaic portrait of the invaders. It's not a flattering image.

Many of the soldiers are dirt-poor and badly educated, with many growing up without access to modern amenities. Many joined the armed forces because they have no future in their backwater towns. The majority have bad training, low morale and no faith in their poorly maintained equipment and their callous or incompetent officers.

When occupying areas, many drank heavily, turning their quarters into shambles, or went around looting anything barely valuable they could get their hands on.

While some civilians acknowledged that they were treated adequately by Russian soldiers, others spoke of casual murder and cruelty inflicted either to feel safe, to satisfy base desires or just for the sake of being cruel.

This was enough to rack up more than 15,000 alleged war crimes as of 1 June by Prosecutor General Iryna Venediktova's reckoning. This ranged from random killings to deliberate murder, to torture and rape of civilians.

Where they're from

Demographic patterns emerge when one looks at Russian soldiers who have been killed or captured in Ukraine.

As of 30 May, the BBC has identified over 3,000 Russian casualties, based on open-source data. Of these, the biggest losses hit the regions of Buryatia, Dagestan, Volgograd, Bashkortostan, Orenburg, Krasnodar, Chelyabinsk and North Ossetia, many of which sit along Russia's southern border, as well as its eastern reaches.

Similar findings appear in a report by iStories Media, a partner of the Organized Crime and Corruption Reporting Project, as well as *The Kyiv Independent*'s review of death reports in Russia's social and traditional media and Telegram channels that purport to list the dead.

Some of these regions are predominantly homes of ethnic minorities. Close to a third of Buryatia's population are Buryats, while about a third of Dagestan residents are Avars. In conversations with *The Kyiv Independent*, Ukrainians in several regions mentioned that significant parts of Russian forces were ethnic Buryats, with a sprinkling of other Siberians.

'Military status can be seen as an escape from the stigma suffered by ethnic minorities,' said Kirill Mykhailov, an expert with the Conflict Intelligence Team, a group of investigative journalists in Russia. 'No one will question if you really are Russian if you are a soldier.'

Chechen forces accompanied the invasion force, but most of them did little fighting and were largely there for 'TikTok PR,' Mikhailov said. On at least one occasion, Kadyrovites have reportedly been used as barrier units, whose job was to prevent retreat and desertion.

But ethnic minorities are far from the only ones who join the military to escape poverty – large numbers of ethnic Russians do the same.

It's also no coincidence that some of the regions with the most known casualties also have the lowest GDP in Russia, including Dagestan, Buryatia and North Ossetia. Bashkortostan and Chelyabinsk are in the middle of the pack of Russian regions sorted by wealth.

The poorer regions also have high unemployment rates. Chechnya, Dagestan and North Ossetia had unemployment rates above 15% while Buryatia's was above 10% in 2020, according to Russia's Statistical Bureau. The official national rate was just above 5% that year.

'The army is the sole stable employer in certain regions,' according to the iStories investigation. 'In regions like this, the army is often the only opportunity for career growth and moving out of their backwater,' Mikhailov added.

The average Russian soldier is poor. Many come from rural areas without modern amenities. According to iStories, less than half of village homes in regions leading by death are equipped with things like hot water or gas.

Kamil Galeev, a Russia-based researcher with the Wilson Center, wrote that the rank and file are 'young guys from small towns and usually underprivileged backgrounds'.

Ukrainian civilians who lived near or among Russian occupiers told *The Kyiv Independent* that many Russian soldiers reacted with surprise, envy and disappointment when they saw how even rural or suburban Ukrainians live.

Multiple residents of a housing complex on the edge of Hostomel, as well as two couples living on a block in Irpin that Russians turned into a base, heard the same sentence from their occupiers: 'You live better than we do. We don't have this at home.' ...

Competence

Those who do fight on the front lines have done a great deal to show the world that the Russian military is a lot less scary than it once seemed, as it let column after column get shot to pieces and failed to achieve objectives against the more lightly armed Ukrainians.

Part of it comes down to training. Taras Chmut, a former Ukrainian marine and head of the Come Back Alive foundation, said about 50–60% of Russia's armed forces have below-average training, with roughly 30% having average training and only about 5% having above average training.

'In general [the training] leaves much to be desired,' agreed Mikhailov. Much of training 'is done halfheartedly, the army never prepared for the war it was about to embark on – remember, it came as a surprise for most of the lowest ranks.'

Airborne troops and marines, who comprise the 'constant readiness troops', were better prepared but still not enough for a war like this, he added.

Low pay, corruption and hazing continue to be problems for the Russian military, according to the OCCRP's April report. Galeev wrote that good, competent officers, who have the trust and support of their men, are antithetical to Putin's desire to maintain absolute power.

He went on to say that as a result, less intelligent officers, leading men with rock-bottom morale, are what the Russian military routinely selects for. Hence its need to rely so much on artillery.

Being a contracted soldier in Russia can be bad enough but conscripts arguably have it even worse. Significant numbers of raw conscripts have been deployed to Ukraine, even though the Kremlin initially denied this.

Mikhailov said that theoretically, two thirds of troops are on contract and the rest are conscripts at any given time; in practice, not all contract slots are filled. The conscripts tend to be poor as 'richer, more privileged ones would dodge the draft', according to Galeev. He added that conscripts who don't know their rights can be pressured into signing a contract.

The system is so ramshackle and the invasion so bungled, that many soldiers and officers have simply refused to follow orders. A senior US defense official told reporters last month that 'mid-grade officers at various levels, even up to the battalion level ... have either refused to obey orders or are not obeying them with the same measure of alacrity that you would expect an officer to obey'.

This doesn't mean that every unit is bad at its job. Illya Bohdanov, a Ukrainian volunteer fighter, told *The Kyiv Independent* how he was sent to reclaim the bodies of a Ukrainian column that was devastated by a Russian ambush, in the area of Bucha and Hostomel early on in the war. The ambushing troops were some of the Russian army's elite.

'In terms of their offensive capability, I was surprised,' said Bohdanov. 'It's unfamiliar territory, you're in a foreign country, you don't even know where you are and to stage such a competent ambush, against regular forces? It impressed me. In general, the Russians fought well.'

Attitude

Still, given all of the above problems, and the shattered promises that Ukraine would fold in under a week, the average Russian soldier was either absolutely miserable or absolutely drunk, according to civilians who spoke to *The Kyiv Independent*.

The Russian soldiers' alleged calls and messages home, which the Ukrainian forces said they intercepted, are full of doom, gloom and terror. Soldiers would describe how they were losing men left and right or how much of their unit was wiped out.

Residents of the Hostomel housing complex said when the Russians arrived, they were proud and cocksure. Soon, that turned into confusion, frustration, then dread. Resident Mykhailo saw a soldier crying. Others jumped at loud noises. 'I saw it in their eyes,' said resident Olena. 'Fear and a lack of understanding of what they're doing here.'

Civilians said that some Russians appeared to believe or at least parrot the notion that they were there as liberators and Ukrainians, by and large, would welcome them. Some did seem confused or crestfallen when that didn't happen.

'One guy got drunk and told stories that he will never forgive himself that he came to Ukraine and did what he did and wants to kill himself every day,' said Victoria Lyashchenko, who lived on a block in Irpin that Russians made into a base.

Her neighbor, a German national who declined to give his name, said the first rotation through the area was made up of very young guys who were 'terrified, we could see it. One of them, 20 years old, even cried on my shoulder.'

The men who came to replace them were different – they were older and determined to enjoy themselves. They stuffed themselves with local food and looted every bottle of alcohol available from local homes, getting hammered and making a big mess on a nightly basis. When that ran out, they started taking their APCs somewhere to get more booze.

'They smashed all the notebooks and tablets and phones, threw them into fires. They ate the food, threw out the scraps with the plates and cups outside. They tore everything apart,' said Lyashchenko. 'We asked if we could give them water to flush the toilets. They said we have no time for that. They threw dirty socks and underwear in the toilets, clogging them.'

This sort of behavior was widespread in Kyiv Oblast. Apartments were torn apart, enormous piles of stuff scattered everywhere. In some homes, the Russians defecated on the floor and left it there or threw it at walls. In one rich man's manor home outside the village of Stoyanka-2, the Russians got into the extensive wine cellar, poured some of it into a small pool and attempted to bathe in it. They drank the rest and trashed the entire property.

Aggression and dehumanization
Some of that energy came out as aggression. Bucha resident Tetiana Oleksandrova described a Chechen soldier that shot a burst of automatic fire into the school basement where she sheltered, killing another woman, as 'furious', with 'the eyes of a jackal'.

Her husband, Andrii Fotchenko, said the young ethnically Russian 'pawns' who anxiously followed him around reminded him of 'baby ducklings'. But these were the same men who earlier threw four flashbangs into a basement they knew was filled with civilians.

One question that tends to come up when discussing Russian troops is their 'adequacy'. Unlike in English, where the word 'adequate' usually means 'sufficient', in Russian and Ukrainian, the adjective is often used to describe a decent, normal person.

Various civilians said that some of the Russians they ran into were 'adequate' people, who just tried to do their jobs and didn't inflict casual cruelty on the residents they captured. Tasia, a mother from a village in Zaporizhzhia, said that when one Russian soldier tried to get his commander to take out her 17-year-old son, the commander disgustedly dismissed the soldier, who was later beaten up by his comrades and transferred elsewhere.

As the world now knows, these were overshadowed by the other soldiers, who were a lot worse. Some of them gunned down individuals or groups of civilians, either because they were hunting them or for no reason at all. Potshots were taken at civilians for entertainment. And then there was all the rape.

In calls and messages between soldiers and their loved ones in Russia, one attitude came up a lot: that Ukrainians aren't really people. Everyone recalls the infamous call where a soldier's girlfriend gave him permission to rape Ukrainian women. In a more recent call, a Russian woman talked about how she would torture and kill Ukrainian children if she had her way. 'I would inject them with drugs, look in their eyes and say die, suffer,' she said.

This falls in line with the Kremlin's message that Ukraine isn't a thing – that its residents are uppity 'Little Russians' that need to be put in their place.

Mikhailov brought up the 'poor work of political officers who never explained what a Nazi is, which is why, per sociologist Greg Yudin, many would assume anyone so much as expressing Ukrainian patriotism is a Nazi and should be treated accordingly'.

Yudin himself wrote that when Russia's 'de-nazification' campaign failed due to brave Ukrainian resistance, the Russians derived 'a natural conclusion from that: Ukrainians turned out to be deeply infected by Nazism'.

'And this is precisely how the message of official speakers has changed recently: We have underestimated how deep Nazism has permeated Ukrainian society. That affects the operational choices by the troops on the ground. Imagine you are a Russian soldier occupying a city in Ukraine ... What are the classifications and distinctions you would use when dealing with the local population?'

'Your basic theory is that this is a land occupied by the Nazis, and you are here to liberate it. Obviously, Nazis will resist; and those resisting are Nazis.'

'This is why I seriously doubt these atrocities are just excesses of war,' he concluded.

10 June 2022

Serhiy Zhadan: 'If Russia wins, there will be no literature, no culture, nothing'

Alexander Query

'C'mon, this way,' Serhiy Zhadan said, climbing the stairs of Kharkiv's Puppet Theater.

We follow the writer's black cigarette jeans and iconic leather jacket through a maze of corridors, almost running after his lean silhouette deep into the cool darkness of empty seats.

Every theater dreams of untold stories.

We were the only spectators in the theater that day, surrounded by empty seats waiting to be filled by an audience who would one day come to listen to stories about Ukraine's victory.

Instead, we watched over a scene of cardboard boxes waiting to be sent to soldiers and civilians on the frontline, in the blue light of a broken-windowed theater converted into a volunteer center on 24 February.

Sitting there among the empty seats and crude forgotten spotlights, I understood why I had traveled halfway across the country to meet Serhiy Zhadan. There was no other way to meet him than in Kharkiv. It's his city, after all.

Since Russia's full-scale invasion began, Zhadan has remained in Kharkiv, Ukraine's second-largest city, doing humanitarian work and conducting numerous interviews in the city he couldn't leave behind.

'The war caught me on the train on my way to Vinnytsia for a concert with the band. We learned about it and came back to Kharkiv,' he said.

'We' being 'Zhadan and the Dogs' ('Zhadan i Sobaky'), the writer's rock band founded in 2007, only one of Zhadan's numerous artistic projects over the years – with literature as his guiding light.

Zhadan looks the part. Only his gray, sleek haircut betrays the passing of time on the 47-year-old writer, easily labeled as Ukraine's *'enfant terrible'*. Writer, poet, musician, humanitarian worker, political activist, Zhadan is on every front avoiding labels as fast as he walks. With 12 poetry books and seven novels, his cult status helped put the country's contemporary literature on the map, especially in eastern Ukraine, where his characters evolve between hallucinated landscapes of war and picaresque quests.

Inspired by the country's 1920s avant-garde, and compared to the likes of William Burroughs, his abrasive style cuts to the chase. 'Let's start by whispering the names, let's weave together the vocabulary of death,' Zhadan wrote in his 2020 poem 'New Orthography', long before Russia's invasion began on 24 February.

Many words were whispered that day. Among them, one unwavering statement: there would be no Ukrainian literature without Ukraine's sovereignty.

'If Ukraine wins, there is some future for us,' he told *The Kyiv Independent*. 'If Russia wins, there will be no literature, no culture, nothing.'

Kharkiv was always Ukrainian

Outside, the eerie silence overwhelming Kharkiv, broken only by the distant sounds of artillery, is a constant reminder of Russia's looming shadow.

The city used to be a vibrant place filled with students from all over the world, taking classes at one of the city's 38 universities. With its student life and numerous coffee shops and bars, Kharkiv was the 'cool' city of eastern Ukraine.

'It was quite a cosmopolitan environment, democratic and open,' Zhadan said. 'And now it's half empty.'

Most of the city center's windows are shattered, with some buildings blown apart by heavy missile strikes. The black, burned skeleton of the Kharkiv Regional State Administration stands on Freedom Square as a monument to Russian dictator Vladimir Putin's brutality.

The windows are missing from Kharkiv's Puppet Theater, where Zhadan has established the headquarters of his volunteer organization. Wood panels and black curtains cover the holes for the time being, like a grieving sign of the city's ordeal.

'The buildings we will rebuild,' Zhadan said. 'The worst thing is not the buildings, but those who have died, because we cannot bring them back.'

Zhadan doesn't have time for art at the moment. 'A lot is happening right now, the last thing I think about now is my art, and I think more about what's happening in my country and how to help,' he said. 'I think reflections and art will take place a bit later.'

Born in now Russian-occupied Starobilsk, near Luhansk, Zhadan spent most of his life in Kharkiv, which stands on the edge of two worlds by its proximity to Russia.

But Kharkiv is not a Russian city, Zhadan said. 'Even though Russia is 40 kilometers from here, Kharkiv has always been Ukrainian.'

If Kharkiv was a character, it would be Enei, said Zhadan. 'Enei is a Cossack and a traveler who has a light and positive character despite everything happening to him,' he said.

Zhadan was referring to the Ukrainian mock-heroic poem 'Eneida' by Ivan Kotliarevsky, a classic in Ukrainian literature published in 1798 that is widely considered to be the first literary work published wholly in modern Ukrainian. In this burlesque parody of Virgil's *Aeneid*, Aeneas is a Ukrainian Cossack.

The poem, which makes Ukrainian school children roll their eyes to the sky, begins with these words: 'Enei was a lively fellow / And quite a Cossack for a lad / For mischief he was more than mellow / While courage above all he had' – a good description of Kharkiv in Zhadan's views.

Kharkiv as a Russian city is mostly a stereotype propagated by Russians themselves, partly supported by Ukraine's own politicians, Zhadan said.

The term 'Russian-speaking Ukrainian' doesn't make sense for Zhadan, as it implies they speak Russian and Ukrainian is a foreign language for them.

Many Kharkiv residents switched to Ukrainian because it's a marker during this war, an effort Zhadan finds moving as they spoke Russian their whole life. 'Speaking Ukrainian is a marker that you're a local, and that you refuse the language of the occupier,' Zhadan said.

The switch to Ukrainian is a natural process that gained momentum after Russia's first invasion of 2014, he said, admitting that Ukraine will always have to fight Russia's dangerous zone of influence. 'It became clear to Ukrainians that we either fight for our identity or be a part of this post-Soviet empire.'

Love poems

For Zhadan, the sole fact of writing in Ukrainian is political. By choosing which language to write in, writers indicate their political and ideological positions.

'That's why even if you write love poems but do it in Ukrainian, you take a certain position in one way or another, it has a political connotation,' he said.

Zhadan predicts this war will divide Ukrainian literature into two periods, pre-war and post-war, but it will take time to see a new opus emerge. 'The reality is too close, too bloody, and too rough to easily talk about,' he said.

Culture is deeply intertwined with politics in Ukraine, and Zhadan, involved in politics since the early 1990s, knows this all too well.

He has taken part in every revolution the country has seen since independence in 1991, becoming a prominent voice of Kharkiv's local EuroMaidan in 2014, fighting against the made-up 'Russian Spring' manufactured by Kremlin proxies in Ukraine's Donbas.

He believes writers have a role to play in the fight against Russia's colonial attitude, by building the country's identity through art. As mediators, writers can't stay idle in such times.

'We are a highly politicized society, which is understandable because we're a postcolonial society and we're trying to build our own identity to escape the influence of the Russian empire.'

This is what distances Ukraine from Russia, he said. 'And Russians know this, which is why from time to time, they try to destroy Ukrainian literature.'

Ukrainian writers paid a hefty price to defend their language, he said, referring to the 'Executed Renaissance', the systematic execution of Ukraine's intelligentsia by Stalin from the 1930s to 1940s.

In the early 1920s, Ukrainian artists and writers settled in Kharkiv, then the capital of Soviet Ukraine, making it an avant-garde hub. But Stalin soon cracked down on Ukrainian intellectuals who threatened the dictator's totalitarian dream of Soviet culture.

Many of these writers and poets lived in the 'Slovo' Building in central Kharkiv, a cooperative built in the late 1920s to house prominent Ukrainian cultural figures. Already seen as a threat, the phone lines were tapped and mass arrests ensued. On 7 March, the building once again came under attack – this time damaged by Russian shelling.

The campaign to exterminate the Ukrainian intelligentsia culminated during the 1936–1938 Great Purge, with 223 writers being imprisoned or executed.

According to estimates, nearly 30,000 Ukrainian intellectuals were repressed during Stalin's Great Purge. In 1930, the works of 259 Ukrainian writers were published, but by 1938 only 36 of those writers remained – the rest were executed, exiled, disappeared, or had committed suicide.

Colonial empire

Zhadan always refers to Russia as 'the empire', a term suiting Russia's colonial behavior towards Ukraine. For Russians, Ukraine is just a part of Russia, Zhadan said.

'Ukraine is just an appendix, a part of Russia, the same people that for some reason they constantly destroy, and Ukrainians have no right to their own independence,' he said. 'And Ukrainians see a history where they are their own people, an independent nation, who was always opposed to the empire.'

Ukrainians want to build an independent and democratic country while Russians feel quite comfortable in totalitarian conditions, Zhadan added.

The 'Executed Renaissance' is just one of many dark chapters in Russia's colonial attitude towards Ukraine – a behavior Zhadan describes as a clash between two countries that are light years away over their perception of past and future.

'In their vision of the past, the main role belongs to Russians, as they monopolized the whole memory of World War II,' a distorted vision they still use today to justify the horrors they inflict on Ukraine.

Yet Russia's invasion showed Ukrainians that they have no other option than to completely disconnect from Russians because any mingling with Russia ends up with the destruction of Ukraine, he said. 'I think Russians have done everything for Ukraine to be destined for its independence and freedom.'

While we were leaving the comfortable darkness of Kharkiv's Puppet Theater for the city, Zhadan's words reverberated in the city's windy streets, intertwined with a far echo of his poem:

To stand and talk about the night
Stand and listen to the voices
of shepherds in the fog
incanting over every single
lost soul.

14 June 2022

Kharkiv residents return home after months spent underground: 'It's scary when there is still shelling'

Asami Terajima

Kharkiv – Weeks after Denys Parkhomenko and his 55-year-old mother moved out of a subway car, it's still hard for them to readjust to normal life.

Moving out of one of Kharkiv's underground metro stations has been especially hard for Parkhomenko's mother, Svitlana, who can't get used to hearing shelling outside.

The two of them had been living in a subway station since 2 March, when their apartment in central Kharkiv was severely damaged by a missile that hit a neighboring building. They were both at home when the strike happened – Parkhomenko was working when he heard the plane and sensed that something was flying in his direction. He trusted his instincts and immediately ran to the corridor.

'If I hesitated, even for a second, I would have been killed,' Parkhomenko said, recalling the moment.

While Russian artillery attacks on Ukraine's second-largest city have decreased compared to the March–April period, indiscriminate shelling continues, resulting in casualties.

In spite of this, following a successful Ukrainian counteroffensive north of Kharkiv, signs of normal life have reappeared in this city, once home to over 1.4 million people.

To ease transportation throughout Kharkiv, Mayor Ihor Terekhov ordered the relaunch of the metro starting on 24 May. Residents were still allowed to stay in a designated space at metro stations and come overnight, but the subway is now running regularly.

After contemplation, Parkhomenko and his mother decided to ask for a temporary place to live since they can't go back to their previous apartment. The city gave them a room in the large residential district of Saltivka, the hardest-hit neighborhood on the edge of Kharkiv that continues to be shelled.

Saltivka sits on the city's northern edge, closest to the front line and keeps getting attacked. 'She [my mother] reacts to the shellings even when she's asleep,' Parkhomenko said worriedly.

Moving out with children

Maria Oblik, 72, still feels uneasy about moving back home as well. Above all, she is worried about the safety of her grandsons, aged 8 and 15.

Until mid-May, she lived with her daughter and two grandchildren inside a tent that they set up in a metro station. The four of them used to sleep inside the tent and occasionally go outside to breathe during breaks in the shelling.

Her daughter and grandsons wanted to leave Kharkiv, but they didn't want to leave without her, and Oblik refused to go anywhere due to her age. Oblik's son is also a soldier fighting in Kharkiv Oblast, and she worries about him every single day.

While her grandsons stayed underground, Oblik would go home regularly, even during the heaviest shelling, to cook warm meals for her family. 'It was scary but I walked [home] for my kids,' the grandmother told *The Kyiv Independent*.

Though her elder grandson began to go home from time to time when the shelling started to fall off, the youngest was still too afraid. The boy refused to leave the subway for months, fearing the sound of shelling. Between the family's move underground on 24 February and their emergence in May, the boy only left the metro station twice to go shower at home ...

But once metro service resumed, they said they were told to pack their tent and go back home.

Weeks after they returned home, Oblik said that shelling continued, though it wasn't as intense. Despite the uncertainty, she said it was good to get back home again and the children began going outside more often. Yet, their fear didn't disappear. 'It's still scary when they are shelling,' she said.

Continuing life underground

For Vitali Bakhmatov, 45, whose flat was blasted by Russia, looking for a place to stay continues to be a challenge.

His apartment is located in Pivnichna Saltivka, an area within the Saltivka district where shelling has been the most intense. The area is still a ghost town – only a few remaining residents live there, still cut off from electricity, heat, and gas. Bakhmatov came to the nearest metro station at about 5:00 a.m. on 24 February after hearing loud sounds of explosions in his neighborhood. 'We didn't know what was happening at the time,' Bakhmatov, a botanist, told *The Kyiv Independent*.

He first came with very little stuff, but after several weeks, he began to go back and forth between his apartment and his temporary bunk bed in the metro, where he spends most of his days. He said it's not possible to live in the apartment anymore because a shell destroyed his staircase and front door. Unlike the others, he says he hasn't been offered temporary boarding, despite having suffered a head injury more than 10 years ago that qualifies him as disabled under Ukrainian law.

There are still about 50 people living inside the metro station near Pivnichna Saltivka, although many people have left for a dormitory, he said.

'Nothing changed,' Bakhmatov said. 'What are we waiting for, we don't know it ourselves.'

Bakhmatov initially wanted to flee to another city, but he couldn't afford the move. 'In our country, if you don't have money, you don't think about going somewhere,' he said. 'There's just no way out.'

'We are sitting here, and we'll watch what will happen next.'

23 June 2022

Fallen activist Roman Ratushnyi and his battle for a better Ukraine
Daria Shulzhenko

A crowd of dozens gathered near the highway in Kyiv's historic Protasiv Yar neighborhood on 16 June.

Many of them knew each other well, united by past rallies against illegal construction in the area. But they were sadly quiet that day, hugging one another occasionally, and wiping off their tears.

As they saw several cars approaching, they kneeled and lighted flares.

There, in one of those cars, was the body of a young Ukrainian activist who had once inspired and united these people and many others to fight for justice.

The cars drove by the freshly painted mural in Protasiv Yar, reading: 'Roman Ratushnyi. Heroes do not die.'

One of the most prominent Kyiv activists, Ratushnyi had been fighting for a better Ukraine since he was 16 years old, first during the EuroMaidan Revolution, then supporting Ukrainian soldiers during Russia's eight-year-long war in Donbas, and later going into civic activism.

He stood up to Ukrainian oligarchs and corrupt officials as a leader of the non-profit 'Let's Protect Protasiv Yar', which fought against illegal construction in the Kyiv park.

'He was a leader and a patriot who drove change and inspired others,' says one of the non-profit's activists, Oleg Nikiforov.

When Russia began its all-out invasion of Ukraine on 24 February, Ratushnyi's friends and loved ones weren't surprised by his decision to fight for the freedom of his homeland.

He joined a local territorial defense unit to protect his native neighborhood, Protasiv Yar – the same area that he used to protect from illegal construction by organizing protests.

Soon, Ratushnyi joined the Ukrainian armed forces. He had been fighting the Russian troops in Sumy Oblast and then at the site of heavy hostilities near Kharkiv.

There, his very last battle for Ukraine took place.

Roman was killed near Izium, Kharkiv Oblast, on 9 June. He was 24 years old.

Although 60–100 Ukrainian soldiers are killed every day according to President Volodymyr Zelensky, this loss reverberated through Kyiv especially strongly.

Ratushnyi had done a lot for Kyiv, but could have done so much more, his friends say. 'He was a great man who sympathized with everyone fighting for freedom, and hated every evil in the world,' says Artur Kharytonov, activist and Ratushnyi's close friend.

'People like Roman are born once in 1,000 years,' says Nikiforov.

Becoming an activist

Ratushnyi was an inspiration for those who knew him personally and even to those who didn't.

Born into a family of Kyiv activist Taras Ratushnyi and journalist and writer Svitlana Povalyaeva, Roman seemed to have little chance of not becoming civic-minded.

When downtown Kyiv was ablaze with massive protests against then-President Viktor Yanukovych during one of the most crucial events in Ukraine's history, the EuroMaidan Revolution, Roman was just 16 years old, studying at one of Kyiv's schools.

That, however, didn't stop him from becoming an active participant in the revolution. 'He was there from day one,' Kharytonov says.

On 30 November 2013, the day that catalyzed the popular uprising, Ratushnyi was among a large group of Ukrainian students violently attacked and beaten by the Berkut riot police. It was back then that his thirst for justice would become stronger than the fear for his own life: Despite injuries and increasing danger, Ratushnyi participated in the protests up until Yanukovych was toppled in February 2014.

'For me, it was not in vain because I see a huge number of positive changes in the country that occurred due to the Maidan,' Ratushnyi said in an interview back in 2018. 'Without Maidan, without showing real resistance to the authorities, these changes would not have happened.'

Just like it changed the mindsets of many Ukrainians, boosting pro-European and patriotic values, the EuroMaidan Revolution changed Ratushnyi as well. After the revolution, Ratushnyi said he started feeling like an 'absolutely free person' in his country. He would later help in identifying some of the Berkut officers and bringing them to justice. 'It was like a very logical way for his becoming, and for our generation as well,' says Roman's friend, architect Ulyana Dzhurlyak.

So when several years after the uprising, a fence appeared near his home in Protasiv Yar, marking yet another illegal construction site in the capital, Ratushnyi, in his early 20s, stood up.

Keep on fighting despite threats

If it wasn't for Ratushnyi, the 20 hectares of Protasiv Yar's sloping woodland not far from Kyiv's downtown would have disappeared under high-rise buildings, according to his friends and fellow activists. 'He began to fight [illegal construction] and with his example showed everyone else what to do,' says Nikiforov, Ratushnyi's friend.

Ratushnyi led a group of protesters and later a non-profit in 2019, when a company linked to controversial former Ukrainian official and businessman Hennadiy Korban attempted to illegally construct three 40-storey buildings at the site of the natural park.

United by Ratushnyi, the group of activists tried to bring the issue into the public eye by holding multiple protests both in the area and near governmental buildings – some of which even ended in clashes with the police and '*titushki*' (thugs) – as well as educating locals on illegal construction and 'fighting the mafia' by holding lectures and movie screenings.

Along with publicity, Ratushnyi said he started getting threats from Korban and his allies. 'They wrote to him directly that "if you can't be bribed, if we can't solve the issue with you, it's easier to kill you",' Nikiforov recalls.

In August 2019, Ratushnyi met with Korban's then-lawyer Andriy Smyrnov, who tried to persuade Ratushnyi not to oppose the project. Nikiforov says he also offered Ratushnyi money, which he refused.

A month after their conversation, Smyrnov was appointed deputy chief of staff for the then newly elected President Volodymyr Zelensky.

Even though Roman later published an audio recording of their conversation, both Smyrnov and Korban denied threatening the activist. In one of his recent interviews, Ratushnyi said that he even met with Zelensky personally, who responded to his complaining about the threats by saying that 'it was before' Smyrnov took a job in the president's office. Smyrnov took the job in September 2019, one month after the alleged threat.

Back then, Nikiforov says, they started to notice some people following Roman. For more than a month, Ratushnyi had to go into hiding, saying that he had received threats to his life.

'But Roman was one of those people who kept fighting no matter what,' says Nikiforov. 'Fighting against corrupt officials, systems, and governments, to rebuild his country.' So he persisted. Not only did he fight for Protasiv Yar, but he supported other activists and initiatives as well.

In March 2021, Ratushnyi was even arrested for what he claimed were trumped-up charges of vandalizing the president's office during a protest demanding the release of then-jailed civic activist Serhiy Sternenko. Nikiforov says it was an attempt to 'get rid of Roman'.

But it failed: thanks to public outcry, Ratushnyi was released from house arrest in April. Following an almost three-year battle with multiple court hearings and protests, Ukraine's supreme court ruled against the developers in early 2022.

Nikiforov recalls Roman saying that even the victory was not a reason to stop: 'One needs to keep on going, to keep on fighting.' And their non-profit plans to follow Ratushnyi's advice. 'We want Roman to be awarded the Hero of Ukraine title, and for the park to be named after him,' Nikiforov says.

The final battle

A bright-minded and excellent strategist, Ratushnyi had no doubt Russia would once again try to wipe out Ukrainian 'national identity'. He was determined to do everything he could to not let it succeed. 'There was no doubt he would go straight to hell [to fight],' says his friend Yevhen Cherepnia. 'Burn all of the Russian subcultures within you ...' Roman would later say. 'Otherwise they will burn you.'

He assembled and headed a volunteer Territorial Defense unit, 'Protasiv Yar', shortly after the full-scale invasion started on 24 February. Nearly a month into the war, after 'gaining some combat experience' in settlements in Kyiv Oblast, Ratushnyi and Cherepnia decided to join the 93rd Mechanized Kholodnyi Yar Brigade of the Ukrainian Ground Forces.

They started by liberating settlements in Sumy Oblast, including the town of Trostianets, and soon headed directly to the site of severe hostilities in Kharkiv Oblast. Roman was distributed to the battalion's special reconnaissance unit. 'Which means being within meters from the enemy,' Cherepnia says.

Besides fighting Russian troops, Ratushnyi had also been collecting equipment and everything needed for his battalion. 'As a soldier, he had the same virtues as a civilian,' Cherepnia says. 'The same fearlessness and determination.'

For the last time, Ratushnyi traveled back home in late May. Kharytonov says he did not want many people to know he was in Kyiv and had a lot to do, just as usual. But something about him had changed, Kharytonov recalls. 'He wanted to return to that hell on the frontline badly,' Kharytonov says. 'Though I felt that it was difficult for him as well.'

Saying goodbye, they took a photograph together, and Ratushnyi left to keep doing what he did the best – fighting for Ukraine. Kharytonov could not abandon the thought that it might be their last photograph together.

Unfortunately, he was not wrong. On 14 June, Ratushnyi's brigade confirmed the terrifying rumors of his death. 'Ambushed by the enemy,' Roman died in combat near Izium, says Cherepnia. One week after that, Ratushnyi's body was finally delivered to his native Kyiv, to his beloved Protasiv Yar.

'I want Ukraine to remember him as an example of a new generation,' says Cherepnia. 'Those who stand for their ideas not in words but actions.'

'Our hope,' people would write on social media after Roman's sudden death. 'He was the best of us ...'

'He would not like it,' says Kharytonov. 'He was very talented but also very humble.'

And yet he 'personified the war in Ukraine', according to Kharytonov.

It now seems that even after his death, Ratushnyi continues fighting for a better future for Ukraine: his mother has asked everyone willing to 'honor the memory' of her son to support Ukrainian cultural and educational facilities like the Taras Shevchenko National Museum, Historical Truth and Novynarnia media outlets, along with National Honored Bandura Band of Ukraine. She has already donated Hr 100,000 to the Historical Truth and Hr 50,000 to 'Your Underground Humanitarian' educational initiative.

Soon, Ratushnyi's name will be inscribed on the map of Kyiv: Volhohradska Street near Protasiv Yar is set to be renamed after the activist.

'You didn't build a house, but you formed a community,' said Roman's father as he stood near the coffin of his son. Ratushnyi was buried in a closed coffin. 'You didn't plant a tree, you saved the park,' he proceeded, trying to hold back tears. 'You didn't have children, but you were not left without descendants ... There is a part of Roman Ratushnyi in every one of us.'

'Heroes do not die,' the crowd could be heard saying in unison throughout the ceremony.

29 June 2022

Despite risks, Ukrainian refugees are coming back home

Thaisa Semenova

Vitallia Mazur, 32, with her then 1-month-old daughter, escaped to Italy in early March, a week after Russian missiles began raining down on Ukrainian cities. Two months later, they returned to Vinnytsia: 'My daughter has been growing up so fast. She started to get used to the environment, to people around her. And the most important people – our relatives, my husband – were thousands of miles away,' she said.

Men under 60 are prohibited from leaving Ukraine under martial law, meaning the vast majority of Ukrainian refugees are women and children, and many families have been separated.

Mazur decided to wait until 9 May, as many observers anticipated Russia would intensify its attacks amid Victory Day celebrations. Just a few days later she was on her way to rejoin her husband in Ukraine.

'Shortly after we crossed the border with Romania and arrived at our hotel in Chernivtsi, we heard the air raid sirens – that terrifying sound I hadn't heard for 60 days. I'm not going to lie, I felt quite anxious,' she recalls. 'But when we finally got to our family home in Vinnytsia, I felt much calmer. The main thing was that I was back with my loved ones, and we would overcome any problems together.'

While the bloodshed has mainly shifted to the east of the country, with Russian troops forced to retreat from the outskirts of Kyiv and Kharkiv, many Ukrainian refugees feel it is safe enough, or at least less dangerous than before, to come back home.

According to United Nations Refugee Agency data, over 8 million people have crossed the border with neighboring countries since the start of Russia's full-scale invasion of Ukraine on 24 February, and more than 3.5 million of them have asked for temporary protection status in EU countries as of 21 June. But the data going in the other direction is 2.8 million, suggesting that about a third of Ukrainians who fled the war may be going home.

This is especially true for cities like Kyiv, where two-thirds of its 4 million residents have already returned, according to Mayor Vitali Klitschko.

Used to air raids

One of those Kyiv residents is Renata Zhupanyn, 24, who fled to Poland in late February.

Before the war, she used to travel a lot, practically living out of a suitcase for three years, searching for the perfect place to settle permanently. She considered Warsaw a good option because she speaks Polish and many of her friends live there. However, in a time of crisis, she realized her hometown Kyiv, not Warsaw, was that perfect place she had been looking for all along. She returned to Kyiv in early June.

She admitted she had no idea what the near future holds for her in Ukraine as there is no corner in the country that is entirely safe from potential Russian missile strikes. But she has almost accepted any fate, saying, 'if the missile hits my house directly, then it's probably meant to be.'

'I can't explain it rationally, but I feel so much better in Kyiv,' she said. 'In Europe, it's good. But my people, my life is in Ukraine. It's quite ironic as I've never thought of myself as a patriot, and I was planning to leave Ukraine eventually. But when I had a chance to emigrate, all I wanted was to go back.'

In a little less than a month at home, Zhupanyn grew accustomed to air raid alerts to the point she rarely reacts to them anymore. Sometimes, she says she even turns off the government app that notifies citizens of air raids so it doesn't disturb her when she is sleeping.

The same goes for Nastia Ladanska, 19, from Lviv, who left for Germany in the early days of the war with her mother and younger siblings but returned home a few weeks ago. She and her husband Andrii rarely go to the bomb shelter when air raids go off. 'I feel safe enough in Lviv. And people around also don't seem to care that much about alerts. Everyone continues to enjoy their coffees on terraces in city center cafes, just minding their own business,' she said.

Ukrainian authorities repeatedly urge citizens not to ignore the air raid alerts. Following a recent missile strike on a shopping mall in the central city of Kremenchuk on 27 June that killed at least 20 people and injured more than 59 others, President Volodymyr Zelensky said that while there were initially 1,000 people in the mall, many managed to get out on time before the missiles hit precisely thanks to the air raid sirens.

'I have little choice'

The war found Maria Berezovets, 21, in Vilnius, Lithuania, where she went to study at a local university as an exchange student. As soon as the war started she intended to go home to Zaporizhzhia in southeastern Ukraine, to be with her mother, who has a spinal fracture, and therefore wouldn't be able to evacuate from the city on her own if needed.

But the host university persuaded her to stay in Vilnius, saying they were responsible for her safety and that she should wait at least until the end of the semester. She agreed to finish her studies but ruled out the option of continuing to live in Lithuania as a refugee.

'During those four months, I kept thinking: "what if the Russians capture the city or bombard it like Mariupol, and mom is there all alone?"' she said, adding that it's hard not to think of worst-case scenarios with Russian troops being in the Zaporizhzhia Oblast since the early days of the war. Currently, Zaporizhzhia Oblast is almost 60% occupied by Russian forces.

Berezovets' mother was against the idea of her coming back while it was still unsafe. 'But I have little choice,' Berezovets said. 'I can't let her be there alone. As long as my mom is in Zaporizhzhia, I will be there, too.'

4 July 2022

Ukrainian artist Liubov Panchenko died after month of starvation in Russian-occupied Bucha

Daria Shulzhenko

One cold day in late March, a Russian shell hit a small barn behind an unremarkable two-storey house in then Russian-occupied Bucha in Kyiv Oblast.

The powerful blast partially destroyed the barn, broke the house's windows, and cracked the entrance door, letting out a small black dog. It rushed down the empty street barking loudly, as if calling for help.

Drawn by the noise, a local resident went outside, despite the fear of being killed by Russian soldiers. He followed the barking dog up to the site of the recent explosion.

There, inside the dilapidated house, a man found an old lady lying unconscious in the cold room.

The woman was Liubov Panchenko, a renowned Ukrainian artist of the 1960s.

Panchenko spent her whole life defending and promoting Ukrainian culture, resisting the Soviet totalitarian regime's censorship by adding folk motifs to her drawings, collages, and clothes as well as speaking the Ukrainian language when it was forbidden.

For that, she was repressed as an artist. While her work was shown alongside other contemporaries, Panchenko never had her own individual exhibit until after the collapse of the Soviet Union.

And for being Ukrainian, she was killed. Russia's war caused her to slowly die of starvation in her beloved hometown of Bucha, where Russian troops killed at least 412 people during the town's occupation in what is now known as the 'Bucha massacre'.

Isolated from the whole world, the 84-year-old artist spent a month under Russian occupation alone, sharing what little food she had with her dog Bonia.

Soon after being found, local volunteers took Panchenko to a hospital in Kyiv, where for nearly a month doctors tried to save her life.

'What we saw at the hospital was a skeleton covered with skin,' says the head of the Ukrainian Sixtiers Dissident Movement Museum Olena Lodzynska, who knew Panchenko personally. 'She was beyond exhausted.'

The artist never recovered. On 30 April, Panchenko died in a hospital in Kyiv.

'She was not broken by the KGB during Soviet times,' said Ukraine's first lady Olena Zelenska. 'But the Russian occupation broke her.' ...

Guilty for being Ukrainian

During one of Russia's multitudinous attempts to silence Ukrainian identity during the Soviet era, Panchenko joined Kyiv's Creative Youth Club, which united a new generation of creative Ukrainian youth who opposed the Soviet authorities known as the Sixtiers.

'It was an attempt of those who just wanted to speak Ukrainian and talk about Ukraine, to gather in one place and do it,' Kulyk says.

Inspired by this community, Panchenko started making traditional folk outfits for Ukrainian choir members and embroidered shirts for her friends and drew portraits of legendary poet Taras Shevchenko, adorning them with his iconic quote from the 'Caucasus' poem – 'fight and you will win'.

By that time, Panchenko's parents finally accepted their daughter's decision to be an artist and their house in Bucha became a welcoming harbor for Ukrainian caroling groups, banned by the Soviet authorities.

'It was the environment that shaped her worldview,' Krupnyk says.

It was also the time when her talent blossomed: In the mid-1960s, Panchenko created an astonishing series of watercolor drawings depicting the Ukrainian Carpathian Mountains and her native Kyiv Oblast, as well as sketches from her trip to the Caucasus. As a clothing designer, Panchenko weaved modern style with traditional folk elements, also using the scraps of fabric to make collages.

Though her works were not totally banned by the Soviet authorities – many of her fashion sketches and embroidery were published in the popular *Soviet Woman* magazine with approval of the magazine's management – Panchenko was often criticized and was even asked to 'change the style of her works'.

'When some Soviet minister told her that it was the time to change her style, she told him that maybe it was the time to change the minister,' says Lodzynska ...

The artist didn't have a single personal exhibition up until 1992, after the fall of the Soviet Union. 'For them, she was guilty of being Ukrainian, for being born in Ukraine, for considering herself Ukrainian and promoting Ukrainian [culture],' Kulyk says.

Killed by Russia

Ever since the death of her husband, Ukrainian artist Oleksiy Oliinyk, in 1994, Panchenko lived alone in her hometown Bucha, occasionally visited by her friends and relatives.

She never had children due to her weak health, which continued to decline over the years. By the time Panchenko turned 84 on 2 February, she was 'almost helpless and needed constant support,' says Krupnyk, who visited the artist on her birthday to present the first digital collection of her work. 'If it wasn't for these inhumane conditions during the occupation of Bucha, I think she would still be alive to witness the print version of the album.'

On the day Russia started its full-scale invasion of Ukraine on 24 February, Panchenko's relatives managed to bring her some food, says Lodzynska. Rozumenko says that before the war, mainly local social workers would bring Panchenko food.

When Russian troops entered and occupied the town, violently killing civilians en masse, it became clear that leaving one's home could be a death trap. It was no longer possible to get to the artist's house. Her beloved dog Bonia was Panchenko's only companion. 'How she was surviving and what she was eating is still a mystery,' Lodzynska says.

Only after her courtyard was hit by a Russian shell, days before Kyiv Oblast was liberated, already unconscious Panchenko was found at her home and then hospitalized. Unable to identify her at the hospital, Lodzynska only found her around two weeks after she was hospitalized. 'She looked just like the victims of concentration camps: Sunken cheeks, thin arms and legs,' Lodzynska says.

Even though Panchenko was awake, the doctor told Lodzynska she wasn't reacting to anything and was getting nutrition intravenously. But when Panchenko saw the flowers in Lodzynska's hands, she instantly reached for them. 'She said "I'm very glad, but sorry that I'm not in a good state,"' Lodzynska recalls. 'As if giving away all her energy with these words.'

In the following days, Panchenko started eating little by little, sparking hope she would survive. Barely talking, she told Lodzynska that Russian soldiers tried to enter her house one day, but she did not let them in. The rest is still unknown ...

'She was killed by Russia,' says Kulyk. 'But her legacy will live on.'

20 July 2022

Inside Ukraine's covert operation to take out elite Wagner Group mercenaries in Donbas

Alexander Khrebet

Editor's Note: The names of the people interviewed by The Kyiv Independent *have been changed in this story to protect their identity, as they have shared sensitive information that could place them and their families in danger.*

Not all of Ukraine's attacks on Russian positions end up circulating on social media like the recent strikes on what Ukraine says are over 30 Russian ammunition depots in the occupied east and south.

There are other, much more discrete operations that Ukraine carries out deep into Russian-occupied territories.

Among these low-profile operations was the destruction of a Wagner Group base 45 kilometers east of the front line in Russian-occupied Kadiivka in Luhansk Oblast in early June.

Russia deployed the Wagner Group, a Russian-controlled mercenary group operating at the Kremlin's request around the world, to eastern Ukraine amid its military's 'heavy losses', the UK Defence Ministry reported on 28 March.

'I was one of the first to find out that they had arrived and were stationed at the local stadium,' Oleh, a resident of Kadiivka, told *The Kyiv Independent*.

Living in a Russian-occupied city for the past eight years, Oleh has been cooperating with Ukrainian authorities, constantly providing them with intelligence. 'I passed this information to the right people,' Oleh said.

As a result, the Ukrainian military hit the base with artillery on 9 June, killing anywhere between 50 and 200 mercenaries according to different estimates and destroying their weapons depot.

The Kyiv Independent has recreated the events of the operation based on conversations with local civilians and sources in intelligence agencies.

Identifying Wagner

Some Ukrainians who remained in Russian-occupied territories have been helping to identify Russian troops, equipment, bases, and depots, Anton, a member of Ukraine's Special Operations Forces, told *The Kyiv Independent*

The Special Operations Forces is a branch of Ukraine's armed forces that conducts reconnaissance missions and covert operations behind enemy lines.

It was through locals that intelligence officers learned in May about the Wagner Group mercenaries stationed in Kadiivka. 'Without them, it would have been impossible,' Anton says. 'The group settled in a local gym. It became clear it wasn't the Russian armed forces, but, let's say, a specific branch of the Russian army.'

The Wagner Group, widely known as a private military company, is controlled by the Kremlin through Russian oligarch Yevgeny Prigozhin, a close friend of Russian President Vladimir Putin, often dubbed 'Putin's chef', because another company of his provides food catering to the Kremlin.

The group consists mostly of former Russian servicemen and has previously been involved in wars and armed conflicts in Ukraine, Syria, the Central African Republic, Mali, Madagascar, Mozambique, and Sudan.

Prigozhin has also been in control of Russian 'troll factories' operating on social media. In 2018, Prigozhin was charged with 'funding and organizing operations for the purpose of interfering with US political and electoral processes, including the 2016 presidential election, and other crimes including identity theft', according to a US court document.

Anton was the first to receive a message from Oleh. 'There is some interesting information. Details later,' the local told him.

Oleh declined to say how he was able to pass the information about Wagner Group's location to Ukraine's Special Forces so as not to endanger future operations. 'Transmission always happens in different ways. One informant may hand over information immediately, another, two weeks later. It's often a matter of chance,' Anton says.

Preparing the operation

After the information is passed along, there are several stages of verification, which generally include open-source intelligence methods. Anton's job is to get tips from locals, verify them, and pass them on to another unit, which then repeats verification. Anton doesn't make decisions on specific targets. He says there are no reports or 'unnecessary paperwork', and a limited number of people are in the loop to prevent the information from leaking. He didn't reveal how the information is verified. Following verification, there is a risk assessment for civilians, after which a final decision is made on the target.

'One of the problems is when a new group of Russians settles on the lower floor of an apartment building. Civilians are living on the upper floors. Russians frequently do it, using civilians as a human shield,' says Anton. 'They can settle between a kindergarten and a school, or inside one of them.'

This time, the Wagner mercenaries in Kadiivka had settled at a stadium in a residential area.

Oleh says a target is never destroyed the day after information is passed along. For the strike on the Wagner base in Kadiivka, preparations took about two weeks – from receiving the tip in May to striking the group on 9 June.

During this time, local residents continuously checked to make sure the mercenaries continued to occupy the building. Those residents have since left the city.

According to Oleh, many locals knew that the Wagner Group was stationed in the city. 'Wagner mercenaries don't know how to keep their mouths shut,' he says. 'They themselves went around and introduced themselves as "an orchestra" or "musicians".' These self-given monikers are references to German composer Richard Wagner whom the group is believed to be named after. 'They were telling local girls, "we are an orchestra on a tour here,"' says Oleh.

Oleh found out exactly where the mercenaries were living at the stadium: in a large gym at the stadium's premises. Under the stadium's tribunes, the mercenaries set up an ammunition depot, with four or five of them standing guard there, and rotating frequently. Videos from the site, published by Russian propagandists after Ukraine hit it, confirm Oleh's description of the place.

'In total, there were about 300 to 400 [mercenaries]. It's hard to say the exact number. I don't think they even know how many of them were in town,' Anton says. It's unknown what this group was doing or preparing to do in the Donbas. Wagner mercenaries are an elite force, more professional and experienced than regular Russian troops or their local collaborators.

Successful strike

Ukraine hit the stadium with artillery on early in the morning on 9 June. The site was destroyed.

The Special Operation Forces' serviceman and his informant disagree on what weapons Ukraine used to hit the stadium. Anton says the strike was carried out with a High Mobility Artillery Rocket System, or HIMARS, recently provided to Ukraine by the US. But Ukraine only officially deployed HIMARS in Donbas in the second half of June. Oleh thinks it was a more obsolete weapon. Russian-controlled proxies reported shelling conducted by a Grad self-propelled multiple rocket launcher. However, photos of the site don't show multiple impact areas that would have been left by this type of rocket launcher.

'The place was immediately cordoned off after the attack,' says Oleh. The local militia was not allowed to enter. Russian officers took over the site. 'Because of this, it was difficult to verify information on casualties. After a laptop was found at the site by a local, it was immediately torn out of his hands by the Russians.'

It took a week to clean up the debris.

Anton puts the number of killed mercenaries at around 250. 'Even for Russia, such high losses of motivated, highly trained fighters is a lot,' says Anton.

Oleh's information from the field is more modest. 'From one hospital, from another, the morgues, there was different data,' Oleh says. 'Rescuers at the scene said there were 50 killed. Some of my sources said the dead were taken to a morgue in Luhansk. There they said that there were 150 bodies.'

The number of survivors is unknown. A few hours before the Ukrainian strike, a part of the group left the site, according to Oleh. Around half of the group, including the ammunition depot guards, remained at the spot.

Russian-controlled proxies reported that 22 civilians were killed in the attack. They reported it as a strike on a residential area, and didn't mention the presence of any military at all, let alone the Wagner Group.

Ukraine said only two civilians were killed as a result of the strike. Oleh agrees with Ukraine's estimation. 'The [Russian-controlled proxies'] number was inflated, there weren't 22 civilians. For some reason, they recorded 20 Wagner mercenaries as civilians,' says Oleh. According to Oleh, the Wagner mercenaries on the site were mostly killed by concrete parts of the building crushing them.

Aftermath

Since the military occupation of Kadiivka began in 2014, Oleh has helped Ukraine in any way possible. He tracked Russian troop movement, handing over sensitive information to Ukrainian special services.

'In 2014, the Ukrainian military was not shooting at bases and warehouses like they do now. Although the data was still transmitted,' he says. 'A couple of months ago, Ukraine hit a base near my town for the first time. I bought a bottle of beer to celebrate. I've been waiting for this for eight years.'

Recently, Oleh has had more and more reasons to celebrate. In his town alone, Ukrainian troops have hit six ammunition depots so far, according to Oleh. The last attack occurred on 14 July, when according to Russian-controlled proxies, Ukraine hit Kadiivka with HIMARS. An ammunition depot caught fire as a result.

Oleh says the new long-range artillery provided by the West is significantly reducing the opportunity for Russian troops to conduct attacks and shelling of Ukrainian territory. Meanwhile, Oleh and others continue their resistance by helping Ukraine far behind the front lines.

22 July 2022

Why is Russia so vulnerable to HIMARS in Ukraine?

Illia Ponomarenko

It's been nearly a month since US-provided High Mobility Artillery Rocket System, or HIMARS, had their long-awaited debut in Ukraine, but their combat record is already extensive.

Using all the heavy and long-range weaponry available to it, including HIMARS, Ukraine began a campaign that has destroyed dozens of significant fuel and munition depots in occupied parts of Ukraine, jeopardizing Russian logistics, vital supplies, and artillery power.

Ukraine's military then moved on to using rockets against Russian-controlled airfields, bridges, and transportation points.

Now, HIMARS are also directly challenging Russia's air defenses, wiping out expensive advanced radars far behind the front lines.

Contrary to its propagandistic bravado, the Russian military has appeared helpless – or at least very vulnerable – to the dozen or so US-provided HIMARS striking the very essence of Russia's military advantage over Ukraine, becoming an important factor in the war.

And as the latest month of hostilities demonstrates, there's little Russia can do about it.

Its own systemic flaws, outdated tactics, lack of initiative, and previous failures in the war leave it few chances to confront the American weapons now in Ukrainian hands.

Russian weak spots

Upon estimates, there are between eight and 12 HIMARS currently on the battlefield in Ukraine. The US on 20 July announced the delivery of four more following the 4th Ramstein meeting of defense ministers. An undisclosed number of M270 MLRS, a similar but heavier truck-mounted system, provided by Western countries, are also already operational in Ukraine, according to Defense Minister Oleksiy Reznikov.

Within just weeks, a few HIMARSs have managed to strip Russia of the majority, if not all of, its most considerable ammunition and fuel depots in Donbas and Ukraine's occupied south.

With almost every nightfall, videos of massive detonations at Russian depots in Kherson Oblast or Donbas pop up on social media.

The situation has even prompted Russian military bloggers to openly raise alarm about escalating munitions hunger, as Russian artillery supremacy was the key behind its incremental advances in Donbas.

What's more, the inception of HIMARS has also allowed Ukraine to make use of its old Soviet Tochka-U ballistic missiles, which had been stashed away by the Ukrainian military due to a lack of heavy weaponry. Now that Ukraine has HIMARS, it can afford to use Tochka-U more often.

Tochka-U systems have an effective range of up to 100 kilometers and are more powerful than HIMARS, but far less precise and much easier to intercept. The Tochkas and HIMARS are spearheading the ongoing campaign to strike deep inside the Russian-held rear.

As part of their expanding hit list, HIMARS were reportedly used to target Russia's 20th Motorized Infantry Brigade headquarters, with the brigade commander Colonel Aleksey Gorobets and two other senior commanders killed on 12 July.

The rockets have also successfully targeted a Repellent-1 on 18 July in Nova Kakhovka and a Podlet K1 in Lazurne, critical Russian air defense radars in Kherson Oblast. Moreover, HIMARS were used in a series of strikes upon the Antonivsky Bridge near Kherson, which rendered a key Russian supply line temporarily unusable on 20 July.

Even before these latest strikes, on 15 July, the Pentagon issued a statement confirming the HIMARS' 'significant impact' on Russia's war in Ukraine. Weeks go by, but Russia has not been seen as effective at countering HIMARS strikes, destroying the systems, or saving their critical infrastructure from them. Russia continues losing near-frontline ammo and fuel dumps, and all of the known confirmed HIMARS attacks have been impactful.

Russia also appears to be incapable of quickly de-concentrating its depots, which could save its munitions in the occupied parts of Ukraine. The Russian military has held on to the outdated Soviet approach of having a hyper-centralized command and control system that doesn't allow for much initiative from medium- and low-rank leaders.

When it comes to ammunition handling, the Russian military is still very dependent on manual labor as soldiers have to load and unload thousands of ammo bundles as they arrive. Russian logistics still fall short of effective communications and automatization, lacking working hands and competent mid-level commanders to cope with a much more complicated depot network.

Moreover, Russian supply lines depend on railway communications, which inevitably keeps them bound to railway stations and junctions. Russian military bloggers have admitted that switching to a more flexible system would take months or even years, which is not a viable solution during the ongoing war.

Russians could make their depots safer by relocating them farther away from the front line.

The high-precision M30/M31 GMLRS rockets used by Ukrainian HIMARS have an effective range of some 85 kilometers. Therefore, locating their depots beyond this dangerous effective range would be the answer to the problem. But by pulling them back, Russia is also greatly complicating its already very problematic logistics.

Russian trucks would have to make it 90 or 100, or even 120 kilometers, to bring supplies to frontline units from dumps instead of the more usual 20 or 30 kilometers. This would take much more time, fuel, and even more manual labor.

According to standard practice, a truck could complete just one round trip daily between a frontline unit and a supply depot located beyond the HIMARS effective range 90 kilometers away from the front line. Withdrawing to new loading areas at safe railroad centers in southern Ukraine would render Russian delivery time between one and a half to two times slower than usual.

But Russia's military keeps running short of trucks, and truck drivers were killed in huge numbers during Russia's early offensive deep inside Ukraine. According to the open source project Oryx documenting Russian war losses, the Russian military has lost at least 1,254 supply trucks and fuel tankers.

Even if they are eventually relocated farther away from the front line, Russian depots would still be threatened by Ukrainian Tochka-U missiles, which have already swept off some of Russia's most giant ammo dumps in Donbas, such as the one in the city of Khrustalniy (formerly Krasniy Luch) in Luhansk Oblast on 18 June.

Should Ukraine be finally provided with 300-kilometer ATACMS missiles, the situation will become even more complicated for Russia ...

2 August 2022

Escaping forced conscription in Russian-occupied Donetsk
Alexander Khrebet

Editor's Note: The names of the people interviewed by The Kyiv Independent *for this story have been changed to protect their identity, as they have shared sensitive information that could place them and their families in danger.*

Stepan didn't see daylight for nearly four months.

Since mid-February, even before Russia's full-scale invasion of Ukraine began, many men of conscription age in Russian-occupied Donetsk, the largest city in Ukraine's Donbas region, went into hiding, fearing what might happen if they stepped outside.

Many of those who dared to walk out were grabbed by local Kremlin-controlled militants and forcibly sent to the front lines to fight against Ukraine. Most of them were sent without any training, equipment, or combat experience.

According to residents who spoke to *The Kyiv Independent*, the city's streets began to empty about a week before Russia launched its full-scale invasion on 24 February. By then, Russian-led militants had already announced a large-scale, forced conscription campaign targeting men between the ages of 18 and 55 in the eastern Ukrainian region they had occupied since 2014.

People started to look for ways to leave the already depopulated city. Several different schemes to smuggle people out emerged just days after men were forced to pick up arms. All of them dangerous and costly.

Stepan, a former resident of Donetsk, told *The Kyiv Independent* he was able to leave after his friends recommended an expensive, yet reliable, guide. 'I fled because it became unrealistic and dangerous to live in Donetsk. You can't go outside because of forced conscription. There is no water, no work,' he said.

Stepan is among the lucky few to have left. Thousands of other men, living in regions occupied by Russian-controlled militants since 2014, have not been so fortunate.

Cannon fodder

The streets of once-busy Donetsk now look empty. In 2014, hundreds of thousands fled Donetsk as Russia took hold of the once prosperous city with a pre-war population of one million. In 2022, a new exodus is taking place as men are fleeing forced conscription.

When local militants began forcibly drafting men from the occupied region in mid-February, some men voluntarily showed up at military registration offices after receiving a notice, believing it was just a formality. It wasn't.

Once the full-scale invasion of Ukraine started on 24 February, Russia used the newly conscripted men from occupied Donbas as cannon fodder in their offensive in eastern Ukraine.

As people stopped showing up at the registration offices, militants began grabbing people right off the streets and bringing them in. Men of conscription age virtually disappeared from the streets, keeping out of sight by staying at home. 'I never went outside. Others were less lucky. People I knew were snatched straight from work or school. Almost immediately they were sent to the [war's] hot spots,' Stepan said.

Many, including Stepan, began looking for a way out of occupied territories.

Getting out

With the battles raging west of Donetsk, the only way out is going east through Russia. Most of the time getting out requires knowing someone who can escort you through the border.

Stepan says the first time you call 'the guide', you need to say you're looking for transportation documents. He says the guide he called was nervous and was afraid of discussing the details on the phone. 'You found me, so you've been told [how it works],' the guide told Stepan.

The guide scheduled the day of the trip. When the day came, he called in the morning and told Stepan the departure time. The car arrived straight at the entrance to Stepan's residential building so that Stepan wouldn't be seen outside.

The militants at the border were in on the scheme and let them pass. Stepan paid a total of 60,000 rubles, equivalent to around $900.

At the Russian border, he was interrogated by the Federal Security Service for several hours. He had to fill out a detailed form about who he was and give up all his social media passwords before eventually being let into the country.

Stepan is now safe in Sweden.

The Kyiv Independent spoke to two other men, Maksym and Yaroslav, who left Donetsk through a similar arrangement.

'If you leave by car, the guide drives. Often these guides are militants dressed as civilians,' Maksym, who left in June for Rostov, told *The Kyiv Independent*. If several people gather for the trip, the cars line up in a column and make their way to the border. The guide's car usually has a special pass on the windshield. With the pass, the car won't be stopped at checkpoints on the way to the border.

According to Maksym, some people leave on their own, bypassing checkpoints through fields. He said that in most cases if a person attempting to flee is stopped at a checkpoint, they can pay a bribe on the spot and get out. Success depends on your wallet, communication skills, and the mood of the militant, Maksym said.

Maksym added that initially, the price to be smuggled out in a packed truck was as low as 20,000 rubles ($370) per person. As the war raged on, the prices increased ...

Yaroslav, who left Donetsk in July and was able to move to Portugal, told *The Kyiv Independent* that he paid $350 in January to have his documents stamped with an 'unfit for service' mark. Today, he says, such a stamp would cost $2,600. 'Few people can afford to pay this,' said Yaroslav, who had no problem entering Russia with an 'unfit for service' stamp.

An explicit war crime

Forced conscription in occupied territories constitutes a war crime according to the Geneva Conventions. It also violates the Rome Statute of the International Criminal Court.

According to human rights activists, Russia has forcibly mobilized up to 100,000 residents of the occupied territories of Donetsk and Luhansk oblasts. Many of them have already been killed. According to the Eastern Human Rights Group, the number of those killed is north of a quarter of those mobilized.

'Forced conscription is sending people to die,' Gunduz Mamedov, former deputy prosecutor general, and expert on international humanitarian law, told *The Kyiv Independent*. 'In Ukraine, forced conscription can lead to up to 12 years in prison [for people involved in the conscription], and if this leads to the person being killed, it is a life sentence.'

Yet it's hard to enforce these laws, says Alyona Luneva, director of advocacy at Ukraine's ZMINA human rights center. 'Ukraine cannot do anything to prevent the forced conscription in the occupied territories,' Luneva told *The Kyiv Independent*. 'Just like with deportation, Ukraine has no legal mechanisms to prevent forced mobilization in occupation.'

This is what Stepan now fears the most. Low on cash and options, his father and friends are still stuck in Russian-occupied Donbas, facing the possibility of forced conscription.

3 August 2022

Battle to end the war: Ukraine's chance to get edge over Russia
Illia Ponomarenko

The third phase of Russia's war on Ukraine is coming.

The first, the Kremlin's brazen blitzkrieg in late February that culminated in the Battle of Kyiv, failed. The months-long Battle of Donbas in Ukraine's east making up the second phase has gotten bogged down, with Russia having barely enough strength to complete the region's capture.

The war's focus has now pivoted to the south.

After over five months of its full-out war, Russia is employing close to 100% of its conventional military power against Ukraine, with only limited results to show for it.

Russia is steadily losing military power as the country struggles to generate high-quality reserves. It has spent the last month refraining from large-scale operations in Donbas and elsewhere, trying to recover from previous battles.

For Ukraine, this hiatus is a window of opportunity.

While Russia is still coming around, Ukraine's military has the chance to deliver a decisive strike that would allow it to gain an edge over Russia and define the course of the rest of the war. In other words, this could be the war's turning point.

This third phase could determine the rest of the war. If successful, it could lead to a fourth phase in which Ukraine defeats Russia.

The Kremlin clearly understands the stakes. It is urgently redeploying much of its forces from Donbas to Ukraine's south, where its positions are the most vulnerable.

The next few months will define the war's outcome, the majority of experts believe.

Limited results

While the fighting in Ukraine's east has been raging since the first day of Russia's full-scale invasion, the region became Russia's primary focus during the war's phase two, the Battle of Donbas, which started mid-April.

Months later, Russia had nearly 78% of Donetsk and Luhansk oblasts under its control, the full seizure of which was repeatedly stated as the new campaign's main goal. However, it had already occupied a total of 30% of the two regions' territory since Russia's invasion of 2014–2015. And this is despite the fact that at the height of the Battle of Donbas, Russia had concentrated close to 65% of its overall military power in Ukraine in northern Donbas.

It's been nearly a month since Russia, following more than 60 days of fighting, finally seized Sievierodonetsk and Lysychansk, the twin cities of Luhansk Oblast, in late June and early July. For the next month, Russian forces took 'an operational pause' to restore their severely depleted units.

Experts polled by *The Kyiv Independent* agree that Russia paid an unreasonably heavy price for their gains in the Battle of Donbas.

The 'pause' continued pretty much until the end of July. During this time, Russia managed to make just tactical gains close to Bakhmut in Donetsk Oblast, such as the capture of the defunct Vuhlehirska power plant by Wagner mercenaries on 26 July.

As the Institute for the Study of War (ISW), a US-based think tank, said on 27 July, the Russian military was capable of sustaining just two significant offensive operations against the cities of Bakhmut and Siversk, respectively.

Other than that, the ISW added, Russia had been unable to sustain 'a similar offensive operational tempo or to make similar territorial gains elsewhere in Ukraine'. The think tank believes Russia's protracted offensive in Donbas will likely culminate before seizing any other major urban areas in Ukraine.

A Russian force of up to 150,000 soldiers is still not enough for all that the Kremlin wants in Ukraine.

Experts believe that Russia made the strategic mistake of dispersing its limited strike force across several axes in Ukraine instead of just one. It had to give up on Kyiv and northern Ukraine and in not withdrawing from the south, Russia was forced to commit a lot of military power at the expense of its offensives in Donbas. 'And thus they fall short of the strength to get 100% results,' said Andriy Zagorodniuk, a former Ukrainian defense minister and currently the head of the Kyiv-based Center for Defense Strategies. 'And we can see that after success in Luhansk Oblast, they're finding it hard to consolidate their gains in Donetsk Oblast. We have spoken to many analysts, including our American colleagues, and most of them have doubts about Russia's ability to seize the whole of Donetsk Oblast.'

New theater

The Battle of Donbas may not be completely over. But the Kherson and the Zaporizhzhia sectors are gaining increasingly stronger significance.

And the Ukrainian military is making incremental gains. According to local Ukrainian authorities, 60 towns and villages have been retaken in tactical strikes all along the 230-kilometer front line of Kherson Oblast as of 3 August.

Ukraine's armed forces have reached the point of openly targeting Russia's ground lines of communications and derailing its infrastructure across the Dnipro River. More than 50 fuel and munition dumps have been destroyed over the last few weeks.

Out of the three bridges that can be used to supply the Russian military in Kherson, two have been rendered unusable with HIMARS strikes. The last bridge to Kherson, the Kakhovska power plant dam, is already within Ukrainian firing range.

The plan of cutting the Russian military off supplies and blocking it in Kherson, discussed for weeks in the media, is slowly moving along.

The growing tension is palpable.

And Russia is reacting. Recently, Russian forces were seen urgently redeploying scores of its troops from Donbas to Crimea in the direction of Kherson or Zaporizhzhia oblasts via the city of Melitopol. According to the Ukrainian authorities, Russia has deployed a total of nearly 25,000 troops to Kherson.

Nearly 10,000 of those troops have been redeployed via the last available concrete crossing in Nova Kakhovka. Russia is also already installing lots of pontoon barges to possibly keep its recently redeployed military grouping supplied.

The redeployment of Russia's VDV airborne units to the south may even halt all Russian offensive operations against Sloviansk, the ISW said on 1 August.

But nonetheless, Russia does have a rather strong, multilayered defense in Kherson, and has brought in urgent reinforcements to Zaporizhzhia Oblast.

A new battle could start anywhere in the swathes of Ukraine's southern steppe. Ukraine may opt to go for Kherson or try and deliver a strike toward Melitopol, a key transportation point with a strategic airfield.

Technical advantage

The war's third stage became possible largely thanks to massive assistance from the West, particularly heavy artillery, munitions, and components.

The Battle of Donbas was a tragedy in itself when, at some point in early summer, Ukrainian artillery ran out completely of its old Soviet munition.

Ukrainian guns went silent in the very heat of Russia's destructive drive to claim Sievierodonetsk. This was a critical point in the war that could have spelled the end of all hope. Stripped of heavy weaponry, Ukraine would have had no serious chance against Russia.

Luckily, this disastrous logistics gap was rather short.

Thanks to massive Western supplies, Ukraine's military managed to quickly switch to NATO-standard artillery pieces and munitions, in all of their variety from different Western militaries. Ukraine also managed to quickly resume the full intensity of its artillery activities with the new Western pieces.

And thanks to ongoing Western supplies, Ukraine is slowly and steadily moving up in terms of its technological power as compared to Russia, which operates far less advanced and precise weaponry, although in larger numbers.

As a result, Russia, in ongoing costly battles, is slowly losing its overall power in Ukraine. More combat units are rendered ineffective and require replenishment, more individual servicemembers refuse to take part in hostilities, and there is more emphasis on irregular mercenaries like the Wagner Group.

However, this does not mean Russia is critically low on combat-capable manpower. Rather, it struggles to generate enough high-quality reserves within a reasonable amount of time.

It is known that Russia is forming the so-called '3rd Army Corps' based in the town of Mulino in Nizhniy Novgorod Oblast.

The 'Corps', according to Ukrainian and Western intelligence, is expected to enlist up to some 10,000–15,000 recruits coming from civilian life with little to no military experience just for the sake of money.

Along with even more dubious and ever less capable 'volunteer battalions' reportedly formed in some of Russia's regions, this force will likely have a very limited effect on the hostilities in Ukraine, experts believe.

Moreover, de-mothballing old hardware and vehicles, which have been collecting dust at Russian bases for decades, is also a far bigger problem than most imagine.

'As is the case with anything, the whole system is only as strong as its weakest part,' said Zagorodniuk. 'If you have like 100 tanks, but just ten trained tank crews – it means, in reality, you have just ten tanks. The Russian military's biggest problem is the organizational capability to generate more strength. The output capacity of their system is just not sufficient. It will have to spend a lot of time mobilizing recruits, training them, commissioning their officers, and so on.'

So while this window of opportunity is open, Ukraine has the chance to gain an edge over Russia while it's still making up for its losses. This must be completed before November, when winter comes in Ukraine and the cold and rain will make it extremely difficult to go on the offense. It is crucial Ukraine not lose this chance. Time is not on Ukraine's side –an endless war of attrition is simply not a choice the country can make.

For the moment it is unclear about where Ukraine can deliver the main strike – leaving Russia guessing and dispersing its forces among all possible areas, exactly what it is doing now.

A concentrated strike along just one axis, with the use of all advantages provided by Western weaponry, could be a success, Zagorodniuk believes.

'But there's an "if",' the expert says. 'Our Western partners have to continue providing us with weapons and hardware at least at the same tempo or even faster. It is important that they do not fall to deliberations.'

'Because each time the war enters a new phase, we have noticed this, they fall into deliberations – if there'll be a success, or if we can do that, and so on. These deliberations tend to become self-inflicting doubt.'

'Besides, there's this "fatigue", a frustration that goes as far as blaming Ukraine for this endless war. So then just give us what we're asking for, and we'll end this war as soon as possible. If anyone is really tired of this war, it's Ukraine.'

5 August 2022

'Torturing people is fun for them': 16-year-old Ukrainian recalls his 3 months in Russian captivity

Daria Shulzhenko

In early April, an unremarkable civilian car drove slowly toward a Russian checkpoint in the occupied town of Vasylivka, Zaporizhzhia Oblast.

It had passed dozens of checkpoints on its way from the occupied city of Melitopol to the Ukrainian-controlled regional capital Zaporizhzhia. None of its passengers expected what was about to happen.

As a Russian soldier approached the car, he spotted a teenage boy checking something on his phone.

'What are you doing, filming me?' the soldier yelled.

He took the boy's phone and pulled him out of the car.

'Should I shoot you right now or smash your phone?' he shouted, pointing his gun at the boy.

The furious soldier dragged the boy to the backyard of a nearby cafe where Russian troops were based, leaving those in the car speechless and terrified.

After an hour of checking his identity, Russian soldiers realized the detainee was a 'jackpot' for them. The boy they captured was Vladyslav Buryak, the son of one of the region's highest-ranking Ukrainian officials – Oleh Buryak, the head of the Zaporizhzhia District State Administration. Until 2020, Buryak was a member of the Russia-friendly Opposition Bloc political party.

The following 90 days in Russian captivity would become nothing but unimaginable horror for the 16-year-old Vladyslav Buryak.

Locked in a tiny dilapidated prison cell in Vasylivka's pre-trial detention center, the boy heard the harrowing screams of Ukrainian prisoners of war being tortured by Russian soldiers. He watched as some of them died after enduring hours of torture and was forced to clean the 'torture room' awash with their blood.

'Every minute there was a very severe challenge because every minute could have been my last,' the boy told *The Kyiv Independent* during an interview alongside his father.

He is not the only Ukrainian minor who has spent a long time in Russian captivity since Russia's all-out war began on 24 February: According to Zaporizhzhia Oblast Governor Oleksandr Starukh, Russians have held captive five minors in Zaporizhzhia Oblast. Two of them remained imprisoned as of the end of July.

A total of 203 children have been recorded missing in Ukraine as of the beginning of August. Most of them went missing in the war's hotspots.

Russia's war has also killed at least 358 children as of 4 August. The numbers are expected to be higher since they don't include casualties in the Russian-occupied territories and areas where hostilities are ongoing.

Among all of Russia's atrocities against Ukrainian children, Buryak's story has a happy ending. On 7 July, he was released.

Family first

Vladyslav Buryak's 'normal and happy' teenage life came to a halt when Russia began its all-out invasion on Ukraine. Buryak's native city of Melitopol, where he lived with his mother and younger sister, was occupied by Russians in the first days of the full-scale war.

Oleh Buryak was already in Zaporizhzhia, where he had moved before the war.

Even though his father had urged Vladyslav and the family to evacuate, the boy wanted to stay in the occupied city to take care of his grandfather, who was sick with late-stage cancer.

'I was with him almost all the time,' he says.

Leaving the city in early March was also too risky since there were too many Russian troops everywhere, according to Vladyslav.

Horrendous sounds of shelling, missile attacks, and street fights became a part of Buryak's everyday life in Melitopol. In between supporting his grandfather and hiding from Russia's attacks, Buryak shared information on local collaborators, Russian tanks, and other machinery movements with his father.

'We agreed that if [Vladyslav] sees that I read the message, he should wait 10 minutes and immediately delete it,' Oleh Buryak says.

When talking on the phone, the two also called themselves by different names so that Russians couldn't identify them.

'I forbade him to call me father or dad,' Oleh says. 'I was worried from day one that sooner or later they would be captured.'

As he was looking for ways to get his son out of the occupied city, Oleh's friend from Melitopol found some local women with whom Vladyslav could evacuate. The boy's mother and sister fled the city a week before him. But he didn't want to leave his grandfather behind until the end.

On 8 April, the day the women were planning to flee Melitopol, Vladyslav's grandfather died.

'I came to hold his hand, kissed him goodbye, and then left,' the boy said.

Comforting the dying

Oleh was at a work meeting when he received a call from a friend. The earth slipped beneath his feet when he heard that Russian soldiers had abducted his son.

'I instantly started thinking of what I could do, what solution I could find,' he says.

For the first few days in captivity, the Russians didn't give Buryak any food or water. Out of stress, he says he didn't even want anything.

Five days later they brought Vladyslav some food and water for the first time. After about two weeks, the Russian soldiers allowed him to take a shower. And only one month after he was imprisoned, Vladyslav was finally allowed to wash his clothes.

But that wasn't the biggest challenge.

'When I got there on the first day, I couldn't understand why someone was screaming so loudly, wildly,' Buryak says. Later he would realize they were Ukrainian prisoners screaming in agony while being tortured by Russian soldiers. 'Most Ukrainian prisoners kept there were members of Territorial Defense units or civilians, who the Russian military tortured and interrogated to get information.'

He remembers that on the fourth day of his imprisonment the Russians threw a 24-year-old man into his prison cell. That man told Vladyslav he was a local priest. He was married and had a little daughter. Russian troops detained him along with members of a local Territorial Defense unit, thinking he was part of it.

The Russian troops tortured the young priest for several hours a day, for two days straight. 'At first, they beat him very hard. Then he was electrocuted. On the second day, they took off his pants, and for another 20 minutes, they beat him on the genitals,' Buryak says. 'He came to the cell in tears. He was stammering and couldn't say anything properly. He used the toilet every three to five minutes, and he practically didn't have a face ... I put him on the bed, covered him with a blanket, hugged him, and supported him.'

Broken by the torture, the priest decided to commit suicide. Vladyslav says he had tried to talk him out of it, and stopped him when he tried to hang himself in the cell. Eventually, the man slit his wrists.

'He didn't think he'd get out of there alive. He thought it would be better to die than endure the torture again,' Buryak says.

There, in a small prison cell, a 16-year-old boy tried to comfort a man who had just slit his wrists with a can lid.

A Russian soldier entered the cell shortly and called a doctor who bandaged his hands and took him away. Buryak never saw the man again. He doesn't know if he survived.

He says that man became one of the reasons he found the strength to survive the horrors of captivity. 'He told me, "Get out from this captivity and tell about everything we've been through",' Buryak says. '"Tell my story so that my death is not in vain."'

'Army of good'

The Russian soldiers never tortured Buryak since he was considered a 'valuable' prisoner they could use in an exchange. Instead, they made the boy work.

'I worked as a kitchen assistant, cleaned the floor, washed the torture room, and collected trash around the prison,' Buryak says.

Vladyslav was forced to clean the so-called torture room up to five times a week. The room was a slightly bigger prison cell where Russian soldiers interrogated Ukrainians, severely beating them with 'iron fittings, rubber batons, and machine guns'.

There, Buryak saw a special tool with wires used for electrocution. He says that Russians often tortured their prisoners by pushing needles underneath their nails, sometimes connecting the needles to the electrocution tool to increase the pain.

He heard Russian soldiers discussing how they would torture their prisoners. Once, he heard them laughing when torturing someone. 'Those people are beasts. [Torturing people] is like fun to them,' Buryak says.

One day when he came to clean the torture room, it wasn't empty as usual. He saw a man hanging from the ceiling with his hands tied with cables. A small bucket with blood stood next to them. The floor was covered in blood, too. 'It was one of the days when I saw [the torture] myself,' he says.

He often heard Russians saying they had come to 'save Ukraine and liberate it from Nazism'. Buryak says they called themselves the 'army of good' and claimed they were 'doing everything for the Ukrainian nation to live well'.

Almost every day, Vladyslav was allowed to spend 10 minutes outside. Other than that, the boy either worked or was locked alone in his prison cell.

Vladyslav spent a total of 48 days in prison. He says that each day, he hoped he wouldn't become the soldiers' next victim.

Oleh says he was doing everything he could to never let that happen.

Never forget

Soon after Vladyslav was captured, his father went public with it. His strategy was to publicize the case so that Russians would value Vladyslav as a prisoner and save his life.

He knew the horrors that his son was exposed to. At one point during the boy's three-month captivity, Oleh was shown a transcript of the testimony of a former prisoner of the jail where Vladyslav was kept. That person had survived two weeks of torture that included sexual violence.

Almost immediately after his son was captured, a Russian officer contacted Oleh to begin what would be an arduous process of negotiations to free Vladyslav.

The officer wanted to exchange the boy for a specific person, 'an adult citizen of Ukraine,' Oleh says. He can't disclose any more details, including whether that exchange took place.

After 48 days in prison, the Russians transferred Vladyslav to a hotel in occupied Melitopol, where he spent another 42 days. While the conditions were much better – there was a toilet and a shower in the room – Vladyslav was still a prisoner, and it wasn't clear whether they would agree to set him free.

Finally, on 4 July, a Russian negotiator agreed to release Vladyslav – three months after he was captured.

Oleh was worried that the Russians might change their mind. Even when Vladyslav called him late on 6 July, saying the Russians said they would let him go the following day, Oleh told him not to get too excited. But on 7 July, Vladyslav was put into one of the civilian cars evacuating from Melitopol.

When he saw his son getting out of the car in the Ukrainian-controlled area of Zaporizhzhia Oblast, Oleh said he felt that 'a piece of his heart returned home'. There, on the road not far from the Russian-occupied settlements, the two stood for several moments, hugging and crying. Vladyslav had made it back home.

Although he is safe now, he will never forget the horrors of captivity he endured. 'Death, horror, destruction – this is what [Russia] represents,' said Vladyslav. 'Nothing more.'

Seeing his son alive and at home with him feels like a personal 'victory' for Oleh.

'Now we need a victory for the country,' Oleh said.

12 August 2022

Why Ukraine struggles to combat Russia's artillery superiority
Illia Ponomarenko

Russian heavy artillery – the Kremlin's deadliest weapon against Ukraine – is still a superior force that has no mercy.

Almost six months into the full-scale invasion, Russian advances remain generally stalled.

But despite much effort with Western-provided advanced weaponry, Russia's artillery force is still inflicting heavy losses on Ukraine and goes unanswered much too often.

Counter-battery fire, the tactic of hunting for and firing at the enemy's artillery pieces, remains a weak spot in Ukraine's military.

The Russian military indeed enjoys very strong numerical superiority. But Ukraine, in turn, often lacks proper organization of counter-battery activities on the battlefield. It also falls short of qualified top-level specialists.

As a result, Russian artillery continues to devastate Ukrainian lines, causing Ukrainian infantry to pay an inflating price in blood …

A weak spot

The progress was notable, but the introduction of superior Western systems has not brought radical changes in Russian superiority.

Russian artillery is still extremely overwhelming and deadly as it continues to shell its way through Ukrainian defenses with extreme power.

Yet another wake-up call occurred on 2 August, just days after the Russian-led militants launched a massive offensive in the town of Pisky, a ruined suburb just northwest of occupied Donetsk next to the city's destroyed airport.

Amid fierce hostilities, Serhiy Gnezdilov, a squad leader with Ukraine's 21st Motorized Infantry Battalion Sarmat, published a headline-making post on his Facebook page.

The soldier's message, full of desperation and anger, describes the horrific situation in Pisky, attacked by Russians.

Within less than 24 hours, according to Gnezdilov, Russian artillery fired nearly 6,500 rounds upon Ukrainian defenses in the town. 'It's beyond one's understanding how some of our infantry manages to survive under this burst of enemy fire,' he wrote.

Russian artillery methodically destroyed Ukrainian concrete defenses without facing any resistance from the Ukrainian side. Ukrainian counter-battery was not working at all, according to the message. 'It's a f*cking slaughter in which the battalion personnel is just deterring the offensive with their bodies,' the soldier wrote.

The Facebook post triggered a stir in Ukrainian media. Shortly after, the Ukrainian command sent reinforcements that gradually stabilized the situation in Pisky. Russian forces currently have nearly a third of the town under their control, following over two weeks of brutal combat.

Despite all the damage done by HIMARSs, Russia, especially in Donbas, is still capable of concentrating its massive artillery power in certain front-line sections.

Speaking on the condition of anonymity, serving Ukrainian artillery officers polled by *The Kyiv Independent* admitted that Ukrainian counter-battery activity remains largely problematic, mainly due to the lack of effective top-level organization.

From their perspective, all main components of counter-battery warfare, especially target acquisition via observation points, radar detection, drones, and sound ranging, need to be improved. And target acquisition must be better synchronized with artillery pieces reacting fast to destroy revealed Russian weapons. And all components need to work as a system and in cooperation with infantry units that should be holding the important local high ground points for artillery, which is often not the case, as artillerists said.

In many cases, Russian successes were ensured not by its overwhelming advantage but by a problematic Ukrainian counter-artillery reaction. 'The infantry has paid for those flaws with its blood,' a Ukrainian artillery officer told *The Kyiv Independent*.

Competent command

Today's Ukrainian top command structure does not have a specific command and control body responsible exclusively for artillery.

Similarly to the General Staff, neither of the four Ukrainian main operational command headquarters ('North,' 'South,' 'East,' 'West') have command in charge of artillery. This is the result of decentralization in the military – the restructuring that was made in an attempt to step away from the over-centralized Soviet military system and towards Western practices.

Before decentralization, top-level structures like army corps command were directly responsible for organizing and running counter-battery warfare. Brigade-level artillery command, in the meantime, was responsible for supporting the infantry on battlefields rather than hunting hostile artillery.

Now, due to lack of centralized command overseeing artillery, there's inconsistency among the Ukrainian units and they have to fix it, says Oleh Zhdanov, a Kyiv-based retired senior artillery officer.

'Each of the larger front line sectors – like Donbas, Zaporizhzhia, or Kherson – should have at least one or two artillery brigades, that's four artillery battalions,' Zhdanov said. 'An artillery brigade would be responsible exclusively for counter-battery warfare within the front line's 100–150-kilometer-long section. It would work as part of the general reconnaissance system. As its forces get fresh data – it immediately goes out to suppress a Russian battery.'

Zhdanov says that each of Ukraine's operational command headquarters should have a competent artillery department responsible for counter-battery warfare within their sectors. But this process also needs to be properly organized, with effective communication between the brain and the muscle, to be able to destroy Russia's most significant advantage over Ukraine.

'The move towards Western methods of working is happening,' said Glen Grant, a retired British Army officer and former adviser to Ukraine's Ministry of Defense. 'But it is hampered by lack of communications, poor organizational structures, and still the heavy hand of the old concepts. What is missing still for Ukraine is to complete the decentralization of control artillery by improving the radio links, creating, equipping, and training more front line observer teams for battalions.'

Grant continued, saying that there is a vital need to create a separate trade of artillery intelligence and ensure that they operate in all brigades and have direct radio or Wi-Fi links to every possible source of data about enemy artillery. 'Finally, we need a high-flying drone flying back from the enemy lines 50–100 kilometers with sideways-looking sensors to identify artillery positions and movement. Some of this is in place, but a better system will save lives and help win the war.'

17 August 2022

Suicide missions, abuse, physical threats: International Legion fighters speak out against leadership's misconduct

Anna Myroniuk and Alexander Khrebet

Disclaimer: The Kyiv Independent is publishing this investigation to shed light on the alleged abuse of power in the leadership of one wing of the International Legion – a legion created for foreign fighters dedicated to defending Ukraine. The members of the Legion's unit say that they reported their commanders' misconduct to Ukrainian law enforcement, the parliament and President Volodymyr Zelensky's Office, but saw no proper reaction and thus turned to journalists as a last resort. Soldiers who pointed at the problems within this unit of the Legion claim they received threats for speaking up. For their safety, we do not disclose their identities.

Top findings
- The leadership of the intelligence-run wing of the International Legion is allegedly implicated in various violations, including abuse, theft, and sending soldiers unprepared on reckless missions.
- One of the unit's commanders and a frequent subject of the soldiers' complaints is an alleged former member of a criminal organization from Poland, wanted at home for fraud. In the Legion's unit, he is involved in coordinating military operations and logistics.
- The legion's fighters accuse him of abusing power by ordering soldiers to loot shops, threatening soldiers with a gun, and sexually harassing the legion's female medics.

In early May, a fighter from Brazil arrived in Ukraine to join the International Legion following President Volodymyr Zelensky's call to 'citizens of the world' to come and help defend Ukraine.

He thought his vast experience in the Brazilian army had prepared him for pretty much any task.

Yet he was neither ready to carry out suicide missions by order of his command, nor to tolerate orders to loot and steal. As a platoon commander of the International Legion, he was ordered to do just that.

The Brazilian officer recalls his subordinates saying, before resigning from the legion: 'We came here to help these people to fight for this country, against this invasion. We didn't come here to do exactly what f*cking Russian people do when they're on Ukrainian soil.'

The Kyiv Independent's investigation reveals endemic problems in one of the International Legion's wings that is overseen by Ukraine's intelligence.

Some of the unit's commanders are implicated in arms and goods theft, sexual harassment, assault, and sending unprepared soldiers on reckless missions, according to multiple sources.

The allegations in this story are based on interviews with legionnaires, written testimonies of over a dozen former and current members of the legion, and a 78-page report they've put together about problems within this particular unit of the International Legion.

For about four months, foreign fighters have been knocking on the doors of high offices asking for help. The report was filed to the parliament, and written testimonies were sent to Zelensky's office. Alyona Verbytska, the president's commissioner for soldiers' rights, confirmed she had received legionnaires' complaints and passed them on to law enforcement.

But authorities, soldiers say, are reluctant to solve the issue.

Failed leadership?

The International Legion, soldiers say, consists of two wings. Ukraine's Ground Forces oversee one. The Defense Ministry's Directorate for Intelligence, known under its Ukrainian acronym GUR, coordinates the other.

The allegations in this report concern the GUR-run wing of the Legion. At its strongest, this unit had up to 500 people, and comprised about one-third of the International Legion, according to *The Kyiv Independent*'s sources among the soldiers. GUR did not respond to *The Kyiv Independent*'s request for comment by publication time.

According to members of the intelligence-run wing of the Legion, their commanders report directly to the head of GUR, Kyrylo Budanov, who Zelensky also appointed to head the intelligence committee in the president's office in late July.

Officially, the GUR wing of the Legion is run by major Vadym Popyk. However, he is not running the unit on his own. The power is in the hands of a few people: Popyk's right hand, major Taras Vashuk (referred to by soldiers as 'young Taras'), an intelligence officer in his late 20s or early 30s, according to the foreign fighters; Vashuk's uncle, also Taras (referred to as 'old Taras') and also an intelligence officer; and 60-year old Sasha Kuchynsky. 'They are like best buds,' an American legionnaire told *The Kyiv Independent* of the three men.

Young Taras, old Taras, and Sasha run the operations of the unit. They send soldiers on missions and coordinate the intelligence wing of the Legion's work. Sasha is also in charge of logistics and supplies.

The legionnaires accuse the trio of various wrongdoings. For the two Tarases, the major complaints concern them sending soldiers on suicide missions.

An American soldier interviewed by *The Kyiv Independent* described a couple of missions that took place near the southern city of Mykolaiv, one of the war's hot spots.

Russian troops discovered their squad's position and started to shell it heavily. The rest of the troops retreated from the secondary position behind them, leaving the squad to hold the front line alone, with no backup. 'We were literally left [behind] and they didn't want to evacuate us,' the soldier said. His fellow soldier, Scott Sibley, was killed, while three others were severely injured on that mission.

Shortly after the squad escaped the shelling, another group from the same unit was ordered to take the same position. 'We told the commander those positions were discovered by Russians ... If we go back there, we are all dead,' the American soldier told *The Kyiv Independent*.

The older Taras did not listen and sent another group to the very same place, the soldier said. The story repeated itself, but this time with four killed, multiple injured, and one taken captive. The captive soldier, Andrew Hill, now faces a fake 'trial' and possible execution in Russian-occupied Donetsk on accusations of being a mercenary.

Sasha Kuchynsky's actions, however, stand out in their breadth of alleged wrongdoing.

Apart from sending fighters to die, legionnaires said, Kuchynsky forced them to help him loot stores. Fighters told *The Kyiv Independent* that he is also a heavy drinker who abuses his subordinates.

Another soldier, an American Jew, told *The Kyiv Independent* that Jewish soldiers experienced antisemitism from Kuchynsky. He emphasized that he did not encounter it from anyone else in the Ukrainian military.

The soldier also says Kuchynsky demanded to have a share of the gear and equipment that the soldier bought for his close peers from the legion. When the soldier refused to give it away, Kuchynsky pointed a gun at him. 'And then Sasha [Kuchynsky] just started yelling, screaming,' the soldier recalled. 'He said, "I know there's stuff here. Give me your stuff".'

'And in front of the translator, he raises his weapon at me. And I was like: "You're gonna shoot me? You're gonna shoot me." And then there's like this kind of look of, honestly, remorse, but like "Oh, f*ck" and he put down his gun,' the soldier went on.

He said that he once met a legionnaire at whom Kuchynsky had also raised a gun.

According to another American legionnaire, Kuchynsky also harassed female medics in their unit, using sexually suggestive language with them. According to the American soldier, the legion's medics complained but nobody did anything about it. The foreign medic he knew that was harassed by Kuchynsky is no longer with the Legion and has since left Ukraine, he said.

When in trouble, legionnaires say, Kuchynsky would turn to Taras Vashuk for a cover-up. 'Sasha would call Taras and get confirmation that he can do whatever he wants to do. And Taras would constantly back him up,' a Scandinavian soldier told *The Kyiv Independent*.

However, to date, Kuchynsky remains in his de facto commanding position in the Legion despite his subordinates' complaints and despite the fact that, according to Ukrainian law, he can't as a foreigner hold executive roles in the army.

When confronted with legionnaires' accusations, Kuchynsky refused to address them. 'It's up to the Military Prosecutor's Office to address these questions,' he told *The Kyiv Independent* over the phone. 'No comments. I'm busy.' He then hung up.

An investigation by the Military Prosecutor's Office wouldn't be the first time Kuchynsky has had trouble with the law.

'Sasha Kuchynsky'

According to *The Kyiv Independent*'s sources inside the legion, Sasha Kuchynsky is not the man's real name. He is allegedly Piotr Kapuscinski, a former member of a criminal organization from Poland, who fled to Ukraine after several run-ins with the law.

Upon request from *The Kyiv Independent*, our colleagues from the Bellingcat investigative journalism group ran an image comparison of the photos of Sasha Kuchynsky, provided by the legionnaires, and photos of Piotr Kapuscinski from Polish media. The results support the conclusion that the photos are of the same person.

In Poland, Kapuscinski is wanted for fraud and faces up to eight years in prison. According to Polish *Gazeta Wyborcza*, he has previously served time.

He fled Poland in 2014, and resurfaced in Ukraine two years later. He was investigated in Ukraine for aggravated robbery and sexual assault in October 2016 but was only charged with robbery. In November 2016, he was detained and spent over a year behind bars.

Warsaw asked Kyiv to extradite Kapuscinski in 2017, but Ukrainian authorities said they would first try him themselves.

He resurfaced again in May 2021, when law enforcement searched his vehicle where they found a semi-automatic pistol and bullets and proceeded to search a building that he used, finding explosives. He faced up to seven years in prison for possession of illegal weapons but was almost immediately released on bail of nearly $2,500.

After the all-out Russian war broke out in February, Kapuscinski joined the military, at which point the courts suspended his case and then paid back his bail in May 2022.

His criminal past did not prevent Kapuscinski from getting into the Legion and obtaining an executive role there. The legislation says all foreign recruits must go through background checks before joining the Ukrainian army. It's not clear whether a criminal record counts as a deal breaker.

In Ukraine, citizens can serve in the military if they have ongoing criminal proceedings or a spent conviction. The law, however, doesn't refer to foreigners. So when a Ukrainian court suspended Kapuscinski's case and paid back his bail, it was applying the same norm that applies to Ukrainians.

In the Legion, Kuchynsky (Kapuscinski) calls himself a colonel and wears a colonel's epaulet, according to the soldiers' testimonies and the photographs of Kuchynsky the legionnaires provided to *The Kyiv Independent*. In fact, foreigners are only allowed to serve in Ukraine's armed forces in the lower ranks, as privates, sergeants, and petty officers.

Since the start of the year, the man who calls himself Sasha Kuchynsky has allegedly gone from a criminal suspect on bail to a free man and de facto commander in a high-profile Ukrainian military unit.

Polish past: Broda, the gangster

According to reports in Polish media, in Poland, Piotr Kapuscinski is known as 'Broda' (Beard), an influential former member of the Pruszków gang, once the largest mafia in the country.

For his alleged wrongdoings in the International Legion, Kuchynsky has already been questioned multiple times. First, by the Security Service of Ukraine (SBU) after threatening one of the American soldiers with a gun. According to the soldier, Kuchynsky didn't face any consequences. Then, by the Military Prosecution Office following other legionnaires' complaints against him, according to *The Kyiv Independent*'s law enforcement sources. The complaints alleged abuse of power, fraud, and assault. Kuchynsky denied the accusations and kept his job. The investigation, however, is ongoing.

Sent to die

The probe into Sasha Kuchynsky, among other episodes, concerns him sending soldiers on what they call a suicide mission in Sievierodonetsk, a key city in Luhansk Oblast that Russian troops seized in late June.

According to the Brazilian fighter who spoke to *The Kyiv Independent*, Kuchynsky's orders were inconsistent. At first, the Brazilian's unit spent two weeks preparing for a demining mission in Zaporizhzhia Oblast, a southern region. In early June, a few days into the mission, they were suddenly moved to another location. Kuchynsky ordered them to go to Sievierodonetsk in the eastern Luhansk Oblast and hold a position close to enemy lines.

Going into one of the war's main hotspots was very different from a demining mission. That wouldn't have been a problem if they were prepared for it, the Brazilian officer said, but they weren't. 'We've been two weeks preparing these guys with all the type of training and metal detectors and anti-mines ... and now you're going to send us to the industrial zone to the urban type of combat. Sasha, this is crazy,' the legionnaire recalls telling his commander.

'I understand. I am with you there, but that's the order,' Kuchynsky reportedly replied.

The Brazilian fighter started planning the operation in Sievierodonetsk, but neither Kuchynsky nor Taras Vashuk, the other commander, gave him any information – which he said they were supposed to – about the situation on the ground. By then, Sievierodonetsk was a center of heavy fighting. Ukrainian troops would retreat from the city a couple of weeks later.

'A lot of questions asked were not answered, like where friendly troops were,' the Brazilian officer said.

Only later did he learn that the previous group sent on this very mission came under friendly fire by Ukrainian soldiers. Another Brazilian legionnaire was killed and they had to retreat.

'We got into the field without knowing what was going on,' the officer said. 'I realized those motherf*ckers won't let us plan,' he said of Sasha and Taras. 'They would just bring us into the middle of the place, dump us there to fight, dump us there to die.'

Upon arrival, a Ukrainian special forces serviceman filled them in. He told the Brazilian that Ukrainian troops are inside the buildings along their way, but they have no established communication with them so they shoot at everyone who breaks through. 'What the f*ck? How are we gonna pass? These [Ukrainian] guys are gonna shoot at us?' the Brazilian said he asked.

'That's right. We need to hide,' the Ukrainian soldier reportedly told him.

They spent four days there instead of the planned two. They ran out of food and water and asked for rotation, but Kuchynsky, who sent them there, wouldn't reply. 'Nobody slept, everybody's super tired. Some of my guys are dehydrated, and one injured guy. And we stood there. That's when Sasha [Kuchynsky] went off the radar,' he said.

Soon someone they didn't know got in touch via radio saying a new group was on their way. The soldiers arrived but then left in the middle of the night without saying anything. The next day, another squad came in to replace them.

The Brazilian believes that Kuchynsky had no plan for their extraction.

'A bunch of wannabes, playing with people's lives,' he said of the unit's leadership. His account of suicide missions is confirmed by other soldiers – both in their conversations with *The Kyiv Independent* and in their official testimonies they filed to the President's Office.

The Brazilian platoon leader and a couple of his soldiers got injured but survived. After finally getting evacuated from Sievierodonetsk, most of the squad fighters decided to quit the Legion. 'We're not f*cking staying. We're leaving,' the fighter recalled them saying.

The team of the Brazilian fighter is not the only one that left the Legion, disappointed. Foreigners quitting the International Legion due to poor organization, lack of equipment, and indefinite contracts have already made headlines across international media.

Shopping mall plunder

Around the time of the Battle of Sievierodonetsk in early June, the legionnaires received a controversial task from Kuchynsky: to drive from their base to a local shopping mall in the front-line city of Lysychansk in Luhansk Oblast and take merchandise from the shops.

'I directly heard Sasha Kuchynsky's order to the soldiers of my unit to break into the shopping center, collect the furniture and electronics as soon as possible and collect all possible valuables along the way,' a Canadian fighter wrote in his statement following the incident.

According to the soldiers' official testimonies obtained by *The Kyiv Independent*, 'Sasha' also told subordinates to take whatever they liked: shoes, women's clothes, jewelry, watches, and electronics. Many soldiers obeyed as they come from professional military backgrounds where they don't question superiors' commands. '[Normally] you should say "yes, sir" and get it done. Because you believe that your commander knows what he's asking you to do ... You just assume that this action is legal, and you're going to go for it. You're not supposed to question it,' the Brazilian legionnaire told *The Kyiv Independent*.

'Locals saw how we loaded the furniture which made me very uncomfortable. It felt like we were robbing them. I didn't come to Ukraine for this,' a testimony of a Columbian soldier reads.

'There were local residents near the shopping mall, one of whom, seeing this, shouted insults, and the others looked at us with reproach and condemnation. I don't know whether it was legal or not but I felt ashamed to carry out the order of Sasha Kuchynsky and take away furniture and valuables from stores during hostilities and in front of local residents who suffered from the war,' a French legionnaire wrote in his statement.

Some soldiers refused to follow the order.

In a video obtained by *The Kyiv Independent*, some foreigners can be heard in the shopping mall questioning the legality of 'Sasha's' orders. 'We will not be implicated by any means as looters. We will not stand for this,' an English-speaking soldier is heard saying. He then tells the crowd that he will not stay in front of the stolen goods and is going downstairs to wait until the car picks him up and drives back to the base.

'Sasha' becomes angry at the soldiers' refusal to carry out his orders. 'Listen, [do not set] conditions for me. This is an order, to stay here and wait for the commander. This is an order. You get it? An order. This is the army,' the Polish commander says in broken Russian.

'I do not find that order lawful. We do not see this as reasonable,' the soldier replies.

The video ends with the soldier saying to his peers: 'Let's go downstairs, guys. We are not playing these games.'

According to the legionnaires, Kuchynsky ordered similar lootings on multiple occasions and Ukrainian soldiers were ordered to participate as well.

The legionnaires don't know where the items were sent to. In a video obtained by *The Kyiv Independent*, one soldier is heard saying in Russian that the furniture and electronics taken from the mall were for their unit's headquarters in Kyiv.

Theft allegations

According to the legionnaires, they regularly witnessed what they believe were suspicious arms movements. 'The car is coming, the cars going, the boxes of weapons coming, the boxes of weapons going,' one of the US soldiers said.

Despite the legion's armory rooms being loaded with all sorts of heavy weaponry and ammunition, the soldiers say they often didn't end up in their hands. 'During my stay in Sievierodonetsk, a civilian vehicle painted in camouflage containing thermal imagers arrived,' a Columbian soldier wrote in his testimony. 'They were not distributed among the soldiers due to their alleged absence. Meanwhile, Sasha Kuchynsky proposed to the military personnel of the International Legion to buy these thermal imagers for $300.'

'I think, Sasha Kuchynsky artificially created the impression of a shortage of some ammunition to illegally enrich himself by providing it to fighters [for money] as if from himself,' another fighter from Columbia wrote in his testimony.

According to him, two of his fellow soldiers damaged their hearing due to the lack of headphones that he knew were in their armory, under Kuchynsky's control.

Soldiers say Kuchynsky would take away part of the ammunition they would independently receive from volunteers and donors. They called it the 'Sasha tax'. 'So you have to give Sasha what he wants. And then you can give [the rest] of this stuff to your guys,' one of the American soldiers said. 'Everything just seems like a cover-up. It's very strange. It feels like an [organized] business.'

The same happened to another American soldier. His shipment arrived at the base while he was on a mission. When he returned, some parcels were gone. 'It was labeled for our team. So basically, simple as that, half of the stuff wasn't there.'

Waiting for solution

The foreign soldiers say they did not want to publicize the crisis in the International Legion and tried to solve the issue behind the scenes.

They first complained to their commanders, then lawmakers, and finally went as far as the President's Office. Since the Legion was created upon Zelensky's order, foreign fighters counted on his administration's support, but did not get much help from there, they said.

Alyona Verbytska, the president's commissioner for soldiers' rights, told *The Kyiv Independent* she had informed her superiors about the legionnaires' complaints. She did not elaborate on who exactly she reported to.

In the President's Office, two people oversee the Legion for Zelensky, according to *The Kyiv Independent*'s sources close to the Office. They are Vitaliy

Martyniuk, a national security expert, and Roman Mashovets, deputy head of the Office and former employee of the GUR intelligence agency.

The President's Office did not reply to *The Kyiv Independent*'s request for comment before publication.

Complaining to the President's Office didn't work out. Things even got worse, the soldiers said, as those who sounded an alarm about the Legion's leadership started to feel under pressure and receive threats.

Meanwhile, many professional members left the unit due to alleged mismanagement and problems with paperwork. The Legion failed to provide some of them with official contracts.

'There were really good special [forces] guys. I mean, not from the regular military. A lot of special [forces] guys literally just said: "No, thank you. We can't work like that anymore",' an American soldier said.

Those who stayed in the unit want it to keep helping Ukraine to stand against Russia. To do it effectively, they believe, the Legion must be reformed under new leadership. 'I have a very, very, very pleasant experience with everybody in the Ukrainian military outside of Sasha and Tarases,' one of the American soldiers said. 'I've always just kind of kept my mouth shut. Just because people like Sasha really discredit all of this.'

1 September 2022

How many tanks does Russia really have?

Illia Ponomarenko

Russia's full-scale invasion of Ukraine is already going down in history as the biggest tank slaughter Europe has seen since World War II.

The Kremlin's reckless and unsuccessful blitzkrieg on Kyiv resulted in the loss of over 1,000 tanks – within just a few weeks after 24 February.

By April, many battlefields in northern Ukraine had become tank cemeteries, with dozens of scorched machines eviscerated by Ukrainian anti-tank squads.

This is a heavy blow for Russia's offensive component, even given its large military. Contrary to its propaganda, Russia's infamously large stockpile of Soviet tanks is little more than a pile of scrap metal unfit to be used in battle.

However, we can not expect Russia to run critically low on tanks anytime soon. Despite heavy losses, Russia still has enough machines to continue waging its war for years.

For Ukraine, this is yet another reason to do everything possible to avoid a protracted, multi-year war for which the Kremlin has many resources.

The debacle

Russia's war against Ukraine has demonstrated that all speculations on the end of the tank era have been somewhat premature. Main battle tanks continue to serve their typical role: supporting the infantry, spearheading assaults, and exploiting breakthroughs, with mechanized infantry following them.

Driven by necessity, Ukraine's military has expanded the role of tanks in combat. Due to a lack of field artillery, many Ukrainian crews practice indirect fire on targets out of the tank's line of sight, howitzer-style.

Meanwhile, Russian forces still rely on tanks as a principal means of concentrated fire support, even during urban warfare.

The ubiquity of relatively inexpensive and handy anti-tank weapons, such as the now-legendary NLAWs, provided to Ukraine by the UK and employed by highly mobile Ukrainian units to ambush Russian convoys, has dramatically challenged the tank's decisive role, however.

US Joint Chiefs of Staff Chairman Mark A. Milley said in mid-June that the international community had provided Ukraine with 97,000 various anti-tank weapons. According to Milley, this is 'more antitank systems than there are tanks in the world'.

The West's significant investment in Ukraine's anti-armor capabilities has resulted in the spectacular failure of Russia's plans for a swift toppling of Ukraine.

At the beginning of its full-scale invasion in February, Russia had around 3,330 operational tanks (2,840 with the ground forces, 330 with its naval infantry, and 160 with its airborne forces), according to the Military Balance 2021 database ... According to Oryx, an online investigative project documenting equipment losses in Russia's war, Russia has lost at least 994 tanks as of 1 September.

However, according to estimates by the Conflict Intelligence Team, an independent Russian online armed conflicts monitor, the Oryx database covers nearly 70% of the total equipment lost in combat by both sides, as it includes only fully verified losses – not every single captured or destroyed vehicle is pictured and documented.

Based on these estimates, Russia has lost nearly 1,300 tanks – an impressive 40% of its total operational tank fleet. This figure coincides with that provided by CNN in May, citing an unnamed senior US defense official, which reported that Russia has lost 'nearly 1,000 tanks' in Ukraine. Official figures provided by Ukraine's military are higher. As of 1 September, six months into Russia's full-scale war, Ukraine has reportedly knocked out 1,997 Russian tanks, which is nearly 60% of Russia's operational tank fleet.

On the other hand, Oryx suggests Ukraine's military has lost 244 tanks, 125 of which were destroyed in combat, and the rest abandoned or seized by

Russian forces. If Conflict Intelligence Team's 70% rule is applied, Ukraine has likely lost over 300 of the nearly 800 tanks it had before 24 February. But Ukraine also has tanks recently acquired from abroad, especially Poland, or captured from Russia.

Rising from the rust

Even the rough estimate provided by Oryx's data shows that Russia has sustained a heavy blow in terms of the technological quality of its tank fleet in Ukraine ... However, Russia still has some 2,000 battle-ready tanks at hand, as well as an enormous amount in storage.

The Military Balance 2021 database says Russian storage facilities have around 10,200 tanks, including various T-72s, 3,000 T-80s, and 200 T-90s. The database's 2016 publication also indicates that Russia has roughly 2,800 Cold War legacy T-55s (the first tank type to feature a nuclear warfare protection system in the 1950s) in storage, as well as 2,500 T-62s and 2,000 T-64s. This means that Russia may have around 17,300 tanks produced between the late 1950s and now.

It likely does – on paper.

In reality, nobody – likely not even Russia – knows precisely how many of those estimated thousands can emerge from the mothballs and be made operational again.

The only way to confirm is to count the tanks sitting at Russian bases. An analysis of Google Maps satellite images of 19 Russian military storage facilities mainly located east of Russia's Ural Mountains by the Ukrainian Military Center, a Ukrainian military defense news site, estimates that 2,299 tanks appear unrestorable.

Stored in the open for decades, they are basically heaps of rusty scrap metal ready for nothing but disposal. Another estimated 1,304 machines are thought to be in a dubious state. 'Those are tanks that can be potentially restored at tank maintenance facilities,' the website wrote on 22 August. 'But they would have to be loaded up a train, transported to a certain tank factory, unloaded, taken to a certain workshop, then examined for defects. What happens next is the search for appropriate parts, some of which are out of production or require new production processes ... This would take a lot of time,' the report concluded.

Another 2,075 tanks seem recoverable, although some would likely need to be taken to tank factories.

An estimated 886 tanks are effectively stored and are likely to be made fully operational.

Many Russian bases also have hangars, which may store up to around 1,330 tanks – in unknown conditions and quantities.

A number of old restored T-62s and T-62Ms have already been seen in Ukraine ...

Given ongoing Western sanctions targeting hi-tech components, Russia will likely have difficulties repairing and modernizing its machines. So it is possible that if Russia continues waging a large-scale war in Ukraine we're going to see a lot of older machines, such as early T-72 or T-80 versions.

In all, Russia has at least 2,000 potentially restorable tanks, meaning it will not run out during its war in Ukraine – even if it has to roll back its relics from the early 1960s.

But Russia also has alternative sources: Belarusian dictator Alexander Lukashenko's regime possesses over 500 modernized T-72 tanks.

13 September 2022

With successful Kharkiv operation, Ukraine turns the war in its favor
Illia Ponomarenko

In warfare, there's no such thing as a miracle.

Yet what happened in early September in the east of Ukraine's Kharkiv Oblast may ascend in history as the Miracle on the Oskil River.

Within a few days, a Ukrainian strike prompted the collapse of the Russian front in the region. To escape a crushing defeat, the Kremlin's forces were forced to withdraw in a stampede from the territory they had held since March.

Ukraine's offensive operation has done more than liberate most of Kharkiv Oblast, as Ukrainian units approach the Russian border. It has exceeded the most optimistic of expectations and rendered one of Russia's strongest military groupings disorganized and combat ineffective.

The battle is an operational success and is bound to have long-lasting consequences for Russia. The loss of Kupiansk and Izium, the two transportation hubs, pulls the plug on Russia's chances of seizing the entire eastern region of Donbas, comprised of Donetsk and Luhansk oblasts.

The collapse also jeopardized Russian defenses in northern Donetsk Oblast, paving the way for new successful attacks by Ukrainian forces in the east.

The war's third phase opens with Ukraine regaining the initiative. Experts say Ukraine has turned the war's tide in its favor, while Russia's power will likely continue to decline in the coming months.

A rapid strike

With everyone's attention fixed on the anticipated Ukrainian counter-strike in Kherson Oblast, the blitz in Kharkiv Oblast came as a surprise.

In late August, when Ukraine's military eventually started its offensive operation in the south, some 25 to 30 Russian battalion tactical groups (BTGs) stood in its way. The Russian forces redeployed to Kherson Oblast included its most-effective airborne units, known in Russia as VDV.

Since Russia still falls short of sufficient quality manpower to hold the 1,000-kilometer front line in Ukraine, those units were relocated to Kherson Oblast at the expense of other frontline sections.

Ukraine's military persuaded the Russian command that Kherson would be its counter-offensive's primary, and likely only, axis. Indeed, experts doubted Ukraine had enough weaponry and hardware for a successful major strike at one frontline section, let alone two or more.

Ukraine has performed well in this battle with operational security (OPSEC), keeping its adversary poorly informed regarding its planned maneuvers and capabilities.

And when the time came, many of Russia's best combat formations ended up isolated in Kherson, with all bridges crossing the Dnipro River ruined as their backs were turned.

The destruction of these bridges means there is no way for Russian forces to withdraw, and there will be a drastic decrease in reinforcements and resupply due to a forced reliance on less effective pontoon crossings across the Dnipro.

Then came something few had expected.

On 6 September, Ukrainian forces launched a rapid advance on Balakliia, Kharkiv Oblast, a city with a pre-war population of 27,000 that Russian troops had occupied since early March. One of Kharkiv Oblast's transport hubs, Balakliia also hosts a giant ammunition depot known as the 65th Arsenal.

Verbivka, a village just north of Balakliia, was liberated by Ukrainian forces within a few hours.

The Ukrainian advance bypassed local cities, leaving Russian garrisons isolated and cut off from their main forces.

The Ukrainian blitz rushed to Volokhiv Yar, a village some 15 kilometers to the northeast of Balakliia, and toward the villages of Kunie and Vesele, 30 kilometers southeast, taking local roads and junctions under its control.

Highly mobile Ukrainian reconnaissance units moved fast ahead of the main Ukrainian forces in Russian-controlled territory using light vehicles, such as US-provided Humvees.

They engaged Russian forces sporadically, wreaking havoc and trying to convince Russian troops that they were attacking from every direction.

The occasional Russian garrison showed little to no resistance in communities along the way.

As early as the next day, Russia's weak Rosgvardia and special police units, short on heavy weaponry, managed to flee Balakliia in time.

While this was already a success, the Ukrainian blitz liberated the town of Shevchenkove, yet another vital junction, followed by the city of Kupiansk, the operation's greatest possible prize. Kupiansk, a major railroad hub, was at the heart of Russia's vital ground line of communication between its territory and occupied Donbas. Cutting off Kupiansk meant derailing Russian supplies in its most critical frontline sector.

Contrary to expectations, Russian forces showed little resistance, and Ukrainian troops managed to break through into Sinkove, a community south of Kupiansk. This move isolated Kupiansk on the western bank of the Oskil River, which divides the city in half.

The Russian front line in Kharkiv Oblast just collapsed within days. The Russian command, taken by surprise, had no choice but to order their combat units to withdraw. Russian soldiers abandoned swathes of hardware and munitions as they hastily left under heavy Ukrainian fire.

Early on 9 September, Ukrainian forces entered Kupiansk.

While this was anticipated to be the operation's most ambitious goal, the rapid Russian collapse made it possible and opened up new opportunities. Two additional Ukrainian strikes from the north and the south put the city of Izium – the most vital Russian-controlled settlement in the region – in the crosshairs.

To avoid being surrounded, some 10,000 Russian troops in Izium were forced to leave overnight by 10 September.

Within a few days, Russia lost its essential pressure point in the Sloviansk–Kramatorsk area of Donetsk Oblast. A Russian advance south from Izium could have cut the entirety of Donbas from the rest of Ukraine and corner the largest Ukrainian military group into a death trap.

Without this critical axis, the chances are high that Russia has lost its only realistic option to seize the rest of Donetsk Oblast, which Russia has repeatedly stated as its primary goal in Ukraine.

Russian forces have captured the entirety of Luhansk Oblast, but it has been struggling to occupy all of Donetsk Oblast, about half of which remains under Ukrainian control. The benefits derived from other axes in Donetsk Oblast near the cities of Bakhmut and Donetsk have been too costly and slow to bring Russia closer to its goal.

The collapse of the Kupiansk–Izium line precipitated Russia's immediate withdrawal from most of Kharkiv Oblast. Ukraine regained control of almost all of the region's border with Russia and some 6,000 square kilometers of its territory.

This is the most significant Ukrainian victory since the Battle of Kyiv in early April.

Humiliating failure

As of 12 September, the Ukrainian operation has slowed down somewhat, likely due to Ukraine's need to consolidate its gains and let its troops have some rest.

The new front line has stabilized along the Oskil River, with Russia still holding the eastern bank.

However, as of 12 September, Ukraine is still active in northern Donetsk Oblast. Capitalizing on the Russian defeat in Izium, Ukrainian forces have remained engaged in the Russian-occupied city of Lyman and retook Sviatohirsk.

In Kharkiv Oblast, Russia failed to surveil the Ukrainian buildup and to redeploy adequate reinforcements to counter rapid Ukrainian advances.

Russia left the front line severely undermanned and weak to try to counter Ukraine's advance in the south. According to Russian military bloggers, local Russian units often had no more than 50% of their members and, in some cases, as little as 20% of their standard personnel capacities.

Ukrainian forces took advantage of this.

Rapid Ukrainian maneuvers put Russian forces under grave threat of isolation and total disorientation.

According to Conflict Intelligence Team, an online Russian investigation group, two large Russian formations in the area, the 11th Army Corps and the elite 1st Guards Tank Army, were rendered disorganized and ineffective due to the battle.

Moreover, according to the United Kingdom's Ministry for Defense, the 1st Guards Tank Army sustained heavy casualties prior to Ukraine's Kharkiv offensive, and it has not fully reconstituted its losses.

Now, severely degraded, the 1st Guards and other formations of Russia's Western Military District withdraw from Ukraine, the ministry said on 13 September, so Russia's conventional force designed to counter NATO is severely weakened, and 'it will take years for Russia to rebuild this capability'.

'Ukraine has turned the tide of this war in its favor,' said the Institute for the Study of War (ISW), a US-based defense think tank, in its 12 September report. 'Kyiv will likely increasingly dictate the location and nature of the major fighting, and Russia will find itself increasingly responding inadequately to growing Ukrainian physical and psychological pressure in successive military campaigns unless Moscow finds some way to regain the initiative.'

Experts now believe that Ukrainian pressure in Kherson Oblast, combined with its rapid counter-offensive in Kharkiv Oblast, presents Russian forces with a terrible dilemma.

'Russia likely lacks sufficient reserve forces to complete the formation of a new defensive line along the Oskil River ... Prudence would demand that Russia pulls forces from other sectors of the battlespace to establish defensive lines further east than the Oskil River to ensure that it can hold the Luhansk Oblast border.'

The Kremlin continues its meaningless, unsuccessful attacks near Bakhmut and Donetsk, refusing to redeploy those forces to mitigate possible new

Ukrainian advances across the Oskil River or Kherson. At the same time, it can't afford to compromise its Kherson defenses for the sake of the Oskil River area.

'Russian President Vladimir Putin risks making a common but deadly mistake by waiting too long to order reinforcements to the Luhansk line,' the ISW said. 'The Ukrainian campaign appears intended to present Putin with precisely such a dilemma and to benefit from almost any decision he makes.'

29 September 2022

Stop using Russia's propaganda language to talk about its war in Ukraine

The Kyiv Independent staff

Editor's note: This editorial presents the opinions of the editorial team of The Kyiv Independent.

In a world polluted with disinformation and manipulations, we all bear responsibility for the words we choose to use.

Unfortunately, some global media and other actors have chosen to act irresponsibly when talking about Russia's war in Ukraine.

On 23–27 September, Russia held what it dubiously calls referendums in Kremlin-occupied parts of Ukraine.

If one listens to Russia, they will hear that Ukrainians living in these territories were given a fair choice: vote for their region to secede from Ukraine and become part of Russia, or against it.

Yet if one has common sense, a pair of eyes, and memory, they would know that:

- There were numerous reports from inside occupied territories about how the vote was conducted: collaborators making house calls accompanied by armed Russian soldiers
- Staged secession referendums are a staple in the Russian invasion textbook: Russia used them in 2014 in Crimea and eastern Ukraine.
- Russia is an authoritarian state that doesn't give its people the right to freely choose their president or government. It would be foolish to assume that Russia would suddenly respect democratic processes and hold free and fair elections in occupied territories it took by force while refusing to grant its own citizens the same basic right.

Even regardless of everything above, no vote organized in invaded territories by an occupying force known for extreme brutality can be considered a real vote.

This didn't stop one of the world's biggest news agencies, Reuters, from publishing a story headlined, 'Big majority said to favor joining Russia in first vote results on future of occupied Ukraine regions'.

One would never know from this headline, or from a similar tweet that Reuters shared to its 25 million followers, that the so-called vote was a sham referendum, held at gunpoint in areas devastated by the invasion, where remaining locals are scared and powerless.

Following a backlash online, Reuters changed the headline to a somewhat better version: 'Moscow's proxies in occupied Ukraine regions report big votes to join Russia'. While it doesn't openly legitimize the referendum, it nonetheless cowardly omits pointing at its staged nature.

Reuters wasn't the only media that made the mistake of reporting the 'referendum' as the real thing. Radio France Internationale did a news story, from Moscow, that reported the results without mentioning the obvious fakeness of the referendum.

Unfortunately, these are not one-off mistakes, but rather, part of a pattern. Global media have been prone to use the language suggested to them by the Russian regime when talking about Ukraine.

The biggest, most irresponsible language mistake of this invasion was made on 24 February, when dozens of the most respected international media outlets reported the beginning of the full-scale invasion as the start of a 'special military operation'.

'Putin announces special military operation in eastern Ukraine,' was the headline that ran on the *Wall Street Journal* as missiles began raining down all across Ukraine.

'Putin authorizes special military operation in Ukraine,' was the headline Reuters found appropriate.

The correct words, of course, were 'war' and 'invades'. Vladimir Putin, a dictator whose regime is built on lies, may choose to call it whatever he wants. But it's our duty as media professionals to not take it at face value, not to amplify or legitimize it.

Proponents of blind journalistic objectivity may decry our attempt to set the record straight. But we believe that no rule should be applied mindlessly. A simplistic approach is to report Putin's words as is – but are we really serving our audience's best interests when we do so? Can anyone seriously claim that the words that come straight out of Putin's mouth – the head of Russian aggression against Ukraine – are objective? We hardly think so.

In Ukraine, we are all too familiar with the world parroting Kremlin propaganda. We have been witnessing the world call Kremlin-led militants in eastern Ukraine 'separatists' since 2014, knowing fully well there were no such 'separatists' in Ukraine's Donbas until Russia decided there should be.

'Russia makes moves to annex separatist regions in Ukraine,' said a recent headline on NPR. The 'separatist regions' in it are Ukrainian territories invaded by Russia.

The truth, based on hard facts, is simple: there are no separatists or separatist regions in Ukraine. Ukraine has never had any real secession movements until Russia staged one in early 2014 to masquerade its invasion of Ukraine.

If you don't believe us, we implore you to do your research. The eastern Ukrainian Luhansk and Donetsk oblasts, the regions making up the Donbas, voted over 80% 'yes' in Ukraine's 1991 referendum for the country's independence from the Soviet Union. According to Ukraine's first President Leonid Kravchuk, who told the story in the interviews, the vote prompted Russia's Boris Yeltsin to ask: 'What, even the Donbas voted yes?' Yes. Full stop.

Now Russia claims these regions have always been Russian and is trying to annex them. The Russian regime will use any lies on its malicious course to preserve its corrupt existence at the cost of disrupting the world – but we shouldn't help it by accepting and using its deceitful language.

This is why we don't refer to the territories occupied by Russian proxies as 'breakaway republics' or by their self-proclaimed names of 'Donetsk People's Republic' or 'Luhansk People's Republic'. These are Ukrainian territories. Calling them otherwise legitimizes the pseudo-formations that are actually nothing but militant groups installed there by Russia.

This is also why we don't call Russia's invasion of Ukraine 'the Ukraine crisis' or 'the Ukraine conflict' – weak and vague terms that dilute the meaning of the events.

We abstain from using all these terms not because we aren't objective, but because they are factually incorrect.

We refrain from using them not because we are Ukrainian journalists and have skin in the game – no, we do so because anything else would mean misinforming readers. In other words, failing at our jobs as journalists.

Since this war is fought on the information battlefield along with the real one, using the correct language that reflects reality is of utmost importance.

Reporting the results of sham referendums without pointing at their nature is tantamount to joining the fight – on Russia's side.

Here's a cheat sheet for filtering out the Kremlin propaganda from one's language:
There is no Ukraine conflict or Ukraine crisis, there is **Russia's war against Ukraine**.
There is no Vladimir Putin's war, there is **Russia's war against Ukraine**.
There is no Russia's special military operation, there is **Russian aggression against Ukraine**.

Russia's war against Ukraine didn't start in 2022, it started in 2014 when Russia invaded and occupied Ukraine's Crimea and Donbas. In 2022, **Russia launched a full-scale invasion of Ukraine** or **an all-out war against Ukraine.**

There is no Donetsk People's Republic (DNR) and no Luhansk People's Republic (LNR), there are **Russian-occupied territories in Ukraine's Donetsk and Luhansk oblasts.**

There are no Ukrainian separatists, there are **Russian-installed proxies/ militants in occupied Ukrainian territories.**

There are no pro-Russian officials (governors, mayors, prosecutors) in occupied Ukrainian territories, there are **Russian-installed proxies in occupied Ukrainian territories.**

There are no separatist regions in Ukraine, there are **Ukrainian territories invaded and occupied by Russia.**

There are no referendums and votes on joining Russia, there are **sham referendums and voting at gunpoint in Russian-occupied Ukrainian territories.**

The mass protests following the announcement of mobilization in Russia were not anti-war protests, they were **anti-mobilization protests in Russia.**

4 October 2022

Life near Russian-occupied nuclear plant: 'I don't know if tomorrow will come'

Alexander Query

Editor's Note: The Kyiv Independent *talked to residents who are still in Russian-occupied Enerhodar and those who recently left but still have family in the city. For their safety, we do not disclose their identities.*

When Russian soldiers captured Enerhodar, the satellite city of the Zaporizhzhia Nuclear Power Plant in early March, it was a shock for Anastasiia, one of roughly 50,000 residents of the city.

'It was horrible to see them in the streets, but for the first two months, they behaved,' she recalled in a conversation with *The Kyiv Independent* in September.

Then the mass abductions and tortures began. 'They torture both men and women,' Anastasiia said. 'They interrogate them and beat them up.'

Anastasiia, who still lives in Enerhodar, says the city has turned into a living hell. She is friends with the nuclear plant workers and active citizens who participated in anti-occupation rallies. She says that those detained by Russian soldiers return from captivity 'barely able to stand'. Some don't return at all. 'Taking your health is the minimum sentence [Russians give you], taking your life is the maximum,' Anastasiia said.

Abductions and torture make it close to impossible for employees to work properly at the local nuclear plant – the biggest one in Europe – that has been a major component of Russia's nuclear blackmail. Workers at the plant put their life on the line to avoid a nuclear catastrophe, but Russian occupation troops keep on abusing them.

Abductions

Enerhodar nowadays resembles a ghost town, according to residents *The Kyiv Independent* spoke to.

Some estimate that roughly half of Enerhodar's 50,000 residents left after Russia captured the city on 4 March.

The remaining residents live in fear of persecution by Russian soldiers. Their most common practice is abduction.

'Many people simply disappear, and some of them are returned for a ransom,' said Anastasiia, who remains in Enerhodar to be with her family who can't leave the city. The ransom can reach up to Hr 50,000, roughly $1,350.

It's a lot of money for Enerhodar, a provincial city where nearly a quarter of the population work at the nuclear power plant. Before the war, the average salary in the region reached $600 a month. So when someone gets detained by Russian soldiers, the community chips in to pay the ransom.

It's unclear to Anastasiia why the Russians persecute the locals. She sees no pattern in who they target.

Their 'protocol', however, is always the same. 'They come at night, they take people to basements and take everything they want from the apartment, and then accuse these people of collaborating with the SBU [Ukraine's Security Service],' she said.

Those working at or near the nuclear plant often become victims of Russian soldiers' torture and abuse. Russians force them to continue to work without pay, food, or sleep, according to Dmytro Orlov, the mayor of Enerhodar. He was forced to flee the city. 'Now they take people directly from the nuclear plant, say that someone betrayed them, and throw them into basements,' he said.

Not everyone survives Russian abuse.

Andriy Honcharuk, a diver at the plant's spent fuel pool, was beaten to death on 29 June because he refused to dive into the pools to check 'if Ukrainian partisans had hidden weapons there'. He died after three days in a coma.

'It's simply unimaginable,' Orlov said of Russian troops' violence against the nuclear plant employees. The head of the nuclear power plant Ihor Murashov was luckier. He was abducted by Russian troops on 30 September, being pulled into a car in broad daylight – and was released four days later.

Andrii, a local business owner, witnessed Russians abducting locals in early July, right before he left. 'Our neighbor was taken away. They didn't even try to hide it,' he said. 'And when we left, three weeks later, he was still kept in a basement somewhere.' Andrii's family and friends remain in the city.

Anastasiia had to be extremely cautious in communicating with *The Kyiv Independent*. According to her, Russian soldiers walk among locals dressed as civilians to spy on them. 'They walk around the city in disguise, listening to what people say,' she said.

She said she never takes her phone with her when she goes out. 'God forbid they take it to check [what's on it]!'

The sham referendums that Russia conducted on 23–27 September in the occupied Ukrainian territories made residents' life even worse, Anastasiia added. 'They went from apartment to apartment, they forced people to vote,' she said. 'They were catching people on the street, and they came to people's workplaces. They pointed a machine gun at them and showed where to put a tick.'

Nuclear plant under threat

Abuses and the resulting stress of nuclear plant workers increases the risk of a nuclear disaster, according to the United Nations' International Atomic Energy Agency (IAEA).

'Ukrainian staff operating the plant under Russian military occupation are under constant high stress and pressure, especially with the limited staff available,' an IAEA report published on 6 September said. 'This is not sustainable and could lead to increased human error with implications for nuclear safety.'

Faltering maintenance could lead to the loss of cooling capacities, culminating in a meltdown of fuel inside an overheated reactor or cooling ponds for spent fuel rods – a scenario similar to the Fukushima disaster in 2011.

Even the spent fuel would spew radioactive particles hundreds of kilometers from the reactor site across southern Ukraine and Russia.

This is why some workers chose to stay despite the risks, Anastasiia said. 'Someone needs to maintain the service at the plant,' she said.

While there are different groups of troops in Enerhodar, the ones in charge of the nuclear plant are reportedly Russian soldiers from the regular army.

Aggressive soldiers

State nuclear agency Energoatom and residents say that both the troops from the regular Russian army and the Kremlin's proxies in Russian-occupied Donetsk and Luhansk oblasts are participating in the persecution of locals in Enerhodar.

Members of Russia's National Guard (Rosgvardia in Russian) were also spotted in the city.

All these groups seem to act separately and don't communicate with each other much, according to locals' observations.

Anastasiia believes that representatives of the FSB, Russia's Federal Security Service, are also in Enerhodar.

According to locals' testimonies, the first batch of Russians that arrived in Enerhodar in March weren't committing atrocities on a massive scale. Soon, a new group of Russian soldiers, police, and security service officers came – that's when the situation got much worse.

The rotation was initiated by the Russian commanders for several reasons. For one, Russian soldiers were 'getting used' to the local population and showing compassion to the locals, Energoatom wrote.

According to local media, looting got worse with every new rotation as soldiers who left the city broke into the apartments of evacuated people and stole their belongings ...

Shellings

Controlling the city doesn't prevent Russians from shelling Enerhodar and its surroundings to put the blame on Ukraine.

'They accuse Ukraine of shelling, but I can see them shelling the city with mortars, tanks, and helicopters,' Anastasiia said.

'Our friends and relatives told us that the Russian troops were not even hiding when they shelled [Enerhodar],' Andrii added.

On 6 September, blasts rang out, and power was cut in Enerhodar, leaving the residents without light and electricity. Some of the city's districts still face frequent blackouts.

Orlov said that some areas in Enerhodar are on the brink of a humanitarian catastrophe. The same neighborhoods have been left without gas for several months.

Constant shelling adds 'enormous pressure' on residents and employees of the plant who already face hardship, according to Anastasiia. 'They go to work under fire, and they can be targeted right at their workplace,' she said.

Regardless of the shelling and the risks, Andrii's parents stayed behind to look after their small hardware store. 'My parents are preparing for winter and repairing the stove in my grandparents' house because most likely there will be no heating there,' he said. 'But they are also thinking of leaving.'

Anastasiia is also faced with a tough choice. She doesn't want to leave her parents alone in the city. 'Russians destroyed our lives, our dreams, and plans,' she said. 'I don't know if tomorrow is gonna come – but hope dies last. We are waiting for a miracle and believe in Ukraine's Armed Forces.'

18 October 2022

Surrounded and desperate: How Russia lost Lyman

Francis Farrell

On a quiet road lined by pine forest leading into the city of Lyman, the remains of a frantic but unsuccessful escape clutter the roadside. Four repurposed civilian cars, burnt-out and upturned, mark the spot where the flight of Russian soldiers met an abrupt end.

Just beside them, the dense green pixel camouflage of charred Russian military uniforms stains the pavement, scattered between personal belongings, toothbrushes, and Moscow metro tickets.

The members of this frantic convoy were fleeing the village of Drobysheve into Lyman, unaware that the latter was already effectively surrounded by the Ukrainian army. Eight Russian soldiers have died here, according to police officers on the ground.

The bodies of those killed on the spot have already been removed from the roadside. Only one member of the party who had crawled into the forest in a hopeless attempt to escape still remained in his final resting place, his hand suspended in the air by rigor mortis.

'He wanted his piece of Ukrainian land,' a police officer on duty at the scene said, 'and he's got it.'

Coming three weeks after Ukraine's lightning counteroffensive in Kharkiv Oblast, on 1 October, the defeat in Lyman was a major setback for Russia's withering war aims for numerous reasons.

Firstly, Ukraine's recapture of Lyman, a city in Donetsk Oblast with a prewar population of 20,000 that had been occupied by Russia since mid-May, proved once again the capacity of Ukraine's forces to conduct large-scale combined arms offensives against an entrenched opponent, this time without the element of surprise.

The loss of Lyman was also particularly embarrassing for Russia's absurd push to annex four more regions of Ukraine on the back of sham referendums. With Ukrainian troops entering the city the day after the illegal annexation was signed into law by Russian dictator Vladimir Putin, jokes flooded the internet about Lyman being 'a part of Russia' for less than 24 hours.

Most morbidly, while official figures are scarce, videos, third-party analysis and anecdotal evidence point towards an astonishing number of Russian soldiers killed in the offensive.

A spokesperson from an unnamed Ukrainian army unit stationed in Drobysheve, who identified himself only as Vladyslav for security reasons, spoke to *The Kyiv Independent* about the chaotic and violent end of Russia's occupation of Lyman.

'According to our data, when Lyman was practically surrounded, there were about 5,000 Russian soldiers in the city,' he said. 'How many of them made it out, how many were caught, how many are still running around, and how many were put to sleep forever, you can think about for yourself.'

Closing the trap

To achieve the final encirclement of Lyman, Ukrainian forces first had to conduct challenging, fiercely contested river crossings at several points along the Siverskyi Donets River, which had served as the line of contact since Russia occupied the northern bank in May.

While one arm of the pincer crossed the river east of Lyman and liberated the town of Yampil, the other crossed near Sviatohirsk, pushing village by village towards Drobysheve.

Artem, an infantry officer stationed on the road into Lyman forbidden to give his full identity, showed *The Kyiv Independent* video footage of the first stages of the crossing. In a relaxed mood, as if on a fishing trip, five infantrymen sit in a small camouflage motorboat as it makes its way out of the bushes to cross the short stretch of water, while the whistle of incoming artillery is heard nearby.

'We took over a month to capture Drobysheve,' Artem, said. 'It was one united operation, and the river was a barrier for us just as it was for them back in May.'

'At first, we could only cross in small groups, one boat at a time ... They were throwing everything at us, Grad rockets, mortars,' Artem, 45, said. 'They couldn't see us, but they knew we were there, and their job was to cover the whole area we could be crossing with fire.'

Deafening fog

On the central street of Drobysheve, hardly a single building remains that has not taken heavy damage from artillery fire. Crude, freshly dug trenches mark the positions where Russian troops attempted to dig in and defend the road. Unlike in the swift push of the Kharkiv Oblast counteroffensive, Ukrainian forces had to pound Russian positions in the town with artillery before infantry was sent in to complete the job.

As always in war, those who suffered most in the hard-fought battles were civilians.

In preparation for counter-offensive operations, the Ukrainian government has consistently called for its citizens to evacuate occupied settlements to safer areas further from the front line. Attached to their homes and without options for alternative accommodation, many residents nonetheless make the choice to stay put.

While Russia took the area in only four days, the Ukrainian operation to liberate it took much longer, with understandably more destruction. 'For twenty days until 30 September, [Ukrainian forces] were hitting us hard,' said Drobysheve resident Nataliia Loboda, 65. 'We hardly came out of our cellars at all. It was scary, even more so than when the Russians came in May.'

For residents of Lyman and the surrounding villages, Ukraine's counter-offensive was only the final chapter of a four-month ordeal, during which their homes were never far away from the front line.

Even in the quieter periods of the Russian occupation of the city, life was rarely lived outside the four dark walls of residents' basements, where they sought refuge both from shelling and from unwanted attention from the Russian proxy soldiers stationed in the city.

'We never strayed far from the cellar,' said Yevhen Tryshkovsky, a 23-year-old resident of Lyman. 'We would run out to turn the pancakes over, and quickly run back inside.'

In this environment of isolation, the occupiers failed to restore basic utilities and did not bother with conducting sham referendums here as the Ukrainian army continued its approach.

Once the battle to retake the city began, the only information that sheltering residents had to go by was the volume of the shelling and gunfire they could hear from street level.

'We had no idea who was shooting and from where,' said Larysa Chaplyna, a 79-year-old resident of Lyman's southern neighborhood. 'The only thing to do was to shake in fear and cry.'

On the sandy hills of Lyman's main cemetery, a scene unfolds that is testament to the danger the city's residents lived under throughout their encounter with Russia's war.

Reminiscent of a similar discovery in liberated Izium, a large makeshift cemetery contains the reburied remains of 187 people who died since Russian forces entered the city in May. The dates on the crosses range from May right through to September, without any noticeable period of relief.

One by one, emergency services workers in hazmat suits unearth the bodies, reburied with the dignity of plastic body bags, unlike in Izium. Early evaluations suggest that most victims died from explosive-related trauma, according to Oleksandra Havrylko, a police press officer at the scene.

Panicked flight
Ukraine's methodical encirclement of Lyman was devastating for the Russian soldiers left in the city. Russian positions on strategic street corners in the city stand hastily abandoned, with pots still on the stove and empty vodka bottles on the table. A few meters away, the body of a Russian soldier with a clean bullet wound to the head lies half-sunken, melting into the sand.

'On the tactical level,' recounted Vladyslav, 'our main aim was to create the worst possible conditions for the enemy in Lyman as long as they stayed there.'

Tetiana Velichko, 53, who conducted the choir at the local house of culture before the invasion and now stood in line for humanitarian aid, said massive strikes started around the city on 18 September.

'It seemed like all parts of the military were here – tanks, rockets, planes, helicopters,' she said. 'The only things missing were the battleships and submarines.'

Videos filmed by the Ukrainian troops who liberated the area showed dozens of destroyed Russian vehicles on the road out of the city. At one location, thirteen corpses were found of wounded Russian troops left for dead, domestic cats scavenging on their bodies as they lay on their stretchers.

'Almost all the roads out of the city were under our fire control,' said Vladyslav. 'If they weren't eliminated in Lyman itself, our soldiers met them with plenty of fire on the way out in the area of Zarichne and Torske.'

Despite their untenable position, the Russian forces in Lyman are understood to have had orders to hold the city at least until the illegal annexation was signed, to avoid political embarrassment for the Kremlin.

'From open sources we know that the Russian soldiers were asking their commanders to allow them to withdraw from Lyman,' said Vladyslav, 'but because Putin had his big speech or whatever it was that evening, they were forbidden from giving the society negative news.'

Nevertheless, some of the more senior Russian ranks began to flee while it was still possible, leaving a mixture of Russian regular troops, proxy forces, and members of the BARS-13 militia unit left in the city to fend for themselves.

'They would keep fighting, even when they had no chances of surviving,' said Vladyslav. 'Some of them chose to change into civilian clothes, hide in basements, and try to blend in with the locals.'

'Our police and security services are doing a good job, and they're still catching them now,' he said. 'That machine gun fire we heard from the forest earlier? That's no exercise, they are still out there.'

The road ahead

After success in Lyman and the surrounding area, the world is watching to see whether the Ukrainian army will be able to push further before winter sets in. The new front lines now roughly follow the border of Luhansk Oblast, which was also declared annexed by Russia together with Donetsk, Kherson, and Zaporizhzhia oblasts.

The next major target in this sector of the front is the town of Kreminna, a key potential staging point for an offensive to retake the larger urban areas of Sievierodonetsk and Lysychansk, which Russia occupied in June after over a month of intense artillery bombardment and urban warfare.

Vladyslav was understandably coy about plans for further Ukrainian offensive operations.

'The enemy will see on the battlefield what the plan is,' he said. 'Every settlement is a different situation, and we are always adapting our tactics. This is our biggest advantage, that we use modern methods and they, for the most part, are stuck in 1945.'

Less than a month after Russia announced the mobilization of 300,000 new soldiers to replenish its badly mauled regular army in Ukraine, untrained conscripts are already being sent to the front en masse.

'Our guys are doing their job,' said Vladyslav. 'If they weren't afraid in the face of a professional army, an amateur army won't change things, whether there is a thousand of them, two thousand, or five coming at you.'

After enduring two fierce battles for their city in the space of five months, locals now face a difficult winter. Many will be forced to remain in their basements with apartment windows blown out and central heating non-existent.

'We don't have anything, no work, no pensions,' said Loboda outside her well-kept garden in Drobysheve. 'We just have the potatoes, cucumbers, tomatoes that we grow ourselves and we make do.'

'I'm just glad that it has become quieter. On the first day after the battles were over I just sat outside in the sun, not doing anything, listening to the silence.'

19 October 2022

Intensified Russian attacks on Ukraine infrastructure unlikely to achieve Kremlin's goals

Oleg Sukhov

Massive Russian missile and drone attacks on Kyiv and energy infrastructure all over Ukraine are becoming a regular occurrence.

One apparent aim of Russian attacks on energy and civilian infrastructure is to bully Ukraine's population into submission.

On 19 October, President Volodymyr Zelensky didn't rule out a potential failure of Ukraine's electricity system. According to the President's Office, the Ukrainian leadership is preparing for 'a number of different scenarios' after over a week of Russian missile and drone strikes on electricity facilities across the country.

Experts believe that Russian dictator Vladimir Putin is also trying to slow down the Ukrainian counteroffensive by attacking the rear. *Meduza*, a Russian independent news outlet, reported that Putin is planning a new offensive in 2023 after newly conscripted Russians reach the front line.

But so far, the strategy does not appear to be working. Ten days after the first major attack on Kyiv in months, there are no signs that Ukrainian public opinion is changing in favor of a peace deal with Russia.

Military experts also add that the attacks have little impact on the situation on the battlefield.

'It doesn't affect the armed forces,' Ukrainian military expert Vyacheslav Tseluiko told *The Kyiv Independent*.

Continuous strikes

On 10 October, Russia attacked Ukraine with 84 missiles and 24 Iranian-made Shahed-136 drones in one of the largest coordinated missile attacks since the full-scale invasion began on 24 February.

At least 19 people, including eight in Kyiv, were killed.

Russia also continued attacking energy infrastructure in different cities.

On 17 October, Russia attacked Ukrainian cities with 43 drones. Russia used 28 drones to attack Kyiv, where a residential building was destroyed. At least five people were killed.

Only half of the missiles targeting Ukraine were shot down on 10 October, but most of the drones were downed on 17 October.

The attacks on Kyiv continued on 18 October, when a Russian missile attack on the city's energy infrastructure killed three people, and 19 October, when 'several missiles' were shot down by air defense, according to the city authorities.

The newly provided German IRIS-T surface-to-air system appeared to be defending Kyiv. Zelensky said the air defense systems were effective and 'performed very well'.

Effects of attacks

The Russian attacks have already had a significant impact on Ukraine's energy infrastructure.

Zelensky said on 18 October that Russia had destroyed 30% of Ukraine's power stations since 10 October. Blackouts in Ukrainian cities have become regular.

Some interpret the attacks to mean that the Kremlin is hoping that Ukraine will be too busy handling a humanitarian catastrophe during the winter heating season, which will halt its counteroffensive.

Yet, military experts argue that the military effects of the Russian attacks are minimal. 'The logic of their actions is terrorist. It's a way to pressure the population,' Tseluiko said. He argued that Russia expects the Ukrainian population to get tired of the war and pressure the government to sue for peace.

The attacks triggered a big public outcry because they hit Kyiv for the first time since July, and the attacks on the capital were more massive this time.

The Kremlin aims to intimidate the residents of Kyiv, where 'the population has become more relaxed, thinking that the war is far away,' Tseluiko said.

Yet the recent attacks on Kyiv are less significant than the constant Russian strikes on many cities closer to the front line, Tseluiko said.

The assault will not have the desired effect because Ukrainians have already experienced eight months of all-out war, according to Tseluiko.

'It's like a pinprick,' he said. 'Ukraine already has immunity to this.'

Running out of missiles?

One of the major consequences of the recent attacks is Russia's diminishing stockpile of missiles.

On 14 October, Ukrainian Defense Minister Oleksiy Reznikov said that Russia had 124 Iskander ballistic missiles left out of the 900 it had before the invasion.

He added that Russia also has 272 Kalibr cruise missiles, compared to 500 before the invasion, and 213 Kh-101 and Kh-555 cruise missiles, compared to the pre-invasion number of 444.

Although these numbers cannot be independently verified, Tseluiko agreed that Russia is running out of missiles.

Since Russian missile production is stagnating, he added that Moscow is switching to Iranian-made drones, which are much cheaper.

Tseluiko added that Russia has to choose between launching a few missiles regularly and launching many missiles but rarely.

'It's an act of desperation,' he said. 'They see that they're losing the war. Russia has spent a major part of its resources but has not achieved any results.'

22 October 2022

How Russia organized its torture chamber network in Kharkiv Oblast
Alexander Query

War veteran Serhii Chepurnyi recently turned 40. This year, he didn't celebrate his birthday.

His hands shaking as he took a cigarette from its pack, Chepurnyi carefully chose his words as he recalled what Russian soldiers did to him when occupying his native village, Velykyi Burluk.

Velykyi Burluk, located roughly 50 kilometers from the Russian border, was swiftly occupied when Russia launched its full-scale invasion of Ukraine on 24 February.

The small settlement was officially liberated on 12 September. A few days earlier, Chepurnyi was freed from a torture chamber in Vovchansk, located within just a few kilometers of Russia.

Chepurnyi spent 44 days in detainment, subjected to Russian torture, electrocution, and beatings on a daily basis.

'Everything was by the hour, everything was planned,' Chepurnyi said of his time in a Russian torture chamber.

His testimony, along with other survivors' accounts from torture chambers in other parts of Ukraine liberated from Russian soldiers, reveals that the torture of civilians was far from a spontaneous act of certain Russian units: it appears to have been a systematic, organized effort to terrorize local populations.

Serhii Bolvinov, Kharkiv Oblast chief investigator, said on 6 October that his team found 22 Russian sites used to torture Ukrainians in Kharkiv Oblast, including in Vovchansk, Kupiansk, Velykyi Burluk, and Izium.

Belkis Wille, a senior crisis and conflict researcher at Human Rights Watch, led a three-week probe in Izium, where the organization interviewed over 100 victims of war crimes.

'Multiple victims shared credible accounts with us of similar experiences of torture during interrogation in facilities under the control of Russian forces and their subordinates, indicating this treatment was part of a policy and plan,' said Wille.

Survivors' testimonies reveal the sheer scale of Russia's highly organized plans to round up Ukrainian war veterans, volunteers, and civilians in a widespread network of torture chambers scattered across Kharkiv Oblast.

Police station torture chamber

As a Ukrainian war veteran who served when Russia invaded Crimea and Donbas in 2014, Chepurnyi knew he had a target on his back.

He served from 2001 as part of compulsory military service and then in the State Border Guard Service until 2014.

He said that Russian soldiers arrested him while he was doing utility work on a road nearby on 28 July. They immediately brought him to Velykyi Burluk's police station, where they made him wait the whole day in a cell without water and access to toilets.

'They took me away at 9 a.m., they didn't give me water or anything,' he said. 'Then, at 10 p.m., they came to me, put a bag on my head, tied my hands, and took me away.'

The Kyiv Independent had access to the Velykyi Burluk police station that Russian forces had taken over during the occupation. The station was heavily damaged during Ukraine's September counteroffensive.

According to Ukraine's open-source intelligence (OSINT) research group Molfar, Velykyi Burluk's police station harbored a battalion of Russia's 200th Separate Motor Rifle Brigade from the 14th Army Corps, servicemen from the 1st and 2nd Army Corps reserve, and a battalion of the 21st Separate Motor Rifle Brigade.

The station's basement revealed a maze of damp makeshift cells with dirty cloths and empty bottles strewn across the floor, where survivors say they were kept before being transferred to other torture chambers in larger cities – Vovchansk and Kupiansk.

Serhiy, a 37-year-old local emergency service worker, who declined to provide his last name in fear of Russia's renewed occupation, told *The Kyiv Independent* that his brother was among those arrested and transferred to Vovchansk.

'He was brought [to the police station] with a bag on his head, he stayed here for several hours and was taken to Vovchansk,' Serhiy said. 'Some were released, and nothing happened, no traces [of torture] were left on them, and some were released, and they were in a very bad shape,' he added about those detained by the Russians.

The fate of many people kept in the Velykyi Burluk police station remains unknown. 'We couldn't even approach [the station], they wouldn't let us,' Serhiy said.

He added that it was easy for Russians to round up Ukrainian war veterans because collaborators provided the Russian soldiers with lists. 'You could see that [some] people cooperated with Russians from the way they behaved.'

He said that everybody was checked at checkpoints surrounding the city, making it impossible to escape if your name appeared on a list.

'Of course, we know who the collaborators are,' he said, adding most of them left with the Russians when Ukraine liberated the village. 'Some stayed there, but the police will find them,' he added. 'Everything will be fine, people will get their due.'

Systematic torture

Russian forces arrested a handful of people, all Ukrainian veterans, in Velykyi Burluk, including Chepurnyi and Serhiy's brothers.

They took them to Vovchansk, three kilometers south of the Russian border.

There, an old factory was turned into a detention center where civilians, including war veterans, were tortured. Serhiy's brother was kept there for 21 days, and Chepurnyi for over a month.

It was visibly painful for Chepurnyi to recall his time in Vovchansk. 'The first interrogation took place at night,' he said.

Chepurnyi showed *The Kyiv Independent* his arms on which he said Russians put electric wires to electrocute him. Russian soldiers were wearing masks, he said. 'They tortured me with electricity, a very high voltage, and beat me hard,' he said. 'The faster they turned [the crank], the higher the voltage.'

'It hurt a lot,' Chepurnyi recalled. Russian soldiers also poured water on his wounds while electrocuting him to make him talk.

Ukrainian officials have accused Russian forces of using old mobile radio telephones as a power source to electrocute prisoners during interrogations. *The Kyiv Independent* spotted a burned Soviet-era radio phone with an apparent wire protruding from its carcass on the floor of one of the first-floor rooms in Velykyi Burluk.

'There was a moment when they said in Russian: "Serhii, your whole life is in your hands. We know where your parents live. Do you understand?"' Chepurnyi said.

Little did he know this first day would become his weekly routine for more than a month.

'They had a rotation there about once a week, and also every Sunday, there were similar interrogations, all the same: electric current, beatings,' he said. 'When they torture you with electricity, you feel no pain from beatings. You only wish your heart doesn't stop, and that's it.'

Chepurnyi was adamant his tormentors were Russians and not from Kremlin proxies in Donetsk and Luhansk oblasts. 'It was the FSB [Russia's Federal Security Service],' he said. 'Their accents were very Russian.'

He said some prisoners surrendered to torture, citing the example of one man who was released after four or five days. He said he thinks this man revealed the position of Ukrainian troops, but Chepurnyi couldn't confirm this information.

Other Ukrainian soldiers confirmed that war veterans had been tortured in Vovchansk, an account also established by locals to Ukrainian media outlet Hromadske, saying 'young guys had been tortured with electric shocks for weeks'.

One of the medics in Vovchansk, who declined to disclose her name, fearing Russia would renew its offensive, concurred. 'They tortured a lot of people,' she told *The Kyiv Independent*, 'but we couldn't approach the victims [to help].'

She said that the Russians had brought their own medical teams that were 'taking care' of the tortured and that the Russian military had set up their own system to handle their victims.

Chepurnyi said that there were around 40 people in his cell, including three war veterans, civilian women, and the six workers from Sri Lanka held captive by Russian forces for months.

'[Russians] served us food by tossing it where we went to the toilet,' he said. 'When they got drunk, they would say: "Where are your Armed Forces? We want to destroy them because we are the strong Russian army."'

But on 10 September, Russians began to flee. They brought the prisoners back into their cells and opened the doors at the last minute.

Chepurnyi, along with other inmates, went to where Russians had kept prisoners' personal documents, and left on foot from Vovchansk, following the signs to Velykyi Burluk before being picked up on the side of the road leading to their hometown.

'Re-education' in Kupiansk

Another Russian torture chamber was established in occupied Kupiansk's police station on the city's main street. Russian forces had their main headquarters across the road.

Both sites were largely destroyed by heavy fighting during Ukraine's counter-offensive.

The smell of sweat mixed with human excrement inside the detention site is still strong. Mattresses covered in dry blood are still present on the floors and benches.

A massive Z and simplistic paintings glorifying Russian soldiers surrounded with the communist hammer and sickles were painted on the walls in a long corridor of doors to the cells where inmates were kept.

Russians packed up to 400 people at once in small cells designed for 140 people in total, according to Ukraine's Security Service (SBU). Russian forces put mattresses under low benches, forcing inmates to crawl under them to sleep. Some inmates were forced to stand.

According to Ukraine's Armed Forces that liberated the town, Russians used the police station as a so-called 're-education' center, forcing prisoners to sing the Russian national anthem daily. The torture chamber had papers taped to the doors with the lyrics.

The uncle of Vladyslav Kaptannyi, a 15-year-old teenager living in Velykyi Burluk, was taken to Kupiansk presumably because he had served in Ukraine's armed forces, Kaptannyi told *The Kyiv Independent*.

'They kidnapped war veterans, took them to Kupiansk, and tortured them there,' he said. *The Kyiv Independent* couldn't directly contact Kaptannyi's uncle and couldn't independently verify the claim.

Many Kupiansk residents, who refused to give their names to *The Kyiv Independent* out of fear of Russian soldiers returning, claimed they didn't know what happened in the police station.

Some recalled Ukrainian veterans being brought there but said they didn't know anything about the accusations of torture and mistreatment.

One of the locals, a retiree, admitted to *The Kyiv Independent* that she was afraid to talk. 'We don't know if they will come back, of course, we're afraid,' she said.

In Velykyi Burluk, Chepurnyi said there is no place for fear in his heart. He wants to recover, go to work, hug his 18-year-old daughter and rebuild his life.

'This torture was tough to survive,' he said. 'I tell you, guys, that they are not humans, they have no pity – they are orcs [a term used in Ukraine for Russian soldiers].'

'I don't feel anything now, only hate,' he said.

Molfar, a Ukrainian open-source intelligence (OSINT) group, contributed to this report by identifying the Russian units that are the alleged perpetrators of Russia's war crimes in formerly occupied territories. Vitalii Poberezhnyi contributed to this report by helping find witnesses of Russia's war crimes.

7 November 2022

How psychologists risk their lives to help victims of Russian attacks

Daria Shulzhenko

When Russia's drone strike hit a residential building in central Kyiv on the morning of 17 October, emergency workers turned up at the scene within minutes.

As rescuers worked to put out the fire and clear out the rubble of the severely damaged high-rise apartment complex, medics provided first aid to the wounded. Police officers documented preliminary casualties.

At the scene, a team of psychologists also worked to provide no less urgent help to the victims: speaking to people who had just experienced an event that could leave potentially devastating effects on their mental health. Some of them may have lost a loved one or their home. For many, the stress of surviving a life-threatening attack can be overwhelming.

Though emergency psychiatric services are often overlooked, they may be just as critical as physical aid after a traumatic experience.

'We go where it is dangerous. It is scary, just like for everybody else. But we know why we are going there,' says 27-year-old Nataliia Andriushchenko, who has been working as a psychologist at the State Emergency Service since 2017. 'We go there to help. We go there to save people,' she adds.

The Russian drone strike on 17 October killed five people, including a young couple expecting a child.

Russia's near-relentless attacks on civilian infrastructure since the start of the full-scale invasion in February have put psychologists with the State Emergency Service on constant alert. Along with other emergency workers, they arrive at the scenes of missile and drone strikes, massive fires, and other disastrous consequences of Russia's brutal attacks.

On alert

Before the full-scale war, psychologists of the Kyiv department of the State Emergency Service were called up to the sites of big accidents or catastrophes, often with many victims, such as a gas explosion that killed five people and destroyed an apartment complex in Kyiv's Pozniaky neighborhood in 2020.

Such calls used to be rare but Russia's war has changed everything.

'If earlier we had to work at the sites of events caused mainly by accidents, now these are targeted attacks on the city,' says Liubov Kirnos, 32, who heads the unit in Kyiv.

Kirnos says that they are now called to every site of Russian drone or missile attack in Kyiv, which often results in the destruction of infrastructure and homes, and the killing of civilians.

Every oblast department of the State Emergency Service has staff psychologists, Kirnos says. There are currently six psychologists working in the capital.

The Kyiv team was called up to work soon after the first explosions were heard in the capital early in the morning of 24 February.

'I will never forget how I felt that day,' Andriushchenko says. 'When everyone was worried about how to flee Kyiv and evacuate their relatives, my number one task was getting to work,' she recalls.

Devoted to helping others, they started working in 'enhanced' mode from day one of the full-scale invasion, switching from the 8-to-5 schedule to 24-hour-shifts.

If nothing happens during a shift, they do their 'regular' job, which includes paperwork, inspecting different units in Kyiv, and training exercises. But whenever their help is needed, psychologists arrive at the site of an attack or other accidents immediately, even if they are not on duty.

'It's not the kind of work that you can go home, switch to something else and not think about it,' Andriushchenko says. 'We must be ready any time.'

According to 28-year-old psychologist Ivanna Davydenko, not only do they have longer shifts and more calls now, but they also have to be 'very careful' at the sites, watching for possible repeated attacks. 'We must be vigilant to protect ourselves and the victims,' she says.

Evacuees and occupation survivors

In early spring, numerous Ukrainians – including those who fled then-occupied towns in Kyiv Oblast – began arriving at the central railway station in Kyiv to take evacuation trains to safer regions in western Ukraine.

At the train station, the emergency service's psychologists encountered victims of Russia's all-out war 'en masse' for the first time.

Kirnos says that many people arriving at the station 'could not remember the last time they ate or drank, as they were under such acute stress'. Some of them looked withdrawn, while others tried to put up a good mood to cheer up their children. Many people were crying.

'The worst thing was not that these people were wounded, but that many of their relatives were killed or missing,' says Davydenko.

Kirnos recalls a man who arrived at the train station with his little daughter. His wife and the girl's mother was killed when Russian troops shelled a line of people waiting to get bread in the city of Chernihiv.

'There were many kids, so we created a special area for them with toys and pencils to distract them while they waited for trains,' Kirnos says.

The psychologists worked with dozens of people at the train station, using various techniques to help them relieve stress. They say that during their time there they saw the unimaginable pain Russia's war had inflicted on civilians.

'We wanted to do everything to make their condition and stay [at the station] at least a little easier,' says Andriushchenko.

In April they went to Borodyanka, a town 40 kilometers northwest of Kyiv that was heavily bombarded and occupied by Russia during the early stages of the all-out war.

In Kyiv Oblast alone, Russian troops killed 1,365 civilians during the month-long occupation, Kyiv Oblast Police Chief Andriy Nebytov reported on 20 October. More graves are still being found in the region.

The psychologists spent nearly a week in Borodyanka, providing support to people 'in conditions of total grief and suffering'. The work was also physically dangerous as Russian troops had scattered the area with mines in the wake of their retreat.

'There was a woman whose son, daughter-in-law, and little granddaughter were killed in a Russian airstrike on a residential building,' Kirnos says. 'She had to wait for a couple of days until their bodies were found under the rubble ... She was in a deep stupor. She sat on a bench, hugged herself, and closed her eyes.'

Kirnos says the doctors could not give her any medication, so the psychologists had to act quickly: by talking to her, Kirnos made the woman open her eyes and helped her to start breathing normally.

In about five minutes, the woman burst into tears. Once she started to reply, the doctors were finally able to give her the medication she needed.

Kirnos says that the lack of psychological first aid at such critical moments can result in depression and post-traumatic stress disorders.

'Our priority is to ensure that a person does not freeze in a certain emotional state,' Andriushchenko says. 'Because if that happens, it can affect their life for a very long time.'

Highest reward

Andriushchenko says that Russia's first-ever attack on Kyiv with kamikaze drones on 17 October was by far the most dangerous for her and her colleagues. While she can not disclose details, Andriushchenko says she calls this day her 'second birthday'.

That morning, Russia attacked Ukraine with 43 drones, 37 of which were shot down. In Kyiv, the attack destroyed a residential building and damaged an office and apartment building next to it.

Psychologists spent nearly 12 hours at the site, helping not only the victims of the strike on the residential building but also those who were hiding in nearby bomb shelters, including children.

To stay sane after seeing all the horrors of Russia's war, psychologists provide each other and their fellow rescuers with mental health assistance. Davydenko says art therapy and physical activity also help her to relieve stress.

Nevertheless, she says she does not regret choosing this job. 'Yes, it is a dangerous, very risky job that requires high emotional stability,' Davydenko says. 'But it is for the sake of other people.'

She says she often gets 'goosebumps' when she hears 'thank you' from the people they have helped. 'This, perhaps, is the highest reward there can be,' she says.

9 November 2022

Voices from the trenches: Ukrainian soldiers near Kherson share what they feel and fear

Igor Kossov

The Kyiv Independent spent some time with units of the 59th Mechanized Brigade who are defending Mykolaiv Oblast and attacking the Russian forces in neighboring Kherson.

These are testimonies of four soldiers, officers and enlisted men, about their day-to-day experiences during the battle for the South. Only first names and callsigns were used to protect the soldiers' identities.

Mykhailo

The higher-ups and military analysts say that the intensity of Russian shelling has gone down significantly in the past few months.

To Senior Lieutenant Mykhailo and his infantrymen, who spend time on the front lines in Kherson Oblast, that may be a stretch.

'They're continuing to shoot us as they shot us before,' says Mykhailo, standing at an entrenched outpost, 15 kilometers in the rear. 'Shells, mortars, cluster munitions. 180 millimeters, 120 millimeters. Tanks.'

The tanks are especially rough. A tank shell announces its arrival with a sudden, shattering blast that gives survivors just seconds to react before the next one. Some tanks' firing rates can be terrifying, the soldiers say.

Indirect-fire weapons often give more of a warning, making a loud noise as they plow through the air. Some Russian artillery rounds and mortars fail to explode, bouncing harmlessly along the ground. 'If only all of them were duds,' Mykhailo says.

'What do we feel?' he muses over the question. 'We pray, each of us sitting in the trench, thinking their own thoughts.'

'We have wounded, shell-shocked, and unfortunately, 200s,' he says, the numerical code for fatalities in this part of the world. 'Here, people are fighting for their land, with their own strength, trying to drive out the enemy.'

Raven

'We just feel like we're at work,' says Voron – Raven in English – who commands a Grad multiple rocket launcher. 'We get our job done, it's all very mundane. There's nothing supernatural about it.'

His unit is one of the instruments of Ukraine's strategy to strike vulnerable Russian positions with rockets and artillery. The Soviet-era vehicle resembles a heavy truck with a rectangular cluster of 40 tubes on the back, able to lob rockets up to 20 kilometers away.

Ukraine does not produce its own Grad munitions and existing stockpiles have to be rationed, Raven says. 'We can't throw ammunition left and right, like we did at the start.'

Raven's detached workmanlike attitude was developed over months of heavy fighting in southern Ukraine.

'The beginning was the hardest – February, March, April. We didn't even know who was shooting at whom. Disinformation, a lack of concrete borders,' he recollects. 'But now we know where the gray zone is and it's a lot easier.'

Still, no one can get too relaxed. Russian artillery and rockets can come at any moment.

'We're doing everything in our power to defeat this enemy,' says Raven. 'We'll fight back for as long as we have the strength, we will hit them as hard as we can for as long as we can so that our children and grandchildren can live calmly and peacefully.'

'We will not allow what our grandfathers allowed to come to pass, when they let us be subjugated under Soviet rule.' ...

Volodymyr

'Want some pea soup?' Volodymyr asks in the makeshift underground trench kitchen. He doesn't take no for an answer, pouring a bowl, cutting off a hunk of bread and pouring a plastic cup full of apple and grape juice.

The space around the small table is packed with shelves, kitchen supplies, military equipment, a stove and a refrigerator. What open wall space remains is covered in drawings contributed by the children of Zhytomyr Oblast, 400 kilometers up north.

The soup is incredible. Volodymyr looks pleased to hear it. But when asked for the recipe, he looks just as pleased to refuse to give it.

As the subject returns to the war, his smile fades and his expression changes. He sinks into thought.

'When you have to bury one of the boys, someone you saw alive just a few days ago, that's the scariest ... Not being wounded. Not being killed, because you wouldn't know what's going on,' he continues. 'But when you have to bury a friend, that's the scariest.'

'I'm talking about Pasha,' he says at length. Pasha was ripped away from him by a Russian attack two weeks ago. The two had completed training together. Pasha was beloved by the unit but he had a melancholy to him. Days before he met his fate, he said, 'I'm not going to be around for very long.'

'When you go through the whole circle with someone ...' Volodymyr trails off. His conclusion, 'that's the scariest', goes unsaid.

21 November 2022

Life slowly returning to Kherson, still without power and water
Asami Terajima

Standing outside her small, dimly lit grocery store, Natalia chain-smokes several cigarettes until a customer finally shows up at the door.

The 48-year-old shopkeeper misses being busy all day. More than a week after Ukrainian forces recaptured her native Kherson, she is still waiting for her long-time customers to show up. After Russia sacked Kherson in early March, the influx of customers at Natalia's store sharply decreased, and so did the quantity and quality of goods sold. 'We had many people coming [before],' Natalia told *The Kyiv Independent*.

When the full-scale war started, her store became a place where people could find much-needed support. 'Elderly women, men would come for milk or for some biscuits ... We would talk about the weather, how we felt, we just supported each other – we are one family.'

'We have lived here for so many years, we know everyone,' she said, referring to fellow residents in her small, largely empty neighborhood.

For most of November, Kherson has been without power, water, and heating. Natalia hopes there will be electricity soon so she can resume selling warm beverages, such as tea, like in the old times.

But her street is still haunted by the war.

Just next to the shop is a former pre-trial detention center that Russians used as a torture chamber. Kherson residents were forcibly dragged there on trumped-up charges, and screams could be heard across the street.

Natalia, who worked everyday during the Russian occupation to serve her customers' needs, said it was 'scary' to hear the screams a few times a week.

Her 22-year-old colleague, Daria, said she did her best to ignore them, fearing consequences from the Russians. 'We understood that one wrong word or move could put us there, too,' Daria said.

After surviving the Russian occupation, Kherson residents grapple with difficult living conditions as they resume life in the city. Some small businesses are now open, mostly grocery stores and cafes, where owners greet fellow Khersonians with a smile.

For the first time in nearly nine months, Kherson residents could openly discuss the war without fearing repercussions. Those who barely left their homes during the occupation enjoy the sunshine and fresh air, sharing a laugh with one another.

The central Freedom Square, where humanitarian aid is handed out, is packed with hundreds of Kherson residents.

Dozens of Kherson residents told *The Kyiv Independent* that they could hardly believe their eyes – the city used to be largely empty after mid-afternoon, and people avoided walking in large groups.

At a larger grocery store located in front of the central square, Bohdan Kosatyy told *The Kyiv Independent* that more than 1,000 customers are shopping every day – compared to a few hundred during the occupation days.

The 27-year-old clerk said that Ukrainian products returned on the shelves for the first time in a long time after months of only seeing 'very limited' Russian products in the shop.

Asked what he enjoys the most about working, Kosatyy said that it's the long-forgotten free interaction with people 'because we are social creatures.' ...

26 November 2022

Empty Kherson art museum in despair after entire collection stolen by Russia

Francis Farrell

Housed in a grand imperial building with a view out onto the Dnipro River, the Kherson Fine Arts Museum once hosted one of the richest collections in all of Ukraine.

As with the rest of Kherson, which had its electricity infrastructure destroyed by withdrawing Russian forces in early November, the halls of the museum are now cold and dark.

Far more tragically, the Kherson Fine Arts Museum has been emptied of all its works by Russian officials. Of the over 14,000 works in its collection, barely anything remains. Russia's withdrawal from Kherson was a well-planned operation, a key component of which was the looting of anything deemed to be of financial or cultural value. The Russian campaign of theft was comprehensive and wide ranging, covering everything from hospital equipment and public monuments to an unfortunate raccoon living in Kherson Zoo.

Stolen equipment and monuments can be replaced, but priceless artworks cannot. All that remains now of the once flourishing museum is the building itself, and inside it, the two last staff members who refused to collaborate with Russia.

Speaking to *The Kyiv Independent* on 16 November in her personal office at the museum, director Alina Dotsenko, 72, steered clear of her old work desk, shuffling closer to the window where the last dim light of the day was making its way in.

'I still can't bring myself to sit where they sat,' she said, referring to her Russian-installed replacement, a local singer called Natalia Desiatova, who oversaw the looting of the museum's collection.

Joy upon the liberation of Kherson comes with a bitter aftertaste for Dotsenko, who had initially fled to Ukrainian-controlled territory in early May, after she had refused to host a Victory Day event held by occupation authorities in the museum.

Dotsenko returned to Kherson in a Security Service convoy on 12 November, a day after Ukrainian troops entered the city, only to arrive at work for all her fears about the museum to be confirmed.

'Are you trying to bring me to tears again?' she said when asked to recall the day. 'I haven't really lived these last few months, I have only worried and worried.'

From intricate 17th century Orthodox icons to works by a multitude of Ukrainian, Russian, and other European masters including Ivan Aivazovsky, Vasily Polenov, Auguste von Bayer and Peter Lely, the museum's collection was Dotsenko's pride and joy. 'We didn't expand our collection for the sake of money or status,' she said, 'but because of what it meant to the city.'

The museum's collection was already in storage when Russia's full-scale invasion was launched on 24 February, as the building was undergoing major restoration works. Calls by Dotsenko to evacuate the collection fell upon deaf ears as Kherson fell to Russian forces in a matter of days ...

Enemies inside

In almost any town or city occupied by Russia in Ukraine, locals are found who, motivated by money, pro-Russian sentiments, or bitterness towards colleagues, are willing to cooperate with the occupying authorities. In the case of the Kherson Fine Arts Museum, the presence of one or two collaborants was pivotal in the stealing of the museum's collection and data.

In the early weeks of the occupation of Kherson, Dotsenko quickly grew concerned that some of the museum staff could soon betray the collection to

Russia. In some cases, Dotsenko sent them on paid leave simply so that they wouldn't be present on the museum grounds.

'I had never trusted them,' she said. 'I grew up a daughter of a border guard, so I had my eyes on them all the time.' One collection worker, Maryna Zhylina, was even fired last year by Dotsenko, who was increasingly concerned by her openly pro-Russian position. 'I had imagined she would leave to Russia, she had a daughter in Moscow,' Dotsenko said. 'She was a good worker but pro-Russian from head to toe.'

With the core of the staff remaining loyal, it took several months before Russian occupation authorities got around to taking over the museum, unlike the neighboring Regional Museum, where director Tetiana Bratchenko immediately chose to collaborate.

'Just see how much we held out!' Dotsenko said with pride. 'They were in the other museum by the beginning of March, but here, not until July!'

When that day came on 19 July, Dotsenko had long left Kherson, and the museum was guarded by accounting and archive worker Hanna Skrypka, 56, a loyal confidant of Dotsenko's. According to Skrypka, armed Russian men came to the museum's doors and demanded the keys from her, 'to open the space and prepare it for the arrival of the new director'. Requests by Skrypka to show some authorizing documents were denied.

After half an hour of stalling the soldiers, the new 'director', Desiatova, arrived. Desiatova was joined by former colleague Anna Koltsova, who had confirmed to the Russians that the collection had not been moved as claimed by Dotsenko, and who had secretly saved copies of the museum's electronic records on her personal computer before the invasion.

'As I understand it, this individual was towards the end of her life and was simply hoping for a taller pedestal to stand on than what she was given by Ukraine,' said Skrypka. 'Traitors, plain and simple.'

Swift and systematic

It was not until the end of October, when the Russian occupation of Kherson was understood to be doomed, that the removal of the museum's entire collection began. 'They were certain that they were here forever,' Dotsenko said, 'but as soon as our soldiers started to come closer, they started to steal everything.'

Starting on 31 October, trucks began to line up outside the museum, accompanied by a mix of Russian soldiers, representatives of the Russian Ministry of Culture and Federal Security Service (FSB) officers in civilian clothes. 'Everything that was in a visible location attracted their eye right away,' said Skrypka. 'Since the so-called "colleagues" of ours who knew where the most valuable artworks were being held, these pieces were taken first according to their instructions.'

Early in the occupation, Dotsenko and Skrypka had tried to hide some of the most valuable works, but the presence of pro-Russian colleagues, Koltsova and Zhylina, rendered these efforts pointless.

'I was trying first to show them some of the Russian artists that weren't as valuable to us personally, in the hope that that would satisfy them,' said Skrypka. 'But the two of them were always there over my shoulder, saying [to the FSB officers] "well have a look at that shelf, why don't you pull out that one ..."'

Two trucks were filled each day with artwork, frames often crudely stacked up against each other with zero care given to proper packaging and temperature controls.

According to Skrypka, the Russians didn't speak much to her, only justifying their theft on the grounds of 'saving' it from the Ukrainian advance, the same message used by local proxy authorities. 'This collection that has been here for many decades, and you are "saving" it?' pondered Skrypka. 'From whom? From the nation who is coming to liberate its own city?'

By the time Skrypka left the museum on 4 November, the removal of over 10,000 works had been accounted for, with more trucks still arriving. 'I didn't say goodbye to them,' said Skrypka of her former colleagues. 'They had planned a big feast to celebrate the completion of the emptying of the museum, and how could I sit and eat with my enemies?'

Dreams of justice

Though shelling of the city has intensified in the two weeks since liberation, residents on the streets of Kherson are largely optimistic that the rest of Ukraine's occupied territories will be successfully liberated. Territory can be won back, but it is hard to look with the same optimism at the chances of returning the priceless artworks of the Fine Arts Museum in Kherson. A museum without its collection and archive is a museum without an identity, and the road ahead is uncertain.

While many of its works have been identified in the pictures from occupied Simferopol, it is not known whether the huge collection has been kept together in its entirety. Given the scale of the theft and lack of care shown to the works, it is not unlikely that some pieces disappeared into private hands on the way.

The museum may be empty, but Skrypka is not short of work. Together with Dotsenko, she must now create a comprehensive digital account of all the looted pieces. 'We need to record everything that was taken, complete with photos,' she said, 'so that if anything happens to show up on a border or at an auction, it can be identified.'

Beyond that, Ukraine's only hope to return the stolen art, which is officially property of the Ukrainian state, is through international efforts now led by the Ministry of Culture. 'When the time eventually comes for peace negotiations, this must be one of the first terms put forward: the return of all artefacts from looted museums,' Skrypka said. 'Of course, they won't agree with it, but we need to be loud about it anyway while other channels are pursued.'

For the foreseeable future though, the Kherson Fine Arts Museum as it once was has ceased to exist.

'I don't have any words to describe their relationship to history, to culture, to human life,' said Skrypka. 'What can you teach children about culture, about respecting other cultures if you not only can't protect your own culture, but simply steal from others and call it your own?'

27 November 2022

Pregnant medic spent 5 months in Russian captivity: 'I feared they would take my child away'

Daria Shulzhenko

Days before giving birth to her first child, Ukrainian military medic Mariana Mamonova was made to board a plane in the Russian city of Taganrog. She was blindfolded and her hands were bound with rope.

'Do you know where they're taking us?' she heard a man sitting next to her ask.

There were dozens of Ukrainian prisoners of war also aboard the plane, although none of them seemed to know their destination.

Many feared they would be transferred to prisons in remote parts of Russia, but their questions were soon answered by a Russian officer.

'Home,' Mamonova responded. 'We're going home.'

She had waited five long months for that very moment.

A medical service captain with the 36th Separate Marine Brigade, Mamonova, 31, was captured alongside fellow Ukrainian soldiers by Russian troops during a combat mission in Mariupol in early April – nearly three weeks after she learned about her pregnancy.

Russian troops locked Mamonova in a prison camp in Olenivka, Donetsk Oblast, where she said she witnessed what is believed to have been a Russian attack that killed over 50 Ukrainian POWs in late July.

Mamonova shared a small, decrepit prison cell with 40 other women and was forced to sleep on the cold floor under one of the bunk beds with nothing but a thin blanket. She said Russian soldiers interrogated her multiple times, threatening to take her baby from her.

She froze and starved in captivity, but she did not lose hope. 'I promised my baby that I wouldn't cry – and I didn't cry until the end,' Mamonova said.

She kept her promise. Tears rolled down Mamonova's face in late September when she arrived in Chernihiv Oblast, a region in Ukraine bordering Russia and Belarus. She had undertaken a 20-hour-long journey from occupied Donetsk to Russia, then to Belarus and finally Chernihiv Oblast.

She was among the 215 Ukrainian defenders released from Russian captivity during a major prisoner exchange on 21 September.

Four days after she returned to Ukraine, Mamonova gave birth to a healthy baby girl named Anna. President Volodymyr Zelensky congratulated her and her newborn in a video address. 'This is more proof that life always triumphs over any evil,' Zelensky said. 'And evil under the Russian flag is no exception to this rule.'

New life amid war

Mamonova and her husband, Lviv-based lawyer Vasyl Mamonov, had planned to have a baby for a while.

The couple met in Mariupol, Mamonov's hometown, in 2020 and got married the following year. While they got accustomed to a long-distance relationship, Mamonova said she had wanted to transfer from Ukraine's east to Lviv to be closer to her husband.

But Russia interrupted her plans.

By 24 February, Mamonova's battalion had already taken up battle position in the village of Shyrokyne, Donetsk Oblast, facing heavy attacks from the Russian army. 'There was nowhere to hide,' she recalled. 'We were covering each other with body armor and helmets and huddled together when the ground shook.'

Throughout those brutal strikes, Mamonova saved lives as she evacuated wounded soldiers from the battlefield.

Her battalion moved to Mariupol, Donetsk Oblast, in early March, stationing at one of the city's giant metallurgical enterprises, the Illich Steel and Iron Works plant. Like the Azovstal steel plant, which had been Ukraine's last stronghold in Mariupol, civilians and soldiers took shelter in the 'bunkers' of the Illich plant.

'It was bombarded more intensively every day, usually from aviation,' Mamonova said. She said the hardest part was losing soldiers that she knew. She recalled one moment when a young soldier who was dying asked her not to tell his mother that he was injured but to reassure her that he was doing well. 'His mother called when his dead body lay in my arms,' Mamonova said. 'She called and called, but we couldn't pick up.'

In Mariupol, surrounded by death, pain, and destruction, Mamonova realized that a new life was growing inside of her – but instead of happiness, she felt fear. 'I knew I had nowhere to go, nowhere to run, no one to ask for help,' she said.

Mamonova did not tell her husband about the pregnancy, as she feared that losing both his wife and child would be 'beyond difficult'.

It was not death that Mamonova feared the most, but Russian captivity.

While working in the military, she had heard many stories of Russian soldiers torturing, beating, and raping women taken prisoner. So when the full-scale war started, she asked a fellow medic to kill her if Russian soldiers captured them.

'No mercy'

One late night in early April, Mamonova and some Ukrainian soldiers were driving on the outskirts of Mariupol when a dozen Russian soldiers stopped their car. 'Hello, comrades. From now on, you are prisoners of war of the Russian Federation,' one of the soldiers said.

Mamonova's heart hammered in her chest as Russian troops started to remove her helmet and armored vest, pointing their guns at them. 'If you decide to run, you will be shot dead immediately,' one Russian soldier said. 'In captivity, you have at least some chance of survival. If you die here, your relatives won't find your body.'

'You realize your life could end in a split second,' Mamonova said. 'The soldiers standing next to you won't help you. You won't help them. That's it, that's the end ...'

For the next three days, the Russian troops locked them in a former grain depot outside Mariupol before transferring them to a prison located around three kilometers east of Olenivka. Since the area fell under Russian occupation in 2014, it has also been used as an internment camp.

Mamonova recalled the squalid conditions of the prison, which she said had 'barbed wire, three high fences so that you don't run away, and mad dogs'. 'Its old cells were not heated. We had to sleep on a cold concrete floor,' Mamonova added. It was in those horrific conditions that she felt her baby kicking for the first time.

Mamonova spent the first two months in a cell with 40 other women – Ukrainian POWs from the National Guard, State Border Service, the Azov regiment, and civilians. She said the cell was meant to fit six people, so there were three women to a single bed, and others were forced to sleep on small benches, a table, or near the toilet.

Russian soldiers only let them take a shower three weeks after they arrived. A month after she was captured, Mamonova was taken outside for the first time 'in a cage, from which you can only see the sky' for 10 minutes.

She said she was starving, having only been given the same tasteless porridge and soup each day. 'It was like a Nazi concentration camp,' she said. 'People who are convicted of certain crimes know when they will get out, but prisoners of war don't.'

Soon, the interrogations started.

Mamonova said she was asked questions wrought by Russian propaganda, such as why Ukraine 'attacked' Donbas in 2014 and why Ukraine does not want to rejoin the Soviet Union. Russian soldiers also threatened to transfer her to a prison in Russia.

They also threatened to take her unborn child to a Russian orphanage, where Mamonova would never find her.

While she was not physically tortured, she heard that Ukrainian soldiers were severely beaten. Russian guards also told her that they were 'kind' as compared to those guarding the pre-trial detention centers in occupied Donetsk. The guards said that in occupied Donetsk, Ukrainian women are guarded by Russian women who 'know no mercy'.

Witnessing the Olenivka explosion

The horrors she endured during Russian captivity escalated on 28 July when Mamonova heard two loud explosions nearby. 'It happened nearly 500 meters from where I was kept,' she said.

The soldiers guarding the women left for the site immediately. 'Nothing was left of your boys there,' they told the POWs when they returned.

Russian proxies occupying the area immediately accused Ukraine of attacking its own soldiers in captivity, claiming US-provided high-precision HIMARS had hit the site. Ukraine denied the allegations. According to Ukraine's Prosecutor General's Office, Russia likely used a thermobaric munition at the Olenivka prison, killing over 50 prisoners of war.

Mamonova said the Russian guards had initially agreed that it was a Ukrainian attack but soon said it was 'something from inside'.

Since the day of the explosion, she feared it could happen to her as well.

In spite of her hardships, Mamonova felt that her baby was growing strong and healthy. Because her due date was approaching, she was transferred to a hospital in occupied Donetsk in August.

While she was treated well at the hospital and was given enough food and medicine, she was petrified at the thought of giving birth in captivity. 'I feared they would take my child to some orphanage and transfer me elsewhere,' she said. 'And then, if they take me for a [prisoner] exchange, no one will return my baby to me.'

She hoped she would be released during a rumored prisoner exchange on 24 August, but she was not. She again grew hopeful in late September when a Russian officer asked Mamonova's doctor if she could be transported in her condition.

As she was taken from Donetsk to Taganrog to board a plane, Mamonova kept telling the Russian officer that she would give birth on the spot if he didn't tell her where they were going. 'He told me: "Don't worry, Mariana, you're going home."'

Days after Mamonova was finally exchanged, the happiness she felt at her release was overcome by a greater one: the birth of her baby girl Anna.

Mamonova said that one day, she will tell her daughter the story about their captivity. But for now, she only wants her to grow up happy 'in a peaceful country'.

After everything Mamonova has been through, she said she would return to service in her battalion. 'Even in Olenivka, I did not regret anything,' she says. 'Because we saved a lot of lives, a lot of soldiers. So it was all worth it.'

30 November 2022

International Legion soldiers allege light weapons misappropriation, abuse by commanders

Anna Myroniuk and Alexander Khrebet

Editor's Note: This follow-up article (see p.255), partly produced in collaboration with the Superwizjer program airing on the Polish TVN channel, sheds light on previously unknown alleged misconduct by the Legion's leadership, reveals that it's of a far-reaching scale and involves both wings of the Legion, subordinated to different agencies. Soldiers who sounded the alarm about problems within the Legion claim to have received threats, gotten denounced, or been kicked out. For their safety, we are protecting their identities. Upon soldiers' request and considering security risks, we no longer identify them by country.

To avoid putting them in additional danger, the commanders in the story are identified by their full name only if they have public profiles or their affiliation with the International Legion has been publicly revealed before.

Top findings

- Multiple legionnaires allege light weapons, including Western-provided arms, go missing. Legionnaires suspect specific commanders of misappropriation.
- Soldiers claim certain commanders threaten them with guns, bully them, and harass them, including sexually.
- Soldiers accuse particular commanders of stealing their personal equipment.
- For flagging the leadership's wrongdoings as well as for being sick, soldiers allegedly get kicked out of the Legion under made-up pretexts like being spies or deserters.

In late spring, a soldier who had traveled across the ocean to join the International Legion following President Volodymyr Zelensky's call to foreign soldiers to join Ukraine's fight against Russia was preparing for deployment to a southern city, then close to the front line, when he heard worrying news coming from the front line.

A fellow fighter told him that his team had suffered casualties in the same area because they lacked a vital weapon component, a Command Launch Unit, or CLU, for an American-made portable Javelin anti-tank missile system.

They had to borrow one from another unit. When they tried to set it in motion, it failed to work. 'They couldn't blow the [Russian] tank off and the tank found them and started shooting at them. It's f*cking frightening,' the now-former legionnaire told *The Kyiv Independent*.

As he was getting ready to head to the same southern city himself, his comrade's experience made him anxious. This story especially worried him since he had just seen a bunch of fully operational computer parts for Javelins at the Legion's base in Kyiv.

Later he realized that it wasn't a one-time incident but a systemic problem where weapons would be missing from where the International Legion's soldiers expected to find them.

Over a dozen other foreign fighters in conversation with *The Kyiv Independent* accused their commanders of stealing small arms and light weapons that they said went missing from the Legion's armory rooms. Some soldiers witnessed arms being loaded into what they described as civilian SUVs to then vanish. It raised suspicions as the drivers often kept the lights off and weren't wearing military clothes, legionnaires said.

This was one of the reasons that led many legionnaires to believe that light weapons were being misappropriated.

'I couldn't help but think that maybe if these weapons were in better hands that would have helped ... or be used to win this war,' one soldier said.

The Kyiv Independent spoke to over 30 sources, including former and current legionnaires, volunteers helping the Legion, and officials. The allegations in this story are based on interviews, written testimonies, official reports, medical records, photos, videos, and audio files.

Pieced together, this evidence alleges that the leadership of both wings of the International Legion, military intelligence-run and army-run, could be implicated in various sorts of misconduct, including harassment and physical threats, illegal expulsion of nonconformists, as well as theft of soldiers' personal equipment and the misappropriation of light weapons.

'The word is out'
Allegations of arms misappropriation are a contentious issue in Ukraine, which depends on Western military aid to successfully fight back Russia's brutal invasion. The issue has appeared in statements opposing weapons

supplies to Ukraine, including in the West, likely in an attempt to tarnish Ukraine's image and undermine arms supplies.

Russian propaganda media outlets spread stories about the alleged theft and trafficking of all sorts of Western arms en masse in Ukraine to discredit both the Ukrainian government and the country's Western allies.

The Kyiv Independent found no evidence backing such claims. The publication, however, collected a body of testimonies showing that specific instances of light weapons and small arms disappearance are linked to the alleged mismanagement by specific commanders in the International Legion.

Investigators who claimed to be affiliated with the UK government are looking into the Western-provided arms allegedly going missing in the Legion, according to *The Kyiv Independent*'s sources.

'The word is out,' said a legionnaire who claims he was helping an unofficial British inquiry into arms going missing in the Legion.

The Embassy neither confirmed nor denied looking into arms disappearances in the Legion, but told *The Kyiv Independent* they 'are conducting a rigorous assessment of the risks associated with providing weapons for the defense of Ukraine'.

The legionnaires who spoke to *The Kyiv Independent* don't know where the light weapons they suggest were stolen might have ended up. They have no evidence they were smuggled out of the country.

Reports on weapons going missing, however, shouldn't be the reason for Western countries to halt military aid to Ukraine, believes Ian Bond, retired British diplomat and the director of foreign policy at the Centre for European Reform.

'All the evidence is that major donated weapons systems are being well looked after and used to good effect against Russian aggression, so there is no reason for the West to suspend deliveries,' Bond told *The Kyiv Independent*.

'Almost every army suffers some level of theft of weapons and ammunition ... Given the fact that Ukraine is fighting a war for national survival, in which Western weapons are playing a vital role, I would be very surprised if many people in the Ukrainian Armed Forces were stealing or illicitly selling the weapons on which their lives depend,' he went on.

The Ukrainian government has shown signs of taking the reports about missing weapons seriously. In July, lawmakers voted to create a committee to oversee Western-donated weapons distribution. The initiative came from Zelensky's right-hand man and head of administration Andriy Yermak.

Lawmaker Oleksandra Ustinova, the head of the committee, told *The Kyiv Independent* that Ukraine's allies are satisfied with how Ukraine is using Western-donated weapons. 'No one suspects us [Ukraine] of stealing and selling weapons,' she said. 'The only questions that are raised are: "Why do you give to Ukraine's armed forces more than to the National Guard?" Technical questions.'

The US Embassy said that they 'have been given considerable access and have seen firsthand' how Ukraine secures Western-provided weapons. However, their 'ability to execute normal enhanced end-use monitoring procedures remains impacted by security conditions'.

Ustinova, however, admitted that tracking small arms like rifles is 'almost impossible'.

A top-ranking official at Ukraine's State Security Service (SBU) agrees. He is now investigating the disappearance of light weapons inside the International Legion, he told *The Kyiv Independent*'s partner in this investigation, Poland's TVN.

'I was approached by the guys who serve in the International Legion. They shared with me the facts about weapons going missing,' said the SBU official in charge of the case. He spoke on condition of anonymity as he is not authorized to comment on the matter.

'From that point on, the subject has caught the attention of our department and we requested information about this subject,' he said of Piotr Kapuscinski, one of the Legion's leaders, who also goes by the name Sasha Kuchynsky.

In an earlier investigation, *The Kyiv Independent* exposed Kapuscinski to be a former Polish gangster who is allegedly involved in theft, looting, and the harassment of soldiers. Kapuscinski refused to speak to *The Kyiv Independent* about the allegations and asked not to call him again.

As the SBU officer learned, his colleagues from another department had already been looking into Kapuscinski before he joined the Legion in around March. The SBU's new investigation into him, launched in August concerns his alleged involvement in arms and humanitarian aid theft. 'It is unclear yet what he does with it, but certain facts indicate that he might be selling it,' the intelligence officer said.

Yet regular legionnaires do not feel like the authorities are taking seriously the Legion's leadership misconduct, including light weapons misappropriation.

No reaction by the Defense Ministry's Directorate for Intelligence, also known under its Ukrainian acronym GUR, and the President's Office followed the August investigation by *The Kyiv Independent* that focused on the military intelligence-run part of the Legion and exposed its commanders, including Kapuscinski's misconduct in various cases.

This time, however, military intelligence seems to be paying attention to the allegations. 'An official internal investigation is ongoing regarding some of the issues raised in your request,' Mykola Krasniy, press secretary of the military intelligence, told *The Kyiv Independent* on 18 November.

According to Krasniy, the investigation was launched on 14 November following *The Kyiv Independent*'s request for comment for this article. He was unable to explain why there was no reaction to the allegations in the August story.

Arms go missing

In conversations with *The Kyiv Independent*, 12 legionnaires accused their commanders of light weapons, small arms and military equipment misappropriation. They provided photographs, reports, and screenshots of the messages they claim to prove these items had disappeared. More legionnaires made similar accusations in written testimonies they filed to their commanders, which have been obtained by *The Kyiv Independent*.

One such episode took place in May. Back then, the leadership of the Legion's 1st battalion, which is under the Ground Forces, changed. Bohdan *(Editor's Note: Bohdan is a military commander who doesn't maintain a public profile. He's not identified by his full name to avoid putting him in additional danger)*, then-commander of the battalion, was out. His successors decided to do an inventory of the battalion's armory room in a heavily attacked northeastern city. It found serious inconsistencies, according to the legionnaires.

'We were told to do it secretly, without anybody noticing because they didn't know who was involved in moving the weapons. So me and a team of guys went down into the bunker ... Did it quickly, got out there, and then passed it to command,' a soldier who was among those conducting the inventory told *The Kyiv Independent*.

The new leadership, he said, 'started panicking' as there were massive discrepancies between what they should have had and what they in fact had.

Citing his commanders, the soldier participating in the inventory said that among the weapons that allegedly went missing were 54 US-made M4 carbines, several anti-tank weapons like RPGs and NLAWs, grenades, a couple of pistols, and a few thousand rounds of ammunition.

'I was not informed about it. I cannot tell anything to you about it as it is an internal matter of Ukraine's armed forces,' Chief of Staff of the 1st Battalion, Anatoliy, told *The Kyiv Independent*, redirecting our journalists to the army press center. He hung up and stopped replying before the journalists had a chance to ask for his last name.

The Kyiv Independent asked the Ground Forces of Ukraine's military to comment on the allegations of missing weapons and misconduct of the Legion's commanders. The Ground Forces' press service refused to comment, saying that 'the requested information falls within the scope of what can contribute to the enemy's awareness of the actions of Ukraine's Armed Forces'.

In a comment to *The Kyiv Independent*, Bohdan denied any wrongdoing and offered his explanation of what happened to the weapons.

'The approximate number of M4s you ask about was moved elsewhere and not all legionnaires know this,' Bohdan said, adding that his transfer of power upon resignation was conducted in accordance with normal procedures and no concerns were raised. 'Weapons were transported to one of the training grounds for the formation of a new unit of legionnaires with the permission of the leadership.'

The Kyiv Independent was unable to verify Bohdan's account.

'When I was commander, a small number of weapons were lost or destroyed during hostilities. An official investigation was immediately ordered, in accordance with the current legislation,' he added.

Another legionnaire responsible for administrative work said that a then-deputy commander of the 1st battalion under the Ground Forces had told him about nearly 50 M4 carbines disappearing. The legionnaire believes it was the same batch that went missing in the northeastern city in question.

'He told me that rifles have a habit of going missing in [names the city],' the legionnaire recalled the commander saying in late June.

He believes the weapons going missing were US-donated. According to the soldier, in April the 1st battalion of the Legion received a batch of 'brand spanking new' M4 carbines that had stamps on them saying 'property of the US government'. The price of M4 carbines in the US can start at $600 and go into thousands, depending on the variant.

Several soldiers link the 54 M4 carbines' alleged disappearance in the northeastern city to Chief Sergeant Nikolay (Mykola) Bakaliuk, who was de facto in charge of the armory room at the time, according to the legionnaires.

'Not even that I am not involved, but there was no sale, theft, or anything else,' Bakaliuk told *The Kyiv Independent*. 'None of the legionnaires is a prosecutor. Only the prosecutor's office can bring charges, and only a court can either confirm or reject them. I will consider everything else as slander.'

'As far as I know, the relevant authorities are already looking into Bakaliuk,' Bohdan said of his former subordinate. 'This does not concern me. Time will tell who stole, and who fought the war.'

Allegations against Bakaliuk

Between September and October, over a dozen soldiers filed formal complaints against Bakaliuk to their leadership, calling for his removal. In these reports, they accuse him of corruption, theft of equipment, and bullying. 'He would repeatedly yell and degrade fellow legionnaires and other Ukrainian service members for what appeared as little or no reason,' one testimony reads.

Broader theft allegations

In April, the soldiers of the intelligence-run wing of the Legion were deployed to a southern city then close to the front line. A big assault operation was coming and they were tasked to assist Ukrainian forces.

They went to the armory room to grab the weapons and ammunition they brought from Kyiv only to discover that the armory was almost empty. 'I saw nothing so I walked out. I was a little in shock,' one soldier said.

According to him, there were eight military sub-units of the Legion at the time in the southern city in question. Every sub-unit brought multiple weapons and placed them in the armory. But in the armory that day, the soldier only saw a handful of small arms left.

The soldiers remembered that, upon arrival in that city, they were ordered to stay in the barracks for about five days before being allowed to go out. 'That's when we assume that the ammunition started to go missing,' he said. He added that his commander told him that Kapuscinski, one of the leaders of the military intelligence-subordinated wing of the Legion, was in charge of the armory room there.

He decided to quit, along with several other soldiers. 'After all the lies and the supplies going missing when we needed them, I had had enough,' he said. 'My spirit was broken. I felt we were just being sent to die with little to no supplies, food, ammunition, you name it, we didn't have it.'

Weapons disappearing in the southern city allegedly raised some concerns outside of the Legion.

One soldier claims that around June or July, a person affiliated with the UK government in Ukraine contacted him asking to check whether the latest shipment of NATO small arms reached the southern city. He claimed to be conducting an unofficial investigation. The investigator specifically mentioned that Piotr (Sasha) Kapuscinski was in charge of the distribution of the supplies from this shipment. 'Kapuscinski was supposedly the one responsible for the warehouses and disseminating the NATO weapons throughout the units in the area. Somehow, some warehouses became emptied,' one soldier said.

Allegations against Kapuscinski's supposed misappropriation of weapons fall under two categories: weapons allegedly going missing from armoires, and weapons taken away directly from the legionnaires without explanation.

When in Kyiv, Kapuscinski was in charge of the dorms and oversaw the armory room, from where the weapons would go missing, too, multiple soldiers said. 'There were two times when NLAWs would come in at night and get unloaded, and they wouldn't be there in the armory the next morning, which is the only place they would be. That was very suspicious,' said a former legionnaire who while giving an interview to *The Kyiv Independent* was participating in Ukraine's counteroffensive in Kharkiv Oblast in September. He got in touch via Starlink. Shelling was heard in the background as he spoke.

There is no chance, he believes, that these weapons were given to some other unit. He believes that they were the only unit in the area at the time and therefore, the only ones who could have used the NLAWs. He said he did not report missing NLAWs to the commanders because he was afraid of Kapuscinski.

Two fighters independently said bayonets or knives for CZ and SCAR-L rifles disappeared from the armory room in Kyiv under Kapuscinski around

April. 'I was thinking that a couple of days ago I saw with my own eyes hundreds of bayonets and now there are none of them in the armory room,' one soldier said of 200–300 bayonets for CZ rifles going missing. He said that it was a popular belief in the Legion that Kapuscinski was taking and selling the weapons.

According to multiple legionnaires, Kapuscinski often ordered them to suddenly hand him their weapons and ammunition and would take them away for good. They obeyed out of fear.

One of the soldiers complained that Kapuscinski had ordered his team of 20–30 people to put all their weapons and equipment in 'garbage piles'. Kapuscinski and his people then allegedly went through the soldiers' stuff, cherry-picked the best, including Legion-issued Glock pistols, and took it away.

In early June, at least a couple of hundred Glock pistols would also vanish from the armory room, said two other legionnaires.

In conversations with *The Kyiv Independent*, seven legionnaires accused Kapuscinski of taking away their personal equipment, including drones, flashlights, and protective gear they bought for themselves. 'He was like a security control that checks your bags and takes stuff,' one legionnaire said of Kapuscinski.

Kapuscinski's room in the Legion's headquarters, legionnaires said, gave them ideas about what his actual dealings might be. 'His room was full of alcohol and stolen stuff. People used to see it when he opened the door and I also saw it,' one fighter said.

'This guy was taking ammunition, rifles, sidearms, firearms, helmets, gear whatever he liked, I guess. He took it to his own personal quarters. And I saw this myself from the second-story window,' another soldier said. This soldier emphasized that there were designated areas where supplies would be kept in storage, and Kapuscinski's room wasn't on that list.

Those who were close to Kapuscinski allegedly received gifts from him, like alcohol, cigarettes, and snacks, from him, according to the soldiers. Soldiers also accused him of offering to trade their equipment for something from the armory room. 'He was just, you know, collecting the best of the best and trading the stuff,' said a legionnaire, who refused Kapuscinski's alleged offer to trade his pistol holster for something from the armory.

In its previous story, *The Kyiv Independent* revealed that Kapuscinski had offered legionnaires to buy equipment from him, such as military thermal imagers, as well as took away half of the equipment they received from volunteers and friends, which they called 'Sasha tax'.

Soldiers claim that Kapuscinski used to order them to carry boxed weapons from the armory to what they described as civilian vehicles. It raised suspicions among some legionnaires as the drivers would often keep the lights off and wear civilian clothes. 'I never saw any papers being signed,' one soldier said.

One of those who participated in it recalled that he carried boxed US-made CZ rifles under Kapuscinski's directions. He also saw NLAW containers and Javelin tubes in the back of the van.

Legionnaires say that amid war, it's easy to move small arms around without anybody noticing. The SBU officer investigating weapons going missing in the military intelligence-run wing of the Legion agrees: 'The country is at war. No one will be surprised if you transport protective gear or weapons.'

'When weapons arrive at a unit, it is official. What happens then is very complicated to establish as it is quite easy to write them off [the weapons] as lost, broken, or destroyed during combat,' he went on.

'It only becomes noticeable when stuff is not available and not getting to the people,' one soldier said. That's also how legionnaires who spoke to *The Kyiv Independent* started noticing it.

A person who used to be responsible for logistics in the Legion claims that often supplies he had delivered did not reach the soldiers on the battlefield. 'You have the guys on the front line, the foreigners themselves, requesting optics or food or X, Y, and Z, whatever ... and then you bring those things to the warehouse,' he said.

A couple of weeks later, the soldiers would request the very same things he had just brought, saying they never received them.

He believes that commanders, who 'inspected every piece of equipment you were bringing', might be behind it.

'When you have some corruption in a unit, making sure that supplies get to the people who need them becomes pretty difficult,' the former logistics officer said.

Untouchables

Since April, the legionnaires had unsuccessfully complained about their leadership misconduct to the parliament and the President's Office. According to them, the parliament did nothing, but the President's Office passed their testimonies to the Luhansk Specialized Military and Defense Prosecutor's Office of the Joint Forces.

In late June, its prosecutors opened a case into Kapuscinski's alleged abuse of power in the Legion. The probe is conducted by the State Bureau of Investigations. It is ongoing and officially has no suspects yet. If found guilty, Kapuscinski faces up to 12 years in prison.

In August, the SBU also opened a probe into Kapuscinski's alleged involvement in arms and humanitarian aid theft, according to *The Kyiv Independent*'s partner TVN's source in the SBU.

Meanwhile, Kapuscinski is wanted in Poland for fraud. Following *The Kyiv Independent*'s August investigation into him, the Polish prosecutors once again requested from their Ukrainian colleagues help in bringing Kapuscinski to justice. '[Kapuscinski] is suspected of committing multiple crimes in Poland, for some of which he was convicted, but did not serve his sentence due to fleeing to the territory of Ukraine,' reads a letter provided to *The Kyiv Independent* by Ukraine's State Bureau of Investigations.

In Ukraine, Kapuscinski was charged with aggravated robbery in 2016 and of illegal arms possession in 2021. After the full-scale Russian war broke out in February, Kapuscinski joined the military, at which point the courts suspended his case.

Despite the accusations and active investigations against him both in Ukraine and Poland, Kapuscinski maintains his high-level position in the Legion, according to *The Kyiv Independent*'s law enforcement and military sources.

'He was untouchable,' a soldier who was among the first to join the Legion, but is no longer there, said of Kapuscinski. 'No matter how many reports I brought [to Kapuscinski's commandment].'

'He was literally behaving like a mafia boss,' another former soldier said of Kapuscinski.

Legionnaires said that backing of the military intelligence (GUR) Major Taras Vashuk helped Kapuscinski get away with stealing and abusing soldiers ... Vashuk did not respond to *The Kyiv Independent*'s request for comment.

For his part, Vashuk has also survived complaints from legionnaires ...

Power abuse

Many legionnaires accused their commanders of harassment, physical threats, and incompetence.

Legionnaires claim that Bohdan planned missions poorly and neglected most of his duties while in charge of the 1st Battalion. Many soldiers flagged Bohdan's drastic mood swings which, they believe, put their lives at additional risk. 'People are telling their families to blame [Bohdan], not the enemy, in case they die,' one legionnaire's testimony reads.

'Screaming at soldiers, telling some of them he doesn't need them. Ukraine doesn't need them,' another soldier told *The Kyiv Independent*. 'He would go from calm and collected to completely flying off the handle.'

Bohdan also allegedly threatened to physically harm his soldiers on a few occasions.

One episode was allegedly caught on tape. In a video secretly recorded by a legionnaire that was leaked to *The Kyiv Independent*, a serviceman threatens to harm a subordinate. While the person isn't clearly seen in the video, legionnaires say that they recognize Bohdan's voice. 'One more word, one more movement. You will be f*cking destroyed,' Bohdan allegedly says to the soldier in English with a heavy accent ... Everybody will say that you just fell down. Suddenly. And you will have a good chance to go to Ukrainian prison. I will call my criminal friends and tell them: "Guys, expect him." I will send them your [ID] and you will have a good time in a Ukrainian prison.'

Bohdan and the legionnaires describe the reason for the altercation differently. The legionnaires say that he was scolding the soldier for refusing to go on a mission while being ill. Bohdan said the issue was that two legionnaires looted locals' houses.

'I mentioned the prison because one of them had something to do with the criminal world. Yes, I was angry because some fight and die, while others steal things from poor people,' Bohdan said, adding that he had passed the information to the local Military Police. Both local Military Police and the Military Prosecution told *The Kyiv Independent* they have no information on such events.

Bohdan also denied that he meant to threaten soldiers with his prison connections: 'I do not have prisoner friends.' Several of his subordinates, however, said that he often bragged about such connections.

In the other wing of the Legion, Kapuscinski often abused his power, too, according to the soldiers. 'He has this style, he would be yelling at people,' one soldier told *The Kyiv Independent*.

He allegedly sexually harassed women, mirroring his past behavior noted in court records in Poland and Ukraine. 'A couple of times he forced me to sit on his lap ... He just pulled me,' a former female legionnaire said. On another occasion, she said, Kapuscinski tried to force her to kiss him, which she refused. One of her comrades backed up her account.

'I personally witnessed Sasha [Kapuscinski] catcalling women in Kyiv in a way that I found astonishing,' another soldier recalled ...

Kicking soldiers out

Many of the legionnaires didn't tolerate their commanders' behavior. Some tried to stand up for themselves. With Kapuscinski, it often resulted in backlash.

'When somebody tries to confront him, he just starts using his own connections and saying stuff like that: "Oh, yeah, you're gonna be kicked out. And now you're not gonna go through Poland safely",' one soldier said. Since the war brought all flights out of Ukraine to a halt, the most common way to travel to and from Ukraine is through Poland.

Often Kapuscinski's threats led to action: he expelled soldiers from the Legion for asking too many questions or confronting him about stealing, according to legionnaires.

Both Kapuscinski and Bohdan kicked out such soldiers under what soldiers claim to be made-up pretexts: Kapuscinski accused soldiers of deserting while

Bohdan would accuse them of spying. 'He was just kicking soldiers out like trash or threatening them that if they cause problems, they are going to have problems with the authorities,' said one soldier who Kapuscinski expelled.

At times it got physical.

Once Kapuscinski, together with an unidentified accomplice, forced a soldier out of the Legion when he was in the hospital undergoing treatment after breaking his neck. The soldier said he was falsely suspected of being a deserter. 'Sasha [Kapuscinski] and his goon came into the hospital, told the doctors to get aside, and physically grabbed me out of the wheelchair ... took me to the base,' a soldier who got expelled recalled. He was one of the two soldiers being kicked out on that day.

Kapuscinski refused to let him take his equipment worth over $3,000, the soldier said, and then drove him to the train station. '[He] put me out on a train to Lviv where I spent the next 18 hours obviously in tremendous pain as I had a broken neck,' he went on.

It wasn't the only time when a soldier from the military intelligence-overseen part of the Legion would get expelled while being sick. Another fighter was shown the door after damaging his meniscus during training without letting him get treatment first. 'Taras forced me out while I had a problem with my knee,' a soldier said of Major Vashuk.

According to this soldier, doctors prescribed him to undergo physiotherapy for a couple of weeks but Vashuk wouldn't greenlight it. 'We have to feed you and you are useless. It is not possible for you to stay out of the game for weeks. You have to leave the Legion,' the soldier recalled Vashuk saying.

Having been expelled from the Legion he went to his home country to recover. He soon returned to fight for Ukraine but outside the Legion, in one of the other formations that allow foreigners to join ranks.

After some time, his knee started hurting like never before. The medics told him he needed urgent surgery, adding that his meniscus should have been operated on months ago when it was first hurt.

Multiple legionnaires complained about not receiving proper medical treatment while serving in Ukraine. Other soldiers red-flagged Vashuk's brutal behavior, too.

In late March, about 30 Georgian soldiers decided to resign after having suffered heavy casualties during what they claimed was a suicide mission they were sent northwest of Kyiv. Vashuk was allegedly unhappy about it. He asked the soldiers to undress and give him their uniforms and backpacks, legionnaires recalled. They refused, arguing it was cold outside. 'Taras kicked my backpack and said: "I don't give a f*ck, take off everything and leave." I stepped forward and told Taras to watch his mouth,' said Nadim Khmaladze, who agreed to be named.

Then Vashuk took out his gun, reloaded it, and pointed at him, Khmaladze said. 'I went towards the gun. I stood in front of him and said: "You b*tch, if you got a gun, shoot",' Khmaladze said. Other legionnaires who were present during the conflict confirmed his recollection of events. Vashuk did not respond to *The Kyiv Independent*'s request for comment.

This was not the first time when an officer of the intelligence-run part of the Legion allegedly raised a gun at a subordinate ...

Like Vashuk and Kapuscinski, Bohdan also often expelled soldiers from the Legion, his subordinates said. According to them, Bohdan kicked multiple soldiers out, accusing them of spying for either their countries or Russia, something they denied.

One company commander had been complaining about their leadership's mismanagement for over a month until in April Bohdan decided to expel him, his testimony reads. He gathered both Ukrainian and foreign officers and proclaimed the soldier in question a spy. 'This "meeting" turned out to be a genuine homemade Stalinist-styled people's court, where Bohdan tried framing me for being a Russian spy,' the legionnaire's report reads. What saved him, he writes, is that 'the foreign officers were not buying any of it'.

Bohdan recalled the events differently: 'I received a report of suspected espionage from other legionnaires. I then reported this to the military counter-intelligence in accordance with the procedure. They [soldiers] were taken from the unit by representatives of the counterintelligence of the SBU. Later I learned that this suspicion was confirmed with evidence.'

The soldier's report reads that he was questioned by two SBU officers who he claims found no 'incriminating material' against him. The SBU press service refused to comment on the matter saying that 'details of counter-intelligence of the SBU cannot be a subject of public discussion'.

The legionnaire eventually resigned. 'I was thoroughly done serving in the Legion. Understandably so, I might add.'

Legionnaires call for change

The endemic abuse of power by the commanders made foreign fighters' service to Ukraine way harder than it could have been.

'For seven months soldiers here have been fighting on two fronts, one is Russia's army, and another one is corruption. The only reason why Ukraine is winning is that Russia is rotten in corruption even more than Ukraine is,' one legionnaire told *The Kyiv Independent*.

The soldiers call upon authorities to reform the Legion. They are afraid that, instead, authorities could just shut it down as an easier solution to end the complaints. 'We do not want the Legion to be closed, but to be reformed by NATO officers able to do so. Getting rid of the Legion will be a loss of opportunity for Ukraine. It has incredible potential, but the leadership must be changed,' the soldier went on.

'There is no trust in the officer structure. And there's no accountability. They don't have to answer to people, there's no checks and balances,' another legionnaire said.

Speaking of Kapuscinski as the most frequent target of complaints, one legionnaire told *The Kyiv Independent*: 'The idea that the Legion was being in some capacity led by a Polish gangster, who was potentially skimming off the top, and that the Ukrainian military leadership or the military intelligence leadership allowed this to happen, I find it, I don't know, infuriating.'

'I have friends that died. I carried the body of one of my friends out of combat. I have other friends who have been emotionally shattered by combat that they saw in Ukraine as part of the Legion and are really struggling with it,' he went on.

'It dishonors the Ukrainian army,' he said of the Legion's leadership misconduct. 'It dishonors the Legion as a whole. And I find it extremely frustrating.'

13 December 2022

Understanding Russia's relentless assault on Bakhmut

Francis Farrell

Water-logged trenches, shredded tree lines, and an undulating, colorless landscape of mud: The visual experience of the battles outside Bakhmut in Donetsk Oblast have proved to transcend centuries.

When Ukrainian machine-gunner Viktor Borinets' photos of conditions on the first line of defense went viral, the comparisons to the notoriously grim trench warfare of World War I wrote themselves.

'It does remind me of the Battle of Verdun, a brutal war of attrition,' Mick Ryan, an ex-Major-General of the Australian Army and Adjunct Fellow at the Center for Strategic & International Studies, told *The Kyiv Independent*. 'It was a deliberate German strategy which had nothing to do with territory or anything else except bleeding the French forces dry.'

Since withdrawing in November from their untenable position on the west bank of the Dnipro River around Kherson, Russian forces have greatly intensified offensive operations in Donetsk Oblast.

Bakhmut, a city with a pre-war population of 71,000, is the prime target of the Russian assault, having stood as a key Ukrainian stronghold on the Donbas front for over five months.

Now, Bakhmut is undoubtedly the scene of the heaviest ongoing fighting in the war. Speaking to *The Kyiv Independent* from a hospital in western Ukraine, a 32-year-old Ukrainian infantryman, known only by his callsign 'Ivan' for security reasons, said that the reality of the fighting outside Bakhmut was in many ways more desperate than the viral images through which it's perceived in Ukraine.

'You feel as if every day could be your last,' said Ivan, who was wounded by Russian mortar fire outside Bakhmut in the first week of December, just seven days after being posted. 'You understand that you could easily die at any moment, and that you count yourself lucky if you are wounded and removed from the battlefield.'

Endless grind

At first glance, the Russian frontal attack on Bakhmut bears similarities to the successful offensive on the nearby cities of Sievierodonetsk and Lysychansk in Luhansk Oblast, occupied back in late June.

Having failed in its early blitzkrieg against Kyiv and fixed its attention on Donbas, Russia looked to leverage its crushing artillery superiority to maul Ukraine's best units and advance in Donbas, kilometer by kilometer.

Cities and villages in the way of the Russian advance were wiped off the face of the earth, becoming harder and more futile for Ukrainian troops to defend, especially when threatened with encirclement, as was the case before the withdrawal from Lysychansk.

Since then, the tactical game has changed. Superior Western equipment has negated the crushing artillery superiority that Russia boasted in early summer, with the US HIMARS multiple-launch rocket system working famously to devastate Russian ammunition dumps and command posts deep behind their lines.

'The Ukrainians are much wiser and more experienced now compared to the period in May,' said Ryan, 'when they were drawn into that point because they had no other option.'

Meanwhile, Ukraine has continued to develop new ways of fighting in this 21st-century trench warfare environment.

Graphic videos of commercial drones dropping bombs on Russian positions from overhead had only just started to appear in summer, with the payload often too weak or inaccurate to cause much more than psychological damage.

Come winter and Ukrainian forces have mastered the art, hitting unaware targets with unnerving accuracy, and rigging larger drones to carry 82mm mortar rounds, capable of clearing a foxhole in one hit.

Recent weeks have shown that Ukraine is not the only side to have updated their tactical approach in Donbas.

Earlier in November, Ukrainian units in the area had reported mindless human wave assaults on their positions, bloating the General Staff's daily casualty figures with hundreds of dead Russian troops.

Now, according to Serhii Cherevatyi, spokesperson for Ukraine's Eastern Military Command, more focus is placed on probing, squad-level raids of under a dozen soldiers creeping over no-man's-land.

'Most of the time they don't make it through,' he said. 'Their main goal is simply to deplete our positions, not to let us relax, and to probe for an opportunity to launch a larger attack.'

Since summer, the Bakhmut sector of the Donbas front line has been dominated by the infamous Wagner Group, a private military formation run by Yevgeny Prigozhin, close confidant of Russian dictator Vladimir Putin.

'For the Russians, the losses they suffer in doing this is not an important factor,' said Cherevatyi. 'The first people that Wagner sends in, for example, are always the convicts and other poorly-trained men, and only behind them come the more professional soldiers.'

Holding for dear life

For those defending Bakhmut, Russia's more cautious tactics bring little relief, as the daily bombardment of Ukrainian positions continues uninterrupted.

Outside the city, the close proximity of Russian and Ukrainian lines, often less than a kilometer apart, means that Russia doesn't even need to use its heavy artillery as much, instead relying on an endless stream of mortar, grenade and rocket launcher fire to pound Ukrainian positions.

For the Ukrainian soldiers tasked with holding the first line, there is little to do but hope that one's trench or dugout doesn't take a direct hit. 'Our first and second lines of defense are relatively stable, but it comes at a great cost,' said Ivan, whose unit and exact posting have been kept undisclosed for security reasons. 'Some units are simply running out of people. From what I saw, in only one fight, we had around 10 of our guys killed, never mind the number of wounded. Not everyone could be extracted from the battlefield, some just bled out where they lay.'

In these conditions, the common belief about Russia's poor effectiveness as a fighting force can quickly melt away. 'They [Ukrainian military leadership] tell everyone about the huge casualties suffered on the Russian side, but from what I could see around Bakhmut, things are more or less OK for them,' said Ivan. 'In terms of the coordination between their brigades and artillery, and their overall unit cohesion, you can tell they are doing very well in this sector because of how difficult it is to fight against them.'

In a period when the General Staff was reporting between 300 and 600 Russian personnel losses per day, Cherevatyi had reported that between 50 and 100 of them were killed every day in the Bakhmut area alone.

While it might not be making large advances, Russia's attritional assault is proving effective in other ways, according to Ivan. 'Morale is beginning to suffer because of the lack of personnel,' he said. 'It's hard to speak of good morale when it's eight below freezing, you are sitting in a trench under fire all day and there is simply nobody to replace you for days on end.'

Still, there is no talk among the troops of retreating from Bakhmut and its outskirts. 'In that respect our resolve is strong,' said Ivan, 'despite – definitely not thanks to – what is going on on the battlefield.'

Cloudy motivations

With Ukraine liberating thousands of square kilometers of territory since Russia made its last significant gains in summer, it may come as a surprise that the Russian army is able to continue to mount brutal offensives like that in Donetsk Oblast.

Further north, Ukraine continues to probe at Russian defenses on the border of Luhansk Oblast, while in the south, a new offensive to slice through Zaporizhzhia Oblast, cutting off Russia's occupied 'land bridge' to Crimea, is also highly anticipated.

Three months after mobilization was announced in Russia, the influx of tens of thousands of conscript soldiers goes some way to explain Russia's enduring potential for offensive operations.

Cherevatyi downplays the role of Russian mobilized troops in the Bakhmut sector, saying that it remains dominated by Wagner forces.

According to Cherevatyi, though, the Wagner assaulting Bakhmut is an outfit almost unrecognizable to the Wagner that was first deployed in Donbas in spring.

'Earlier on, Wagner were a much more professional outfit, with better-equipped troops who had combat experience in Syria and Africa, and played a highly specialized role in the war here,' he said.

Now, as Wagner ups its assault on Donbas, the group serves as a conduit from Russia's prison system to the trenches in Ukraine. 'These formations have suffered great losses, which is why they have had to fill their ranks with so many convicts,' Cherevatyi added.

Specifically because Bakhmut has been Wagner's designated sphere of operations for so long, the city is often seen as a personal prize for Prigozhin, who presumably seeks to further raise his favor with Putin vis-à-vis the Russian Defense Ministry and military leadership.

'It is hard to see what they are really trying to achieve other than carrying out the order they were given, to take Bakhmut regardless of the costs,' said Ryan, who recently authored an analysis of Russian commander Sergei Surovikin in Ukraine. 'It displays an inflexibility in the Russian system and it shows a misalignment between what's going on in the battlefield and what the Russians are really trying to achieve in Ukraine.'

If breakthrough could be achieved, though, taking Bakhmut would be an undeniably significant achievement for Russia. 'Bakhmut is the opening to Kostiantynivka, Pokrovsk, Siversk, Kramatorsk,' said Cherevatyi of Russia's long-term aims in Donetsk Oblast. 'These are the key goals of the push to take Donbas, and if they were ever to succeed, they will look at where to go further.'

According to the Institute for the Study of War (ISW), while the capture of Bakhmut would be significant, Russian forces would nonetheless struggle to advance deeper into Donetsk Oblast.

Overall, Cherevatyi still holds that the prime objective is political. 'These attacks make sense for Putin, for his hold on power,' he said. 'He started this full-scale war, leveraged 20 years of propaganda about us [Ukrainians and Russians] being one people, and now they can't even take Bakhmut; it's a huge hit to his reputation if he fails.'

Uncertain winter

Over the winter, it has long been clear that both armies will face their own set of challenges.

What has been broken is the expectation that the arrival of winter will bring with it an operational pause as both sides dig in, conserving strength for the spring campaign.

'I don't agree with the US intelligence assessment that not much is going to happen over winter now,' said Ryan. 'First, they underestimated their ability to conduct offensives, and now they're underestimating Ukraine's capacity to conduct winter operations, when they have the initiative and it makes perfect sense for them to do so.'

Rather, the winter equation is one of waiting for the waterlogged ground to freeze, allowing armored vehicles to once again maneuver with ease.

'At the moment, in the east, the war is one of maneuver and careful counter-attacks,' said Cherevatyi. 'Things depend a lot on the weather.'

While Russia continues to grind up against Bakhmut, early signs point to the chance of a Ukrainian breakthrough soon near Kreminna, 52 kilometers north of Bakhmut in Luhansk Oblast.

Independent analysts show Ukrainian forces making incremental gains on both sides of the town, cutting off a key resupply route from the town of Svatove. Meanwhile, Luhansk Oblast Governor Serhii Haidai said on 11 December that Ukrainian troops had already reached the outskirts of Kreminna, though this remains to be confirmed by the Ukrainian military.

Both the ISW and the UK Defence Ministry have conceded the possibility of Russia taking Bakhmut, but both have assessed that the costs incurred will far outweigh the benefits.

Overall, the winter campaign in the Donbas looks to remain in this state of flux. 'They are looking for opportunities to concentrate their forces for an attack,' said Cherevatyi. 'We are not only watching them closely, but also looking for our own opportunities. In the end, as simple as it is, the side which is better able to prepare for and carry out operations on a tactical level will have the initiative.'

16 December 2022

Ukrainian teacher risked prison in Siberia to expose collaborators in occupied Snihurivka

Alexander Khrebet

When Russian forces seized her town, chemistry teacher Natalia Vorobiova had a choice: collaborate and be left alone or defy them and risk everything.

She chose defiance.

Even after Russia's Federal Security Service (FSB) threatened to abduct and imprison her in Siberia, she continued to refuse to teach a Russian curriculum. When some other teachers chose to work with the Russians, she tried to collect their names and turn them over to Ukrainian authorities.

Her attitude was on display on 1 September, the first day of the school year, when she stood in front of her school, wearing her vyshyvanka, a traditional Ukrainian embroidered shirt. The school was closed due to Russian occupation, but Vorobiova wanted to send a message. 'I am Ukraine, and I will work for Ukraine,' Vorobiova recalled telling the FSB operatives who came to cajole and threaten her.

Snihurivka, a railway hub on the western bank of Inhulets River and the northern gate to Kherson, was occupied by the Russian troops on 19 March, after 16 days of heavy fighting against Ukrainian forces and crowds of civilians blocking roads into the town.

Vorobiova and her fellow educators from local schools were left with an unenviable choice: continue to teach under the Russian flag or look for another job. Usually, the only other available work was selling produce at local markets.

Vorobiova, who had previously taught chemistry in two Snihurivka schools, chose the market.

Saving the Ukrainian flag

When Russian troops occupied Snihurivka, they took over both schools where Vorobiova had worked before the full-scale invasion.

One of these schools had displayed a Ukrainian flag, donated and autographed by the 28th Mechanized Brigade of Ukraine's Ground Forces. When

Russian soldiers moved in, they took the flag out of its display and threw it on the floor to step on.

'I distracted a Russian soldier, grabbed the flag, and shoved it up my sleeve,' Vorobiova told *The Kyiv Independent*. 'I do not know what was driving me.' When she got home, she put the flag in a glass jar and buried it in the ground among some berry bushes.

In late June, Vorobiova told a colleague she was hiding the flag. 'When two FSB operatives showed up at my place, I thought that my colleague had exposed me to the Russians,' Vorobiova said. But the Russians were there because of her other activities.

Informing on collaborators

The occupying forces had started recruiting teachers to keep the schools open. By offering promotions and other benefits, they succeeded in recruiting over a dozen teachers – in an attempt to relaunch at least one of the schools.

Vorobiova continued her resistance. 'I advised parents not to attend Russian schools,' she said, showing *The Kyiv Independent* two Russian school advertisements that she tore down.

In the meantime, Vorobiova began putting together a list of teachers that agreed to continue working with the Russians.

In late June, she came to one of the schools where she worked before the occupation and asked her colleague to provide their names, as her list was still incomplete. 'I was told "this is confidential information",' Vorobiova said. She threatened to report the colleague to the headquarters of Vitaliy Kim, the governor of Mykolaiv Oblast.

Several hours later, two FSB operatives showed up at her house and started questioning her. When one of them looked inside her phone, asking where she saved Kim's number, 'that moment I realized who turned me in', Vorobiova said.

Regardless, Vorobiova said she did not hold back in front of the operatives. 'I told them how I was cursing out the Russian soldiers at the checkpoints inside the town,' she recalled.

Vorobiova then admitted that she was providing the teachers' names and other information to the deputy head of the Snihurivka military administration and her former student, Ivan Kukhta.

'For transferring that kind of information, you face five years in Siberia,' Vorobiova said she was told.

According to Vorobiova, seeing that intimidation doesn't work, the FSB officer tried to recruit her. When Vorobiova said no, he leaned on the threats. 'Passing on information can be very unfortunate for you,' she recalls hearing. They asked her to reconsider, giving her until 1 September to comply.

Vorobiova never agreed. She was banned from coming close to the town administration building during the occupation. All four checkpoints inside Snihurivka had notices identifying her as a threat.

Closed schools

Vorobiova said that the entire staff of one of her schools refused the Russians' offers to continue working, disgusted by teachers who agreed.

Larysa Olekhova, the Ukrainian language and literature teacher in the vocational lyceum, was among those who refused the Russian demands. 'Russian soldiers had an insulting attitude towards the Ukrainian language and our territory. They kept telling us that this land is Russia, not Ukraine,' Olekhova told *The Kyiv Independent*, standing in line at a humanitarian aid distribution point in Snihurivka.

'This will be Russia, and you will teach the Russian language,' a Russian soldier told Olekhova.

'I told them I am a pensioner and can stay retired. I would never do it,' Olekhova said.

Because of the fighting, the Russians in Snihurivka hadn't managed to open the schools by 1 September. A month later, on 1 October, the schools were still closed. The Russians had scheduled the next school opening day for 4 December. But Ukrainian troops reached the town prior.

Locals said that almost all Russian troops left Snihurivka on 8 November. Two days later, Ukraine's 131st Reconnaissance Battalion liberated the town, raising the Ukrainian flag. At the same time, the 28th Mechanized Brigade was liberating Kherson, some 50 kilometers to the south.

'We prayed for our Armed Forces to free us, and our soldiers liberated us. Although there are difficulties, we breathe and live easier,' Olekhova said.

20 December 2022

Ukraine enters 2023 with frail upper hand over Russia

Illia Ponomarenko

In December 2021, most forecasting in the media did not give Ukraine much of a chance in case of Russia's full-scale invasion.

Ten months after it started on 24 February 2022, experts and media discuss where Ukraine will strike next, and what else Russia can do to save itself from a humiliating ultimate defeat in this war.

In the year 2022, two large militaries clashed in the biggest battle since World War II, involving a mix of modern warfare and brutal trench slaughter.

Despite all odds, Ukraine managed to do the unthinkable, having successfully repelled the initial Russian blitz, then withstanding the bloodletting war of attrition, and then retaking the strategic initiative.

Ukraine has destroyed the myth of Russian invincibility and persuaded the West to fully support its case instead of making yet another deal with the Kremlin. It has forced the 'almighty' Russia to go to extremes and – unsuccessfully – adhere to general mobilization, nuclear threats, and overt terror bombing to make Ukraine surrender.

The war enters 2023, with Ukraine having a slight advantage over the greatly degraded Russian military, mainly thanks to the extensive Western military aid. Chances are high that the next months of winter and spring 2023 are going to be decisive for the war's general outcome.

Ukraine is going to continue with its effort to retake the occupied land via new offensive operations.

And it is likely that the Kremlin, in a bid to save face in the increasingly critical situation, is preparing one more all-out attack upon Ukraine – such as the second massive rush on Kyiv in early 2023.

The failed blitz

In many ways, the war's outcome was predestined as soon as it became clear that Russia's all-out grand offensive of February and March had failed.

The monstrously overconfident Russian plan put a stake on a sweeping paralyzing strike coming from multiple axes along a 1,500-kilometer-long contact line. Russia, which had over 100 battalion tactical groups on the ground, went all-in, expecting little to no resistance in Ukraine.

Russia wanted the takeover to be quick and relatively easy, with the main goal to seize Kyiv, all of the country's key cities and facilities, and then install a Russian-backed puppet government.

Given that Russia never had enough military power for a long and hard war of conquest, a shock-and-awe blitzkrieg was the only realistic way to victory. But it failed. Ukraine managed to sustain the first massive missile strike and retain its armed forces, including air defense, operational and effective.

Ukraine also managed to retain the central government and local authorities, and eluded a societal collapse.

Using the tactics of highly mobile and flexible combat groups, the Ukrainian military managed to inflict devastating losses on numerous vulnerable Russian convoys moving on roads deep into Ukrainian territory.

Then, large Russian forces impeded by poor logistics and Ukrainian ambushes gradually bogged down in hard fighting in the suburbs of Kyiv, Chernihiv, and Sumy, losing time and a lot of resources. From the very beginning of the full-scale invasion, Russia failed to achieve dominance in the air.

The result was predestined within the first ten days of the battle of Ukraine's north – Russia's forces had to leave before it was too late.

The blitz was successful in Ukraine's south, which quickly fell to Russia within the expanse between Kherson and the outskirts of Mariupol. But the stubborn defense of Mykolaiv and Voznesensk stopped the Russian advance northwest to seize Odesa.

The Ukrainian success in the Battle of Kyiv made Russia leave some 40% of the territories seized after 24 February.

It also laid the first pillar of Ukraine's potential future victory in the war – it ruined the Russian blitz and won time for a general mobilization. Moreover, the month-long brutal fighting seriously degraded many of Russia's best and most effective combat formations thrown against Kyiv or Kharkiv.

Seizing initiative

Ukraine had sustained the first and the most dangerous strike. This made the Kremlin narrow its megalomaniac goals and focus on the east of Ukraine.

Following the Battle of Kyiv, the front line was reduced to nearly 1,000 kilometers, but the Kremlin clearly didn't have enough force for the entire duration. So it regrouped and created an unprecedented concentration of military power, mainly artillery, under the disguise of 'the liberation of Donbas'.

The Battle of Donbas, which has been ongoing since mid-April, saw Russian territorial gains at the price of the region's utter destruction and depopulation. But Russia failed to encircle the large Ukrainian military grouping in Donbas. And it had to narrow its goals, again and again, storming cities in costly frontal attacks and devastating artillery sprees.

In this new stage of the war, Ukraine also managed to withstand and exhaust Russian forces in grueling urban warfare, although it had also sustained heavy losses. And during this battle, Kyiv also managed to secure the second key factor of its possible future victory – the full-fledged Western military support, which had evolved from slight supplies of anti-tank weapons and firearms to extensive consignments of modern artillery and munitions.

Without Western artillery coming in large numbers, Ukraine would have run out of old Soviet-standard munitions within a very short period of time and essentially lose a chance to prevail in the longer run.

Moreover, in the Battle of Donbas, Russia was spending its manpower and resources so lavishly for the sake of purely political and propagandistic goals that it essentially degraded its immediately available offensive capability in the war.

After months of a brutal battle for Sievierodonetsk and Lysychansk, Russia eventually gained the dead ruins of former twin cities and could proudly declare the full capture of Luhansk Oblast. But since July, Russia's military had been so exhausted that it lost its ability to carry out new and successful large-scale operations for many months.

By mid-July, the front line stabilized.

But against expectations, this was not a stalemate. Thanks to Western aid, the Ukrainian military had accumulated resources in late August and launched a strike in the southern Kherson Oblast, which diverted the most combat-capable Russian forces. Then, Ukraine suddenly inflicted a crushing defeat to weaken Russian forces in the northeastern Kharkiv Oblast.

The Russian stampede in Kupiansk and Izium, Kharkiv Oblast, essentially spelled the end to Russian chances to seize central Donbas in the foreseeable future. Russians have lost the possibility to move further south from Izium towards Barvinkove and eventually isolate the Kramatorsk–Sloviansk area from the rest of the country and then destroy the Ukrainian military group in this giant pocket.

Then the successful Ukrainian counteroffensive operation in Lyman, Donetsk Oblast, ultimately proved that the Ukrainian military had seized the initiative in the war.

The successful tactics of derailing Russian logistics and command structures with US-provided HIMARS (High Mobility Artillery Rocket System) strikes eventually resulted in the largest Ukrainian military success since the Battle of Kyiv – the liberation of Kherson city and surrounding areas in mid-November. Kherson was the only regional capital that Russia managed to occupy since 24 February.

The Ukrainian autumn campaign had achieved 100% of its realistic agenda before the coming of the rainy season and wintertime. Moreover, it has given a clear answer to the question of whether the Ukrainian military is capable of large offensive operations along with stubborn defense.

Winter for war

By winter, the Ukrainian military has won the strategic initiative – yet another key component for victory.

The Russian lack of high-quality military power has seemingly become so severe that it resolved to mobilization – a very belated and politically risky step the Kremlin tried to avoid for many months despite obvious setbacks on battlefields. Besides, it gave a go to Wagner Group, operating near Bakhmut, to illegally recruit prior convicts, as well as continued nuclear intimidation and missile terror attacks on Ukraine's vital infrastructure.

The Kremlin is trying to buy some time and slow down Ukrainian advances with units reinforced with barely trained manpower.

As of mid-December, muddy weather conditions still prevent both sides from trying to make any substantial territorial gains.

In the upcoming winter and spring campaigns, the Ukrainian military is yet to lay another key pillar of its possible victory – the ability to hold on to its strategic advantage over the adversary and also to continue carrying out new successful counter-offensive operations. That would derail Russia's own plans for 2023.

The upcoming winter campaign will come as soon as stable frosty weather finally prepares the ground for maneuvers. It remains an open question where the Ukrainian command decides to try and strike next.

To Ukraine, the most attractive and most obvious goal is Melitopol, a city in Zaporizhzhia Oblast which is the key transportation point of the Russian-occupied south and also the gate to Crimea. Another potential target is Svatove, the liberation of which could undermine the Russian military presence in the north of Luhansk Oblast. And one more possibility is Volnovakha, another important railroad communication point between Donetsk and Mariupol.

The Ukrainian command's choice between these three goals will probably open the year 2023, along with the war of logistics and the challenge of fighting in the winter environment. And then the spring campaign may be decisive for the war's outcome.

In his recent interview with the Economist, Ukraine's Chief Commander Valerii Zaluzhnyi suggested that Russia prepares some 200,000 fresh troops for a new large-scale offensive in January, February, or March 2023. From his point of view, this will undoubtedly include yet another massive attack on Kyiv from Belarusian territory.

Therefore, the commander said, the Ukrainian military needs extensive Western military assistance, including hundreds of tanks, vehicles, and artillery pieces, to successfully repel the new attack and regain all territories occupied by Russia after 24 February.

According to the Institute for the Study of War (ISW), a US-based defense think tank, Russian President Vladimir Putin may be setting conditions for such an attack in the winter of 2023.

But, according to the group's report published on 15 December, such an attack is 'extraordinarily unlikely to succeed'.

The ongoing Russian efforts with brutal fighting near Bakhmut and Avdiivka and massive missile attacks fail to coerce Ukraine into negotiations or concessions. Still, the think tank believes the attack from Belarusian territory is 'not imminent at this time'.

Moreover, when it comes to the direct involvement of the Belarusian military – which many have been speculating about recently – the possibility of that remains also 'extraordinarily unlikely' in the foreseeable future', the think tank believes.

'A Belarusian intervention in Ukraine, moreover,' the ISW said, 'would not be able to do more than draw Ukrainian ground forces away from other parts of the theater temporarily given the extremely limited effective combat power at Minsk's disposal.'

27 December 2022

In occupied Chornobaivka, doctor shortage forced driver to become wounded people's last hope

Asami Terajima

Hours before the Ukrainian forces arrived to liberate this village outside Kherson on 11 November, a breathless local man sprinted into its one small hospital.

The morning's shelling had hit his neighbor – the local saw him screaming, covered in blood. With no mobile service or any other utilities in Chornobaivka, the man had to run 600 meters to summon emergency medical support.

The occupation had stressed the small hospital to its limit. Its medical supplies were dwindling and most of its doctors had already fled, leaving only the director and a family doctor, along with a few junior personnel. The depleted staff had to take on many new responsibilities just to keep the place running.

That's how Petro Omelchuk, 65, a driver by profession, found himself thrust into the role of emergency service worker during the occupation. On 11 November, he was at the reception desk, when the wounded man's neighbor burst through the door.

Omelchuk and two nurses immediately got into a car, as the neighbor pointed the way to the scene of the attack. When they got there, the driver immediately saw a man lying in the yard, impaled through the stomach by a 15-centimeter long piece of shrapnel.

'The house was scattered, and he was buried under shrapnel and glass,' Omelchuk told *The Kyiv Independent* at the Chornobaivka hospital, now back under Ukrainian control, a few weeks after the incident.

Omelchuk wrapped the wounded man in a blanket and carried him into his car. He then drove 10 kilometers to the regional hospital in Kherson, cutting through the dirt roads to get there quicker.

Something was off about that day. The Russian checkpoint between Kherson and Chornobaivka was gone, and there were no soldiers to be seen. But Omelchuk said he was so focused on driving that he didn't have time to consider why the checkpoint was missing, not with his passenger still bleeding and crying out in pain.

Shortly after dropping off the victim at the Kherson hospital, Omelchuk was informed that the wounded man had died. Omelchuk only found out when he returned home to Chornobaivka that the victim was his acquaintance with whom he often talked at the local market.

He didn't recognize him because of the dirt and blood covering the victim's face.

On the same day, an elderly woman was also wounded in Chornobaivka in the same round of shelling, with the shrapnel cutting deep into her leg. Omelchuk was informed that a resident drove her to Kherson. She also didn't survive.

Omelchuk said that both would have lived if they had access to doctors and proper medicine in the village.

Run-down hospital

Once a peaceful village, home to nearly 10,000 people, Chornobaivka is now strewn with the trauma of Russian occupation.

Neither the local authorities nor residents were ready for the full-scale war. Chornobaivka had no ambulance even before the full-scale invasion. Patients in critical conditions would be taken to Kherson due to the lack of medical equipment for complex surgeries in the village.

By early March, Russian troops had established control over Kherson and the surrounding areas, strictly controlling the movement in and out of the city. The local hospital would have to do its best.

The first weeks of occupation were particularly difficult for the hospital. The casualty rate was at its peak due to shelling. Treating wounded civilians while continuing to help regular patients with their illnesses proved to be an immense challenge.

That's why Omelchuk, whose usual job consisted of medical supply delivery and helping less mobile patients get to the hospital, had to learn how to carefully carry patients with excessive bleeding into a car and drive in a way that causes minimal stress.

Omelchuk understood the risks of working under occupation. There was a time when he thought about leaving Chornobaivka because of the massive number of Russian tanks and soldiers in the village.

Despite the threat of Russians taking away his car or abducting him, he continued to drive back and forth between Kherson and Chornobaivka to bring medical supplies. He was always available if someone needed to be driven to the hospital in Kherson.

Omelchuk drove a regular white car with the words 'help' in Ukrainian and a medical cross.

It's still a mystery to Omelchuk why he was allowed to continue working. '[Maybe] they just felt sorry for me that I was small and old,' he said.

Omelchuk said he doesn't know how many times he brought patients to Kherson. 'It's impossible to remember everything,' he said, recounting the trauma he experienced.

One such experience happened in May. There was a badly wounded mother screaming for her 34-year-old son until she was taken to the hospital. She died in the Kherson regional hospital without finding out that her son was found dead under the rubble of a destroyed house the next day, Omelchuk recalled.

'They were good, young people,' he said.

Choosing to stay behind

Throughout the occupation, at least 18 civilians were killed and 28 were wounded in Chornobaivka, according to village council data seen by *The Kyiv Independent*.

Among the slain were two 23-year-olds, brutally shot dead by Russian soldiers on the streets on 4 March.

'I never thought that I would issue such death certificates,' the small hospital director, Olena Kasatkina said, referring to the day she signed the paper for the murdered young men's relatives.

As head of the facility, the 62-year-old said it was important to keep the basic services running despite the overwhelmed hospital's limitations 'because people get sick and ask for help'. Besides treating the wounded, the medical staff also took care of patients ill with Covid-19 and cardiovascular diseases.

'Every day, whether [Russian troops] shell or don't shell [Chornobaivka], we leave home and head to work,' Kasatkina told *The Kyiv Independent*.

The biggest challenges of running the small hospital under Russian occupation involved the unstable utilities and shortages of even the most basic medicines, like pills to lower blood pressure, according to Kasatkina.

The center was able to treat less critical patients and hand out some basic medicine for free, as the supplies were provided from Kherson, and the staff received salaries via Ukrainian bank cards from the National Health Service of Ukraine, Kasatkina said. But that didn't solve all their problems, as there were big gaps in the availability of almost everything.

It was 'very difficult morally' to continue working even if Russian troops didn't directly threaten the hospital staff, Kasatkina said. Yet she continued to work to care for patients.

It was only in May that Russian troops began patrolling the center of the village, both on foot and by car. They took over the village council administrative building on 2 May and began putting the Russian flag everywhere.

The Russians also came to the hospital. They threatened the staff that they would 'shoot down the building' if the Russian flag on the hospital was taken down, according to Omelchuk. The staff immediately took the flag down as soon as Ukrainian soldiers arrived on 11 November.

Kasatkina's lowest points were 'when a person is dying, but [Russians] don't let the ambulance through'.

Despite the threat of working independently while Chornobaivka was occupied, the hospital staff said they did their best to continue the operations of the only medical facility for the village's predominantly-elderly residents. 'We did what we could,' Kasatkina said.

28 December 2022

A glance into Kherson's underground resistance during Russian occupation

Igor Kossov

Editor's Note: We don't reveal the real names of the people interviewed for this story due to the sensitive nature of their activities that puts them in direct danger. In the story, names were assigned to them for storytelling purposes.

Kherson was liberated because Ukraine forced Russians to accept they could not hold the city with their dwindling supplies and growing body count.

Part of that was achieved by Ukrainian forces running the Russians ragged, continuously destroying their supply lines and command centers. But an important role was also played by people who were inside Kherson during the occupation. From sending targeting coordinates to assassinating ranking Russians and collaborators, Ukrainian informants and partisans made sure that the invaders never got too comfortable.

With Russians constantly on the hunt for partisans, it was extremely dangerous to be one. Many Ukrainians who did this kind of work were abducted, tortured, and even killed. Many remain in Russian hands somewhere on the other side of the Dnipro River, where Russian forces retreated in November.

The Kyiv Independent spoke with people in Kherson who took part in underground resistance work to varying degrees. They spoke of how partisans and other civilians did their work while hiding in plain sight, constantly waiting for a squad to kick down their doors. Many details, including their identities, have been deliberately omitted for their security.

'When a soldier gets wounded, he gets evacuated to a hospital,' said a man going by the name Doron, who coordinated a partisan cell in Kherson in the occupation. 'Sabotage and reconnaissance types can't retreat. You are already in a trap, surrounded by FSB and Russian agents. You have nowhere to run.'

Resistance activity in occupied Kherson took many different forms – including spreading Ukrainian symbols, spying on the Russians, smuggling in concealed weapons and using those weapons to kill the invaders.

Information about this kind of work is so limited and individual contributions were so varied, that overgeneralizing would be misleading, as would sorting resistance members into definitive categories.

Friendly fire could also be a concern.

'Partisan is a slippery term. When liquidating a person, you have to [be sure] not to blast one of your own. Any person in the structure of the occupier could be our agent,' said Doron. 'Partisans can kill you, even if you are an agent.'

The quality of informants varied as well. 'Kostiantyn', who works in Ukrainian intelligence, said he received reports from many types of people ranging from street junkies to ordinary observant citizens, to more valuable sources like taxi drivers, employees of certain industries and people who worked among the occupation authorities.

For example, a woman identifying herself as 'Masha', who worked for several days in Kherson's regional administration building during the occupation, said people would spy for Ukraine by leaving hidden recording devices in offices or meeting rooms.

Behind enemy lines

Doron was well placed to become a guerilla and spy. Before the invasion, he was a comfortable Kherson native, with the appropriate background to do this kind of work and remain calm under pressure. He also knew a lot of different people in the city.

Before the full-scale invasion, he spoke to authorities about preparing for the Russians' arrival. He said that visiting the local territorial defense recruitment office left him very underwhelmed. 'One guy was drunk. Another guy taped a knife to his leg with scotch tape,' he recalled.

According to Doron, Ukrainian intelligence left Kherson and other places poorly prepared to resist the Russians. Usually, when anticipating the possibility of captured territory and partisan resistance, hidden stashes of weapons and supplies should be prepared in advance. 'There were no weapons, explosives, nothing in the areas that would be occupied,' said Doron.

He decided to put up resistance, in coordination with Ukrainian intelligence. When Russia invaded the city in early March, he stayed in Kherson, knowing that if he left and came back, it would arouse the Russians' suspicion. There were others, who would do the same. As the trap closed around them, some of them formed into cells.

'The main factor was having the balls,' Doron said of the criteria for his cell's recruitment. 'My whole unit ... was tested for courage and readiness.'

One way to test someone's courage was to hand them a grenade and ask them to lob it into a building full of FSB operatives, he said. 'They go to do it, you stop them.'

Courage was very much needed with the constant threat of arrest and interrogation hanging overhead. Russian operatives were known for various forms of torture, including extreme ones like attaching electrodes to the penis.

'Every day, you wake up at 4 a.m. and you wait for someone to come for you,' said Doron. 'My neighbors were collaborators. I saw how the FSB went to the house across the street all the time. They would come and [the neighbor] would already be waiting outside.'

Starting in March, when the city was captured, Doron said he would collect information from multiple sources and pass it onto Ukraine's special forces, saying there could be up to five attacks per day that used the coordinates he passed on.

The observers spread out to constantly monitor the main routes for the arrival of Russian combat vehicles, especially the Antonovsky Bridge. This gave them a clear idea of what the Russians were bringing across the river and where they were doing it. They also found out where Russians would build pontoon bridges.

'I had one call at night: there are four Bayraktars in the air – what should they hit?' Doron recalled.

Because only Russian data networks were available on occupied land, partisans used VPNs and secure apps like Signal to communicate. 'Kostiantyn' said that sometimes the app Threema was also used.

'Kostiantyn' showed pictures that informants sent him through these apps, including targets' cars, the remains of a bombed booth and some Google Maps screen grabs with addresses pointed out. In one picture, the target building was circled by a pink heart.

'They [Russians] didn't like Signal,' said 'Yuriy', another Khersonian who smuggled weapons into occupied territory. 'If they found Signal on your phone, you were a partisan.'

Doron and members of his group didn't just sit at home in Kherson. Their assignments would send them to different corners of the occupied part of Kherson Oblast. For example, if an agent disappeared from contact, they would drive over to double-check their status.

They also had to transport weapons like grenade launchers and assault rifles, many of which were smuggled in from outside the occupied territory, donated or sold by private citizens. They were concealed inside personal vehicles in imaginative ways or buried under innocuous objects.

Weapon transporters had to be very calm and casual, when passing through the many Russian checkpoints along their way.

Every trip and meeting had to have a cover story, such as going fishing, visiting a friend to get drunk, or coming to help fix something. Each story required the correct props – fishing rods, packed food, liquor, power tools or whatever fit the narrative. When moving about, they left their work phones at home and carried burner ones, used only to access content that appeared inane and non-threatening like entertainment sites or internet porn.

Protecting main working devices was critical, as the FSB was very good at pulling any information it wanted off phones, even ones that had been smashed or in pieces.

Much of the prep work was in service to the more impactful partisan work of sabotage and assassination. Individual members of resistance cells had limited information by design and assassination work was also segmented for the same reason.

'Everything was divided up. One guy leaves an explosive at the property, a second guy watches it, a third guy puts it on the car,' said Doron. 'The watcher then reports that the car is moving and the fourth guy then presses the button.'

The difficulty of eliminating someone was in direct proportion to their value. Top collaborators were protected by the FSB, often transported in armored vehicles, which were inspected for bombs, Doron said. But even less important targets could take some studying.

'You would look at how they move around, their lifestyle, whom they know. You look for a weak point,' said Doron.

The killings, either with assault rifles, bombs or targeted artillery, whittled down Russians and alleged collaborators throughout the entire occupation.

As an example, 'Yuriy' said that his acquaintance in April gunned down blogger Valeriy Kuleshov, who was accused of pro-Russian views and working with top Russian collaborator Kyrylo Stremousov.

Stremousov himself, whom the Russians had made the deputy head of their occupation authority, died just as Russia was about to pull out of Kherson in November. The Russians' official report was that he died in a car crash.

Doron said the most high-profile death in which he was involved was that of Lieutenant General Yakov Rezantsev, commander of Russia's 49th Combined Arms Army. Doron's cell got word that Rezantsev would be at the Chornobaivka airfield on 25 March. The Ukrainian forces took him out with an artillery strike, according to presidential adviser Oleksiy Arestovych.

While Doron managed to last and evade capture, many people who did any kind of resistance work in Kherson weren't so lucky. Doron said he had heard of people being tortured to insanity or death by the Russians.

Ukraine is working on setting these prisoners free.

Personal note from Oleksiy Sorokin, senior editor

'I knew the Ukrainian people would resist'

Civil resistance was expected. After three revolutions where people self-organized, first against the communist regime, then against a fraudulent electoral count, and later against a president slipping into authoritarianism, Ukrainians know how to fight. In 2014, when Russia launched its invasion, and the Ukrainian army was demoralized and incapable of defending the country, it was the volunteer battalions that defended the country in the east; it was also the volunteers who provided them with equipment, food, medicine and moral support.

During the months leading to war, the slogan 'Ukrainians will resist' was nationwide. Everyone knew that, no matter how the Ukrainian armed forces would perform, Ukrainians, equipped with Molotov cocktails, would fight. Russia's biggest mistake was that they didn't believe Ukrainians when they were told point-blank that they were up for the fight. The Territorial Defense units are a good example. Corruption was reported in them ... not to avoid the army, but to get enrolled into the units! Days into the war, the units were packed, with officers asking people to stop coming to conscription centers.

I expected the civil resistance and was 100% sure that Russia would lose from the moment it decided to move in, because it would have to deal with a country 40 million people strong that hates them to their guts. The Ukrainian armed forces, however, are performing way above expectations. We were told, in Ukraine, that the Ukrainian army was well prepared, that the country had been gearing up for a potential Russian offensive for eight years. However, corruption and lack of competent military leadership in the past cast doubt about the Ukrainian military capability. I was wrong and I'm happy that I underestimated the military.

Being an editor allows me to work in the safety of an office, and to live in a country at war without actually seeing the war. I don't want to live and work like that. I feel that to do a proper job as an editor and manager of a news outlet amid an ongoing war, I need to see the war. I need to witness what our reporters witness on the front lines, in destroyed villages, what they feel when they talk to people who lost everything. I need to see war, so I can report on it.

The Kyiv Independent, this news outlet that several people (including myself) built from scratch over the dead body of an oligarchy-controlled *Kyiv Post*, became the most influential voice coming from Ukraine. This comes with a responsibility. We hold on to the high-quality standards preached in the *Kyiv Post* and make it our distinct feature – high-quality journalism from

Ukraine. The other side of it is having a handful of days off since the war began and maybe a dozen since 8 November 2021.

I've traveled a bit since 24 February and I have recorded some stories that people told me. One was a man in the Shevchenkove village, in Mykolaiv Oblast, several kilometers west of Kherson Oblast. When I asked him why he and his wife were living in this village, constantly shelled by Russian troops, he told me that his son was fighting in Mariupol. Their friends sent them a link showing their son on Russian TV as a prisoner of war. He told me that they will wait for their son in their house, so that when he is released, he can come home. It was back in May, and I hope he's been a part of a prisoner exchange. I really hope that all of our men and women kidnapped by Russia will return home.

Ukraine will obviously win. This is a fight between the future and the past, the long-dead Soviet imperialism and the freedom, democracy and dignity of people who respect themselves and the place they live. Russia can occupy the land, erect Lenin statues and fly Soviet flags, but it doesn't have a future to offer. Russia is a walking corpse that is bound to fold.

However, despite Ukraine's victory being obvious in the long run, it's unknown how many people will have to die because of Russia. We don't know how long the war will last, and how long Ukrainian territories will live under occupation. I expect it will get worse, much worse, before it can get better. Ukraine can only win this war. Its spirit and willpower will outlast anything Russia tries to impose.

29 December 2022

How volunteers risk their lives to rescue abandoned animals amid war

Daria Shulzhenko

When Ukrainian soldiers were entering the village of Yampil in Donetsk Oblast after five months of Russian occupation, they discovered an abandoned zoo on the outskirts.

Dozens of animal corpses, either killed by Russian troops or dead of starvation, were lying throughout the zoo's territory. But in one locked cage, they noticed an animal that was still fighting for its life.

'[The bear] was in terrible condition. Five more days and we wouldn't have saved him,' says Olena Bila, a volunteer who came to the bear's rescue in late September, shortly after Ukrainian soldiers called for volunteers to help.

When Bila arrived at the site, she saw the bodies of killed wolves, foxes, and empty cages that she believed had belonged to lions. She found the bear locked in a tiny cell, neglected, thin, and 'drowning in his excrement'.

'He was concussed,' Bila says, adding that a shell had exploded near his cage. 'It was hard to look at.'

Bila and her team had to act quickly to move the animal, since Russian troops could open fire against the liberated village at any moment. Luckily, the mission was successful. Bila says the bear now lives in 'good conditions' at a zoo in the Polish city of Poznan and feels better.

They named him Yampil after the village he was found in.

According to the United Nations, over 13 million Ukrainians have been forced to flee their homes since the beginning of Russia's all-out war, including 7 million refugees and 6.5 million internally displaced. Countless animals were left behind, forced to fight for survival amid Russian attacks and cold weather.

For many of them, the only chance to survive is to be rescued by Ukrainian volunteers, who risk their lives traveling to front-line settlements and liberated territories to save abandoned cats and dogs, farm animals, and wild ones.

'Most humanitarian missions and charities are aimed at helping people, and I can understand that,' says volunteer Kateryna Arisoy.

'But I believe that all creatures deserve to live,' she adds. '[Animals] suffer no less than people, and in some cases – even more.'

'Ukrainians who care'

For Arisoy, the battle to save animals started over a decade before Russia launched its full-scale invasion of Ukraine. In 2011, she co-founded a small animal shelter in her home town of Bakhmut, Donetsk Oblast.

'I was so naive to think that we had already survived the hardest times [the Russian invasion of Donbas in 2014–2022],' Arisoy says, adding that she had never expected the all-out war to hit Bakhmut so hard.

She fled Bakhmut in April amid non-stop Russian attacks but well before it became the focus of some of the heaviest fighting along the entire front line. Since then, she has returned to the city multiple times to help animals, 'those who can't ask for help'.

In the city of Dnipro, where Arisoy temporarily found a new home, she joined the Vetmarket Pluriton, a team of volunteers that help and rescue animals affected by the war. Arisoy says volunteers often get calls from locals telling them where the help is needed.

The volunteers started by rescuing animals from the liberated towns of Irpin and Bucha outside Kyiv. When fighting intensified in the east of Ukraine, they began traveling to Bakhmut and other settlements in the area.

Bila, on the other hand, was 'far from volunteering' before the full-scale invasion: in the early days of the war, she and her husband had to shut down their small business in Kyiv Oblast and 'devote themselves to helping others' by joining the team of UAnimals, a nonprofit that advocates for animal rights.

On 8 March, during one of their missions near the capital, Ukrainian soldiers showed them a small wounded puppy that had recently come to them. 'We took him and started treating his wounds,' Bila says. 'When you look into his eyes, you can drown. We decided to keep him.'

The puppy turned out to be a Bernese Mountain Dog. They named him Baron. He has accompanied them during every 'evacuation, under shelling, and in all the front-line hot spots'. 'He goes ahead of us during rescue missions,' Bila says. 'He is always on alert. When we are loading animals [into their mini-bus], and he hears [shells] flying towards us, he starts barking, warning us to hide.'

During another mission, they once stopped at a gas station, where a Ukrainian family with a little daughter spotted a cute puppy the couple had just rescued from a war-torn settlement. 'We offered for them to take that puppy, but they refused, saying it was too big of a responsibility,' Bila says.

After they had driven 100 kilometers from the gas station, a car appeared behind them and honked for them to stop in the middle of the highway. 'It was the same family we had offered the puppy,' Bila says. 'When we left, the girl started crying, persuading her parents to keep it. So they chased us for more than 100 kilometers to get this puppy. It was adorable.'

In September, Bila went to the liberated city of Izium in Kharkiv Oblast. She says Ukrainian soldiers rescued 10 dogs there and decided to adopt all of them into their families. 'We brought the dogs to their new families, not shelters,' Bila says. 'They are happy now, waiting for the soldiers to return.'

'There are many Ukrainians who care about animals, even despite the horrors of the war,' Bila adds.

Striking difference

Seeing Ukrainian soldiers treat animals kindly and rescue them amid heavy fighting touches Bila's heart deeply. 'Our soldiers are humane, kind-hearted, and brave. If they see that an animal needs help, even if it's in a dangerous place, they will still try to save it,' she says. 'That distinguishes our soldiers [from the Russian troops].'

Volunteers say that the difference is especially striking in the settlements liberated from the Russian occupation.

When Arisoy visited the Yampil zoo and the nearby nature reserve shortly after the area's liberation, she was shocked to see what Russians left of the place she used to enjoy. 'Russian soldiers were based there during the occupation. Most of the animals died of hunger or from shelling,' she says. 'But Russians also ate many animals,' she says, adding that they learned about that from locals.

Upon arrival at the reserve, Arisoy saw 'skins, torn-off heads, and bones' of a deer, ostrich, and bison. There, she also saw the remains of her 'favorite alpaca'. 'As soon as I saw the skin, I immediately recognized who it was and almost fainted,' she says.

Out of nearly 200 animals at the zoo and the reserve, only two horses, four donkeys, a couple of pigs and six piglets, a llama, a wild bear, a goat, a duck, and a cat survived the Russian occupation. Arisoy says volunteers evacuated them all.

At the zoo, she says they also found a corpse of a camel that died of starvation: 'Only bones remained,' Arisoy says.

Bila assumes Russian soldiers were also 'killing animals for fun', as volunteers found wild animals 'shot dead in their cages' at the zoo. She says it was the first time she saw animals that had been shot dead.

Though most of the animals they rescue have been abandoned by their owners escaping the war, there are some whose owners had been killed. From one of the liberated half-ruined settlements of Kharkiv Oblast, Bila rescued a dog with a litter of small puppies.

The dog's owner, a local veterinarian, was killed in a Russian airstrike on the village, she says. His house was destroyed, but his pets somehow survived the attack. Now, other volunteers take care of the pets and look for new homes for them.

There are countless similar stories all over Ukraine, Bila says. That's why she and her husband work almost non-stop to rescue as many as possible, often putting their lives in danger.

Risking lives

Arosoy says animal rescue missions during war mean constant threats to their lives.

'We come under fire all the time,' she says, adding that a rocket fell in front of their car when they were driving near Bakhmut recently. Bila agrees, saying that recently they evacuated five horses from a farm in liberated Kherson under the heavy shelling. When they were on a mission to rescue a bear from Bakhmut, a projectile fell nearly 10 meters away from them, Bila says. Luckily, it didn't explode.

'Something protects, perhaps, because we are on such a good mission – saving the lives of our animals,' Bila says.

But Russian attacks are not the only threats the volunteers face. 'Three members of our team were taken prisoner by the Russian troops when they went to Lysychansk to evacuate children and a local animal shelter,' Arisoy says.

Russian forces captured Lysychansk, the last Ukrainian holdout in Luhansk Oblast, after heavy fighting, in early July. Arisoy says their volunteers were in the city at that time. She can not disclose details but says they are still in captivity.

Despite the many challenges and risks they are facing, Bila says there 'was not a second she regretted becoming a volunteer'. 'It is so heartwarming when you save a life and see an animal that is grateful to you,' she says. 'They can't say anything, but how they look at you shows gratitude for being saved.'

5 January 2023

As Battle of Bakhmut nears culmination, Ukraine's artillery gasps for more ammo

Illia Ponomarenko

It's the last days of December and the heat of the holiday season. But an artillery battalion with Ukraine's 24th Mechanized Infantry just couldn't care less. For them, it's like Groundhog Day – just another day of war that keeps repeating over and over.

From their place in an abandoned village in Donetsk Oblast, they support Ukrainian infantry repelling Russian frontal attacks in Bakhmut. The site of the most grueling battle of Russia's war in Ukraine so far, Bakhmut has been drawing comparisons with World War I's deadly Battle of Verdun.

A 122-millimeter 2S1 self-propelled howitzer Gvozdika is waiting in the bushes, the dry grass around it charred after the gun's multiple shots there.

The gun is on standby. The artillerymen are in an abandoned house nearby, where they try to keep close to the cellar. The radio buzzes: a warning comes that Russians counter-shot some of this battery's guns this morning, 'so you guys better watch out'.

Time after time, other Ukrainian howitzers rattle the air. The thunder of impact rolls through the steppe, and plumes of whitish smoke rise on the horizon. The artillery duel between Russians and Ukrainians is brutal. Russian artillery is attacking from Opytne, a town just south of Bakhmut.

'Hey, did you see what happened to those dudes from our regiment the other day?' one of the crew tells his mates.

'By some miracle, the recon told them Russians were about to target their area. So they took cover at the last minute. But their machine is absolutely down. A knock-out hit.'

He pulls out a picture of a burning 2S1 howitzer on his smartphone.

'Shit happens, but they are all fine now.'

Tanks, Humvees, and seen-it-all 4x4 trucks roar time and again near the house as they try to dash through the unbelievable swamps of dirt roads.

The radio buzzes again.

'Ah, f*ck,' the artillerymen drop their cigarettes and rush to the gun.

Two rounds are requested. The infantry fighting in Bakhmut need urgent support.

The howitzer gets loaded. The coordinates have been adjusted.

'Fire!' the gun's commander shouts.

The old Soviet howitzer spits out a shot, instantly filling the air with smoke and the smell of expelled propellant. And one more time. The work is done – for now.

The crew get back to the same rhythm of waiting in a cold abandoned house for command. The wait may last a few minutes or painfully endless hours.

The grueling Battle of Bakhmut lasts for five months, but Russian forces, despite insane pressure and massive losses, have not yet managed to capture the important city, the local transportation hub and one of key fortresses of Donbas. Their slow advances finally got them to the city's outskirts – in many ways due to their overwhelming artillery power.

But over recent weeks, Russian advances in the area have been dying down.

The Battle of Bakhmut is likely culminating.

According to international monitors, Russian forces appear to be losing their biggest advantage over Ukraine – the seemingly near-endless stocks of artillery munitions. After so many months of inadequately costly effort to encircle the Ukrainian fortress city, even popular Russian war bloggers admit the acute munitions hunger that is now impeding their advances.

Ukrainian forces on the ground confirm the rapidly decreasing activity of Russian artillery.

But meanwhile, Ukrainian artillery, despite extensive Western supplies, also struggles to make its best due to lack of munitions, especially when it comes to old Soviet standards.

On the ground, this results in horrific losses among Ukrainian infantry holding the ground for months.

'This is good for us'

Behind this grid of artillery guns pounding Russian lines around the clock, there's just one man.

He sits at a desk in front of a laptop and an iPad in a townhouse close to the howitzers. The room is heated hot with a stove, and he is sipping coffee from his mug. This humble working place is a priority target for Russian counter-battery activity.

The man, Stepan, is watching the real-time picture of the battlefield, transmitted by the drones in the air. He coordinates the artillery strikes delivered at requests of infantry.

His iPad shows fields of black and green surrounding Bakhmut. As far as the drone's electric eye can see, everything up to the horizon is a giant moonscape of black impact holes.

Time and again, new plumes of smoke rise up in the field from fresh impacts.

'Our godawful Starlink just isn't working the way it should,' the specialist says as he angrily digs into his laptop.

'How am I supposed to work when the internet is so damn slow?'

As simple as that, the Ukrainian military shares the picture from drones with other units via link-only live streams on YouTube.

Russia initiated the Battle of Bakhmut in August, following the failure of its attempts to advance in other axes, particularly in Donbas.

After months of intense frontal attacks, spearheaded by Russia's notorious military company Wagner Group, it has become the meaning of devastating losses on both sides.

After five months of fighting, Russian forces near Bakhmut have only advanced between 6 and 12 kilometers east and south of the city. Since September, they have stood at the eastern outskirts of Bakhmut.

But neither frontal attacks nor attempts to isolate the Bakhmut garrison from the north (via Soledar) and the south (via Kurdiumivka) have had limited results, although they put the city closer to the downfall.

According to Ukrainian intelligence, in December, Russia had concentrated 40 battalion tactical groups and the largest artillery force in the area.

After the Russian military's spectacular failures in Kharkiv and Kherson, the battle for Bakhmut has become the Kremlin's only realistic chance to get a victory that can be used to reinforce the pro-war propaganda.

For this sake, the Wagner Group, headed by increasingly powerful Kremlin insider Yevgeny Prigozhin, is going as far as the mass recruitment of convicts in Russian prisons to be thrown in the meat grinder of Bakhmut.

In December, it felt like Bakhmut might fall soon.

Russian forces made gains south of the city, aiming to sever the vital road running west to the city of Kostiantynivka. Had they succeeded, Ukrainian forces would have to withdraw from the city to avoid a death trap.

Russian forces managed to enter the eastern outskirts of Bakhmut in December. But on 21 December, the day after President Volodymyr Zelensky made a surprise visit to the city, Ukrainian forces managed to carry out a tactical counter-attack and drive Russia out of the city.

And then on 27 December, the head of Ukraine's military intelligence, General Kyrylo Budanov, was seen visiting his scouting troops deployed in Bakhmut just 600 meters from Russia's lines.

Many indicators allege that Russia's pressure in Bakhmut is finally reaching its limits.

Ukrainian forces are sustaining between 3 and 8 infantry attacks in the area daily, according to troops on the ground. But over the last few weeks, Russians were seen switching to using small squads of between 10 and 15 men instead of company or battalion-sized tactical groups.

Besides, Russian airborne units were also reportedly deployed to the Bakhmut area to augment the Wagner Group, seriously degraded after months of costly attacks.

Another factor is the reportedly diminishing Russian artillery power.

In late December, Budanov said that the daily spending of Russian artillery in combat dropped from 60,000 to between 19,000 and 20,000 rounds by the end of 2022.

Moreover, according to the general, by March 2023, these issues will be even more obvious.

On 24 December, the United Kingdom's Ministry of Defence also said Russian forces currently lack the necessary stockpile to support large-scale offensive operations and sustain defensive operations in Ukraine.

Rumors on deteriorating munitions have been circulating for quite some time in Russian pro-war Telegram channels. An escalation came on 27 December, when the Wagner Group released a video in which two militants insult Russia's Chief of General Staff Valeriy Gerasimov and accuse him of severe lack of artillery munitions in the Bakhmut area.

Conflict Intelligence Team (CIT), an open-source investigations group, however, says the current situation is precipitated by poor and ineffective logistics rather than the physical absence of munitions in Russia's stockpile per se.

'The intensity has definitely dropped several-fold, that's true,' artillery specialist Stepan told *The Kyiv Independent* near Bakhmut, as Ukrainian howitzers kept booming behind the house windows.

'Including in terms of counter-artillery activity. Which is good for us.'

From the Ukrainian side, however, the situation is no better.

Especially when it comes to Soviet-standard munitions, the main stocks of which had been largely depleted back in summer. According to the 24th Brigade artillerists, at the beginning of Russia's war, each battery used to get up to 150 full loads of munitions a day (which corresponds to up to 6,000 rounds). Now they're getting only up to 30 full loads a day.

'We need every single 122-millimeter round anywhere in the world so we could go on helping our infantry. We do everything we can, but we don't have much ammo,' Ukrainian artillerists say.

'You just can't have enough rounds in this war.'

According to the Institute for the Study of War (ISW), a US-based defense think tank, the depletion of the Russian stockpile 'will likely in part prevent Russian forces from maintaining a high pace of operations in the Bakhmut area in the near term'.

From the ISW's perspective, the most brutal battle of this war is likely culminating.

'US military doctrine defines culmination as the "point at which a force no longer has the capability to continue its form of operations, offense or defense",' the ISW said on 29 December. 'And "when a force cannot continue the attack and must assume a defensive posture or execute an operational pause". If Russian forces in Bakhmut have indeed culminated, they may nevertheless continue to attack aggressively. Culminated Russian forces may continue to conduct ineffective squad-sized assaults against Bakhmut, though these assaults would be very unlikely to make operationally significant gains.'

Moreover, according to a British intelligence report issued on 3 January, over the previous 10 days Ukraine had committed fresh reinforcements to the Bakhmut area. And Russian attacks by the Wagner Group intensified in mid-December, but were poorly supported.

'Russian offensive operations in the area are now likely being conducted at only platoon or section level,' the British Ministry of Defense said.

'It is unlikely Russia will achieve a significant breakthrough near Bakhmut in the coming weeks.'

'We don't want to just die'

Once one of the best-looking cities of the industrial part of Donbas, the famous manufacturer of salt, Bakhmut is dead now.

Almost no building is left intact. Some buildings are completely razed to ashes, with giant, meters-deep impact holes next to them. Most are damaged but still standing. The street signs wrecked with shell fragments still tell the story of vibrant life in the very recent past.

The apocalyptic streets are empty and silent, except for the roar of artillery guns and the buzz of drones high above. Every now and then, one of the few remaining locals is seen in the street, often carrying bags of humanitarian aid.

According to the military-civilian administration responsible for the area, some 90% of residents have fled. But some 8,700 civilians out of a pre-war population of over 70,000 are still hiding in ruins.

Off and on, Ukrainian tanks drive slowly through the streets of rubble and rusty anti-tank hedgehogs.

All hell is breaking loose on the other side of the Bakhmutka River, which divides the city in half. Russians are standing just at the gates, but they have not broken through.

The infantry of Bakhmut – sick, tired, full of bitter resentment – has its own point of view on what's going on with the most monstrous and dramatic battle of Russia's war.

'It's hard even to describe our death toll in there,' soldiers say as they get back to the line after a long-awaited yet short rest in the rear.

'It's beyond horrific, it's something a sane human mind can't imagine. We repel at least three major attacks every single day.'

'And Russians roll on, and on, and on, and on. They never stop throwing their scum at us. Sometimes we can hear Wagner commanders talk on communications: "Run to the Ukrainian trenches, and whoever makes it – you know what to do."'

Soldiers gladly pass an opened bottle of whiskey to journalists. They are just dying to spend a minute talking to a new face before they have to move on.

'It's such a mess.' They get emotional.

'What they write about us on the internet, all the glorious victories, is so different from what we see here every day. Where is our artillery, what are they even doing? It's a complete mess. We don't give a f*ck if that's Wagner or anyone else, we'll keep fighting anyway.'

'But we want to fight and win, not just fight and die sooner or later.'

5 January 2023

Covered by dead bodies of his relatives, 4-year-old boy survives Russian attack

Daria Shulzhenko

When Russian forces opened fire on the peaceful village of Oskil, Kharkiv Oblast, on 27 March, Svitlana Voshchana realized her friend's home was under attack. When the attack stopped, she rushed to their home, hoping the family had managed to hide. Stepping into their yard, she saw the house severely damaged – its walls, windows, and doors were in pieces. Next to the partially destroyed building, standing on a pile of broken bricks, was a small child – her friend's four-year-old grandson Mykyta. His winter jacket was torn, but he was not crying.

'I asked him where his grandmother was,' Voshchana recalls. 'He said, so quietly: "She is dead."'

When she turned to look at what remained of the cellar, she saw something 'beyond terrifying'.

'I saw them, lying very close to each other, four dead bodies,' Voshchana says.

Her friends had not managed to hide from the Russian artillery strike that morning. Mykyta's mother, Liudmyla Chibis, aged 36, his sister, Karyna, aged 7, and his grandparents, Volodymyr and Vira Serdiuchenko, aged 69 and 64, were all killed on 27 March.

Mykyta saw the dismembered bodies of his family, says Voshchana. The young boy had crawled out from underneath his family's dead bodies. Injured, cold, and scared, he wandered alone among the rubble that was left of his grandparents' home until Voshchana found him.

'When I took him in my arms, he said: "I have been waiting for you for so long. I knew that you would save me,"' she says.

There were no other casualties due to the attack that day.

A few days later, Russian forces occupied Oskil, a village in Kharkiv Oblast with a pre-war population of 3,000 residents located just east of Izium. Oskil remained under Russian occupation until September when Ukrainian forces liberated most of Kharkiv Oblast in its surprise counteroffensive.

After nearly seven months of occupation, Oskil residents still consider the 27 March strike one of the most horrifying tragedies Russia inflicted on their village.

No safe place

Mykyta's grandparents' house in Oskil had always been the family's favorite place to gather, says Daria Sviatenko, Mykyta's eldest cousin. The entire family sought refuge there shortly after Russia launched its full-scale invasion of Ukraine on 24 February. Before the war, the family had been scattered between Kharkiv, Izium, and several other homes in Oskil.

'We thought it would be safer in the village,' Sviatenko says.

They were soon proven wrong as Russian jets started to fly over Oskil. 'It was horrifying,' she recalls.

After spending over a week hiding in their basement with no mobile connection, power, or 'access to civilization', Sviatenko's mother, Olena, decided to flee Russia's war with her children. Although she tried to persuade her relatives to evacuate, they refused. 'My grandparents didn't want to leave their home,' Sviatenko says, adding that her aunt, Liudmyla Chibis, was afraid to flee with her children. The family had heard stories of Russian troops killing civilians as they tried to evacuate from occupied areas.

On 5 March, Sviatenko and her children fled Oskil to a town in Poland where their father worked at the time.

After they left, Russian forces began to shell Oskil more heavily. The village, divided by the Oskil River, was soon partially occupied by the Russian army.

On 10 March, the first Russian tanks entered the street where the family lived, and the 'nightmare' began, says Voshchana.

Gripped by fear

The family home's windows were covered with pieces of old fabric, and the doors were locked from the inside when several Russian soldiers entered the yard one day in March.

When he spotted the soldiers, young Mykyta climbed onto a chair near the window and bravely shouted: 'Glory to Ukraine.'

'They all got so scared and took him away from the window,' Voshchana recalls.

Luckily, the Russian soldiers had not heard him. They tried to open the front door but soon left, she adds.

During that period, Ukrainian forces repelled Russian attempts to advance toward a local hydroelectric station outside the village, Voshchana says. As they withdrew, Russian troops abandoned three tanks on the street where Voshchana and the Serdiuchenko family lived.

The evening before the attack, Voshchana says she had spotted a Russian drone following her near her home. She believes Russian forces were surveying the area in an attempt to spot Ukrainian troops. 'Our soldiers were on the opposite bank [of the Oskil River],' she says. 'There were no Ukrainian soldiers on our street.'

Later that same day, Voshchana made her regular visit to her longtime friend Vira Serdiuchenko, Mykyta's grandmother. 'We were sitting at their place, talking about how brave Mykyta had been when the Russians came,' Voshchana says. 'All of a sudden, the first blast hit.'

Voshchana looked up at the ceiling and could see the sky – the explosion had damaged the roof, as well as shattered the windows and cracked the front door.

'The children started to cry out of fear,' she says.

While the family had a small basement in their home, Mykyta's grandfather, Volodymyr, thought it better to hide in the cellar outside to avoid being killed 'under the rubble of the building.' Voshchana decided to return home quickly.

The moment she left their house, another shell exploded nearby. Voshchana says she somehow managed to return home and hide in her yard.

Russian troops shelled the residential street for about half an hour, she notes. When the attack appeared to quiet down, Voshchana rushed back to the Serdiuchenko's home. Despite seeing the many craters formed from the shells on her way, she says she 'could not have imagined the tragedy that had already happened'.

When Mykyta told her that his grandmother had died, Voshchana says she first thought she had died from a heart attack amid the heavy shelling. 'The fear gripped me,' Voshchana says, as he told her that his mother had also died.

Next to the cellar, she says she saw their four dead bodies, all of them mutilated. She remembers Volodymyr's blood-soaked and ripped hat: 'The explosion was very close to them. There was no chance of survival.'

Four-year-old Mykyta was the only one to have survived the Russian strike.

'He got out from underneath [his family's bodies] and climbed atop a pile of bricks,' Voshchana says. 'That was where I found him.'

Coping with trauma

After the attack, Voshchana says troops from the local, territorial defense forces retrieved Mykyta's family's bodies and buried them amid ongoing shelling in a shared grave at the village's cemetery.

Mykyta was taken to a local doctor's home, where his injured arm and hip were treated.

Olha Shamaida, an Oskil resident and acquaintance of Mykyta's family, came to visit the young boy. 'He was terrified and cold,' she recalls. 'He even asked me, "Will you warm me up?"'

She took him home.

A mother of three, Shamaida says she did her best to help Mykyta cope with the trauma caused by Russia's attack. 'He didn't sleep for two weeks,' Shamaida says. 'He was remembering those horrible explosions.'

Several months later, Mykyta's aunt, Olena Sviatenko, managed to evacuate him from still-occupied Oskil and gain legal custody of him. Mykyta, now five years old, lives with his aunt's family in Poland.

Mykyta's cousin, Daria Sviatenko, says Mykyta understands that his loved ones were killed and that he misses them a lot. 'He does not cry, but he understands everything.'

Sometimes, she says, Mykyta opens up and talks about the tragedy. 'I only survived because my mama and sister covered me,' he once said.

8 January 2023

Even after sanctions, Russian economy can pay for war

Oleg Sukhov

The Russian economy has faced unprecedented sanctions since the Kremlin launched the full-scale invasion of Ukraine on 24 February.

The latest events – the West's embargo on seaborne oil and price cap on Russian oil sales worldwide – are seen as a blow to the Russian economy, whose backbone is the energy industry.

But, paradoxically, Russia's economy has not collapsed and is unlikely to do so in the foreseeable future, analysts say.

The cap is too high, Europe isn't the only market, while Russia's stocking of revenues from oil and gas sales will keep the economy afloat.

Russia's ability to fund its war against Ukraine may remain unchanged. Instead of reducing war spending, the Kremlin is likely to redirect resources from the civilian sector toward the defense industry, experts say.

Russia's economy is expected to become increasingly militarized as the Kremlin seeks to supply its invasion force in Ukraine.

This means that the civilian sector will shrink further, and living standards will fall, but the war won't end.

Oil sanctions

Since Russia launched its full-scale invasion on 24 February, the West has cut off some Russian banks from the SWIFT messaging network, banned high-tech exports to Russia, and frozen $300 billion in Russia's foreign exchange reserves.

The latest blow dealt to the Russian economy is an unprecedented sanctions package against Russian oil.

The US and UK banned Russian oil imports in March, and the EU followed suit on 5 December.

The EU will also start implementing an embargo on Russian oil products starting from 5 February.

The embargo on oil products will be extremely painful for Russia because it will not be able to supply them to China and India, which are exporters – not importers – of oil products, Mikhail Krutikhin, a Russian-born oil and gas analyst based in Sweden, told Ukrainian political blogger Olena Kyryk in December.

On 5 December, G7 and the EU started implementing a $60 per barrel price cap on Russian oil.

Since the EU, the UK, and the US have previously banned the imports of Russian seaborne crude, the price cap mostly applies to other countries that still buy Russian oil. Insurers for the oil market, which are mostly based in the West, are banned from dealing with Russian oil priced above the cap.

In Europe, several landlocked countries – the Czech Republic, Hungary and Slovakia – also continue to buy Russian petroleum shipped via pipelines.

Ukrainian oil and gas analyst Oleksandr Kharchenko told *The Kyiv Independent* that China and India would not be able to compensate for the drop in Russian oil supplies to Europe because transportation costs for shipping oil to Asia would be much greater.

Russian dictator Vladimir Putin further shot himself in the foot by issuing a decree on 27 December to ban oil and oil product exports to countries that comply with the price cap. However, it is unclear how stringently the ban will be applied since the decree's wording allows the Kremlin to provide loopholes and exemptions.

Andrei Movchan, a Russian-born economist based in London, told *The Kyiv Independent* that he believes the Russian ban is just a face-saving measure that will not be enforced in practice and will not affect oil exports.

Bypassing sanctions

There is also the possibility that Russia may try to bypass the oil sanctions, partially neutralizing the embargo and the price cap.

'Russian oil companies may seek to bypass the oil price cap by selling oil to markets that do not implement the cap,' Jack Sharples, a research fellow at the Oxford Institute for Energy Studies, told *The Kyiv Independent*. 'However, sales to other markets, further away, will entail higher transportation costs and likely lower profits. Much will depend on Russia's access to oil tankers that are not following the sanctions prohibiting the transportation of Russian oil, especially the "dark fleet" that was used to bypass sanctions on Iranian oil exports.'

Movchan said that Russia might be able to export at least the same amount of oil in violation of sanctions as Iran, which has been successfully evading Western sanctions for decades.

Iran has been exporting between 1 million and 2 million barrels of oil per day in recent years.

Kharchenko said that the West should strengthen the sanctions by improving the mechanism for monitoring and cracking down on Russia's attempts to evade them.

Natural gas industry

Since the beginning of the invasion, Russia has also lost most of its European market for its natural gas – the main source of gas giant Gazprom's revenue.

Russia's Nord Stream 2 gas pipeline via the Baltic Sea to Germany was completed in 2021, but Berlin banned its launch due to the Russian invasion of Ukraine.

Gazprom's Nord Stream 1 gas pipeline had operated until September when it stopped working after a series of bombings. The organizers of the sabotage remain unknown.

Russia also contributed to halting its gas exports to Europe by trying to force European countries to pay for its gas in rubles and halting supplies to the countries that refused.

Before the Nord Stream bombings, Gazprom had also halted and reduced its gas supplies via the pipeline several times due to alleged repairs. The measures were seen by Russia's critics as an attempt to pressure and blackmail Europe.

On 19 December, the EU agreed to impose a price cap on both Russian and non-Russian gas at $180 per megawatt hour starting from 15 February.

Czech Prime Minister Petr Fiala described the deal as 'very important,' saying it aims 'to secure affordable energies for European households and businesses'.

The decrease in the significance of the European market is seen as a huge blow to Gazprom.

Russia will not be able to reorient its gas exports to China because there are not enough pipelines in that direction, Kharchenko said. Nor does Russia have enough liquefied natural gas (LNG) plants to ship its gas by sea, and it does not have the technology to build such plants either, he added.

Is the Russian economy on the verge of collapse?

Economists say that the sanctions dealt a major blow to Russia's oil and gas industry and its entire economy, whose backbone is the energy sector.

Russia's oil output is expected to halve in 2023, while Russia's budget revenues are expected to fall by 30%, Krutikhin said.

Although the Russian economy is going to suffer, economists say that an economic collapse is unlikely.

'It currently seems unlikely that the reduction in gas exports to Europe and oil sanctions will lead to an economic collapse in Russia,' Sharples said.

'The reduction in tax revenues from the oil and gas sector will lead the government to draw upon its National Wealth Fund and increase the annual deficit of the federal budget at a time when the government is also looking for funds to pursue its war in Ukraine.'

Sharples argued that the costs of the war and the Western sanctions would 'have an economic impact on Russia that will likely be felt to a far greater extent in the medium-term future than in the short-term.'

Movchan said that imports and investments had fallen, and Russia's central bank would have to print more money, leading to a higher rate of inflation.

However, the sanctions are not a 'catastrophe' for the Russian economy, and there will be no shortage of foreign currency, he added.

'Russia is self-sufficient in terms of resources,' he said.

Movchan said that Chinese imports would replace Western ones, and Russia would gradually turn into an economic satellite of China.

Competent management

The Russian economy's ability to survive has also been attributed to the competence of Putin's team of 'liberal economists'.

These include Elvira Nabiullina, head of Russia's central bank, and German Gref, the CEO of Russia's state-controlled Sberbank.

Russia's economy has turned out to be stronger than expected.

In April, Russia's Finance Ministry expected the country's economy to fall by 12% in 2022, according to sources cited by Bloomberg.

But Russian Finance Minister Anton Siluanov said on 29 December that Russia's GDP would eventually fall by a mere 2.7% in 2022.

The Russian ruble plummeted after 24 February but then rose to the highest level since 2014 in September as the authorities introduced draconian foreign currency controls, while oil and gas revenues increased and imports fell.

Despite the heavy EU sanctions targeting Russian energy, Moscow received a record revenue from energy exports in 2022 due to high prices.

The ruble fell to an eight-month low in December after the oil sanctions came into effect, and imports, including Turkish ones, rose.

If the Russian economy continues to be run wisely, there will be no collapse, Sergei Sazonov, a Russian-born political philosopher at Estonia's Tartu University, told *The Kyiv Independent*.

'But any government can destroy the economy by making stupid decisions,' he added.

Military economy

As Russia is waging its war against Ukraine, it also seeks to militarize its economy to boost the war effort.

Putin has repeatedly instructed the military-industrial complex to step up production.

However, analysts say that so far, it's not clear if Russia has managed to significantly increase its production of weapons since there is little information.

Movchan argued that Russia is capable of building a wartime economy. It can manufacture some missiles and start producing military drones, he said.

Movchan and Sazonov said that the militarization of the economy would not be on the scale of World War II when the whole industry was transformed to supply products for the war machine.

The Soviet Union had a militarized planned economy from the very beginning, and its industrialization was aimed at creating a powerful war machine, Sazonov said. In contrast, Russia's more complicated market economy is harder to mobilize for military purposes, he added.

The United States' highly advanced market economy was also successfully transformed into a war machine during World War II, but it was also very different from Russia's.

'The US economy was much more powerful,' Sazonov said. They had a high level of competence and gigantic experience in organizing mass production.'

Funding the war

The purpose of the sanctions was to deprive Russia of its ability to fund its war against Ukraine. However, experts say that Russia's ability to fund the war may remain virtually unchanged.

'The reduction in oil and gas sector revenues will mean that as the government continues the war, it will deplete its savings and accrue debt more rapidly,' Sharples said. 'In time, this could undermine the ability of the government to fund the war.'

But he added that 'it is also possible that the government will face the more difficult financial circumstances by prioritizing military spending and cutting back elsewhere, such as spending on health, welfare, and education'.

'If so, the Russian population will increasingly bear the costs of the war,' Sharples added.

Movchan argued that the sanctions would not have 'any impact' on Russia's ability to finance the war machine.

The war against Ukraine is a 'priority task' for Russia, and it will redirect resources from the civilian sector to the war effort and print money to fund the war, he said.

Sazonov said that Russia would not spend less on the war even if its revenue fell dramatically. Instead, he said that it will reorient its resources, forcing living standards to fall.

Impact of sanctions

Sazonov believes the economic sanctions would not affect Russia's ability to wage war.

'There were no examples when a country's will to wage war was crushed by economic pressure,' he said.

Nazi Germany did not lose its ability to wage war even when it was completely isolated and was being bombed by the Allies at the end of World War II, Sazonov said.

He also cited the examples of Iran, which has been able to survive and wage wars for decades despite Western sanctions, and North Korea, which has been isolated for decades but managed to create a nuclear bomb.

'The idea that it's possible to defeat Russia economically is a dead-end,' Sazonov said. 'Russia has all the basic resources inside the country – food, fuel, and ammunition.'

The only way to defeat Russia is for the West to dramatically increase the production of weapons and supply them to Ukraine, he added.

The idea that the Western sanctions and Russia's economic problems will lead to regime change is questionable.

Sazonov argued that Russians' resentment with falling living standards would not lead to any coup, uprising, or revolution. Putin has destroyed all independent elites and is strong enough to crush any dissent, he said.

But Georgy Satarov, a Russian political analyst, told *The Kyiv Independent* that regime change is unpredictable, and economic difficulties may be one of the numerous factors that can lead to a coup or revolution.

'The [1917] February Revolution started after a women's revolt in bread lines,' he said. 'A hundred years later, this may be one of the many factors that will become the trigger.'

16 January 2023

Russian missile attack on Dnipro destroys families as death toll rises
Asami Terajima

Editor's note: The Kyiv Independent does not publish the last names of all interviewees to protect their identity.

With dark purple bruises around her eyes, 81-year-old Lidiia packed whatever she could fit into a plastic shopping bag and left home in a hurry on 15 January.

A day after a Russian missile struck an apartment complex not too far from the center of Dnipro in central-eastern Ukraine, residents were allowed to briefly visit home to collect their valuables while first responders were still on site.

More than 30 people are still missing as of 9 p.m. on 15 January, President Volodymyr Zelensky said in an address.

Russia launched its deadliest attack on Dnipro on 14 January, killing at least 30 people, including a 15-year-old girl, and wounding 73, according to the latest figures. Of the 30 patients still hospitalized, 12 are in critical condition, local authorities said.

The attack was part of another widespread Russian attack across Ukraine that targeted several cities, including Kyiv, Kharkiv, Odesa, Kryvyi Rih, and Vinnytsia.

Lidiia's apartment was located about 15 meters from the epicenter of the attack. Her section of the building still stands, but all of the rooms in her apartment suffered from the blast wave, leaving glass shattered across the floors.

When Russia's Kh-22 missile with a 950-kilogram warhead smashed into a building in a commuter town at around three o'clock in the afternoon, Lidiia was sitting on her bed alone in the apartment.

Lidiia was facing her bedroom window when she heard a 'sharp and very loud sound', and something hit her head, she told *The Kyiv Independent*.

She believes it was 'a fragment of something' in the room that flew into her face due to the blast wave. The fragment left a large bump on her forehead.

Despite the pain in her eyes, Lidiia stayed in the room for about 40 minutes until the cold temperature in the room became too difficult to bear. There was no electricity, mobile network, and heating following the attack, which meant the injured couldn't call for help.

After escaping the damaged apartment building on her own, Lidiia called a taxi to her relatives' place and later went for an X-ray. 'They were all horrified,' Lidiia said, referring to how her relatives reacted when they saw her after the missile strike.

She was later diagnosed with a concussion and is currently undergoing medical treatment.

Awaiting rescue

For Vladyslav Soloviov, 29, the screams of those caught under the rubble he heard following the attack are something he will never forget.

Soloviov was standing near his apartment door at the time, waiting for his wife to finish getting ready. They were going to a nearby grocery store. The powerful blast threw Soloviov out of the door. His wife was in the bathroom at the time of the attack. Neither of them suffered any serious injuries.

Despite hearing the loud sound of an explosion and the ground shaking, Soloviov said that the couple didn't immediately realize their apartment had been hit. 'You don't know how it feels when a missile is shot at you,' Soloviov said. But what he saw outside the window wiped his doubts away. The ex-law enforcement officer, who now works as a volunteer, said he only saw a column of smoke, but 'nothing was visible'.

The couple closed all doors and stayed in a room to hide from the smoke, wearing masks, until the rescuers found them. He said the two waited around 20–30 minutes.

First responders went door to door to help victims. Soloviov said he felt it would be unsafe to climb down alone due to the smoke and broken glass everywhere. He tried to send a message to emergency services that they were awaiting rescue, but there was no cellphone service or internet.

Soloviov believes the couple would have had less chance of survival if they had left their home earlier. The part of the apartment building that was hit fell onto the path they would have taken to the grocery store, he said. 'If we had been outside, then most likely, we would have been buried under the rubble of the apartment,' Soloviov said.

Families torn apart

Russia's Kh-22 missile, originally designed to destroy aircraft carriers, struck the residential building as many families were at home to meet the Orthodox New Year.

In just seconds, 72 apartments were completely destroyed, and more than 230 apartments were damaged, according to Dnipropetrovsk Oblast Governor Valentyn Reznichenko's preliminary data.

The Soviet-era apartment complex attacked has 16 entrances and was home to about 1,700 people.

Russia previously used the same Kh-22 missile when it struck a shopping mall in Kremenchuk in June, killing at least 20 people.

Similar to the attack on Kremenchuk, the 24 January missile strike in Dnipro has destroyed families. Rescuers said a large crowd of people waited outside the building, hoping that it would be their loved ones who would be rescued next. Some still don't know the fate of their family members.

Anastasiia Shchvets, 23, was one of those who lost her family in the attack, her father's decades-long colleague who works at Toyota Center in Dnipro told *The Kyiv Independent*.

According to Oleksandr Kornyenko, Shchvets was home with her mother and father when their apartment building collapsed. The parents were killed in the kitchen while the daughter, who was in the bathroom, miraculously survived, he added.

Kornyenko said that the family was likely at home because Shchvets's father, 46, took sick leave from work. He was supposed to return to work on 16 January.

The daughter was immediately hospitalized after rescuers found her and is now with an aunt, Kornyenko said. He said he spoke with her on the phone late on 14 January, and she was understandably fragile and in shock.

The death of Shchvets's parents was confirmed by her grandmother on 15 January, according to Kornyenko.

Mykhailo Kurenovskyi, a well-known professional boxing coach who lived on the top floor of the apartment building, was also killed by the strike.

Vitaliy Fedorenko, whose six-year-old son was coached by Kurenovskyi, said the coach's wife and his daughters had just left home when the missile attack happened.

Kurenovskyi was supposed to come with the mother and daughters but decided to take more time and promised to catch up with them later. His body was found under the rubble on 15 January, according to Fedorenko.

Fedorenko said Kurenovskyi was 'the best coach' and a great person with whom he'd often talk about the future of their children.

Rescue operations

As soon as the missile struck the building, rescuers and volunteers arrived quickly to help the victims.

The emergency response team operated in the most difficult parts, the 1st to 4th floors, of the collapsed building, crawling to find survivors. The rest – including the local Territorial Defense brigade volunteers – divided into groups of three to four people and used ladders to find any sign of life.

First responder Serhii Harmash, 27, said it was becoming more difficult to find survivors when he took the night shift at 12 a.m.

Harmash worked 14 hours non-stop. He found a survivor toward the end of his shift, at around 11 a.m. on 15 January. The young woman was in her kitchen on the fourth floor and had yelled for help for about four hours, so she couldn't speak or walk when he found her, he said.

Cuts are the most common injury among the wounded, Harmash said. Among the killed, there were many bodies with missing parts, a head included, he added.

There were wounded people who have died because they were forced to stay in the cold weather for too long, Harmash said. 'Every death is horrifying,' Harmash said. 'People lived here peacefully, and then this happened.'

Harmash said in total, he had recovered six dead bodies.

Meanwhile, co-commanders of the local Territorial Defense brigade volunteers, Oleksandr, 43, and Konstyantyn, 50, said it was difficult to convince relatives to wait outside the building.

The relatives, many of whom had just miraculously survived the attack, tried to go back into the building to find their loved ones, the co-commanders said.

Konstyantyn said the most horrifying thing he experienced while participating in the rescue efforts was finding 'parts of bodies' lying in the courtyard. He said collected them and put them in a bag.

The co-commanders went inside the building together to look for the wounded. They were able to rescue an elderly woman and man on floors higher up.

The couple was in shock, but the commanders remembered the elderly man telling them that he was going to find his cane and make 'the president of the neighboring country' pay back.

18 January 2023

Harder than ever: How power outages affect people with disabilities in Ukraine

Daria Shulzhenko

On 18 December, Kyiv resident Tetiana Venhlinska was without power at home for 10 hours straight. The blackout was imposed following another large-scale missile strike in a series of Russian attacks on Ukraine's energy infrastructure.

For most Kyiv residents, the long power outage was likely a mere annoying inconvenience. But for Tetiana Venhlinska's mother, 75-year-old lung cancer patient Yeva Venhlinska, it was a life-and-death situation.

Yeva Venhlinska was diagnosed with advanced lung cancer in 2017. For the last three years, her life has depended on a stationary oxygen concentrator running non-stop to provide oxygen flow.

During blackouts, she uses portable versions of the device. But hours into the unexpectedly long power outage on 18 December, she only had around 30–40 minutes of battery left, according to her daughter.

That's when Tetiana Venhlinska called a costly private medical company that took her mother to life-saving hospice.

Yeva Venhlinska's blood oxygen level had fallen to a critical 80% (95–100% is considered healthy) by the time she was connected to an oxygen device in the ambulance. 'That helped save her life,' Tetiana Venhlinska says. 'Otherwise, she would have just suffocated.'

There were over 2.7 million people with disabilities in Ukraine as of June 2021, according to the State Statistics Service. That numbler includes nearly 164,000 children.

Russia's repeated attacks on energy infrastructure across Ukraine, which have killed dozens of people and caused electricity, water, and heating cut-offs, have made Yeva Venhlinska's life and the lives of millions of other people with disabilities and those who rely on special medical equipment, harder than ever. 'It affects them a lot,' says Serhiy Rashchenko, the head of a rehabilitation center in Odesa whose son uses a wheelchair.

Rashchenko says that with no power, it has become more challenging for people with disabilities to take care of themselves, prepare food, exercise, and even leave the house since elevators can't function without electricity. 'It's difficult not only physically but morally to withstand this pressure,' Rashchenko says. 'When no one can help you, and you sit at home with no power, no water, nothing. I see suicidal thoughts all around.'

Oxygen for mother

Tetiana Venhlinska says they had short power cuts at home at the early stage of Russia's full-scale invasion of Ukraine, which began on 24 February. They lasted from 30 minutes to two hours, she says.

Back then, Venhlinska raised money to purchase a car battery that kept her mother's oxygen concentrator running for about two hours without electricity, in an attempt to prepare for 'short-term emergencies'. Aware of their situation, a local charity also donated a portable oxygen concentrator to the family. Working at minimum capacity, the portable concentrator can run for nearly seven hours, Venhlinska says. But the amount of oxygen her mother needs can drain the battery in just three, she adds.

Since Russia began targeting Ukraine's energy system with missiles and drones in October, frequent lasting blackouts have become a real challenge for the family. 'The last three months have been a constant stress to us,' Venhlinska says. 'It is impossible to predict how long the blackout will last, whether it will be four, seven, or nine hours ... Each time, we tried to save as much [oxygen] as possible because we don't know when the power will be back on.'

Getting less oxygen also seriously affects her mother's overall health. 'Imagine that you don't have enough oxygen. You try not to breathe,' Venhlinska says. 'She gets exhausted,' she goes on. '[She] tries not to move much, freezes, and just waits [for the power to be back on].'

The night of 18 December was the longest amount of time Venhlinska did not have electricity at home. It was two days after Russia unleashed its seventh large-scale attack on energy infrastructure across Ukraine.

The strike 'significantly' increased electricity shortage in the system, which was substantial even before that, the state grid operator Ukrenergo said at the time. For Yeva Venhlinska, it was life-threatening.

Her daughter called the ambulance when the portable oxygen concentrator was already working at the lowest capacity, and had only 40 minutes until the battery ran out. Medical workers had to carry her down from the seventh floor of their apartment building since the elevator was not running. 'I paid for the private ambulance and private hospice that was ready to receive us in the middle of the night,' she says.

According to Venhlinska, state-run hospices 'accept people only by appointment', have long queues of patients waiting to get in, and their wards are already full of those 'who need pain relief, who are in agony'.

If the lengthy blackouts caused by Russian attacks continue, Venhlinska says she doesn't know what to do. 'Constant power cuts were very exhausting and painful for my mother. It was torture,' she says.

'Five times harder'

The everyday well-being of Rashchenko's son Mykhailo depends not only on the three people taking care of him but on the uninterrupted power supply at his home as well.

Back in 2015, then-16-year-old Mykhailo got into a road accident that led to multiple injuries, including nine bone fractures, that put him in a coma. His father says Mykhailo's brain injury severely affected his health.

Since then, Mykhailo has used a wheelchair and has needed constant care. Rashchenko says his son can't chew on his own, so the food they make for Mykhailo needs to be ground in a mixer. Physical exercises that involve special exercise machines twice a day are 'critical' for his health, says Rashchenko. Though it was tough, Rashchenko says the family managed to organize their lives so that Mykhailo could get the care that he needs.

Russia's fifth large-scale missile attack across Ukraine on 23 November, which damaged critical infrastructure and caused blackouts in much of the country and even neighboring Moldova, interrupted the Rashchenko family's routine. Following the attack, they did not have power for 70 hours straight, Rashchenko says.

'My parents live near the hospital, and they have power all the time,' he says. 'So I had to go to their place to prepare food [for Mykhailo] and go back home.'

Since Mykhailo's exercise machines require electricity to work, the family had to simulate exercising by stimulating his muscles with their hands, 'which was not really effective', Rashchenko says.

During that time, Rashchenko says they could not bathe Mykhailo normally, since the water supply requires electricity. They also could not take him outside for a breath of fresh air since the elevator wasn't working.

Rashchenko – who works with people with disabilities every day and whose rehabilitation center currently helps nearly 100 people in Odesa – says that those people with disabilities who have no one to take care of them should consider finding a way to flee abroad, at least for some time until Russian attacks on Ukraine's energy infrastructure are over. 'It's always been hard, but now it's five times harder,' he says.

Charging hearing aids

The four-year-old son of Kyiv Oblast resident Anna Sytnyk lost his hearing following a severe Covid-19 infection in 2020. Without hearing aids, he can barely hear anything now. 'A blackout is the worst thing that can happen to us because hearing aids need to be charged daily,' Sytnyk says.

The devices that the little Roman uses for hearing can work for up to 12 hours.

'We take him to the kindergarten at 8 a.m., and he hears everything until 8 p.m. thanks to hearing aids,' says Sytnyk. 'Then they need to be charged.'

Due to the illnesses that Roman endured as a little child, he also needs to use an electronic nebulizer for inhalation whenever he gets a cold and starts coughing, his mother says.

Three days after Russia unleashed another missile strike on Ukraine's civilian infrastructure on 23 November, six million people were still facing electricity shortages, according to President Volodymyr Zelensky.

Sytnyk's family was among them. She says they did not have power for 68 hours straight. Back then, the family did not have a power generator and was unable to heat the house with two little children in it, not to mention prepare food and charge Roman's hearing aids. At that time, Roman also had a cough and needed to use his nebulizer to relieve the symptoms.

'You can not even imagine how difficult it was,' Sytnyk says. 'We could never believe that in the 21st century, such a thing could happen. That we can be simply cut off from the world.'

Luckily, a gas station nearby that had power came to the family's rescue. There, Sytnyk says, Roman was able to use his nebulizer. She also left the expensive hearing aids at the gas station to charge for up to six hours so that her son could use them at kindergarten the next day. Sytnyk says the gas station employees treated her nicely, understanding the difficulty of the family's situation. She says that even when crowded, people at the gas station always let her and Roman use a plug socket to turn the nebulizer on.

Despite all the difficulties her family went through in the past months, Sytnyk says she 'would rather stay without power for 100 or 200 hours' than have anything to do with Russia. 'Anything other than to pay in Russian rubles and to be with Russia,' she adds.

25 January 2023

Ukraine war latest: US, Germany to send dozens of tanks to Ukraine, Kyiv admits the loss of Soledar

Asami Terajima

Key developments on 25 January

- Germany to send 14 Leopard 2 tanks for Ukraine, green light for other countries to deliver
- US announces decision to send 31 Abrams tanks to Ukraine
- Zelensky thanks US for 'important step on the path to victory'; Germany for 'important and timely' decision
- Ukraine confirms withdrawal from Soledar, Donetsk Oblast

President Volodymyr Zelensky's 45th birthday turned into a historic day for Ukraine, with the US and Germany vowing to send scores of advanced Western tanks after a long wait.

On 25 January, Germany promised to supply 14 Leopard 2 tanks to Ukraine, while the US announced the transfer of 31 Abrams tanks.

Germany also authorized other countries, such as Poland, to export their stock of Leopards to Ukraine – encouraging NATO allies to confirm their readiness to send their tanks as well.

A number of European nations have made their promises already. Poland, Norway, Finland, and Spain have said they would be ready to provide Ukraine with long-anticipated Leopards.

While the Netherlands doesn't own any, Dutch Prime Minister Mark Rutte said on 25 January that his country is prepared to purchase Leopards in order to transfer them to Ukraine.

Zelensky thanked Germany and the US for their decision to provide Ukraine with tanks but reiterated that it was important to move on to the next step. He said the main aspects of the next procedure are making sure that the delivery of the tanks is timely and that sufficient quantity would be provided. 'We must form such a tank fist, such a fist of freedom, after the blows of which tyranny will no longer rise,' Zelensky said in his evening address. 'Together – just like we make a decision today.'

After the weapon delivery announcements, Russia began launching airstrikes in multiple regions across Ukraine late on 25 January.

Head of Ukraine's President's Office Andriy Yermak said that the air defense was working to shoot down incoming targets.

Moscow has repeatedly threatened Western nations against supplying tanks to Ukraine, claiming they would 'regret' making such a decision.

An army of Western tanks would give Ukraine a major equipment advantage over Russia, whose troops rely on Soviet ones.

Leopards for Ukraine

The day began with Germany confirming that it would send its powerful Leopard tanks to Ukraine and authorized other countries, such as Poland, to send their own stocks.

German Defense Minister Boris Pistorius said after a morning cabinet meeting that it would take about three months for the Leopards to arrive in Ukraine. But a program for Ukrainian troops to train on Leopards is set to begin soon.

Berlin said in a statement that European allies would organize two battalions of Leopards. A battalion typically consists of about 40 tanks, meaning that Ukraine could expect to receive approximately 80 Leopards in the nearest future.

ABC News reported on 24 January, citing unnamed sources familiar with the matter, that 12 countries were prepared to send about 100 Leopards to Ukraine upon Berlin's consent.

The exact quantity of Western tanks that Ukraine would get in the nearest future is unclear, but it is likely to be lower than what Kyiv had anticipated.

Along with other equipment, Ukraine needs 300 main battle tanks to conduct counter-offensive operations, Ukraine's Commander-in-Chief Valerii Zaluzhnyi and Defense Minister Oleksii Reznikov said in December.

Mounting pressure

Pressure had been mounting for Berlin to greenlight the transfer of the Leopards after France and the UK made their vows earlier in January.

Poland has particularly pressed on Germany in public, with Prime Minister Mateusz Morawiecki accusing Berlin of 'wasting time'. He said Poland was ready to send Leopards to Ukraine regardless of Germany's will.

The Russian embassy in Germany immediately labeled Berlin's decision 'extremely dangerous', saying it took the war to a 'new level of confrontation'. Moscow is likely pressing on Berlin's repeatedly stated fears that sending Leopard tanks could lead to a direct confrontation with Russia.

Later on 25 January, US President Joe Biden announced a long-awaited decision to send 31 of his country's most advanced battle tanks, M1 Abrams, to Ukraine. Training of Ukrainian soldiers will begin 'as soon as possible', but the delivery could 'take time', he added.

The training for Ukrainian troops on M1 Abrams tanks could start in 'weeks, not months', White House National Security Council spokesperson John Kirby said at a news conference.

The US's delivery promise came a few days after US lawmakers called for giving Ukraine Abrams tanks, as they sought to push Germany into green-lighting Leopards for Ukraine.

Multiple Western media reports, citing unnamed American and German officials, revealed that Germany was ready to provide Ukraine with Leopards if the US went ahead with Abrams.

German Defense Minister Pistorius dismissed the reports, saying that he was not aware of such a link.

Compared with Soviet tanks, which Ukraine and Russia currently use on the battlefield, the mobility and firepower of Western equipment could help Ukraine launch more counter-offensive operations. 'Western states' provision of main battle tanks to Ukraine will help enable Ukraine to conduct mechanized warfare to defeat the Russian military and liberate Ukrainian territory,' the Institute for the Study of War (ISW), a US defense think-tank, said in its 24 January report.

Admitting the loss of Soledar

For the first time, the Ukrainian military acknowledged that it had withdrawn from the salt-mining town of Soledar, located 10 kilometers north of Bakhmut – a fiercely contested city Russia has tried to capture for months.

Ukrainian troops had to retreat from Soledar 'to save the lives of the personnel', and they are now strengthening defense on the outskirts of the town, Serhiy Cherevatyi, a spokesman for Ukraine's Eastern Military Command, said on 25 January.

Cherevatyi did not indicate when Ukrainian troops had withdrawn.

While the Russian Defense Ministry claimed victory over Soledar on 13 January (and Wagner's mercenaries on 11 January), it remained unclear how much of the town Ukraine still controlled.

Ukrainian authorities continued to deny Russia's claim about its victory over Soledar, dismissing it as part of the Kremlin's propaganda campaign to show tangible results to its public.

However, international observers and independent military analysts have confirmed Russia's capture of Soledar as early as mid-January.

The UK Defence Ministry said in its intelligence briefing that 'Ukrainian forces had highly likely withdrawn' from Soledar by the end of 16 January, leaving Russian troops and Wagner Group mercenaries in control of the town.

The ministry added in its 18 January report that retreating Ukrainian forces 'have likely established new defensive lines to the west' of Soledar.

Ukrainian drone unit commander Robert 'Magyar' Brovdy also reported on his Telegram channel that Russian assault units captured the last Ukrainian stronghold – an industrial zone on the western part of the town – at around

5.30 p.m. on 16 January. He added that the front line was outside the administrative border from now on.

Capturing Soledar could help Russian forces encircle Bakhmut from the north, but it doesn't guarantee Moscow's success since Ukraine still controls areas (including main roads) west of the city, according to military analysts. Russia already controls areas east and south of Bakhmut.

If Russians were to capture Bakhmut, they would be able to threaten the two other Ukrainian strongholds in Donetsk Oblast – Kramatorsk and Sloviansk.

After nearly six months of deadly trench warfare around Bakhmut, US and Western officials are 'urging Ukraine to shift its focus' from Bakhmut to a potential counter-offensive in the country's south, CNN said on 24 January.

Citing Western and Ukrainian officials, CNN reported that the Western allies are advising Ukraine to use a different counter-offensive style that involves 'billions of dollars in new military hardware recently committed by Western allies'. '[Bakhmut] is less attractive militarily, in terms of any sort of infrastructure, than it might have been if it had not been this destroyed,' a senior US official told CNN last week.

Nearly 11 months into its full-scale invasion, Russia has begun changing tactics – relying on assault groups of 140 to 160 people – rather than making advances with battalions, much larger in size, Deputy Military Intelligence Chief Vadym Skibitsky said in an interview published on 23 January.

Russian forces are launching 'powerful artillery strikes' to 'completely destroy' Ukrainian defenses, 'wave after wave', according to Skibitsky.

Skibitsky added that the same tactic was used by the Kremlin-controlled notorious Wagner Group 'first in Bakhmut, then in Soledar (when Russia intensified its offensive in early January)'.

The *New York Times* reported on 24 January, citing satellite images and video footage, that Wagner was suffering extremely heavy casualties in the war in Ukraine.

Citing a satellite image from 24 January, the *NYT* said that the number of burial plots in a cemetery known to hold Wagner mercenaries' bodies has increased by nearly seven times compared to what was seen on satellite imagery just two months ago.

Ukrainian forces are also reported to have been suffering heavy casualties in the area.

For Russia, the capture of Soledar was its first noticeable success since it captured the last Ukrainian strongholds of Sievierodonetsk and Lysychansk in Luhansk Oblast in June and July.

EPILOGUE

By the staff of The Kyiv Independent

Writing an epilogue feels strange when we know that our story, and the story of Ukraine, is only just beginning.

When we created *The Kyiv Independent* just months before Russia's full-scale invasion of Ukraine, we knew we were facing an uphill battle. We thought, however, that we'd be fighting an unfavorable media market and threats to freedom of speech. We never expected that our country would soon become the place of the deadliest war in Europe since World War II.

One can't be prepared for something like that. We weren't. There are no textbooks for surviving as a newsroom in the epicenter of a war.

So we navigated the crisis following our instincts. We did what we felt was right: stayed on duty and served as the world's window into the events on the ground. On this path, filled with sleepless nights and anxiety-ridden days, we have been driven by our mission.

Because of our hard work and bold choices, we succeeded. We went from an underdog to one of the best-known independent media outlets in the region, almost overnight. It was an unexpected, immense success against all odds.

Yet a far more important story of unexpected success was meanwhile developing around us. The story of Ukraine.

In February 2022, in the build-up to Russia's invasion, a sense of gloom and despair was in the air. Embassies were fleeing Kyiv. Foreign journalists were ordered to catch the next flight home. Western leaders, as we now know, were effectively saying farewell in conversations with their Ukrainian counterparts. It felt like we, Ukrainians, were being left alone to face an overwhelmingly stronger attacker.

When the invasion started on the early morning of 24 February, global TV networks talked not of *if* Kyiv would fall, but *when*. The world didn't believe in us, didn't believe that Ukrainians could withstand the attack.

And yet – that's exactly what happened. Ukraine, the largest country in Europe but very small when compared to Russia, stopped the invaders and, over the course of the next year, took back at least 40% of the territories Russia had invaded since 24 February.

With all its strength and enormous resources, Russia was humiliated.

Ukraine's success has been largely possible thanks to the world's support in the form of military and humanitarian aid, as well as sanctions on Russia and its allies.

But the support hasn't been coming fast enough. The weapons arrive after months of diplomatic work. Neither have sanctions been enough to strangle the Russian economy – a year later, it can still pay for its war.

We have been writing at *The Kyiv Independent* from day one of the war: this is not a war between two countries, but between two polar sets of values. The outcome of this war will determine not only the future of Ukraine, but of the world.

Will democracy preserve the dominant place in the world order, or will it give way to repressive authoritarian regimes?

The ending of this story has not yet been written. The stories in this book are just a first draft of history – the new history of a new Ukraine. We at *The Kyiv Independent* consider it a privilege to have a part in writing it.

THE KYIV INDEPENDENT

Become a patron of *The Kyiv Independent* and support independent journalism in Ukraine

www.patreon.com/kyivindependent